TAKING SIDES

Clashing Views on
Global Issues

FIFTH EDITION

Selected, Edited, and with Introductions by

James E. Harf
University of Tampa and Maryville University

and

Mark Owen Lombardi
Maryville University

McGraw-Hill
Higher Education

Boston   Burr Ridge, IL   Dubuque, IA   New York   San Francisco   St. Louis
Bangkok   Bogotá   Caracas   Kuala Lumpur   Lisbon   London   Madrid   Mexico City
Milan   Montreal   New Delhi   Santiago   Seoul   Singapore   Sydney   Taipei   Toronto

The *McGraw·Hill* Companies

McGraw-Hill
Higher Education

TAKING SIDES: CLASHING VIEWS ON GLOBAL ISSUES, FIFTH EDITION

Published by McGraw-Hill, a business unit of The McGraw-Hill Companies, Inc., 1221 Avenue of the Americas, New York, NY 10020. Copyright © 2009 by The McGraw-Hill Companies, Inc. All rights reserved. Previous edition(s) 2004–2009. No part of this publication may be reproduced or distributed in any form or by any means, or stored in a database or retrieval system, without the prior written consent of The McGraw-Hill Companies, Inc., including, but not limited to, in any network or other electronic storage or transmission, or broadcast for distance learning.

Some ancillaries, including electronic and print components, may not be available to customers outside the United States.

Taking Sides® is a registered trademark of the McGraw-Hill Companies, Inc.
Taking Sides is published by the **Contemporary Learning Series** group within the McGraw-Hill Higher Education division.

1 2 3 4 5 6 7 8 9 0 DOC/DOC 0 9 8

MHID: 0-07-351534-5
ISBN: 978-0-07-351534-2
ISSN: 1536-3317

Managing Editor: *Larry Loeppke*
Senior Managing Editor: *Faye Schilling*
Developmental Editor: *Jill Peter*
Editorial Assistant: *Nancy Meissner*
Production Service Assistant: *Rita Hingtgen*
Permissions Coordinator: *Shirley Lanners*
Senior Marketing Manager: *Julie Keck*
Marketing Communications Specialist: *Mary Klein*
Marketing Coordinator: *Alice Link*
Project Manager: *Sandy Wille*
Design Specialist: *Tara McDermott*
Cover Graphics: *Kristine Jubeck*

Compositor: ICC Macmillan
Cover Image: © Corbis/Royalty Free

Library of Congress Cataloging-in-Publication Data

Main entry under title:
  Taking sides: clashing views on controversial global issues/selected, edited, and with
  introductions by James E. Harf and Mark Owen Lombardi.—5th ed.

Includes bibliographical references and index.
1. Globalization. 2. International relations, 3. global environmental change. 4. Population.
5. Emigration and immigration. I. Harf, James E., *ed.* II. Lombardi Mark Owen, *ed.* III. Series.
303

www.mhhe.com

Preface

This volume reflects the changing nature of the contemporary world in which we live. Not only are we now witnessing a dramatic leap in the *scope* of global change, but we are also experiencing a *rate* of change in the world unparalleled in recorded history. Change in the international system is not a new phenomenon. Since the creation in the early 1500s of a Euro-centric world system of sovereign nation-states that dominated political, economic, and social events throughout the known world, global change has been with us. But earlier manifestations of change were characterized by infrequent bursts of system-changing episodes followed by long periods of "normalcy," where the processes and structures of the international system demonstrated regularity or consistency.

First, the Catholic church sought to recapture its European dominance and glory during the Middle Ages in a last gasp effort to withstand challenges against its rule from a newly developed secularized and urbanized mercantile class, only to be pushed aside in a devastating continental struggle known as the Thirty Years' War and relegated to irrelevant status by the resultant Treaty of Westphalia in 1648. A century and a half later, the global system was again challenged, this time by a French general turned emperor, Napoleon Bonaparte, who sought to export the newly created utopian vision of the French Revolution beyond the boundaries of France to the rest of the world. Napoleon was eventually repelled by a coalition of major powers intent on preserving the world as these countries knew it.

Soon the eighteenth-century Europe was being transformed by the intrusion of the Industrial Revolution on the daily lives of average citizens and national leaders alike. Technological advances enhanced the capacity of countries to dramatically increase their military capability, achieving the ability to project such power far beyond their national borders in short time. Other threats to the existing world order also emerged. Nationalism began to capture the hearts of various country leaders who sought to impart such loyalties to their subjects, while new ideologies competed with one another as well as with nationalism to create a thirst for alternative world models to the existing nation-state system. The result was another failed attempt by a European power, this time Germany, to expand its influence via a major war, later to be called World War I, throughout the continent. The post-war map of Europe reflected major consequences of the abortive German effort.

Almost immediately, the international system was threatened by a newly emergent virulent ideology of the left intent on taking over the world. Communism had gained a foothold in Russia, and soon its leaders were eager to transport it across the continent to the far corners of the globe, threatening to destroy the existing economic order and, by definition, its political counterpart. Shortly thereafter, a competing virulent ideology from the right and fascism emerged. Under its manipulation by a new German leader, Adolph Hitler, the international system was once again greatly threatened. Six long years of war and unthinkable levels of devastation and destruction followed, until the fascist threat turned back. The scourge of communism persisted, however, until late in the millennium, when it also virtually disappeared, felled by its own weaknesses and excesses.

In the interim, new challenges to global order appeared in the form of a set of issues unlike no other during the 500-year history of the nation-state system. The nature of these global issues and the pace at which they both landed on the global agenda and then expanded were to quickly affect the international system. This new agenda took root in the late 1960s, when astute observers began to identify disquieting trends: quickening population growth in the poorer sectors of the globe, growing disruptions in the world's ability to feed its population, increasing shortfalls in required resources, and expanding evidence of negative environmental impacts, such as a variety of pollution evils. Some of these issues—like decreasing levels of adequate supplies of food, energy, and water for example—emerged as a result of both increased population growth and increased per capita levels of consumption. Dramatic population increases, in turn, resulted in changes in global population dynamics—increasing aged population or massive new migration patterns. The emergence of this set of new issues was soon followed by another phenomenon, globalization, which emphasized increasing speedy flows of information through innovative technology and a resultant diffusion of regional cultures throughout the globe and the emergence of a global macro-culture. Globalization not only affected the nature of the international system in these general ways, but also influenced both the manner in which these global issues impacted the system and how the latter addressed them.

The major consequence of the confluence of these events is the extent to which and the shortened time frame in which the change affects them. No longer is the change measured in centuries or even decades. It is now measured in years or even months. No longer are likely solutions to such problems simple, known, confined to a relatively small part of the globe, and capable of being achieved by the efforts of one or a few national governments. Instead, these global issues are characterized by increased rapidity of change, increased complexity, increased geographical impact, increased resistance to solution, and increased fluidity.

One only has to compare the world as it existed when these issues first appeared to the world of today to grasp the difference. When students first began to study these issues in the early 1960s, their written analysis was accomplished either by putting pen to pad or by engaging an unwieldy typewriter. Their experience with a computer was limited to watching a moon landing through the eyes of NASA Mission Control. The use of phones was relegated to a location where a cord could be plugged into a wall socket. Their written correspondence with someone beyond their immediate location had a stamp on it. Their reading of news, both serious and frivolous, occurred via a newspaper. Visual news invaded their space in 30-minute daily segments from three major TV networks. Being entertained required some effort, usually away from the confines of their home or dorm room. Today, of course, the personal computer and its companion, the Internet, have transformed the way students learn, the way they communicate with one another, and the way they entertain themselves.

The age of globalization has accelerated, affecting and transforming trends that began over three decades ago. No longer are nation-states the only actors on the global stage. Moreover, their position of dominance is increasingly challenged by an array of other actors—international governmental organizations, private international groups, multinational corporations, and important individuals—who might be better equipped to address newly emerging issues (or who might also serve as the source of yet other problems).

An even more recent phenomenon is the unleashing of ethnic pride, which manifests itself in both positive and negative ways. The history of post-Cold War conflict is a history of intrastate, ethnically driven violence that has torn apart those countries that have been unable to deal effectively with the changes brought on by the end of the Cold War. The most insidious manifestation of this emphasis on ethnicity is the emergence of terrorist groups who use religion and other aspects of ethnicity to justify bringing death and destruction on their perceived enemies. As national governments attempt to cope with this latest phenomenon, they too are changing the nature of war and violence. The global agenda's current transformation, brought about by globalization, demands that our attention turn towards the latter's consequences.

The format of *Taking Sides: Clashing Views on Controversial Global Issues*, Fifth Edition, follows the successful formula of other books in the Taking Sides series. The book begins with an introduction to the emergence of global issues, the new age of globalization, and the effect that 9/11 and the international community's response to the world that ushered in the twentieth century. It then addresses 20 current global issues grouped into four parts. Population takes center stage in Part 1 because it not only represents a global issue by itself, but it also affects the parameters of most other global issues. Population growth, aging, location, and policy making are considered. Part 2 addresses a range of problems associated with global resources and their environmental impact. Parts 3 and 4 feature issues borne out of the emerging agenda of the twenty-first century. The former part examines widely disparate expanding forces and movements across national boundaries, such as global pandemics as well as new communication and information devices exemplified by MySpace and YouTube. Part 4 focuses on new security issues in the post-Cold War and post-September 11 eras, such as whether the world is headed for a nuclear 9/11 or China will become the next superpower.

Each issue has two readings, one pro and one con. The readings are preceded by an issue *introduction* that sets the stage for the debate and briefly describes the two readings. Each issue concludes with a *postscript* that summarizes the issues, suggests further avenues for thought, and provides *suggestions for further reading*. At the back of the book is a listing of all the *contributors to this volume* with a brief biographical sketch of each of the prominent figures whose views are debated here.

We wish to acknowledge the research assistance of Kaylyn Wilkin in helping us with this most recent edition.

Changes to this edition This fifth edition represents a significant revision. Four of the 20 issues are completely new: *"Do MySpace and YouTube Make Private Globalization Democratized?"* (Issue 15); *"Is Religious and Cultural Extremism a Global Security Threat?"* (Issue 18); *"Is a Nuclear Iran a Global Security Threat?"* (Issue 19); and *Will China Be the Next Superpower?"* (Issue 20). In six of the remaining sixteen issues, one or both selections were replaced to bring the issues up to date.

James E. Harf
University of Tampa
and
Maryville University

Mark Owen Lombardi
Maryville University

Contents In Brief

Contents

YES: **Michael Meyer,** from "Birth Dearth," *Newsweek*
(September 27, 2004)   *4*

NO: **Danielle Nierenberg and Mia MacDonald,** from "The
Population Story . . . So Far," *World Watch Magazine* (September/
October 2004)   *10*

Michael Meyer, a writer for *Newsweek International*, argues that the new
global population threat is not too many people as a consequence of
continuing high growth rates. On the contrary, declining birth rates will
ultimately lead to depopulation in many places on Earth, a virtual
population implosion, in both the developed and developing worlds.
Danielle Nierenberg, a research associate at the Worldwatch Institute,
and Mia MacDonald, a policy analyst and Worldwatch Institute senior
fellow, argue that the consequences of a still-rising population have
worsened in some ways because of the simultaneous existence of
fast-rising consumption patterns, creating a new set of concerns.

Issue 2.   **Should the International Community Attempt
to Curb Population Growth in the Developing
World?   20**

YES: **Robert S. McNamara,** from "The Population Explosion,"
The Futurist (November/December 1992)   *22*

NO: **Steven W. Mosher,** from "McNamara's Folly: Bankrolling
Family Planning," *PRI Review* (March–April 2003)   *28*

Robert McNamara, former president of the World Bank, argues in this piece
written during his presidency that the developed countries of the world and
international organizations should help the countries of the developing
world reduce their population growth rates. Steven W. Mosher, president of
the Population Research Institute, an organization dedicated to debunking
the idea that the world is overpopulated, argues that McNamara's World
Bank and other international financial lending agencies have served for
over a decade as "loan sharks" for those groups and individuals who were
pressuring developing countries to adopt fertility reduction programs for
self-interest reasons.

UNIT 2 GLOBAL RESOURCES AND THE ENVIRONMENT 83

Rosegrant and colleagues conclude that if current water policies continue, farmers will find it difficult to grow sufficient food to meet the world's needs. Lomborg contends that water is not only plentiful but is a renewable resource that, if properly treated as valuable, should not pose a future problem.

UNIT 3 EXPANDING GLOBAL FORCES AND MOVEMENTS 169

This 2007 report by the UN's Office on Drugs and Crime provides "robust evidence" that "drug control is working" and "the world drug problem is being contained." Ethan Nadelmann argues that prohibition has failed by not treating the "demand for drugs as a market, and addicts as patients," resulting in "boosting the profits of drug lords, and fostering narcostates that would frighten Al Capone."

The document from the World Health Organization lays out a comprehensive program of action for individual countries, the international community, and WHO to address the next influenza pandemic. H. T. Goranson, a former top national scientist with the U.S. government, describes the grave dangers posed by global pandemics and highlights flaws in the international community's ability to respond.

Janie Chuang, practitioner-in-residence at the America University Washington College of Law, suggests that governments have been finally motivated to take action against human traffickers as a consequence of the concern over national security implications of forced human labor movement and the involvement of transnational criminal syndicates. Dina Francesca Haynes, associate professor of law at the New England School of Law, argues that none of the models underlying domestic legislation to deal with human traffickers is "terribly effective" in addressing the issue.

Meredith and Hoppough argue that the data supports the conclusion that globalization works for both rich and poor. They particularly point to the growing middle class in many countries throughout Asia, Africa and Latin America to support this conclusion. Weber et al. argue that globalization and the American predominance that drives it amplify a myriad of evils including terrorism, global warming, and interethnic conflict creating a less stable and less just world community.

Julia Galeota contends that the world today is flooded with American culture, and while some would argue that this is simply a matter of tastes and choices, she argues that it is a strategy to impose American principles and ideals on the world community and as a result destroy other cultures. Philippe Legrain is a British economist who presents two views of cultural imperialism and argues that the notion of American cultural imperialism "is a myth" and that the spreading of cultures through globalization is a positive, not negative, development.

Brain argues that the Internet and elements like MySpace, YouTube, and others allow for instant dissemination of information, response, and change empowering millions in the marketplace of things and ideas. He contends that top-down control is melting away amidst this onslaught and everyone is becoming their own creator, critic, and controller, thus democratizing everything from corporate products to tastes and politics. Keen contends that the Internet is destroying culture and rubbing outlines between knowledge and whimsy, experts and neophytes. He argues that MySpace and YouTube do not empower, but rather water down, values and ideals such that a lowest common denominator prevails, leading to less democracy and not more.

UNIT 4   THE NEW GLOBAL SECURITY DILEMMA   299

Mark Krikorian argues that immigration and security are directly and inexorably linked. He contends that the nature of terrorism is such that individual and small group infiltration of our U.S. borders is a prime strategy for terrorists, and thus undermines individual calls for relaxed or open immigration. Daniel T. Griswold argues that by coupling security and immigration, we simplify a complex issue and, in fact, do little to enhance security while we demonize a huge segment of the population who are by and large law abiding and not a threat.

David Krieger, president of the Nuclear Age Peace Foundation, argues that a nuclear 9/11 is very likely in a U.S. city due to the prevalence of nuclear weapons and the failure of nuclear member states to adequately enforce a true non-proliferation regime. Graham Allison, noted international scholar, argues that a nuclear 9/11 is preventable, provided that the United States and other states halt proliferation to states predisposed toward assisting terrorists, particularly North Korea.

Solomon argues that when religious extremism, which is a security threat in and of itself, is merged with state power, the threat to global security is potentially catastrophic and must be met with clear and uncompromising policies. He contends that this is present across all religions, and he uses both a born-again George Bush and a fundamentalist Mahmoud

Ahmadinejad as his examples. Telhami, on the other hand, does not argue that religious extremism is the threat, but rather that global security threats are from political groups with political agendas and not extremism as such.

Correlation Guide

The *Taking Sides* series presents current issues in a debate-style format designed to stimulate student interest and develop critical thinking skills. Each issue is thoughtfully framed with an issue summary, an issue introduction, and a postscript. The pro and con essays—selected for their liveliness and substance—represent the arguments of leading scholars and commentators in their fields.

Taking Sides: Clashing Views on Global Issues, 5/e is an easy-to-use reader that presents issues on important topics such as *global population, global resources and the environment, expanding global forces and movements*, and *the new global security dilemma*. For more information on *Taking Sides* and other *McGraw-Hill Contemporary Learning Series* titles, visit www.mhcls.com.

This convenient guide matches the issues in **Taking Sides: Global Issues, 5/e** with the corresponding chapters in two of our best-selling McGraw-Hill Political Science textbooks by Boyer and Rourke.

Taking Sides: Global Issues, 5/e	International Politics on the World Stage, Brief, 8/e by Boyer/Rourke	International Politics on the World Stage, 12/e by Rourke
Issue 1: Are Declining Growth Rates Rather Than Rapid Population Growth Today's Major Global Population Problem?	**Chapter 1:** Thinking and Caring about World Politics **Chapter 6:** Power and the National States: The Traditional Structure **Chapter 12:** Preserving and Enhancing the Global Commons	**Chapter 1:** Thinking and Caring about World Politics **Chapter 8:** National Power and Statecraft: The Traditional Approach **Chapter 12:** National Economic Competition: The Traditional Road **Chapter 14:** Preserving and Enhancing Human Rights and Dignity **Chapter 15:** Preserving and Enhancing the Biosphere
Issue 2: Should the International Community Attempt to Curb Population Growth in the Developing World?	**Chapter 12:** Preserving and Enhancing the Global Commons	**Chapter 15:** Preserving and Enhancing the Biosphere
Issue 3: Is Global Aging in the Developed World a Major Problem?	**Chapter 6:** Power and the National States: The Traditional Structure **Chapter 12:** Preserving and Enhancing the Global Commons	**Chapter 8:** National Power and Statecraft: The Traditional Approach
Issue 4: Does Global Urbanization Lead Primarily to Undesirable Consequences?		
Issue 5: Do Environmentalists Overstate Their Case?	**Chapter 12:** Preserving and Enhancing the Global Commons	**Chapter 15:** Preserving and Enhancing the Biosphere
Issue 6: Should the World Continue to Rely on Oil as a Major Source of Energy?	**Chapter 6:** Power and the National States: The Traditional Structure **Chapter 10:** Globalization in the World Economy **Chapter 11:** Global Economic Competition and Cooperation **Chapter 12:** Preserving and Enhancing the Global Commons	**Chapter 8:** National Power and Statecraft: The Traditional Approach **Chapter 15:** Preserving and Enhancing the Biosphere

Issue 7: Will the World Be Able to Feed Itself in the Foreseeable Future?	**Chapter 8:** International Law and Human Rights: An Alternative Approach	**Chapter 7:** Intergovernmental Organizations: Alternative Governance
	Chapter 12: Preserving and Enhancing the Global Commons	**Chapter 14:** Preserving and Enhancing Human Rights and Dignity
Issue 8: Is the Threat of Global Warming Real?	**Chapter 1:** Thinking and Caring about World Politics	**Chapter 1:** Thinking and Caring about World Politics
	Chapter 12: Preserving and Enhancing the Global Commons	**Chapter 15:** Preserving and Enhancing the Biosphere
Issue 9: Is the Threat of a Global Water Shortage Real?	**Chapter 12:** Preserving and Enhancing the Global Commons	**Chapter 15:** Preserving and Enhancing the Biosphere
Issue 10: Can the Global Community "Win" the Drug War?		
Issue 11: Is the International Community Adequately Prepared to Address Global Health Pandemics?	**Chapter 8:** International Law and Human Rights: An Alternative Approach	**Chapter 14:** Preserving and Enhancing Human Rights and Dignity
	Chapter 10: Globalization in the World Economy	
Issue 12: Do Adequate Strategies Exist to Combat Human Trafficking?	**Chapter 8:** International Law and Human Rights: An Alternative Approach	**Chapter 14:** Preserving and Enhancing Human Rights and Dignity
Issue 13: Is Globalization a Positive Development for the World Community?	**Chapter 2:** The Evolution of World Politics	**Chapter 2:** The Evolution of World Politics
	Chapter 5: Globalization and Transnationalism: The Alternative Orientation	**Chapter 5:** Globalism: The Alternative Orientation
	Chapter 7: International Organization: An Alternative Structure	**Chapter 12:** National Economic Competition: The Traditional Road
	Chapter 10: Globalization in the World Economy	**Chapter 13:** International Economic Cooperation: The Alternative Road
	Chapter 12: Preserving and Enhancing the Global Commons	
Issue 14: Is the World a Victim of American Cultural Imperialism?	**Chapter 8:** International Law and Human Rights: An Alternative Approach	**Chapter 14:** Preserving and Enhancing Human Rights and Dignity
Issue 15: Do MySpace and YouTube Make Private Globalization Democratized?		
Issue 16: Does Immigration Policy Affect Terrorism?	**Chapter 9:** Pursuing Security	
Issue 17: Are We Headed Toward a Nuclear 9/11?	**Chapter 9:** Pursuing Security	**Chapter 10:** National Security: The Traditional Road
		Chapter 11: International Security: The Alternative Road
Issue 18: Is Religious and Cultural Extremism a Global Security Threat?	**Chapter 4:** Nationalism: The Traditional Orientation	**Chapter 4:** Nationalism: The Traditional Orientation
	Chapter 5: Globalization and Transnationalism: The Alternative Orientation	**Chapter 5:** Globalism: The Alternative Orientation
	Chapter 9: Pursuing Security	
Issue 19: Is a Nuclear Iran a Global Security Threat?	**Chapter 3:** Level of Analysis	**Chapter 3:** Levels of Analysis and Foreign Policy
	Chapter 6: Power and the National States: The Traditional Structure	**Chapter 8:** National Power and Statecraft: The Traditional Approach
	Chapter 9: Pursuing Security	**Chapter 12:** National Economic Competition: The Traditional Road
Issue 20: Will China Be the Next Superpower?	**Chapter 1:** Thinking and Caring about World Politics	**Chapter 1:** Thinking and Caring about World Politics
	Chapter 2: The Evolution of World Politics	**Chapter 2:** The Evolution of World Politics
		Chapter 8: National Power and Statecraft: The Traditional Approach

Introduction

Global Issues in the Twenty-First Century

James E. Harf
Mark Owen Lombardi

Threats of the New Millennium

As the new millennium dawned, the world witnessed two very different events whose impacts are far reaching, profound, and in many ways shape the discourse of global issues. One episode was the tragedy of 9/11, a series of incidents that ushered in a new era of terrorism. It burst upon the international scene with the force of a mega-catastrophe, occupying virtually every waking moment of national and global leaders throughout the world and seizing the attention of the rest of the planet's citizens who contemplated both the immediate implications and the long-term effects of a U.S. response. The focused interest of national policymakers was soon transformed into a war on terrorism, while average citizens sought to cope with changes brought on by both the tragic events of September 2001 and the global community's response to them. Both governmental leaders and citizens continue to address the consequences of this first intrusion of the new millennium on a world now far different in many ways since the pre-9/11 era.

The second event was less dramatic and certainly did not receive the same fanfare, but still has both short- and long-term ramifications for the global community in the twenty-first century. This was the creation of a set of ambitious millennium development goals by the United Nations. In September 2000, 189 national governments committed to eight major goals in an initiative known as the UN Millennium Development Goals (MDG): eradicate extreme poverty and hunger; achieve universal primary education; promote gender equality and empower women; reduce child mortality; improve maternal health; combat HIV/AIDS, malaria and other diseases; ensure environmental sustainability; and develop a global partnership for development. This initiative was important not only because the UN was setting an actionable 15-year agenda against a relatively new set of global issues, but also because it signified a major change in how the international community would henceforth address such problems confronting human-kind. The new initiative represented recognition of: (1) shared responsibility between rich and poor nations for solving such problems; (2) a link between goals; (3) the paramount role to be played by national governments in the process; and (4) the need for measurable outcome indicators of success. The UN Millennium Development Goals initiative went virtually unnoticed by much of the public, although governmental decision-makers involved with the United Nations understood its significance. Jay Leno of NBC's Tonight show would have a field day questioning passersby on the street about their knowledge of this UN initiative.

These two major events, although vastly different, symbolize the world in which we now find ourselves, a world far more complex and more violent than either the earlier one characterized by the Cold War struggle between the United States and the Soviet Union, or the post-Cold War era of the 1990s, where global and national leaders struggled to identify and then find their proper place in the post-Cold War world order. Consider the first event, the 9/11 tragedy. It reminds us all that the use and abuse of power in pursuit of political goals in earlier centuries is still a viable option for those throughout the world who believe themselves disadvantaged because of various political, economic, or social conditions and structures. The only difference is the perpetrators' choice of military hardware and strategy. Formally declared wars fought by regular national military forces committed (at least on paper) to the tenets of just war theory have now been replaced by a plethora of "quasi-military tactics" whose defining characteristics conjure up terrorism, perpetrated by individuals without attachments to a regular military and/or without allegiance to a national government and country, and who do not hesitate to put ordinary citizens in harm's way.

On the other hand, the second event of the new century, the UN Millennium Goals initiative, symbolizes the other side of the global coin, the recognition that the international community is also beset with a number of problems unrelated to military actions or national security, at least in a direct sense. Rather, the past three or four decades have witnessed the emergence and thrust to prominence of a number of new problems relating to social, economic, and environmental characteristics of the citizens that inhabit this planet. These problems impact the basic quality of life of global inhabitants in ways very different from the scourges of military violence. Yet they are just as dangerous and just as threatening. And they also unite us as global citizens in the same way that terrorism separates us. At the heart of this global change affecting the global system and its inhabitants for good or for ill is a phenomenon called globalization.

The Age of Globalization

The Cold War era, marked by the domination of two superpowers in the decades following the end of World War II, has given way to a new era called globalization. This new epoch is characterized by a dramatic shrinking of the globe in terms of travel and communication, increased participation in global policy making by an expanding array of national and non-state actors, and an exploding volume of problems with ever-growing consequences. While the tearing down of the Berlin Wall almost two decades ago dramatically symbolized the end of the Cold War era, the creation of the Internet, with its ability to connect around the world, and the fallen

World Trade Center, with its dramatic illustration of vulnerability, symbolize the new paradigm of integration and violence.

Globalization is a fluid and complex phenomenon that manifests itself in thousands of wondrous as well as disturbing ways. In the past 10 years, national borders have shrunk or disappeared, with a resultant increase in the movement of ideas, products, resources, finances, and people throughout the globe. This reality has brought with it great advances and challenges. For example, the ease with which people and objects move throughout the globe has greatly magnified fears like the spread of disease. The term "epidemic" has been replaced by the phrase "global pandemic," as virulent scourges unleashed in one part of the globe now have greater potential to find their way to the far corners of the planet. The world has also come to fear an expanded potential for terrorism, as new technologies combined with increasing cultural friction and socioeconomic disparities have conspired to make the world far less safe than it had been. The pistol that killed the Austrian Archduke in Sarajevo in 1914 ushering in World War I has been replaced by the jumbo jet used as a missile to bring down the World Trade Center and with it, to snuff out the lives of thousands of innocent victims. We now live in an era of global reach for both good and ill, where a small group or an individual can touch the hearts of people around the world with acts of kindness or can shatter their dreams with acts of terror.

This increase in the movement of information and ideas has ushered in global concerns over cultural imperialism and religious/ethnic wars. The ability both to retrieve and to disseminate information in the contemporary era will have an impact in this century as great as, if not greater than, the telephone, radio, and television in the last century. The potential for global good or ill is mind-boggling. Finally, traditional notions of great-power security embodied in the Cold War rivalry have given way to concerns about terrorism, genocide, nuclear proliferation, cultural conflict, and the diminishing role of international law.

Globalization heightens our awareness of a vast array of global issues that will challenge individuals as well as governmental and nongovernmental actors. Everyone has become a global actor and so has policy impact. This text seeks to identify those issues that are central to the discourse on the impact of globalization. The issues in this volume provide a broad overview of the mosaic of global issues that will affect students' daily lives.

What Is a Global Issue?

We begin by addressing the basic characteristics of a *global issue*.[1] By definition, the word *issue* suggests disagreement along several related dimensions:

1. whether a problem exists and how it comes about;
2. the characteristics of the problem;

---

[1]The characteristics are extracted from James E. Harf and B. Thomas Trout, *The Politics of Global Resources*, Duke University Press, 1986. pp. 12–28.

3. the preferred future alternatives or solutions; and/or
4. how these preferred futures are to be obtained.

These problems are real, vexing, and controversial because policymakers bring to their analysis different historical experiences, values, goals, and objectives. These differences impede and may even prevent successful problem solving. In short, the key ingredient of an issue is disagreement.

The word *global* in the phrase *global issue* is what makes the set of problems confronting the human race today far different from those that challenged earlier generations. Historically, problems were confined to a village, city, or region. The capacity of the human race to fulfill its daily needs was limited to a much smaller space: the immediate environment. In 1900, 90 percent of all humanity was born, lived, and died within a 50-mile radius. Today, over 30 percent of the world's population travel to one or more countries. In the United States, 75 percent of people move at least 100 miles away from their homes and most travel to places their grandparents could only dream about.

What does this mobility mean? It suggests that a vast array of issues are now no longer only local or national but global in scope, including but not limited to food resources, trade, energy, health care, the environment, disease, conflict, cultural rivalry, populism, and nuclear Armageddon.

The character of these issues is thus different from those of earlier eras. First, they transcend national boundaries and impact virtually every corner of the globe. In effect, these issues help make national borders increasingly meaningless. Environmental pollution or poisonous gases do not recognize or respect national borders. Birds carrying the avian flu have no knowledge of political boundaries.

Second, these new issues cannot be resolved by the autonomous action of a single actor, be it a national government, international organization, or multi-national corporation. A country cannot guarantee its own energy or food security without participating in a global energy or food system.

Third, these issues are characterized by a wide array of value systems. To a family in the developing world, giving birth to a fifth or sixth child may contribute to the family's immediate economic well-being. But to a research scholar at the United Nations Population Fund, the consequence of such an action multiplied across the entire developing world leads to expanding poverty and resource depletion.

Fourth, these issues will not go away. They require specific policy action by a consortium of local, national, and international leaders. Simply ignoring the issue cannot eliminate the threat of chemical or biological terrorism, for example. If global warming does exist, it would not disappear unless specific policies are developed and implemented.

These issues are also characterized by their persistence over time. The human race has developed the capacity to manipulate its external environment and, in so doing, has created a host of opportunities and challenges. The accelerating pace of technological change suggests that global issues will proliferate and will continue to challenge human beings throughout the next millennium.

In the final analysis, however, a global issue is defined as such only through mutual agreement by a host of actors within the international community. Some may disagree about the nature, severity, or presence of a given issue. These concerns then become areas of focus after a significant number of actors (states, international organizations, the United Nations, and others) begin to focus systematic and organized attention on the issue itself.

Defining the Global Issues Agenda

At the time of writing this book, the outcome of the 2008 U.S. presidential election is uncertain. Whether the next president is a republican or a democrat, we believe that it is critical that he or she embraces this new global issues agenda and validates the centrality of these issues not only as they relate to U.S. policy, but also as to how they affect global security and sustainability. How the new president meets these issues and concerns will be a central element in defining his or her effectiveness and legacy.

The Nexus of Global Issues and Globalization

Since 1989, the world has been caught in the maelstrom of globalization. Throughout the 1990s and into the twenty-first century, scholars and policymakers have struggled to define this new era. As the early years of the new century ushered in a different and heightened level of violence, a sense of urgency emerged. Some have analyzed the new era in terms of the victory of Western or American ideals, the dominance of global capitalism, and the spread of democracy vs. the have-nots of the world who use religious fanaticism as a ploy to rearrange power within the international system. Others have defined it simply in terms of the multiplicity of actors now performing on the world stage, and how states and their sovereignty have declined in importance and impact vis-à-vis others, such as multinational corporations, and nongovernmental groups like Greenpeace and Amnesty International. Still others have focused on the vital element of technology and its impact on communications, information storage and retrieval, global exchange, and attitudes, culture, and values.

Whether globalization reflects one, two, or all of these characteristics is not as important as the fundamental realization that globalization is the dominant element of a new era in international politics. The globalization revolution now shapes and dictates the agenda. To argue otherwise is frankly akin to insisting on using a rotary phone in an iPhone world. This new period is characterized by several basic traits that greatly impact the definition, analysis, and solution of global issues. They include the following:

- an emphasis on information technology;
- the increasing speed of information and idea flows;
- the ability of global citizens to access information at rapidly growing rates and thus empower themselves for good or for ill;

- a need for greater sophistication and expertise to manage such flows;
- the control and dissemination of technology; and
- the cultural diffusion and interaction that come with information expansion and dissemination.

Each of these areas has helped shape a new emerging global issues agenda. Current issues remain important and, indeed, these factors help us to understand them on a much deeper level. Yet globalization created a new array of problems that is reshaping the global issues landscape and the dialogue, tools, strategies, and approaches that the next U.S. president and indeed all global actors will take.

For example, the spread of information technology has made ideas, attitudes, and information more available to people throughout the world. Americans in Columbus, Ohio, had the ability to log onto the Internet and speak with their counterparts in Kosovo to discover when NATO bombing had begun and to gauge the accuracy of later news reports on the bombing. Norwegian students can share values and customs directly with their counterparts in South Africa, thereby experiencing cultural attitudes firsthand without the filtering mechanisms of governments or even parents and teachers. Scientific information that is available through computer technology can now be used to build sophisticated biological and chemical weapons of immense destructive capability, or equally to promote the dissemination of drugs and medicines outside of "normal" national channels. Ethnic conflicts and genocide between groups of people are now global news, forcing millions to come to grips with issues of intervention, prevention, and punishment. And terrorists in different parts of the globe can communicate readily with one another, transferring plans and even money across national and continental boundaries with ease.

Globalization is an international system and it is also rapidly changing. Because of the fluid nature of this system and the fact that it is both relatively new and largely fueled by the amazing speed of technology, continuing issues are constantly being transformed and new issues are emerging regularly. The nexus of globalization and global issues has now become, in many ways, the defining dynamic of understanding global issues. Whether it is new forms of terrorism, new conceptions of security, expanding international law, solving ethnic conflicts, dealing with mass migration, coping with individual freedom and access to information, or addressing cultural clash and cultural imperialism, the transition from a Cold War world to a globalized world helps us understand in part what these issues are and why they are important. But most importantly, this fundamental realization shapes how governments and people can and must respond.

Identifying the New Global Issues Agenda

The organization of this text reflects the centrality of globalization. Parts 1 and 2 focus on the continuing global agenda of the post-Cold War era. The emphasis is on global population and environmental issues and the nexus between these two phenomena. Has the threat of uncontrolled world population growth subsided or will the built-in momentum of the past 30 years override any recent strides in slowing birth rates in the developing world? Should the international community continue to address this problem? Is global aging about to unleash a host of problems for governments of the developed world? Is rapid urbanization creating a whole new set of problems unique to such urban settings? Do environmentalists overstate their case or is the charge of "crying wolf" by environmental conservatives a misplaced attack? Is the world running out of natural resources or is the concern of many about resource availability, be it food, oil, water, air, and/or pristine land, simply misguided? Should the world continue to rely on oil or should the search for viable alternatives take on a new urgency? Will the world be able to feed itself or provide enough water in the foreseeable future? Is global warming for real?

Part 3 addresses the consequences of the decline of national boundaries and the resultant increased international flow of information, ideas, money, and material things in this globalization age. Can the global community win the war on drugs? Is the international community prepared for the next global health pandemic? Has this community also designed an adequate strategy to address human trafficking? Is globalization a positive or negative development? Does the explosion of the Internet in forms like MySpace and YouTube aid or hinder democratization?

Part 4 addresses the new global security dilemma. Does immigration policy affect terrorism? Are we headed for a nuclear 9/11? Are cultural and ethnic wars the defining dimensions of conflict in this century? Is this the China century? Can nuclear proliferation be stopped? Has U.S. hegemony rendered the United Nations irrelevant?

The revolutionary changes of the last few decades present us with serious challenges unlike any others in human history. However, as in all periods of historic change, we possess significant opportunities to overcome problems. The task ahead is to define these issues, explore their context, and develop solutions that are comprehensive in scope and effect. The role of all researchers in this field, or any other, is to analyze objectively such problems and search for workable solutions. As students of global issues, your task is to educate yourselves about these issues and become part of the solution.

Internet References . . .

Population Reference Bureau

The Population Reference Bureau provides current information on international population trends and their implications from an objective viewpoint. The PopNet section of this Web site offers maps with regional and country-specific population information as well as information divided by selected topics.

http://www.prb.org

United Nations Population Fund (UNFPA)

The United Nations Population Fund (UNFPA) was established in 1969 and was originally called the United Nations Fund for Population Activities. This organization works with developing countries to educate people about reproductive and sexual health as well as about family planning. The UNFPA also supports population and development strategies that will benefit developing countries and advocates for the resources needed to accomplish these tasks.

http://www.unfpa.org

Population Connection

Population Connection (formerly Zero Population Growth) is a national, nonprofit organization working to slow population growth and to achieve a sustainable balance between Earth's people and its resources. The organization seeks to protect the environment and to ensure a high quality of life for present and future generations.

http://www.populationconnection.org

The CSIS Global Aging Initiative

The Center for Strategic and International Studies (CSIS) is a public policy research institution that approaches the issue of the aging population in developed countries in a bipartisan manner. The CSIS is involved in a two-year project to explore the global implications of aging in developed nations and to seek strategies on dealing with this issue. This site includes a list of publications that were presented at previous events.

http://www.csis.org/gai/

The Population Council

The Population Council is an international, nonprofit organization that conducts research on population matters from biological, social science, and public health perspectives. It was established in 1952 by John D. Rockefeller, III.

http://www.popcouncil.org

The Population Institute

The Population Institute is an international, educational, non-profit organization that seeks to voluntarily reduce excessive population growth. Established in 1989 and headquartered in Washington, D.C., it has members in 172 countries.

http://www.populationinstitute.org

Global Population

*I*t is not a coincidence that many of the global issues in this book emerged at about the same time as world population growth exploded. No matter what the issue, the presence of a large and fast-growing population alongside it exacerbates the issue and transforms its basic characteristics. In the new millennium, declining growth rates, which first appeared in the developed world but are now also evident in many parts of the developing world, pose a different set of problems. The emergence of a graying population throughout the globe, but particularly in the developed world, has the potential for significant impact. And the rapid growth within urban areas of the developing world continues to pose a different set of problems. The ability of the global community to respond to any given issue is diminished by certain population conditions, be it an extremely young consuming population in a poor country in need of producers, an expanding urban population whose local public officials are unable to provide an appropriate infrastructure, a large working-age group in a nation without sufficient jobs, or an ever-growing senior population for whom additional services are needed.

Thus we begin this text with a series of issues directly related to various aspects of world population. It serves as both a separate global agenda and as a context within which other issues are examined.

- Are Declining Growth Rates Rather than Rapid Population Growth Today's Major Global Population Problem?

- Should the International Community Attempt to Curb Population Growth in the Developing World?

- Is Global Aging in the Developed World a Major Problem?

- Does Global Urbanization Lead Primarily to Undesirable Consequences?

ISSUE 1

Are Declining Growth Rates Rather than Rapid Population Growth Today's Major Global Population Problem?

YES: Michael Meyer, from "Birth Dearth," *Newsweek* (September 27, 2004)

NO: Danielle Nierenberg and Mia MacDonald, from "The Population Story . . . So Far," *World Watch Magazine* (September/ October 2004)

ISSUE SUMMARY

YES: Michael Meyer, a writer for *Newsweek International,* argues that the new global population threat is not too many people as a consequence of continuing high growth rates. On the contrary, declining birth rates will ultimately lead to depopulation in many places on Earth, a virtual population implosion, in both the developed and developing worlds.

NO: Danielle Nierenberg, a research associate at the Worldwatch Institute, and Mia MacDonald, a policy analyst and Worldwatch Institute senior fellow, argue that the consequences of a still-rising population have worsened in some ways because of the simultaneous existence of fast-rising consumption patterns, creating a new set of concerns.

Beginning in the late 1960s, demographers began to observe dramatic increases in population growth, particularly in the developing world. As a consequence, both policymakers and scholars focused on projections of rising birth rates and declining death rates, the consequences of the resultant increased population levels, and strategies for combating such growth. By the mid-1970s, growth rates, particularly in the developing world, were such that the doubling of the world's population was predicted to occur in only a few decades. Consensus on both the resultant level of population growth and its implications was not immediately evident, however. And indeed, as the last millennium was coming to an end, a billion people were added to the world's population in just 12 short years. Contrast this time frame with the fact that it had taken all of recorded history until 1830 for the planet to reach a population of one billion and 100 years for the second billion.

In the last decade of the millennium, however, something unforeseen happened. Population growth slowed, not only in the developed sector of the globe but also in the developing world. The U.N. Population Fund lowered its short-term and long-term projections. With the turn of the century, individual demographers began to change their calculations as well with the turn of the century as the release of yearly figures suggested the need to do so.

More specifically, no longer could observers simply place all developing countries into a high-growth category and reserve the low-growth category for countries of the developed world. It had become clear that an increasing number of poorer countries had begun to experience a dramatic drop in fertility as well as growth rates.

These recent trends have been surprising, as most observers had long believed that the built-in momentum of population growth in the last third of the twentieth century would have major impacts well into the new century. The logic was understandable, as numbers do matter. They contain a potential built-in momentum that, if left unchecked, creates a geometric increase in births. For example, let us assume that a young third-world mother gives birth to three daughters before the age of 20. In turn, each of these three daughters has three daughters before she reaches the age of 20. The result of such fertility behavior is a nine-fold (900 percent) increase in the population (minus a much lower mortality-rate influence) within 40 years, or two generations. Contrast this pattern with that of a young mother in the developed world, who is currently reproducing at or slightly above/below replacement level. Add a third generation of fertility, and the developing-world family will have increased 27-fold within 60 years, while the developed-world family's size would remain virtually unchanged.

Thus, problems relating to population growth may, in fact, be at the heart of most global issues. If growth is a problem, control it and half the ecological battle is won. Fail to control it, and global problem-solvers will be swimming upstream against an ever-increasing current. It is for this reason that the question of "out-of-control" population growth was selected to be the first issue in this volume.

Michael Meyer describes how families in both the developed and developing worlds are choosing to have fewer children and chronicles what he believes to be an array of negative consequences associated with this population transition. Danielle Nierenberg and Mia MacDonald argue that even though the rate of growth has declined, the latter is applied to a much larger base than at any time in history, including the last century.

YES ↵

Birth Dearth

Everyone knows there are too many people in the world. Whether we live in Lahore or Los Angeles, Shanghai or Sao Paulo, our lives are daily proof. We endure traffic gridlock, urban sprawl and environmental depredation. The evening news brings variations on Ramallah or Darfur—images of Third World famine, poverty, pestilence, war, global competition for jobs, and increasingly scarce natural resources.

Just last week the United Nations warned that many of the world's cities are becoming hopelessly overcrowded. Lagos alone will grow from 6.5 million people in 1995 to 16 million by 2015, a miasma of slums and decay where a fifth of all children will die before they are 5. At a conference in London, the U.N. Population Fund weighed in with a similarly bleak report: unless something dramatically changes, the world's 50 poorest countries will triple in size by 2050, to 1.7 billion people.

Yet this is not the full story. To the contrary, in fact. Across the globe, people are having fewer and fewer children. Fertility rates have dropped by half since 1972, from six children per woman to 2.9. And demographers say they're still falling, faster than ever. The world's population will continue to grow—from today's 6.4 billion to around 9 billion in 2050. But after that, it will go sharply into decline. Indeed, a phenomenon that we're destined to learn much more about—depopulation—has already begun in a number of countries. Welcome to the New Demography. It will change everything about our world, from the absolute size and power of nations to global economic growth to the quality of our lives.

This revolutionary transformation will be led not so much by developed nations as by the developing ones. Most of us are familiar with demographic trends in Europe, where birthrates have been declining for years. To reproduce itself, a society's women must each bear 2.1 children. Europe's fertility rates fall far short of that, according to the 2002 U.N. population report. France and Ireland, at 1.8, top Europe's childbearing charts. Italy and Spain, at 1.2, bring up the rear. In between are countries such as Germany, whose fertility rate of 1.4 is exactly Europe's average. What does that mean? If the U.N. figures are right, Germany could shed nearly a fifth of its 82.5 million people over the next 40 years—roughly the equivalent of all of east Germany, a loss of population not seen in Europe since the Thirty Years' War.

From *Newsweek*, vol. 144, issue 13, September 27, 2004, pp. 54–61. Copyright © 2004 by Newsweek. Reprinted by permission via PARS International.

And so it is across the Continent. Bulgaria will shrink by 38 percent, Romania by 27 percent, Estonia by 25 percent. "Parts of Eastern Europe, already sparsely populated, will just empty out," predicts Reiner Klingholz, director of the Berlin Institute for Population and Development. Russia is already losing close to 750,000 people yearly. (President Vladimir Putin calls it a "national crisis.") So is Western Europe, and that figure could grow to as much as 3 million a year by midcentury, if not more.

The surprise is how closely the less-developed world is following the same trajectory. In Asia it's well known that Japan will soon tip into population loss, if it hasn't already. With a fertility rate of 1.3 children per woman, the country stands to shed a quarter of its 127 million people over the next four decades, according to U.N. projections. But while the graying of Japan (average age: 42.3 years) has long been a staple of news headlines, what to make of China, whose fertility rate has declined from 5.8 in 1970 to 1.8 today, according to the U.N.? Chinese census data put the figure even lower, at 1.3. Coupled with increasing life spans, that means China's population will age as quickly in one generation as Europe's has over the past 100 years, reports the Center for Strategic and International Studies in Washington. With an expected median age of 44 in 2015, China will be older on average than the United States. By 2019 or soon after, its population will peak at 1.5 billion, then enter a steep decline. By midcentury, China could well lose 20 to 30 percent of its population every generation.

The picture is similar elsewhere in Asia, where birthrates are declining even in the absence of such stringent birth-control programs as China's. Indeed, it's happening despite often generous official incentives to procreate. The industrialized nations of Singapore, Hong Kong, Taiwan and South Korea all report subreplacement fertility, says Nicholas Eberstadt, a demographer at the American Enterprise Institute in Washington. To this list can be added Thailand, Burma, Australia and Sri Lanka, along with Cuba and many Caribbean nations, as well as Uruguay and Brazil. Mexico is aging so rapidly that within several decades it will not only stop growing but will have an older population than that of the United States. So much for the cliche of those Mexican youths swarming across the Rio Grande? "If these figures are accurate," says Eberstadt, "just about half of the world's population lives in subreplacement countries."

There are notable exceptions. In Europe, Albania and the outlier province of Kosovo are reproducing energetically. So are pockets of Asia: Mongolia, Pakistan and the Philippines. The United Nations projects that the Middle East will double in population over the next 20 years, growing from 326 million today to 649 million by 2050. Saudi Arabia has one of the highest fertility rates in the world, 5.7, after Palestinian territories at 5.9 and Yemen at 7.2. Yet there are surprises here, too. Tunisia has tipped below replacement. Lebanon and Iran are at the threshold. And though overall the region's population continues to grow, the increase is due mainly to lower infant mortality; fertility rates themselves are falling faster than in developed countries, indicating that over the coming decades the Middle

East will age far more rapidly than other regions of the world. Birthrates in Africa remain high, and despite the AIDS epidemic its population is projected to keep growing. So is that of the United States.

We'll return to American exceptionalism, and what that might portend. But first, let's explore the causes of the birth dearth, as outlined in a pair of new books on the subject. "Never in the last 650 years, since the time of the Black Plague, have birth and fertility rates fallen so far, so fast, so low, for so long, in so many places," writes the sociologist Ben Wattenberg in "Fewer: How the New Demography of Depopulation Will Shape Our Future." Why? Wattenberg suggests that a variety of once independent trends have conjoined to produce a demographic tsunami. As the United Nations reported last week, people everywhere are leaving the countryside and moving to cities, which will be home to more than half the world's people by 2007. Once there, having a child becomes a cost rather than an asset. From 1970 to 2000, Nigeria's urban population climbed from 14 to 44 percent. South Korea went from 28 to 84 percent. So-called megacities, from Lagos to Mexico City, have exploded seemingly overnight. Birthrates have fallen in inverse correlation.

Other factors are at work. Increasing female literacy and enrollment in schools have tended to decrease fertility, as have divorce, abortion and the worldwide trend toward later marriage. Contraceptive use has risen dramatically over the past decade; according to U.N. data, 62 percent of married or "in union" women of reproductive age are now using some form of nonnatural birth control. In countries such as India, now the capital of global HIV, disease has become a factor. In Russia, the culprits include alcoholism, poor public health and industrial pollution that has whacked male sperm counts. Wealth discourages childbearing, as seen long ago in Europe and now in Asia. As Wattenberg puts it, "Capitalism is the best contraception."

The potential consequences of the population implosion are enormous. Consider the global economy, as Phillip Longman describes it in another recent book, "The Empty Cradle: How Falling Birthrates Threaten World Prosperity and What to Do About It." A population expert at the New America Foundation in Washington, he sees danger for global prosperity. Whether it's real estate or consumer spending, economic growth and population have always been closely linked. "There are people who cling to the hope that you can have a vibrant economy without a growing population, but mainstream economists are pessimistic," says Longman. You have only to look at Japan or Europe for a whiff of what the future might bring, he adds. In Italy, demographers forecast a 40 percent decline in the working-age population over the next four decades—accompanied by a commensurate drop in growth across the Continent, according to the European Commission. What happens when Europe's cohort of baby boomers begins to retire around 2020? Recent strikes and demonstrations in Germany, Italy, France and Austria over the most modest pension reforms are only the beginning of what promises to become a major sociological battle between Europe's older and younger generations.

That will be only a skirmish compared with the conflict brewing in China. There market reforms have removed the cradle-to-grave benefits of the planned economy, while the Communist Party hasn't constructed an adequate social safety net to take their place. Less than one quarter of the population is covered by retirement pensions, according to CSIS. That puts the burden of elder care almost entirely on what is now a generation of only children. The one-child policy has led to the so-called 4-2-1 problem, in which each child will be potentially responsible for caring for two parents and four grandparents.

Incomes in China aren't rising fast enough to offset this burden. In some rural villages, so many young people have fled to the cities that there may be nobody left to look after the elders. And the aging population could soon start to dull China's competitive edge, which depends on a seemingly endless supply of cheap labor. After 2015, this labor pool will begin to dry up, says economist Hu Angang. China will have little choice but to adopt a very Western-sounding solution, he says: it will have to raise the education level of its work force and make it more productive. Whether it can is an open question. Either way, this much is certain: among Asia's emerging economic powers, China will be the first to grow old before it gets rich.

Equally deep dislocations are becoming apparent in Japan. Akihiko Matsutani, an economist and author of a recent best seller, "The Economy of a Shrinking Population," predicts that by 2009 Japan's economy will enter an era of "negative growth." By 2030, national income will have shrunk by 15 percent. Speculating about the future is always dicey, but economists pose troubling questions. Take the legendarily high savings that have long buoyed the Japanese economy and financed borrowing worldwide, especially by the United States. As an aging Japan draws down those assets in retirement, will U.S. and global interest rates rise? At home, will Japanese businesses find themselves competing for increasingly scarce investment capital? And just what will they be investing in, as the country's consumers grow older, and demand for the latest in hot new products cools off? What of the effect on national infrastructure? With less tax revenue in state coffers, Matsutani predicts, governments will increasingly be forced to skimp on or delay repairs to the nation's roads, bridges, rail lines and the like. "Life will become less convenient," he says. Spanking-clean Tokyo might come to look more like New York City in the 1970s, when many urban dwellers decamped for the suburbs (taking their taxes with them) and city fathers could no longer afford the municipal upkeep. Can Japanese cope? "They will have to," says Matsutani. "There's no alternative."

Demographic change magnifies all of a country's problems, social as well as economic. An overburdened welfare state? Aging makes it collapse. Tensions over immigration? Differing birthrates intensify anxieties, just as the need for imported labor rises—perhaps the critical issue for the Europe of tomorrow. A poor education system, with too many kids left behind? Better fix it, because a shrinking work force requires higher productivity and greater flexibility, reflected in a new need for continuing job training, career switches and the health care needed to keep workers working into old age.

In an ideal world, perhaps, the growing gulf between the world's wealthy but shrinking countries and its poor, growing ones would create an opportunity. Labor would flow from the overpopulated, resource-poor south to the depopulating north, where jobs would continue to be plentiful. Capital and remittance income from the rich nations would flow along the reverse path, benefiting all. Will it happen? Perhaps, but that presupposes considerable labor mobility. Considering the resistance Europeans display toward large-scale immigration from North Africa, or Japan's almost zero-immigration policy, it's hard to be optimistic. Yes, attitudes are changing. Only a decade ago, for instance, Europeans also spoke of zero immigration. Today they recognize the need and, in bits and pieces, are beginning to plan for it. But will it happen on the scale required?

A more probable scenario may be an intensification of existing tensions between peoples determined to preserve their beleaguered national identities on the one hand, and immigrant groups on the other seeking to escape overcrowding and lack of opportunity at home. For countries such as the Philippines—still growing, and whose educated work force looks likely to break out of low-status jobs as nannies and gardeners and move up the global professional ladder—this may be less of a problem. It will be vastly more serious for the tens of millions of Arab youths who make up a majority of the population in the Middle East and North Africa, at least half of whom are unemployed.

America is the wild card in this global equation. While Europe and much of Asia shrinks, the United States' indigenous population looks likely to stay relatively constant, with fertility rates hovering almost precisely at replacement levels. Add in heavy immigration, and you quickly see that America is the only modern nation that will continue to grow. Over the next 45 years the United States will gain 100 million people, Wattenberg estimates, while Europe loses roughly as many.

This does not mean that Americans will escape the coming demographic whammy. They, too, face the problems of an aging work force and its burdens. (The cost of Medicare and Social Security will rise from 4.3 percent of GDP in 2000 to 11.5 percent in 2030 and 21 percent in 2050, according to the Congressional Budget Office.) They, too, face the prospect of increasing ethnic tensions, as a flat white population and a dwindling black one become gradually smaller minorities in a growing multicultural sea. And in our interdependent era, the troubles of America's major trading partners—Europe and Japan—will quickly become its own. To cite one example, what becomes of the vaunted "China market," invested in so heavily by U.S. companies, if by 2050 China loses an estimated 35 percent of its workers and the aged consume an ever-greater share of income?

America's demographic "unipolarity" has profound security implications as well. Washington worries about terrorism and failing states. Yet the chaos of today's fragmented world is likely to prove small in comparison to what could come. For U.S. leaders, Longman in "The Empty Cradle" sketches an unsettling prospect. Though the United States may have few military competitors, the technologies by which it projects geopolitical power—from laser-guided missiles and stealth bombers to a huge military infrastructure—may gradually become too expensive for a country facing massively rising social entitlements in an era of slowing global economic growth. If the war on terrorism turns out to be the "generational struggle" that national-security adviser Condoleezza Rice says it is, Longman concludes, then the United States might have difficulty paying for it.

None of this is writ, of course. Enlightened governments could help hold the line. France and the Netherlands have instituted family-friendly policies that help women combine work and motherhood, ranging from tax credits for kids to subsidized day care. Scandinavian countries have kept birthrates up with generous provisions for parental leave, health care and part-time employment. Still, similar programs offered by the shrinking city-state of Singapore—including a state-run dating service—have done little to reverse the birth dearth. Remember, too, that such prognoses have been wrong in the past. At the cusp of the postwar baby boom, demographers predicted a sharp fall in fertility and a global birth dearth. Yet even if this generation of seers turns out to be right, as seems likely, not all is bad. Environmentally, a smaller world is almost certainly a better world, whether in terms of cleaner air or, say, the return of wolves and rare flora to abandoned stretches of the East German countryside. And while people are living longer, they are also living healthier—at least in the developed world. That means they can (and probably should) work more years before retirement.

Yes, a younger generation will have to shoulder the burden of paying for their elders. But there will be compensations. As populations shrink, says economist Matsutani, national incomes may drop—but not necessarily per capita incomes. And in this realm of uncertainty, one mundane thing is probably sure: real-estate prices will fall. That will hurt seniors whose nest eggs are tied up in their homes, but it will be a boon to youngsters of the future. Who knows? Maybe the added space and cheap living will inspire them to, well, do whatever it takes to make more babies. Thus the cycle of life will restore its balance. . . .

Danielle Nierenberg and
Mia MacDonald

➡ **NO**

The Population Story . . . So Far

Forty years ago, the world's women bore an average of six children each. Today, that number is just below three. In 1960, 10–15 percent of married couples in developing countries used a modern method of contraception; now, 60 percent do.

To a considerable extent, these simple facts sum up the change in the Earth's human population prospects, then and now. In the mid-1960s, it was not uncommon to think about the human population as a time bomb. In 1971, population biologist Paul Ehrlich estimated that if human numbers kept increasing at the high rates of the time, by around 2900 the planet would be teeming with sixty million billion people (that's 60,000,000,000,000,000). But the rate of population rise actually peaked in the 1960s and demographers expect a leveling-off of human numbers this century.

Every couple of years the United Nations Population Division issues projections of human population growth to 2050. In 2002, U.N. demographers predicted a somewhat different picture of human population growth to mid-century than what the "population bombers" thought likely a generation ago. World population, growing by 76 million people every year (about 240,000 people per day), will pass 6.4 billion this year. The latest U.N. mid-range estimate says there will be about 8.9 billion people on Earth by 2050. And, according to this new scenario, total population will begin to shrink over the next hundred years.

These numbers are leading some people to say that the population bomb has been defused. A few nations, such as Italy and Japan, are even worried that birth rates are too low and that their graying populations will be a drain on the economy. (Some studies suggest that China, the world's most populous country, may also "need" more people to help support the hundreds of millions who will retire in coming decades.)

We're not out of the woods yet. While the annual rate of population growth has decreased since 1970—from about 2 percent to 1.3 percent today—*the rate is applied to a much larger population* than ever before, meaning that the added yearly increments to the population are also much larger. These numbers show that the largest generation in history has

From *World Watch Magazine*, September/October 2004, PP. 14–17. Copyright © 2004 by Worldwatch Institute. Reprinted by permission. www.worldwatch.com.

arrived: 1.2 billion people are between 10 and 19. In large measure, it will be their choices—those they have, and those they make—that determine where the global population meter rests by mid-century.

Population × Consumption

Potential for catastrophe persists. In many places, population growth is slowly smoldering but could turn into a fast burn. Countries as diverse as Ethiopia, the Democratic Republic of Congo, and Pakistan are poised to more than double their size by 2050 even as supplies of water, forests, and food crops are already showing signs of strain and other species are being squeezed into smaller and smaller ranges. Arid Yemen will likely see its population quadruple to 80 million by 2050. The U.N. estimates that populations in the world's 48 least-developed countries could triple by 2050. And if the world's women have, on average, a half a child more than the U.N. predicts, global population could grow to 10.6 billion by mid-century.

But it is a mistake to think that population growth is only a problem for developing countries. While consumption levels need to increase among the 2.8 billion people who now live on less than $2 a day, high rates of population growth combined with high levels of consumption in rich countries are taking a heavy toll on the Earth's natural resources:

- Carbon dioxide levels today are 18 percent higher than in 1960 and an estimated 31 percent higher than they were at the onset of the Industrial Revolution in 1750.
- Half the world's original forest cover is gone and another 30 percent is degraded or fragmented.
- Industrial fleets have fished out at least 90 percent of all large ocean predators—tuna, marlin, swordfish, cod, halibut, skate, and flounder—in just the past 50 years, according to a study in *Nature* in 2003.
- An estimated 10–20 percent of the world's cropland, and more than 70 percent of the world's rangelands, are degraded.

As global consumption of oil, meat, electricity, paper products, and a host of consumer goods rises, the impact of population numbers takes on a new relevance. Although each new person increases total demands on the Earth's resources, the size of each person's "ecological footprint"—the biologically productive area required to support that person—varies hugely from one to another. The largest ecofootprints belong to those in the industrialized world.

Further, new demographic trends can have significant impacts as well. Since 1970, the number of people living together in one household has declined worldwide, as incomes have risen, urbanization has accelerated and families have gotten smaller. With fewer people sharing energy, appliances, and furnishings, consumption actually rises. A one-person household in the United States uses about 17 percent *more* energy per person than a two-person home.

And while some nations are getting nervous about declining birth rates, for most of the world the end of population growth is anything but imminent. Although fertility rates are ratcheting down, this trajectory is not guaranteed. Projections of slower population growth assume that more couples will be able to choose to have smaller families, and that investment in reproductive health keeps pace with rising demand. But along the route to the eventual leveling-off of global population, plateaus are possible. And smaller families are not guaranteed in countries where government resources are strained or where health care, education, and women's rights are low on the list of priorities.

In the West African country of Niger, for example, the availability of family planning and reproductive health services has declined, while birth rates have increased. According to a recent report by the World Bank, the average woman in Niger will give birth to eight children in her lifetime, up from seven in 1998 and more than women in any other nation. Niger is already bulging with young people; 50 percent of the population is under age 15 and 70 percent is under 25.

Biology ≠ Destiny

A series of global conferences in the 1990s—spanning the Rio Earth Summit in 1992, the Cairo population conference (1994), the Beijing women's conference (1995), and the UN's Millennium Summit in 2000—put issues of environment, development, poverty, and women's rights on the global policy table. As a result, discussions of the relationship between growing human numbers and the Earth's ability to provide are increasingly framed by the realities of gender relations. It is now generally agreed that while enabling larger numbers of women and men to use modern methods of family planning is essential, it is not sufficient. Expanding the choices, capacities, and agency of women has become a central thread in the population story. Consumption—what we need and what we want—is, too.

Many studies have shown that women with more education have smaller, healthier families, and that their children have a better chance of making it out of poverty. Likewise, wealthier women and those with the right to make decisions about their lives and bodies also have fewer children. And women who have the choice to delay marriage and childbearing past their teens tend to have fewer children than those women—and there are millions of them still—who marry before they've completed the transition from adolescence. Equalizing relations between women and men is also a social good: not only is it just, but a recent World Bank report found that in developing countries where gender equality lags, efforts to combat poverty and increase economic growth lag, too.

Yet women's rights and voices remain suppressed or muted throughout the world. Over 100 million girls will be married before their 18th birthdays in the next decade, some as young as 8 or 9. Early childbearing is the leading cause of death and disability for women between the ages of 15 and 19 in developing countries. At least 350 million women still lack access to a full range of contraceptive methods, 10 years after the Cairo conference yielded a 20-year plan to balance the world's people with its resources. Demand for services will increase an estimated 40 percent by 2025.

The assault of HIV/AIDS is also increasingly hurting women: more than 18 million women are living with HIV/AIDS, and in 2003 women's rate of infection for the first time equaled men's. In the region hardest hit, sub-Saharan Africa, 60 percent of adults living with HIV are women. Two-thirds of the world's 876 million illiterates are women and a majority of the 115 million children not attending grade school are girls. In no country in the world are women judged to have political, economic, and social power equal to that of men.

Even in the United States, women's reproductive rights are increasingly constrained by the growing number of restrictions and conditions on choice imposed by state and federal laws. Like the U.S. lifestyle, the current Administration's blinkered view of sexuality has gone global. The United States has withheld $34 million from the U.N. Population Fund (UNFPA) every year of the Bush Administration due to a dispute over abortion. And the "global gag rule," a relic of the Reagan presidency reimposed by President Bush, binds U.S. population assistance by making taboo any discussion of abortion in reproductive health clinics, even in countries where it is legal.

The impacts reach more deeply than the rhetoric: due to the loss of U.S. population funds, reproductive health services have been scaled back or eliminated in some of the world's poorest countries, precisely where fertility rates are highest and women's access to family planning most tenuous. In Kenya, for instance, the two main providers of reproductive health services refused to sign a pledge to enforce the gag rule, with the result that they lost funds and closed five family planning clinics, eliminating women's access to maternal health care, contraception, and voluntary counseling and testing for HIV/AIDS. In Ethiopia, where only 6 percent of women use modern methods of contraception, the gag rule has cut a wide swath: clinics have reduced services, laid off staff and curtailed community health programs; many have suffered shortages of contraceptive supplies.

Need ↑ Funds ↓

A recent study by UNFPA and the Alan Guttmacher Institute estimated that meeting women's current unmet need for contraception would prevent each year:

- 23 million unplanned births;
- 22 million induced abortions;
- 1.4 million infant deaths;

- 142,000 pregnancy related-deaths (including 53,000 from unsafe abortions); and
- 505,000 children losing their mothers due to pregnancy-related causes.

The non-medical benefits are not quantified but are considerable: greater self-esteem and decision-making power for women; higher productivity and income; increased health, nutrition, and education expenditures on each child; higher savings and investment rates; and increased equality between women and men. We know this from experience: recent research in the United States, for example, ascribes the large numbers of women entering law, medical, and other professional training programs in the 1970s to the expanded choices afforded by the wide availability of the Pill.

Despite these benedits, vast needs go unmet as the Cairo action plan remains underfunded. The United States is not the only culprit. UNFPA reports that donor funds for a basic package of reproductive health services and population data and policy work totaled about $3.1 billion in 2003—$2.6 billion less than the level agreed to in the ICPD Program. Developing country domestic resources were estimated at $11.7 billion, a major portion of which is spent by just a handful of large countries. A number of countries, particularly the poorest, rely heavily on donor funds to provide services for family planning, reproductive health, and HIV/AIDS, and to build data sets and craft needed policies.

A year from now, donors will be expected to be contributing $6.1 billion annually, $3 billion more than what has already been spent. "A world that spends $800 billion to $1 trillion each year on the military can afford the equivalent of slightly more than one day's military spending to close Cairo's $3 billion external funding gap to save and improve the lives of millions of women and families in developing countries," says UNFPA's executive director, Thoraya Obaid. But as the world's priorities lie in other arenas, it is looking increasingly unlikely that the Cairo targets—despite their modest price tag in a world where the bill for a war can top $100 billion—will be met.

But it isn't only poor people in developing countries who will determine whether the more dire population scenarios pass from speculation to reality. Family size has declined in most wealthy nations, but the U.S. population grew by 32.7 million people (13.1 percent) during the 1990s, the largest number in any 10-year period in U.S. history. At about 280 million people, the United States is now the third most populous nation in the world and its population is expected to reach 400 million by 2050. A recent study suggests that if every person alive today consumed at the rate of an average person in the United States, three more planets would be required to fulfill these demands.

Whether or not birth rates continue to fall, consumption levels and patterns (affluence), coupled with technology, take on new importance. The global consumer class—around 1.7 billion people, or more than a quarter of humanity—is growing rapidly. These people are collectively responsible for the vast majority of meat-eating, paper use, car driving, and energy consumption on the planet, as well as the resulting impact of these activities on its natural resources. As populations surge in developing countries and the world becomes increasingly globalized, more and more people have access to, and the means to acquire, a greater diversity of products and services than ever before.

It is the combined effect of human numbers and human consumption that creates such potent flash-points. Decisions about sexuality and lifestyle are among the most deeply personal and political decisions societies and their citizens can make. The fate of the human presence on the Earth will be shaped in large part by those decisions and how their implications unfold in the coming years. This population story's ending still hasn't been written.

POSTSCRIPT

Are Declining Growth Rates Rather than Rapid Population Growth Today's Major Global Population Problem?

The growth issue can be structured most simply as one of an insurmountable built-in momentum vs. dramatic change in fertility attitudes and behavior. Demographers are correct when they assert that the population explosion of the latter part of the twentieth century had the potential of future fertility disaster because of the high percentage of the population who are either in the middle of or about to enter their reproductive years. They are also correct when they assert that the last decade has witnessed major transitions away from high growth rates, even in many parts of the developing world.

The key word is "potential." Its relevance grows out of the built-in momentum that has caused the developing world's actual population to rise substantially in the last thirty-five years despite a decline in the growth rate. In its 2001 analysis of population patterns, the United Nations suggested that population growth in the first half of the twenty-first century would increase by over 50 percent, or by more than 3 billion (United Nations, *World Population: The 2000 Revision—Highlights* 2001). This was higher than its projections of just two years earlier, due primarily to higher projected fertility levels in countries that are slow to show signs of fertility decline.

The entire growth of the first half of the twenty-first century would take place in the developing world, according to the study. It acknowledged that population would also grow in the developed world during the first 25 years of the new century, but then it would decline to levels approximating 2000 by mid-century. On the other hand, despite lowering birth rates in the less developed world, the built-in momentum would result in a 65 percent projected growth (from 4.9 billion in 2000 to 8.1 billion in 2050) during the first half of the century.

The U.N. revised its earlier predictions in 2002, tempering projections for future growth (*World Population Prospects: The 2002 Revision*). The executive director of the U.N. Population Fund explained it by suggesting that "men and women in larger numbers were making their own decisions on birth spacing and family size, contributing to slower population growth."

A perusal of the Population Reference Bureau's *2007 World Population Data Sheet* confirms, however, that while the developed world is growing slowly (1.6 million per year), the developing world is continuing its rapid growth (80 million per year at current rates). Birth rates, while falling worldwide, are still high enough in the poorer sectors of the globe to ensure continued high growth for some time into the future.

It has become increasingly clear that today's youth will not produce at the same level as their parents and grandparents, based on the evidence of the last quarter-century. Two factors are at work here. The demographic transition is evident in those countries of the developing world that are experiencing economic growth. Birth rates have dropped significantly, leading to lowered growth rates. In over one-third of the world's countries, containing 43 percent of the globe's population, women are having no more than two children on average. But while the rates are higher than those for the newly industrializing countries of the third world, growth rates for the remaining developing countries have also dropped in a large number of cases. In the latter situation, policy intervention lies at the heart of such lowered rates. The latter effort has been spearheaded by the United Nations and includes the work of many non-governmental organizations as well. In global conferences held every 10 years (1974, 1984, and 1994), the entire international community has systematically addressed the problem of third-world fertility, admittedly from different perspectives. Yet world population is still growing at a 1.2 percent rate, adding 80 million people annually.

Acknowledging declining birth rates still begs the question: Is there still a built-in momentum that will lead to negative consequences? William P. Butz addresses this question in *The Double Divide: Implosionists and Explosionists Endanger Progress Since Cairo* (Population Reference Bureau, September 2004). The Implosionists argue that falling birth rates throughout the world is the most important variable. They suggest that the biggest global population challenge in the immediate future will be how to cope with the wide range of challenges confronting countries with declining fertility rates. The Explosionists counter that there will still be substantial population growth, even in those countries that have recently begun to experience low birth rates. To them, world leaders and organizations must not ignore those problems that emerge from populations whose percentage of young are still quite high. Two who share the implosionist position are David R. Francis ("Now, Dangers of a Population Implosion," *Christian Science Monitor*, October 7, 2004) and Denis Dutton ("Now It's the Population Implosion," *New Zealand Herald*, July 23, 2003). On the other hand, Werner Fornos advances the explosionists' position in "A Global Concern: A Population Crisis Still Looms" (*International Herald Tribune*, January 14, 2004).

A book that focuses on the demographic divide is Paul A. Laudicina's *World Out of Balance* (McGraw-Hill, 2004). Two important books advocating the implosionist position are Phillip Longman's *The Empty Cradle: How Falling Birthrates Threaten World Prosperity and What to Do About It* (Basic Books, 2004) and *The End of World Population Growth in the 21st Century:*

New Challenges for Human Capital Formation and Sustainable Development (Wolfgang Lutz, Warren Sanderson, and Sergei Scherbov, eds., Earthscan Publishers, 2004). Two books advancing the explosionist thesis are *No Vacancy: Global Responses to the Human Population Explosion* (Michael Tobias, Bob Gillespie and Elizabeth Hughes, eds., Hope Publishing House, 2006) and K. Bruce Newbold's *Six Billion Plus: World Population in the Twenty-First Century* (Rowman & Littlefield Publishers, 2006).

In a sense, both viewpoints are correct as each acknowledges declining birth rates in the developing world and an eventual leveling-off of growth there. Their disagreement does point out dramatic implications of ever so slight variations in both the timing and the degree of fertility reduction among the poorer countries.

The United Nations (www.un.org/popin) serves as an authoritative source on various population data, whether historical, current, or future oriented. One of the U.N. agencies, the United Nations Population Fund or UNFPA (www.unfpa.org), issues an annual *State of the World Population,* as well as other reports.

Two Washington private organizations, the Population Reference Bureau (PRB) (www.prb.org) and The Population Institute (www.populationinstitute.org), publish a variety of booklets, newsletters, and reports yearly. Admittedly, these sources tend to emphasize the continued urgency rather than the seeds of progress, although recent articles have described the positive aspects of the current population transition. One particularly useful PRB publication is *World Population Beyond Six Billion* (*Population Bulletin,* March 1999). Three other important PRB publications are: *Global Demographic Divide* (Mary M. Kent and Carl Haub 2005); *Transitions in World Population* (March 2004); and *World Population Highlights: Key Findings from the PRB's 2007 World Population Data Sheet* (2007). A particularly succinct discussion of this "demographic divide" is found in PRB's *The Demographic Divide: What It Is and What It Means* (Mary Mederios and Carl Haub, 2008). Other sources focus on either success stories or the potential for success growing out of recent policy intervention. The Population Council of New York (www.popcouncil.org) falls into the latter category.

For over a decade, until the death of one of the participants, two individuals took center stage in the debate over population growth and its implications. Paul Ehrlich led the call for vigorous action to curb population growth. His co-authored works, *The Population Bomb* (1971) and *The Population Explosion* (1990), advanced the notion that the Earth's resource base could not keep pace with population growth, and thus the survival of the planet was brought into question. The late Julian Simon's *Population Matters: People, Resources, Environment, and Immigration* (1990) and *The Ultimate Resource 2* (1996) challenge Ehrlich's basic thesis. Simon's place in the debate appears to have been assumed by Ronald Bailey, science correspondent for *Reason* magazine. Two important publications of Bailey are *Global Warming and Other Eco-Myths* (Forum, 2002) and *Earth Report 2000* (McGraw-Hill, 2000).

A succinct, centrist, and easily understood analysis of the future of world population can be found in Leon F. Bouvier and Jane T. Bertrand,

World Population: Challenges for the 21st Century (1999). The annual *State of the World* volume from the Worldwatch Institute typically includes a timely analysis on some aspect of the world population problem.

Numerous web sites can be found under world population on www. msn.com (type in "world population web sites").

ISSUE 2

Should the International Community Attempt to Curb Population Growth in the Developing World?

YES: Robert S. McNamara, from "The Population Explosion," *The Futurist* (November/December 1992)

NO: Steven W. Mosher, from "McNamara's Folly: Bankrolling Family Planning," *PRI Review* (March–April 2003)

ISSUE SUMMARY

YES: Robert McNamara, former president of the World Bank, argues in this piece written during his presidency that the developed countries of the world and international organizations should help the countries of the developing world reduce their population growth rates.

NO: Steven W. Mosher, president of the Population Research Institute, an organization dedicated to debunking the idea that the world is overpopulated, argues that McNamara's World Bank and other international financial lending agencies have served for over a decade as "loan sharks" for those groups and individuals who were pressuring developing countries to adopt fertility reduction programs for self-interest reasons.

The history of the international community's efforts to lower birth rates throughout the developing world goes back to the late 1960s, when the annual growth rate hovered around 2.35 percent. At that time, selected individuals in international governmental organizations, including the United Nations, were persuaded by a number of wealthy national governments as well as by international nongovernmental population agencies that a problem of potentially massive proportions had recently emerged. Quite simply, demographers had observed a pattern of population growth in the poorer regions of the world quite unlike that which had occurred in the richer countries during the previous 150–200 years.

Population growth in the developed countries of the globe had followed a rather persistent pattern during the last two centuries. Prior to the Industrial Revolution, these countries typically experienced both high birth rates and death rates. As industrialization took hold and advances in the quality of life for citizens of these countries occurred, death rates fell, resulting in a period of time when the size of the population rose. Later, birth rates also began to decline, in large part because the newly industrialized societies were better suited to families with fewer children. After awhile, both birth and death rates leveled off at a much lower level than during preindustrial times.

This earlier transition throughout the developed world differed, however, from the newer growth pattern in the poorer regions of the globe observed by demographers in the late 1960s. First, the transition in the developed world occurred over a long period of time, allowing the population to deal more readily with such growth. On the other hand, post-1960s' growth in the developing world had taken off at a much faster pace, far outstripping the capacity of these societies to cope with the changes accompanying such growth.

Second, the earlier growth in the developed world began with a much smaller population base and a much larger resource base than did the developing world, again allowing the richer societies to cope more easily with such growth. The developing world of the 1960s, however, found percentages of increase based on a much higher base. Coping under the latter scenario proved much more difficult.

Finally, industrialization accompanied population change in the developed world, again allowing for those societies to address resultant problems more easily. Today's developing world has no such luxury. New jobs are not available, expanded educational facilities are non-existent, unsatisfactory health services remain unchanged, and modern infrastructures have not been created.

The international community formally placed the population issue—defined primarily as excessive birth rates in the developing world—on the global agenda in 1974 with the first major global conference on population, held in Bucharest, Romania. There was much debate over the motives of both sides. Both rich and poor countries eventually pledged to work together.

In the first selection, Robert McNamara argues that high population growth is exacerbating an already dire set of conditions in the developing world and that the industrialized countries of the globe should embark on a massive assistance program to help the "have-not" countries reduce fertility. In the second selection, Steven Mosher views the efforts of organizations such as the United Nations Population Fund much differently. In his view, these organizations have always sought to impose birth-control methods on the developing world in the misguided name of "virtuous and humanitarian motives," while attacking the motives of their opponents as self-serving or worse.

YES ↵

Robert S. McNamara

The Population Explosion

For thousands of years, the world's human population grew at a snail's pace. It took over a million years to reach 1 billion people at the beginning of the last century. But then the pace quickened. The second billion was added in 130 years, the third in 30, and the fourth in 15. The current total is some 5.4 billion people.

Although population growth rates are declining, they are still extraordinarily high. During this decade, about 100 million people per year will be added to the planet. Over 90% of this growth is taking place in the developing world. Where will it end?

The World Bank's latest projection indicates that the plateau level will not be less than 12.4 billion. And Nafis Sadik, director of the United Nations Population Fund, has stated that "the world could be headed toward an eventual total of 14 billion."

What would such population levels mean in terms of alleviating poverty, improving the status of women and children, and attaining sustainable economic development? To what degree are we consuming today the very capital required to achieve decent standards of living for future generations?

More People, Consuming More

To determine whether the world—or a particular country—is on a path of sustainable development, one must relate future population levels and future consumption patterns to their impact on the environment.

Put very simply, environmental stress is a function of three factors: increases in population, increases in consumption per capita, and changes in technology that may tend to reduce environmental stress per unit of consumption.

Were population to rise to the figure referred to by Sadik—14 billion—there would be a 2.6-fold increase in world population. If consumption per capita were to increase at 2% per annum—about two-thirds the rate realized during the past 25 years—it would double in 35 years and quadruple in 70 years. By the end of the next century, consumption per capita would be eight times greater than it is today.

Some may say it is unreasonable to consider such a large increase in the per capita incomes of the peoples in the developing countries. But per capita income in the United States rose at least that much in this century, starting from a much higher base. And today, billions of human beings across the globe are now living in intolerable conditions that can only be relieved by increases in consumption.

A 2.6-fold increase in world population and an eightfold increase in consumption per capita by 2100 would cause the globe's production output to be 20 times greater than today. Likewise, the impact on non-renewable and renewable resources would be 20 times greater, assuming no change in environmental stress per unit of production.

On the assumptions I have made, the question becomes: Can a 20-fold increase in the consumption of physical resources be sustained? The answer is almost certainly "No." If not, can substantial reductions in environmental stress—environmental damage—per unit of production be achieved? Here, the answer is clearly "Yes."

Reducing Environmental Damage

Environmental damage per unit of production can—and will—be cut drastically. There is much evidence that the environment is being stressed today. But there are equally strong indications that we can drastically reduce the resources consumed and waste generated per unit of "human advance."

With each passing year, we are learning more about the environmental damage that is caused by present population levels and present consumption patterns. The superficial signs are clearly visible. Our water and air are being polluted, whether we live in Los Angeles, Mexico City, or Lagos. Disposal of both toxic and nontoxic wastes is a worldwide problem. And the ozone layer, which protects us all against skin cancer, is being destroyed by the concentration of chlorofluorocarbons in the upper atmosphere.

But for each of these problems, there are known remedies—at least for today's population levels and current consumption patterns. The remedies are costly, politically difficult to implement, and require years to become effective, but they can be put in place.

The impact, however, of huge increases in population and consumption on such basic resources and ecosystems as land and water, forests, photosynthesis, and climate is far more difficult to appraise. Changes in complex systems such as these are what the scientists describe as nonlinear and subject to discontinuities. Therefore, they are very difficult to predict.

A Hungrier Planet?

Let's examine the effect of population growth on natural resources in terms of agriculture. Can the world's land and water resources produce the food required to feed 14 billion people at acceptable nutritional levels? To do so would require a four-fold increase in food output.

Modern agricultural techniques have greatly increased crop yields per unit of land and have kept food production ahead of population growth for several decades. But the costs are proving to be high: widespread acceleration of erosion and nutrient depletion of soils, pollution of surface waters, overuse and contamination of groundwater resources, and desertification of overcultivated or overgrazed lands.

The early gains of the Green Revolution have nearly run their course. Since the mid-1980s, increases in worldwide food production have lagged behind population growth. In sub-Saharan Africa and Latin America, per capita food production has been declining for a decade or more.

What, then, of the future? Some authorities are pessimistic, arguing that maximum global food output will support no more than 7.5 billion people. Others are somewhat more optimistic. They conclude that if a variety of actions were taken, beginning with a substantial increase in agricultural research, the world's agricultural system could meet food requirements for at least the next 40–50 years.

However, it seems clear that the actions required to realize that capacity are not now being taken. As a result, there will be severe regional shortfalls (e.g., in sub-Saharan Africa), and as world population continues to increase, the likelihood of meeting global food requirements will become ever more doubtful.

Similar comments could be made in regard to other natural resources and ecosystems. More and more biologists are warning that there are indeed biological limits to the number of people that the globe can support at acceptable standards of living. They say, in effect, "We don't know where those limits are, but they clearly exist."

Sustainability Limits

How much might population grow and production increase without going beyond sustainable levels—levels that are compatible with the globe's capacity for waste disposal and that do not deplete essential resources?

Jim MacNeil, Peter Winsemaus, and Taizo Yakushiji have tried to answer that question in *Beyond Interdependence,* a study prepared recently for the Trilateral Commission. They begin by stating: "Even at present levels of economic activity, there is growing evidence that certain critical global thresholds are being approached, perhaps even passed."

They then estimate that, if "human numbers double, a five- to ten-fold increase in economic activity would be required to enable them to meet [even] their basic needs and minimal aspirations." They ask, "Is there, in fact, any way to multiply economic activity a further five to ten times, without it undermining itself and compromising the future completely?" They clearly believe that the answer is "No."

Similar questions and doubts exist in the minds of many other experts in the field. In July 1991, Nobel laureate and Cal Tech physicist Murray Gell-Mann and his associates initiated a multiyear project to try to understand how "humanity can make the shift to sustainability." They point out that "such a change, if it could be achieved, would require a series of transitions in fields ranging from technology to social and economic organization and ideology."

The implication of their statement is not that we should assume the outlook for sustainable development is hopeless, but rather that each nation individually, and all nations collectively, should begin now to identify and introduce the changes necessary to achieve it if we are to avoid costly—and possibly coercive—action in the future.

One change that would enhance the prospects for sustainable, development across the globe would be a reduction in population growth rates.

Population and Poverty

The developing world has made enormous economic progress over the past three decades. But at the same time, the number of human beings living in "absolute poverty" has risen sharply.

When I coined the term "absolute poverty" in the late 1960s, I did so to distinguish a particular segment of the poor in the developing world from the billions of others who would be classified as poor in Western terms. The "absolute poor" are those living, literally, on the margin of life. Their lives are so characterized by malnutrition, illiteracy, and disease as to be beneath any reasonable definition of human dignity.

Today, their number approaches 1 billion. And the World Bank estimates that it is likely to increase further—by nearly 100 million—in this decade.

A major concern raised by poverty of this magnitude lies in the possibility of so many children's physical and intellectual impairment. Surveys have shown that millions of children in low-income families receive insufficient protein and calories to permit optimal development of their brains, thereby limiting their capacity to learn and to lead fully productive lives. Additional millions die each year, before the age of five, from debilitating disease caused by nutritional deficiencies.

High population growth is not the only factor contributing to these problems; political organization, macroeconomic policies, institutional structures, and economic growth in the industrial nations all affect economic and social advance in developing countries. But intuitively we recognize that the immediate effects of high population growth are adverse.

Our intuition is supported by facts: In Latin America during the 1970s, when the school-age population expanded dramatically, public spending per primary-school student fell by 45% in real terms. In Mexico, life expectancy for the poorest 10% of the population is 20 years less than for the richest 10%.

Based on such analyses, the World Bank has stated: "The evidence points overwhelmingly to the conclusion that population growth at the rates common in most of the developing world slows development. . . . Policies to reduce population growth can make an important contribution to [social advance]."

A Lower Plateau for World Population?

Any one of the adverse consequences of the high population growth rates—environmentally unsustainable development, the worsening of poverty, and the negative impact on the status and welfare of women and children—would be reason enough for developing nations across the globe to move more quickly to reduce fertility rates. Taken together, they make an overwhelming case.

Should not every developing country, therefore, formulate long-term population objectives—objectives that will maximize the welfare of both present and future generations? They should be constrained only by the maximum feasible rate at which the use of contraception could be increased in the particular nation.

If this were done, I estimate that country family-planning goals might lead to national population-stabilization levels that would total 9.7 billion people for the globe. That is an 80% increase over today's population, but it's also 4.3 billion fewer people than the 14 billion toward which we may be heading. At the consumption levels I have assumed, those additional 4.3 billion people could require a production output several times greater than the world's total output today.

Reducing Fertility Rates

Assuming that nations wish to reduce fertility rates to replacement levels at the fastest possible pace, what should be done?

The Bucharest Population Conference in 1974 emphasized that high fertility is in part a function of slow economic and social development. Experience has indeed shown that as economic growth occurs, particularly when it is accompanied by broadly based social advance, birth rates do tend to decline. But it is also generally recognized today that not all economic growth leads to immediate fertility reductions, and in any event, fertility reduction can be accelerated by direct action to increase the use of contraceptives.

It follows, therefore, that any campaign to accelerate reductions in fertility should focus on two components: (1) increasing the pace of economic and social advance, with particular emphasis on enhancing the status of women and on reducing infant mortality, and (2) introducing or expanding comprehensive family-planning programs.

Much has been learned in recent years about how to raise rates of economic and social advance in developing countries. I won't try to summarize those lessons here. I do wish to emphasize, however, the magnitude of the increases required in family planning if individual countries are to hold population growth rates to levels that maximize economic and social advance.

The number of women of childbearing age in developing countries is projected to increase by about 22% from 1990 to 2000. If contraception use were to increase from 50% in 1990 to 65% in 2000, the number of women using contraception must rise by over 200 million.

That appears to be an unattainable objective, considering that the number of women using contraception rose by only 175 million in the past *two* decades, but it is not. The task for certain countries and regions—for example, India, Pakistan, and almost all of sub-Saharan Africa—will indeed be difficult, but other nations have done as much or more. Thailand, Indonesia, Bangladesh, and Mexico all increased use of contraceptives at least as rapidly. The actions they took are known, and their experience can be exported. It is available to all who ask.

Financing Population Programs

A global family-planning program of the size I am proposing for 2000 would cost approximately $8 billion, with $3.5 billion coming from the developed nations (up from $800 million spent in 1990). While the additional funding appears large, it is very, very small in relation to the gross national products and overseas development assistance projected for the industrialized countries.

Clearly, it is within the capabilities of the industrialized nations and the multilateral financial institutions to help developing countries finance expanded family-planning programs. The World Bank has already started on such a path, doubling its financing of population projects in the current year. Others should follow its lead. The funds required are so small, and the benefits to both families and nations so large, that money should not be allowed to stand in the way of reducing fertility rates as rapidly as is desired by the developing countries.

The developed nations should also initiate a discussion of how their citizens, who consume seven times as much per capita as do those of the developing countries, may both adjust their consumption patterns and reduce the environmental impact of each unit of consumption. They can thereby help ensure a sustainable path of economic advance for all the inhabitants of our planet.

Steven W. Mosher   ➡ **NO**

McNamara's Folly:
Bankrolling Family Planning

At the same time that Reimert Ravenholt was setting up his "powerful population program," the nations of Western Europe, along with Japan, were being encouraged by the administration of President Lyndon B. Johnson to make family planning a priority of their own aid programs. International organizations, primarily the UN and its affiliated agencies, were also being leveraged on board. Together, they helped to create and maintain the illusion that the international community was solidly behind population control programs. (It wasn't, and isn't, as we shall see.) But it was the World Bank and its billions that was the real prize for the anti-natalists. And they captured it when one of their own, Robert McNamara, was appointed as President in 1968.[1]

McNamara Moves In

McNamara came to the World Bank from the post of Secretary of Defense, where he had unsuccessfully prosecuted the Vietnam War by focusing on "kill ratios" and the "pacification of the natives" instead of victory. A former automobile executive, he was prone to cost-cutting measures which sometimes proved to be false economies, as when he decreed that a new class of ship—the fleet frigate—should have only one screw instead of the customary two. This saved the expense of a second turbine and drive train, but the frigate—known to the Navy as McNamara's Folly—lacked speed, was hard to berth, and had to be retired early.[2] The population policies he was to advocate suffered from similar defects.

When the Boards of the World Bank and the International Monetary Fund convened on October 1 of that year, President Johnson made a surprise appearance.[3] Technology in the underdeveloped nations, he said, had "bought time for family planning policies to become effective. But the fate of development hinges on how vigorously that time is used."

No More People

The stage was now set for McNamara to get up and attack the "population explosion," saying that it was "one of the greatest barriers to the economic growth and social well-being of our member states." The World Bank would no longer stand idly by in the face of this threat, McNamara said, but would:

> Let the developing nations know the extent to which rapid population growth slows down their potential development, and that, in consequence, the optimum employment of the world's scarce development funds requires attention to this problem. Seek opportunities to finance facilities required by our member countries to carry out family planning programs. Join with others in programs of research to determine the most effective methods of family planning and of national administration of population control programs.[4]

It quickly became evident that "the optimum employment of the world's scarce development funds" meant in practice that the World Bank, the International Monetary Fund (IMF), and its network of regional development banks would act as loan sharks for the anti-natalists, pressuring sovereign nations into accepting family planning programs on pain of forfeiting vital short-term, long-term, and soft loans.[5] This practice is well known in the developing world, as when a Dhaka daily, *The New Nation,* headline read, "WB [World Bank] Conditions Aid to Population Control."[6]

McNamara also began providing loans for population and family planning projects, including those which involved abortion (both surgical and through abortifacient chemicals). By 1976 the National Security Council (NSC) was able to praise the World Bank for being "the principal international financial institution providing population programs."[7] Details are hard to come by, however. The World Bank is one of the most secretive organizations in the world, besides being effectively accountable to no one. It is known that there is a carefully segregated population division, which reportedly employs approximately 500 people. But those who work on conventional development projects are not privy to what goes on in this division, which is off-limits to all but those who work there.[8]

Fewer People, More Money

A rare inside look at the organization's activities in this area is provided by a recent World Bank report, entitled *Improving Reproductive Health: The Role of the World Bank.* Written in a distinctly self-congratulatory tone, the document reveals that the Bank has spent over $2.5 billion over the last twenty-five years to support 130 reproductive health projects in over 70 countries. Indonesia and Lesotho, for example, have been the site of "'information, education and communication' campaigns about sex and reproductive health." India has been the beneficiary of several different programs, which the report claims have "helped bring India two-thirds of the way towards her goal of replacement level fertility." No mention is made of the fact that the Indian campaigns have been notorious for their coercive tactics. Or that McNamara visited India at the height of the compulsory sterilization campaign in 1976 to congratulate the government for its "political will and determination" in the campaign and, one would suspect, to offer new loans.[9]

The World Bank also promotes abortion. *Improving Reproductive Health* openly admits that, since the 1994 Cairo Conference on Population and Development, the first of the World Bank's goals in the area of reproductive health has been "providing access and *choice* in family planning." [italics added] Except for its candor, this promotion of abortion should come as no surprise. In Burkina Faso, for example, we are told that World Bank projects have included "mobilizing public awareness and political support" [that is, lobbying] for abortion and other reproductive health services.

The Bank has long been accused of pressuring nations, such as Nigeria, into legalizing abortion. In 1988, for example, abortion was virtually unthinkable as an official family planning practice in Nigeria. As recently as 1990, the Planned Parenthood Federation of Nigeria was forced to defend itself against allegations that it promoted the sale and use of "contraceptives" that were abortifacient in character. A year later—and two months after approval of a $78 million World Bank population loan—the government announced proposals for allowing abortion under certain circumstances.[10]

Population control loans skyrocketed after the Cairo conference. The Bank reported that, in the two years that followed, it had "lent almost $1 billion in support of population and reproductive health objectives."[11] And the numbers have been climbing since then. But even this is just the tip of the iceberg. As Jacqueline Kasun notes, "Given the conditions which the bank imposes on its lending, the entire $20 billion of its annual disbursements is properly regarded as part of the world population control effort."[12]

No More Reform

Despite his predilection for population control, McNamara never abandoned more conventional aid modalities, roads, dams, power plants, and the like. Not so James Wolfensohn, who became the head of the Bank in 1995. Asked at the 1996 World Food Summit in Rome how the World Bank understood its mission towards the developing world, Wolfensohn replied that there was a "new paradigm" at the Bank. "From now on," Wolfensohn said, "the business of the World Bank will not be primarily economic reform, or governmental reform. The business of the World Bank will primarily be social reform." The Bank has learned, he added, that attempting to reform a nation's economics or government without first reforming the society "usually means failure."

The benefits to nations who are willing to fall into line in the "civil society" will be immediate and intensely attractive. "The World Bank will be willing to look favorably on any reasonable plan for debt reduction—and even debt forgiveness," Wolfensohn told the assembled reporters, "provided that the nation in question is willing to follow a sensible social policy." Wolfensohn went on to tell reporters that population control activities are a *sine qua non* for any social policy to be considered "sensible."[13]

The World Bank is also, according to Wolfensohn, prepared to begin "directly funding—not through loans" certain NGOs in the countries involved, to further ensure that governments adopt "sensible social policies." Thus fueled with money from the World Bank, the heat these favored NGOs will be able to generate on their governments to adopt, say, population control programs, including legalized abortion, will be considerable.[14] Of course, other international organizations, not to mention USAID and European aid agencies, have been using this tactic for many years with great effect. Recalcitrant governments (who may innocently believe that they do not have a population "problem") are thus sandwiched between the demands of international lenders and aid givers on the one hand, and the demands of "local" NGOs—loud, persistent and extremely well-funded—on the other.

Rapid Spread of Programs

With the U.S., international organizations, and an increasing number of developed countries now working in tandem to strong-arm developing countries into compliance, anti-natalist programs spread with startling rapidity. Bernard Berelson, the head of the Population Council, happily reported in 1970 that:

> In 1960 only three countries had anti-natalist population policies (all on paper), only one government was offering assistance [that is, funding population control programs overseas], no international organizations was working on family planning. In 1970 nearly 25 countries on all three developing continents, with 67 percent of the total population, have policies and programs; and another 15 or so, with 12 percent of the population, provide support in the absence of an explicitly formulated policy . . . five to ten governments now offer external support (though only two in any magnitude); and the international assistance system is formally on board (the U.N. Population Division, the UNDP, WHO, UNESCO, FAO, ILO, OECD, the World Bank).[15]

The recklessness with which Ravenholt, McNamara and others forced crude anti-natal programs upon the developing world dismayed many even within the movement. Ronald Freedman, a leading sociologist/demographer, complained in 1975 that, "If reducing the birth rate is that important and urgent, then the results of the expanded research during the 1960s are still *pathetically inadequate. There are serious proposals for social programs on a vast scale to change reproductive institutions and values that have been central to human society for millennia.*"[16] [italics added] This was social engineering with a vengeance, Freedman was saying, and *we don't know what we are doing.*

With even committed controllers saying "Slow down!" one might think that the anti-natalists would hesitate. But their army had already been assembled and its generals had sounded the advance; it could not be halted now. Even Freedman, rhetorically throwing up his hands, conceded that "many people . . . are eager for knowledge that can be used in action programs aimed at accelerating fertility decline," and that the programs would have to proceed by "a process of trial and error." The *trials* of course would be funded by the developed world; while the *errors*, murderous and costly, would be borne by poor women and families in the developed world.

What justification was offered for this massive investment of U.S. prestige and capital in these programs? Stripped of its later accretions—protecting the environment, promoting economic development, advancing the rights of women—at the outset it was mostly blatant self-interest. McNamara, who headed an organization ostensibly devoted to the welfare of the developing countries, had told the World Bank's Board of Governors in 1968 that "population growth slows down their potential development." But he told the *Christian Science Monitor* some years later that continued population growth would lead to "poverty, hunger, stress, crowding, and frustration," which would threaten social, economic, and military stability. This would not be "a world that anyone wants," he declared.[17] It was certainly not the world that many in the security establishment wanted, as secret National Security Council deliberations would soon make starkly clear.

Cold War Against Population

As the populations of developing world countries began to grow after World War Two, the U.S. national security establishment—the Pentagon, the Central Intelligence Agency, the National Security Agency, and the National Security Council—became concerned. Population was an important element of national power, and countries with growing populations would almost inevitably increase in geopolitical weight. This was obviously a concern in the case of countries opposed to U.S. interests, such as the Soviet Union and China. But even allies might prove less pliable as their populations and economies grew. Most worrisome of all was the possibility that the rapidly multiplying peoples of Asia, Africa, and Latin America would turn to communism in their search for independence and economic advancement *unless their birth rate was reduced.* Thus did population control become a weapon in the Cold War. . . .

Earth First (People Last): Environmental Movement Signs On

Every sorcerer deserves an apprentice. Hugh Moore, grand wizard of the population explosion, got his in the person of a young Stanford University entomologist by the name of Paul Ehrlich. In the very first sentence of his very first book Ehrlich proved beyond all doubt that he had already mastered Moore's panic-driven style. "The battle to feed all of humanity is over," he wrote. "In the 1970s the world will undergo famines—hundreds of million of people will starve to death in spite of any crash programs embarked upon now."[18]

In fact, he had gone Moore one better, as overzealous acolytes are prone to do. His book should have been named *The Population Explosion*, instead of *The Population Bomb*, for according to Ehrlich the "bomb" had already gone off and there was nothing to do now but wait for the inevitable human die-back. "Too many people" were chasing "too little food."[19] The most optimistic of Ehrlich's "scenarios" involved the immediate imposition of a harsh regimen of population control and resource conservation around the world, with the goal of reducing the number of people to 1.5 billion (about a fourth of its current level) over the next century or two. Even so, about a fifth of the world's population would still starve to death in the immediate future.

Such a prediction took pluck, for when the book appeared in 1968 there was no hint of massive famine on the horizon. The days of Indian food shortages were past. (We wouldn't learn about China's man-made calamity until a decade later.) The Green Revolution was starting to pay off in increased crop yields. And experts like Dr. Karl Brandt, the Director of the Stanford Food Research Institute, rebuked Ehrlich, saying that "Many nations need more people, not less, to cultivate food products and build a sound agricultural economy . . . every country that makes the effort can produce all the food it needs."[20]

But it wasn't his forecast of a massive human die-off that catapulted Ehrlich into the front rank of environmental prophets. (In a motif that has since become familiar, the book left readers with the impression that this might not be such a bad thing.) Rather it was his startling claim that our reckless breeding had jeopardized earth's ability to support life. All life, not just human life. Our planet was literally dying. Not only were the Children of Earth killing ourselves, we were going to take Mother with us as well.

The Population Bomb

Heavily promoted by the Sierra Club, *The Population Bomb* sold over a million copies. Ehrlich became an instant celebrity, becoming as much of a fixture on the "Tonight Show" as Johnny Carson's sidekick Ed McMahon. He command[ed] hefty lecture fees wherever he went (and he went everywhere), and always drew a crowd. People found it entertaining to hear about the end of the world. Likening the earth to an overloaded spaceship or sinking lifeboat, issuing apocalyptic warnings about the imminent "standing room only" problem, he captured the popular imagination. His prescriptions were always the same: "Join the environmental movement, stop having children, and save the planet."[21]

While Ehrlich fiddled his apocalyptic tunes, Moore burned to commit the growing environmental movement firmly to a policy of population control. His ad campaign, still ongoing, began suggesting that the best kind of environmental protection was population control. "Whatever Your Cause, It's a Lost Cause Unless We Control Population," one ad read. "Warning: The Water You are Drinking May be Polluted," read another, whose text went on to equate more people with more pollution. A third, addressed to "Dear President Nixon," claimed that "We can't lick the environment problem without considering this little fellow." It featured a picture of a newborn baby.

Birth of Earth Day

Moore went all out for the first Earth Day in 1970, printing a third of a million leaflets, folders, and pamphlets for campus distribution. College newspapers received free cartoons highlighting the population crisis and college radio stations a free taped show (featuring Paul Ehrlich). With his genius for marketing, Moore even announced a contest with cash awards for the best slogans relating environmental problems to what he called "popullution" [population pollution]. Students on over 200 campuses participated. The winner, not surprisingly, was "People Pollute."[22]

By 1971 most of the leading environmental groups had signed on to the anti-natal agenda, having been convinced that reducing the human birth rate would greatly benefit the environment. Perhaps it was their interest in "managing" populations of other species—salmon, condors, whales, etc.—that predisposed them to impose technical solutions on their own species. In any event, many of them were population hawks, who believed that simply making abortion, sterilization and contraception widely available was not enough. "Voluntarism is a farce," wrote Richard Bowers of Zero Population Growth as early as 1969. "The private sector effort has failed . . . [even the expenditure] of billions of dollars will not limit growth." Coercive measures were required. He proposed enacting "criminal laws to limit population, if the earth is to survive."[23]

Those who held such views were not content to merely stop people from multiplying, they demanded radical reductions in human numbers. The group Negative Population Growth wanted to cut the-then U.S. population of 200 million by more than half, to 90 million.[24] Celebrated oceanographer Jacques Cousteau told the *UNESCO Courier* in 1991, "In order to stabilize world populations, we must eliminate 350,000 people per day." Garrett Hardin of "The Tragedy of the Commons" fame opined that the "carrying capacity" of the planet was 100 million and that our numbers should be reduced accordingly. (Do we pick the lucky 100 million by lottery?) To carry out these decimations, Malthusian solutions are proposed, as when novelist William T. Vollman stated that, "there are too many people in the world and maybe something like AIDS or something like war may be a good thing on that level."[25] And lest we have compunctions about resorting to such measures, we should bear in mind, as Earth First! Founder Dave Foreman wrote, "We humans have become a disease, the Humanpox."

The Feminist Dilemma

The most radical of the feminists had a different definition of disease. Why should women be "subject to the species gnawing at their vitals," as Simone de Beauvoir so memorably wrote in her feminist classic *The Second Sex?* Why endure pregnancy at all, if contraception, sterilization and, especially, abortion, could be made widely available? With the legalization of abortion in the U.S. in 1973, feminists increasingly looked overseas, eager to extend their newfound rights to "women of color" elsewhere in the world. They had read their Ehrlich as well as their Beauvior, and knew that the world had too many people, or soon would. But family planning, especially abortion, provided a way out. "Let us bestow upon all the women of the world the blessing that we women in the privileged West have received—freedom from fear of pregnancy," the feminists said to themselves. "We will, at the same time and by the same means, solve the problem of too many babies. For surely impoverished Third World women do not actually want all those children they are bearing. Patriarchy has made them into breeding machines, but we will set them free."

Abortion "Needs" Appear

At the time, the population control movement remained ambivalent over the question of abortion. Hugh Moore had long wanted it as a population control measure, but Frank Notestein was still arguing in the early 1970s that the Population Council should "consistently and firmly take the anti-abortion stance and use every occasion to point out that the need for abortions is the proof of program failure in the field of family planning and public health education."[26]

But the women's movement would not be put off with the promise of a perfect contraceptive. They knew, better than anyone (and often from painful personal experience) that contraception, because of the inevitable failures, *always* led to abortion. As Sharon Camp of the Population Crisis Committee wrote "both abortion and contraception are presently on the rise in most developing countries."[27]

Abortion was, in the end, accepted by most controllers because it came to be seen as a necessary part of the anti-natal arsenal. The Rockefeller Commission, established by President Nixon, wrote that "We are impressed that induced abortion has a demographic effect wherever legalized" and on these grounds went on to call for "abortion on demand."[28] The Population Council followed the Commission in endorsing abortion as a means of population control by 1975.

In the end, feminist advocacy of abortion had proven decisive. The feminists had given the population control movement an additional weapon, abortion, to use in its drive to reduce human fecundity, and encouraged its aggressive use.

Third World Women

At the same time, it was soon apparent to many feminists that birth control was not an unmixed blessing for Third World women, who continued to be targets of ever-more aggressive programs in places like Indonesia, India, and Bangladesh. They began to demand further changes in the way programs were carried out, starting with male contraceptives and more vasectomies. Frank Notestein wrote of the feminists that, "As second-generation suffragists they were not at all disposed to allow the brutish male to be in charge of contraception. Women must have their own methods!" But more recent feminists "complain violently that the men are trying to saddle the women with all the contraceptive work. You can't please them if you do, and can't please them if you don't."[29]

Although expressed somewhat crudely, Notestein's comment pointed out the dilemma faced by feminists. On the one hand, they sought to impose a radically pro-abortion agenda on population control programs, whose general purpose—fertility reduction—they applauded. On the other they tried to protect women from the abuses that invariably accompanied such programs. But with the exception of the condom, other methods of contraception all put the burden on women. Vasectomies could easily be performed on men, but it was usually the woman who went under the knife to have her tubes tied. And abortions could only be performed on women. So, as a practical matter, the burden of fertility reduction was placed disproportionately on women. And when programs took a turn towards the coercive, as they were invariably prone to do in the Third World, it was overwhelmingly women who paid the price.

Feminist complaints did lead to some changes, but these were mostly cosmetic. Population controllers did learn, over time, to speak a different language or, rather, several different languages, to disguise the true, anti-natal purpose of their efforts. When Western feminists need to be convinced of the importance of supporting the programs, reproductive rights rhetoric is the order of the day. Thus we hear Nafis Sadik telling Western reporters on the eve of the 1994 U.N. Conference on Population and Development that the heart of the discussion "is the recognition that the low status of women is a root cause of inadequate reproductive health care." Such language would ring strange in the ears of Third World women, who are instead the object of soothing lectures about "child-spacing" and "maternal health." Population control programs were originally unpopular in many Middle Eastern countries and sub-Sarahan countries until they were redesigned, with feminist input, as programs to "help" women. As Peter Donaldson, the head of the Population Reference Bureau, writes, "The idea of limiting the number of births was so culturally unacceptable [in the Middle East and sub-Saharan Africa] that family planning programs were introduced as a means for promoting better maternal and child health by helping women space their births."[30] James Grant of the U.N. Children's Fund (UNICEF), in an address to the World Bank, was even more blunt: "Children and women are to be the Trojan Horse for dramatically slowing population growth."[31]

Corrupted Feminist Movement

The feminists did not imagine, when they signed onto the population control movement, that they would merely be marketing consultants. It is telling that many Third World feminists have refused to endorse population control programs at all, arguing instead that these programs violate the rights of women while ignoring their real needs. It must be painful for Western feminists to contemplate, but their own movement has been used or, to use Betsy Hartmann's term, "co-opted," by another movement for whom humanity as a whole, and women in particular, remain a faceless mass of numbers to be contracepted, sterilized, and aborted. For, despite the feminist rhetoric, the basic character of the programs hasn't changed. They are a numbers-driven, technical solution to the "problem of overpopulation"—which is, in truth, a problem of poverty—and they overwhelmingly target women.

This is, in many respects, an inevitable outcome. To accept the premise that the world is overpopulated and then seek to make the resulting birth control programs "women-friendly," as many feminists have, is a fateful compromise. For it means that concern for the real needs of women is neither the starting point of these programs, nor their ultimate goal, but merely a consideration along the way. Typical of the views of feminists actively involved in the population movement are those of Sharon Camp, who writes, "There is still time to avoid another population doubling, but only if the world community acts very quickly to make family planning universally available and to invest in other social programs, like education for girls, which can help accelerate fertility declines."[32] Here we see the population crisis mentality in an uneasy alliance with programs for women which, however, are justified chiefly because they "help accelerate fertility declines."

The alliance between the feminists and population controllers has been an awkward affair. But the third of the three most anti-natalist movements in history gave the population controllers new resources, new constituencies, new political allies, a new rhetoric, and remains a staunch supporter even today.

Population Firm Funding

Over the past decade the Population Firm has become more powerful than ever. Like a highly organized cartel, working through an alphabet soup of United Nations agencies and "nongovernmental organizations," its tentacles reach into nearly every developing country. It receives sustenance from feeding tubes attached to the legislatures of most developed countries, and further support through the government-financed population research industry, with its hundreds of professors and thousand of students. But unlike any other firm in human history, its purpose is not to produce anything, but rather to destroy—to destroy fertility, to prevent babies from being conceived and born. It diminishes, one might say, the oversupply of people. It does this for the highest of motives—to protect all of us from "popullution." Those who do not subscribe to its ideology it bribes and browbeats, bringing the combined weight of the world's industrial powers to bear on those in countries which are poor.

In 1991, the U.N. estimated that a yearly sum of $4.5 to $5 billion was being directed to population programs in developing countries. This figure, which has grown tremendously in the last 10 years, includes contributions from bilateral donors such as the U.S., the European nations and Japan, from international agencies like those associated with the UN, and from multilateral lending institutions, including the World Bank and the various regional development banks. It includes grants from foundations, like Ted Turner's U.N. Foundation, and wealthy individuals like Warren Buffet.

Moreover, a vast amount of money not explicitly designated as "population" finance is used to further the family planning effort. As Elizabeth Liagin notes, "During the 1980s, the diversion of funds from government non-population budgets to fertility-reduction measures soared, especially in the U.S., where literally hundreds of millions from the Economic Support Funds program, regional development accounts, and other non-population budgets were redirected to "strengthen" population planning abroad."[33]

More Money Spent

An almost unlimited variety of other "development" efforts—health, education, energy, commodity imports, infrastructure, and debt relief, for example—are also used by governments and other international agencies such as the World Bank, to promote population control policies, either through requiring recipient nations to incorporate family planning into another program or by holding funds or loans hostage to the development of a national commitment to tackle the "over-population" problem.

In its insatiable effort to locate additional funds for its insatiable population control programs, USAID has even attempted to redirect "blocked assets"—profits generated by international corporations operating in developing nations that prohibit the transfer of money outside the country—into population control efforts. In September 1992, USAID signed a $36.4 million contract and "statement of work" with the accounting firm Deloitte and Touche to act as a mediator with global corporations and to negotiate deals that would help turn the estimated $200 *billion* in blocked assets into "private" contributions for family planning in host countries. The corporations would in return get to claim a deduction on their U.S. tax return for this "charitable contribution." The Profit initiative, as it is fittingly called, is not limited to applying its funds directly to family planning "services," but is also encouraged to "work for the removal" of "trade barriers for contraceptive commodities" and "assist in the development of a regulatory framework that permits the expansion of private sector family planning services." This reads like a bureaucratic mandate to lobby for the elimination of local laws which in any way interfere with efforts to drive down the birth rate, such as laws restricting abortion or sterilization.[34]

U.S.'s Real Foreign Aid Policy

Throughout the nineties, the idea of the population controllers that people in their numbers were somehow the enemy of all that is good reigned supreme. J. Brian Atwood, who administered the U.S. Agency for International Development in the early days of the Clinton administration, put it this way: "If we aren't able to find and promote ways of curbing population growth, we are going to fail in *all* of our foreign policy initiatives." [italics added] (Atwood also went on to announce that the U.S. "also plans to resume funding in January [1994] to the U.N. Fund for Population Activities (UNFPA).")[35] Secretary of State Warren Christopher offered a similar but even more detailed defense of population programs the following year. "Population and sustainable development are back where they belong in the mainstream of American foreign policy and diplomacy." He went on to say, in a line that comes right out of U.S. National Security Study Memo 200, that population pressure "ultimately jeopardizes America's security interests." But that's just the beginning. Repeating the now familiar litany, he claimed of population growth that, "It strains resources. It stunts economic growth. It generates disease. It spawns huge refugee flows, and ultimately it threatens our stability. . . . We want to continue working with the other donors to meet the rather ambitious funding goals that were set up in Cairo."[36]

The movement was never more powerful than it was in 2000 in terms of money, other resources, and political clout.

Losing Momentum

Like a wave which crests only seconds before it crashes upon the shore, this appearance of strength may be deceiving. There are signs that the anti-natal movement has peaked, and may before long collapse of its own overreaching. U.S. spending on coercive population control and abortion overseas have long been banned. In 1998 the U.S. Congress, in response to a flood of reports about human rights abuses, for the first time set limits on what can be done to people in the name of "voluntary family planning."[37] Developing countries are regularly denouncing what they see as foreign interference into their domestic affairs, as the Peruvian Congress did in 2002. Despite strenuous efforts to co-opt them, the opposition of feminists to population control programs (which target women) seems to be growing.[38] Many other groups—libertarians, Catholics, Christians of other denominations, the majority of economists, and those who define themselves as pro-life—have long been opposed.

As population control falls into increasing disrepute worldwide, the controllers are attempting to reinvent themselves, much the same way that the Communists in the old Soviet Union reemerged as "social democrats" following its collapse. Organizations working in this area have found it wise to disguise their agenda by adopting less revealing names. Thus Zero Population Growth in June 2002 became Population Connection, and the Association for Voluntary Surgical Contraception the year before changed its name to Engender Health. Similarly, the U.N., in documents prepared for public consumption, has recently found it expedient to cloak its plans in language about the "empowerment of women," "sustainable development," "safe motherhood," and "reproductive health." Yet the old anti-natal zeal continues to come through in internal discussions, as when Thoraya Obaid affirmed to her new bosses on the U.N. Commission on Population and Development her commitment to "slow and eventually stabilize population growth." "And today I want to make one thing very clear," she went on to say. "The slowdown in population growth does not mean we can slow down efforts for population and reproductive health— quite the contrary. If we want real progress and if we want the projections to come true, we must step up efforts . . . while population growth is slowing, it is still growing by 77 million people every year."[39] And so on.

Such efforts to wear a more pleasing face for public consumption will in the end avail them nothing. For, as we will see, their central idea—the Malthusian notion that you can eliminate poverty, hunger, disease, and pollution by eliminating the poor—is increasingly bankrupt.

Reducing the numbers of babies born has not and will not solve political, societal and economic problems. It is like trying to kill a gnat with a sledgehammer, missing the gnat entirely, and ruining your furniture beyond repair. It is like trying to protect yourself from a hurricane with a bus ticket. Such programs come with massive costs, largely hidden from the view of well-meaning Westerners who have been propagandized into supporting them. And their "benefits" have proven ephemeral or worse. These programs, as in China, have done actual harm to real people in the areas of human rights, health care, democracy, and so forth. And, with falling birth rates everywhere, they are demographic nonsense. Where population control programs are concerned, these costs have been largely ignored (as the cost of doing business) while the benefits to people, the environment, and to the economy, have been greatly exaggerated, as we will see. Women in the developing world are the principal victims.

Notes

1. The World Bank is to a large degree under the control of the United States, which provides the largest amount of funding. This is why the head of the World Bank is always an American. The activities of the Bank are monitored by the National Advisory Council on International Monetary and Financial Policies—called the NAC for short, of the Treasury Department. The 1988 annual report of the NAC states that "the council [NAC] seeks to ensure that . . . the . . . operations [of the World Bank and other international financial institutions] are conducted in a manner consistent with U.S. policies and objectives . . ." International Finance: National Advisory Council on International Monetary and Financial Policies, Annual Report

to the President and to the Congress for the Fiscal year 1988, (Wash., D.C., Department of the Treasury), Appendix A, p. 31. Quoted in Jean Guilfoyle, "World Bank Population Policy: Remote Control," *PRI Review* 1:4 (July/ August 1991), p. 8.

2. I served on board a ship of this class, the USS Lockwood, from 1974–76. As the Main Propulsion Assistant—the officer in charge of the engine room—I can personally attest that this fleet frigate, as it was called, was anything but fleet. On picket duty, it could not keep up with the big flattops that it was intended to protect from submarine attacks.

3. The 1968 meeting was 23rd joint annual meeting of the Boards of Governors of the World Bank and the International Monetary Fund. The two organizations always hold their annual meetings in tandem, underscoring their collaboration on all matters of importance.

4. McNamara moderated his anti-natal rhetoric on this formal occasion. More often, he sounded like Hugh Moore, as when he wrote: "the greatest single obstacle to the economic and social advancement of the majority of the peoples in the underdeveloped world is rampant population growth. . . . The threat of unmanageable population pressures is very much like the threat of nuclear war. . . . Both threats can and will have catastrophic consequences unless they are dealt with rapidly." *One Hundred Countries, Two Billion People* (London: Pall Mall Press, 1973), pp. 45–46. Quoted in Michael Cromartie, ed., *The 9 Lives of Population Control,* (Washington: Ethics and Public Policy Center, 1995), p. 62. McNamara never expressed any public doubts about the importance of population control, although he did once confide in Bernard Berelson that "many of our friends see family planning as being 'too simple, too narrow, and too coercive.'" As indeed it was—and is. Quote is from Donald Crichtlow, *Intended Consequences: Birth Control, Abortion, and the Federal Government in Modern America,* (Oxford: Oxford University Press, 1999), p. 178.

5. See Fred T. Sai and Lauren A. Chester, "The Role of the World Bank in Shaping Third World Population Policy," in Godfrey Roberst, ed., *Population Policy: Contemporary Issues* (New York: Praeger, 1990). Cited in Jacqueline Kasun, *The War Against Population,* Revised Ed. (San Fransisco: Ignatius Press, 1999), p. 104.

6. 7 September 1994, p. 1. Cited in Kasun, p. 104.

7. U.S. International Population Policy: First Annual Report, prepared by the Interagency Task Force on Population Policy, (Wash., D.C., U.S. National Archives, May 1976). Quoted in Jean Guilfoyle, "World Bank Population Policy: Remote Control," *PRI Review* 1:4 (July/August 1991), p. 8.

8. Personal Communication with the author from a retired World Bank executive who worries that, if his identity is revealed, his pension may be in jeopardy.

9. Peter T. Bauer and Basil S. Yamey, "The Third World and the West: An Economic Perspective," in W. Scott Thompson, ed., *The Third World: Premises of U.S. Policy* (San Francisco: Institute for Contemporary Studies, 1978), p. 302. Quoted in Kasun, p. 105.

10. See Elizabeth Liagin, "Money for Lies," *PRI Review,* July/October 1998, for the definitive history of the imposition of population control on Nigeria;

The Nigerian case is also discussed by Barbara Akapo, "When family planning meets population control," *Gender Review,* June 1994, pp. 8–9.

11. Word Bank, 1995 Annual Report, p. 18. Quoted in *PRI Review* 5:6 (November/December 1995), p. 7.

12. Kasun, p. 277.

13. David Morrison, "Weaving a Wider Net: U.N. Move to Consolidate Its Anti-Natalist Gains," *PRI Review* 7:1 (January–February 1997), p. 7.

14. Ibid.

15. Bernard Berelson, "Where Do We Stand," paper prepared for Conference on Technological change and Population Growth, California Institute of Technology, May 1970, p. 1. Quoted in Ronald Freedman, *The Sociology of Human Fertility: An Annotated Bibliography* (New York: Irvington Publishers, 1975), p. 3. It's worth noting that Freedman's book was a subsidized product of the institution Berelson then headed. As Freedman notes in his "Preface," the "staff at the Population Council were very helpful in reading proof, editorial review, and making detailed arrangements for publication. Financial support was provided by the Population Council." (p. 2.)

16. Freedman, p. 4.

17. *Christian Science Monitor,* 5 July 1977. He went on to say that, if present methods of population control "fail, and population pressures become too great, nations will be driven to more coercive methods."

18. Paul R. Ehrlich, *The Population Bomb* (New York: Ballantine books, 1968).

19. The first three sections of Ehrlich's book were called, "Too many people," "Too little Food," and "A Dying Planet."

20. *Is there a Population Explosion?*, Daniel Lyons, (Catholic Polls: New York, 1970), p. 5.

21. Ehrlich has continued on the present day, writing one book after another, each one chock full of predictions of imminent disasters that fail to materialize. People wonder why Ehrlich doesn't learn from his experiences? The answer, I think, is that he has learned very well. He has learned that writing about "overpopulation and environmental disaster" sells books, *lots* of books. He has learned that there is no price to pay for being wrong, as long as he doesn't admit his mistakes *in print* and glibly moves on to the next disaster. In one sense, he has far outdone Hugh Moore in this regard. For unlike Moore, who had to spend his own money to publish the original *The Population Bomb,* Ehrlich was able to hype the population scare *and* make money by doing so. He is thus the archetype of a figure familiar to those who follow the anti-natal movement: the population hustler.

22. Lawrence Lader, *Breeding Ourselves to Death,* pp. 79–81.

23. Richard M. Bowers to ZPG members, 30 September 1969, Population Council (unprocessed), RZ. Quoted in Critchlow, p. 156.

24. In later years, as U.S. population continued to grow, NPG has gradually increased its estimate of a "sustainable" U.S. population to 150 million. See Donald Mann, "A No-Growth Steady-State Economy Must Be Our Goal," NPG Position Paper, June 2002.

25. Quoted in David Boaz, "Pro-Life," *Cato Policy Report* (July/August 2002), p. 2.

26. Frank Notestein to Bernard Berelson, 8 February 1971, Rockefeller Brother Fund Papers, Box 210, RA. Quoted in Critchlow, p. 177. These concerns, while real enough to Notestein, apparently did not cause him to reflect on the fact that he was a major player in a movement that "detracted from the value of human life" by suggesting that there was simply too much of that life, and working for its selective elimination.

27. Population Action International, "Expanding Access to Safe Abortion: Key Policy Issues," Population Policy Information Kit 8 (September 1993). Quoted in Sharon Camp, "The Politics of U.S. Population Assistance," in Mazur, *Beyond the Numbers,* p. 126.

28. Critchlow, p. 165.

29. Frank Notestein to Bernard Berelson, April 27, 1971, Notestein Papers, Box 8, Princeton University.

30. Peter Donaldson and Amy Ong Tsui, "The International Family Planning Movement," in Laurie Ann Mazur, ed., *Beyond the Numbers* (Island Press, Washington, D.C., 1994), p. 118. Donaldson was, at the time, president of the Population Reference Bureau, and Tsui was deputy director of the Carolina Population Center.

31. World Bank 1993 International Development Conference, Washington, D.C., 11 January 1993, p. 3. Also quoted in *PRI Review* (September–October 1994), p. 9.

32. Sharon Camp, "Politics of U.S. Population Assistance," in *Beyond the Numbers,* pp. 130–1. Camp for many years worked at the Population Crisis Committee, founded by Hugh Moore in the early sixties. It has recently, perhaps in recognition of falling fertility rates worldwide, renamed itself Population Action International.

33. Quoted from Elizabeth Liagin, "Profit or Loss: Cooking the Books at USAID," *PRI Review* 6:3 (November/December 1996), p. 1.

34. Ibid., p. 11.

35. John M. Goshko, "Planned Parenthood gets AID grant . . . ," *Washington Post,* 23 November 1993, A12–13.

36. Reuters, "Christopher defends U.S. population programs," Washington, D.C., 19 December 1994.

37. The Tiahrt Amendment.

38. See Betsy Hartmann, *Reproductive Rights and Wrongs* (Boston: South End Press, 1995).

39. Thoraya Ahmed Obaid, "Reproductive Health and Reproductive Rights With Special Reference to HIV/AIDS," Statement to the U.N. Commission on Population and Development, 1 April 2002.

POSTSCRIPT

Should the International Community Attempt to Curb Population Growth in the Developing World?

There are at least two basic dimensions to this issue. First, should the international community involve itself in reducing fertility throughout the developing world? That is, is it a violation of either national sovereignty (a country should be free from extreme outside influence) or human rights (an individual has the right to make fertility decisions unencumbered by outside pressure, particularly those from another culture)? And second, if so, what should its motives be? To put it another way, is advocacy of population control really a form of ethnic or national genocide?

McNamara answers these questions with the same set of arguments. His belief that the international community has an obligation to get involved is based on his assessment of the resultant damage to both the developing world where such high levels of growth are found and the rest of the world that must compete with the poorer countries for increasingly scare resources. For McNamara, a 2.6-fold increase in population and an 8-fold increase in consumption per capita (by the end of the twenty-first century) would result in a 20-fold impact on nonrenewable and renewable resources. He cites the projected agricultural needs to demonstrate that the Earth cannot sustain such consumption levels. Additionally, McNamara suggests that other consequences include environmentally unsustainable development, worsening of poverty, and negative impacts on the welfare of women and children. They appear to make an overwhelming case for fertility reduction. And the cost of policy intervention is small, in his judgment, compared to both gross national products and overseas general development assistance. And finally, given the projections, the developing world ought to embrace such policy intervention for its own good.

Those who oppose such intervention point to several different reasons. The first, originally articulated at the 1974 Bucharest conference, argues that economic development is the best contraceptive. The demographic transition worked in the developed world and there was no reason to assume that it will not work in the developing world. This was the dominant view of the developing countries at Bucharest, who feared international policy intervention, and at the same time wanted and needed external capital to develop. They soon came to realize that characteristics particular to the developing world in the latter part of the twentieth century meant that foreign aid alone would not be enough. It had to be accompanied by fertility reduction programs, wherever the origin.

Second, some who oppose intervention do not see the extreme negative environmental consequences of expanding populations. For them, the pronatalists (those favoring fertility reduction programs) engage in inflammatory discourse, exaggerated arguments, and scare tactics devoid of much scientific evidence.

Mosher goes further in the second selection, accusing McNamara, who served as U.S. Secretary of Defense during the Vietnam era, of using his position as one of the most important leaders in the international financial lending world to help prevent continuing population growth in the developing world because of its potential threat to the national security of countries like the United States. He also concludes that the interventionists are engaged in social engineering, not economic development.

And finally, cultural constraints can counteract any attempt to impose fertility reduction values from the outside. Children are valued in most societies. They, particularly male heirs, serve as the social security system for most families. They become producers at an early age, contributing to the family income.

McNamara is correct if one assumes that no changes—technological, social, and organizational—accompany predicted population growth. But others would argue that society has always found a way to use technology to address newly emerging problems successfully. The question remains, though: Are the current problems and the world in which they function too complex to allow for a simple solution?

The bottom line is that each has a valid point. Environmental stress is a fact of life, and increased consumption does play a role. If the latter originates because of more people, then fertility reduction is a viable solution. Left to its own devices, the developing world is unable to provide both the rationale for such action and the resources to accomplish it. The barriers are too great. While the international community must guard against behavior that is or appears to be either genocidal in nature or violates human rights, it must nonetheless move forward.

An excellent account of the 1994 Cairo population conference's answer to how the international community ought to respond is found in Lori S. Ashford's *New Perspectives on Population: Lessons from Cairo* (1995). Other sources that address the question of the need for international action include William Hollingworth's *Ending the Explosion: Population Policies and Ethics for a Humane Future* (1996), Elizabeth Liagin's *Excessive Force: Power, Politics, and Population* (1996), and Julian Simon's *The Ultimate Resource 2* (1996). In 2003, the UN Commission on Population and Development held a weeklong meeting on educating people to curb population growth. More recent calls for action include top Australian and British scientists, according to several Internet blogs.

There are both United Nations and external analyses of the Cairo conference and assessments of progress made in implementing its Plan of Action. The United Nations Population Fund's web site (www.unfpa.org)

has a section entitled *ICPD and Key Actions*. There you will find numerous in-house analyses of both the conference and post-1994 action. In the broader UN Web site (www.un.org/popin), one finds a major study, *Progress Made in Achieving the Goals and Objectives of the Program of Action of the International Conference on Population and Development.* An external assessment is the Population Institute's report entitled *The Hague Forum: Measuring ICPD Progress Since Cairo* (1999). See its Web site at www.populationinstitute.org.

ISSUE 3

Is Global Aging in the Developed World a Major Problem?

YES: Pete Engardio and Carol Matlack, from "Global Aging," *Business Week* (January 31, 2005)

NO: Rand Corporation, from "Population Implosion?" Research Brief, Rand Europe (2005)

ISSUE SUMMARY

YES: This *Business Week* cover story outlines the aging of the population in both the developed world and the newly emerging economies, suggesting that the time for action is now.

NO: This Rand Corporation study suggests that because of declining fertility, European populations are either growing more slowly or have actually begun to decline. Although these trends "portend difficult times ahead," European governments should be able to confront these challenges successfully.

T he developed world is now faced with an aging population brought on by declining birth rates and an increasing life expectancy. The phenomenon first appeared during the last quarter of the previous century with the demographic transition from high birth and death rates to lower rates. The drop in death rates in these countries was a function of two basic factors: (1) the dramatic decline in both infant mortality (within the first year of birth) and child mortality (within the first five years) due to women being healthier during pregnancy and nursing periods, and to the virtually universal inoculation of children against principal childhood diseases; and (2) once people reach adulthood, they are living longer, in large part because of medical advances against key adult illnesses.

Declining mortality rates yield an aging population in need of a variety of services—heath care, housing, and guards against inflation, for example—provided, in large part, by the tax dollars of the younger, producing sector of society. As the "gray" numbers of society grow, the labor force is increasingly called upon to provide more help for this class.

Declining birth and death rates mean that significantly more services will be needed to provide for the aging populations of the industrialized world, while at the same time, fewer individuals will be joining the workforce to provide the resources to pay for these services. However, some experts say that the new work force will be able to take advantage of the skills of the more aged, unlike previous eras. In order for national economies to grow in the information age, an expanding workforce may not be as an important prerequisite as it once was.

However, the elderly and the young are not randomly distributed throughout society, which is likely to create a growing set of regional problems. In the United States, for example, the educated young are likely to leave the "gray belt" of the north for the Sun Belt of the south, southwest and west. Who will be left in the older, established sectors of the country that were originally at the forefront of the industrial age to care for the disproportionately elderly population? What will happen 30 and 40 years from now, when the respective sizes of the young and the elderly populations throughout the developed world will yield a much larger population at the twilight of their existence? Although the trend is most evident in the richer part of the globe, people are also living longer in the developing world, primarily because of the diffusion of modern medical practices. But unless society can accommodate their skills of later years, they may become an even bigger burden in the future for their national governments.

A 2001 report, *Preparing for an Aging World: The Case for Cross-National Research* (National Academy of Sciences), identified a number of areas in which policymakers need a better understanding of the consequences of aging and resultant appropriate policy responses. Unless national governments of the developed world can effectively respond to these issues, the economic and social consequences can have a significant negative impact in both the aging population cohort as well as throughout the entire society. This theme was reiterated in a major report of the Population Reference Bureau in March 2005 (*Global Aging: The Challenge of Success*), suggesting three major challenges of an aging population: (1) economic development issues, (2) health and well-being issues, and (3) the challenge of enabling and supportive environments.

In the first selection, the *Business Week* international cover story suggests that "the graying of the baby boom generation" represents "one of the greatest sociological shifts in history," the inevitable changing demographics of a much higher percentage of the population falling into the elderly category. This, in turn, will create "significant challenges" to society to maintain and improve the quality of life for seniors as well as for the entire population of the developed world. In the second selection, the Rand Corporation study suggests that because of declining fertility, European populations are either growing more slowly or have actually begun to decline. Although these trends "portend difficult times ahead," European governments should be able to confront these challenges successfully.

YES ↩ Pete Engardio and Carol Matlack

Global Aging

J enny François doesn't have the world's most glamorous job. For 20 years she has commuted 45 minutes to the office of insurer Macif in Agen, France, where she punches data from insurance forms into a computer. But in the not-too-distant future, François and hundreds of millions of people like her in the industrialized world could look back at the early 21st century as the beginning of the end of a wonderful era, when even average workers could retire in reasonable comfort in their still-vigorous 50s. Thanks to France's generous pension system, François, 58, is in "pre-retirement." For the past three years she has worked just two days a week and still collects $1,500 a month—more than 70% of her old full-time salary. Her pay will decline only slightly when she reaches 60. "The system is great for me," François says, "and I think it should be every worker's right."

Lower Living Standards

It's already clear that the system will be far less generous to future retirees in France and elsewhere. And the message isn't going down easy. To avert a looming fiscal crunch, President Jacques Chirac's government in 2003 enacted new rules requiring people to work longer to qualify for benefits. The government endured a national wave of strikes. Italy and Germany also witnessed massive protests after their governments proposed similar measures. Despite electoral setbacks, Japanese Prime Minister Junichiro Koizumi still vows to ram through proposals to hike pension taxes from around 14% of pay to 18% by 2017 and to slash benefits from 59% of average wages now to 50%. In the U.S., the political debate is just starting to heat up over President George W. Bush's proposal to let workers park some of their Social Security contributions in personal investment accounts. Finland, South Korea, Brazil, and Greece all have recently moved or proposed to trim benefits, extend retirement ages, and hike workers' pension contributions.

The rollback of pension promises is just one symptom of one of the greatest sociological shifts in history: The graying of the baby-boom generation. The ranks of 60-year-olds and older are growing 1.9% a year—60%

faster than the overall world population. In 1950 there were 12 people aged 15 to 64 to support each one of retirement age. Now the global average is nine. It will be only four-to-one by mid-century, predicts the U.N. Population Div. By then the elderly will outnumber children for the first time. Some economists fear this will lead to bankrupt pensions and lower living standards.

That's why even more cutbacks in retirement benefits are likely. "I don't even want to think about my children's pensions," says Lina Iulita, 72, referring to Italy's hugely underfunded system. "There won't be enough money coming in." In Iulita's town of Dormeletto, on the shore of Lake Maggiore, coffee bars are jammed with seniors. The town's over-75 population has doubled since 1971, and there are one-third fewer children under 6. Local schools and gyms have closed, while senior citizens' clubs are flourishing.

The trend has drawn the most attention in Europe and in Japan, where the working-age population will decline by 0.6% this year. By 2025 the number of people aged 15 to 64 is projected to dwindle by 10.4% in Spain, 10.7% in Germany, 14.8% in Italy, and 15.7% in Japan. But aging is just as dramatic in such emerging markets as China—which is expected to have 265 million 65-year-olds by 2020—and Russia and Ukraine. Western European employers won't be able to count on the Czech Republic, Hungary, and Poland for big pools of low-cost workers forever: They're aging just as quickly. Within 20 years, East Asia's dynamic tigers will be youthful no longer. South Korea, Thailand, Taiwan, Singapore, and Hong Kong will have a median age of 40. Indonesia, India, Brazil, Mexico, the Philippines, Iran, and Egypt will still boast big, growing pools of workers for two decades. But they're on the same demographic curve and will show the effects of an aging population a generation or two later. "The aging workforce is the biggest economic challenge policymakers will face over the next 20 years," says Monika Queisser, a pension expert at the Organization for Economic Cooperation & Development.

The same basic factors are driving this shift: declining fertility and longer lifespans. Both are signs of enormous progress in the 20th century. With rare exceptions—such as impoverished Sub-Saharan Africa—birth control and better opportunities for women have lowered birth rates from five or six children per female in the 1950s to as few as one or two today. A fertility rate of 2.1 is seen as the population breakeven point. Over the same period, great advances in health care have added two full decades to the world's average life span, to age 66 now.

For most of the postwar era, the combination of baby booms, healthier populations, and smaller families amounted to what economists call the "demographic dividend," a tremendous, once-only chance to spur rapid development in nations with the right pro-growth policies. As boomers flooded into the workforce—first in the West and Japan, then Latin America and East Asia—they provided the labor for economic take-offs. Then, as they became parents, boomers had fewer children. So adults had more money to spend on goods and services and invest in their families' education.

But analysts and policymakers are starting to obsess over the flip side of the story: What happens when the baby boom becomes the geezer glut? How successfully this transition is managed around the world could determine the rise and fall of nations and reshape the global economy. Two key ingredients of growth are increases in the labor force and productivity. If countries can't maintain the size of their labor forces—say, by persuading older workers to retire later, getting stay-at-home wives to find jobs, or taking in more immigrants—they must boost productivity to maintain current growth levels. That will be a particular challenge in Europe, where productivity growth has averaged just 1.3% since 1995.

By these measures the U.S. is in relatively healthy shape despite the hand-wringing over Social Security and Medicare. Because of a slightly higher fertility rate and an annual intake of 900,000 legal immigrants, America's population should grow from 285 million now to 358 million in 2025. And the U.S. median age will rise just three years, to 39, over the next quarter-century, before the aging of America really starts to accelerate. The U.S. also has one of the world's most diversified retirement systems, including Social Security, company pensions, 401(k) savings plans that are largely invested in stocks, and private retirement insurance policies.

Nations with insolvent pension systems or insufficient private nest eggs, meanwhile, could face "an unprecedented societal crisis," warns OECD Secretary General Donald J. Johnston. Analysts say pension systems in Europe, Asia, and Latin America will start running into serious funding problems in a decade or two. Further down the road, some economists fear inadequate retiree savings will lead to lower consumption and asset values. The McKinsey Global Institute predicts that by 2024, growth in household financial wealth in the U.S., Europe, and Japan will slow from a combined 4.5% annual clip now to 1.3%. That will translate into $31 trillion less wealth than if the average age were to remain the same. Higher productivity would help, says McKinsey Global Director Diana Farrell. But without radical changes in labor and pensions, U.S. output per worker would have to be at least twice as high as the 2.6% McKinsey projects for the next decade, in part because workers will be a smaller portion of the population. "You would need numbers way north of what we can reasonably expect," says Farrell.

Wharton School finance professor Jeremy J. Siegel also contends that productivity won't be enough to offset the rise in number of retirees. Most pensions now index benefits to wages, rather than inflation, "and wages tend to rise with productivity," he notes. "As wages go up, people will demand higher benefits, so you essentially are chasing your tail." Siegel, famous for his bullishness on investing in blue-chip stocks for the long run, also worries about what will happen when future retirees try to liquidate their nest eggs en masse. To keep asset values from plummeting, Siegel predicts that heavy investments from newly affluent emerging markets such as India and China will have to flow into U.S. stocks, property, and bonds.

Whether such scenarios play out, of course, is anyone's guess. Aging's impact on financial markets isn't well understood, and predicting what the economy will be like in three years, much less three decades, is hard enough. Some argue that only modestly higher productivity will be able to offset demographic shifts and that worrymongers use overly pessimistic assumptions of medical costs. And, with enough political will, certainly governments can do plenty to ameliorate the social and economic fallout. "Most of the debate now is about benefits and taxes, but other levers can be pulled to make the problem more tractable," says Richard M. Samans, a managing director at the World Economic Forum.

The Future Is Now

From Stockholm to Seoul to Santiago, policymakers are seeking to boost private savings in stock and bond funds, lure young immigrant workers, find cheaper ways to provide elder care, and persuade companies to hire or retain older workers. On their own, none of these approaches is seen as a practical solution: Germany would have to more than double its annual intake of 185,000 foreigners to make up for fewer births, while immigration to Japan, now just 56,000 a year, would have to leap elevenfold. And slashing pensions enough to guarantee long-term solvency would mean political suicide. But a combination of sensible changes might make a big difference.

Developing nations with young and growing populations, meanwhile, face other issues. India is on pace to catch up and pass China's 1.4 billion population in three decades, for example. The trouble is, 40% of Indians drop out of school by age 10. Efforts to greatly expand education could determine whether India is a future economic superpower or if it will be burdened with the world's biggest population of poor illiterates. In Iran, an explosion of educated youth now joining the workforce could fuel a takeoff—or foment political strife if there are no jobs.

Why the sudden attention to a demographic trend that has been obvious for decades? In part, it's because the future is already dawning in many nations. In South Korea and Japan, which have strong cultural aversions to immigration, small factories, construction companies, and health clinics are relying more on "temporary" workers from the Philippines, Bangladesh, and Vietnam. In reality they are becoming permanent second-class citizens. In China's northern industrial belt, state industries are struggling over how to lay off unneeded middle-age workers when there is no social safety net to support them.

Across Europe, meanwhile, baby boomers such as Jenny François in France are retiring in droves—even though the first of this generation won't reach 65 until 2011. Most of Europe's state-funded pension systems encourage early retirement. Now, 85.5% of adults in France quit work by age 60, and only 1.3% work beyond 65. In Italy, 62% of adults call it quits by age 55. That compares with 47% of people who earn wages or salaries until they are 65 in the U.S. and 55% in Japan. With jobless rates still high, there's been little urgency to change. "I feel like I am in good enough shape to work, but there isn't enough work to go around," says Uwe Bohn, pouring a cup of coffee in his 12th-floor apartment in a drab Berlin highrise. Bohn, 61, retired four years ago after losing his civil-engineering job and failing for years to find steady work.

Dire Math

But financial pressures and the prospect of future labor shortages are spurring action. In France, business groups, unions, and the government will begin talks in February aimed at changing early-retirement rules. "We must correct fundamental aspects of that system," says Ernest-Antoine Seillière, chairman of French industrial investment firm Wendel Investissement and head of French employer group MEDEF.

With smart policies, older workers can be a boon to the economy, contends gerontologist Françoise Forette, president of the International Longevity Center in Paris. Research shows that better health care means today's veteran workers can remain productive much longer, especially with training, Forette says. "And if people work longer, there is no pension bomb—even in Europe." A World Economic Forum study to be released at its annual meeting from Jan. 26–30 in Davos, Switzerland, suggests labor shortfalls are solvable. Europe and Japan could make up for the decline in workers by keeping workers from retiring before 65 as well as by raising participation rates of women and people in their mid-20s to U.S. levels.

Some European countries are making progress. In Finland, new government and corporate policies are boosting the average retirement age. No longer is Italian home-appliance maker Indesit Co. coaxing older workers to retire early to make room for younger recruits. Instead, it's teaching its over-50 staff in its seven Italian factories new skills, such as factory and supply-chain management. So far the program is going smoothly, says Indesit human-resource director Cesare Ranieri. Luxembourg-based steelmaker Arcelor, which until 1991 offered early retirement at 92% of pay at age 50, says it has more than doubled productivity since raising the age to 60. Among other things, it hiked salaries for veterans who agreed to extra training and made it easier for them to work part time. "The policy proved very successful," says Arcelor human-resources manager director Daniel Atlan.

What really has pushed aging to the top of the global agenda, though, are ballooning fiscal gaps in the U.S., Europe, Japan, and elsewhere that could worsen as boomers retire. While U.S. Social Security is projected to remain solvent until at least 2042, the picture is more dire in Europe. Unlike the U.S., where most citizens also have private savings plans, in much of Europe up to 90% of workers rely almost entirely on public pensions. Benefits also are generous. Austria guarantees 93% of pay at retirement, for example, and Spain offers 94.7%. Without radical change, pensions and elder-care costs will jump from 14% of industrial nations' gross domestic product to 18% in 35 years, warns Washington's Center for Strategic & International Studies.

Fortunately, the global public appears to be bracing itself for rollbacks. Polling agency Allensbach reports that 89% of Germans don't believe their pensions are safe, from 63% a decade ago. Surveys of workers 25 and over by Des Moines financial-services provider Principal Financial Group (PFG) found that just 26% of French and 18% of Japanese are confident that their old-age system will pay the same benefits in the future as today.

Japanese workers such as Yumiko Wada certainly aren't in denial. "Old people today get quite a good pension, so they don't have a problem," says Wada, 30, an office employee in Tochigi. "But I wonder who will support us when we get old." Shunichi Kudo, 35, a salesman at a Fukuoka map-publishing house, says he agrees with Koizumi's plan to raise premiums and lower retiree benefits. "It's going to be difficult, and I don't like it, but I understand why it's happening," Kudo says.

The basic math of Japan's demographic profile is dire. Already, 17 of every 100 of its people are over 65, and this ratio will near 30 in 15 years. From 2005 to 2012, Japan's workforce is projected to shrink by around 1% each year—a pace that will accelerate after that. Economists fear that, besides blowing an even bigger hole in Japan's underfunded pension system, the decline of workers and young families will make it harder for the nation to generate new wealth: Its potential annual growth rate will drop below 1%, estimates Japan Research Institute Ltd. chief economist Kenji Yumoto, unless productivity spikes.

Japan's fiscal mess is so serious that it's hard to see an alternative to drastic future cuts. In 1998, Prime Minister Ryutaro Hashimoto hiked pension and social security contributions and the value-added tax, cutting disposable income by about $88 billion, or 2.5%. Japan's economy hasn't been the same since. Shock therapy is a "recipe for recessions," says Jesper Koll, chief Japan economist at Merrill Lynch & Co. (MER). Now, Tokyo plans to raise workers' burden by a more modest 0.3% of gross domestic product each year until 2017. Will that be enough to enable to Japan to meet its obligations to retirees? Probably not, Koll predicts, but Japanese citizens will endure that as well. "At the end of the day, part of the solution is going to be reduced contractual obligations," he says.

Shoring up public pensions is hardly the only avenue nations are exploring. In developing countries, privately managed savings accounts have been the rage. Two decades ago, nearly every Latin American nation had pay-as-you-go systems like Social Security, but more generous. Some granted civil servants retiring in their 50s full salaries for life. Widening budget deficits changed that. In 1981, Chile replaced its public system with retirement accounts funded by worker contributions and managed by private firms. Urged to follow suit by the World Bank, 11 other Latin nations introduced similar features. The movement also spread through Eastern Europe. The upsides have been enormous: Chile helped plug a big fiscal budget deficit, has mobilized $49 billion of pension-fund assets that make it easier for companies and governments to fund investments in the local currency with bond offerings, and most workers have some retirement benefits. Mexico and other Latin nations have seen similar payoffs.

Privatization alone is no panacea, however. For starters, private managers charge fees that often devour one quarter of workers' funds—prompting calls for fee limits and greater regulation. Also, private funds are leaving many workers virtually uncovered, either because they don't contribute much or work in the so-called informal sector of small, unregistered businesses. In Mexico, only 38% of the 32.6 million accounts are active, receiving monthly deposits from workers, employers, and the government. Of Brazil's 68 million workers, meanwhile, 56% are in the informal economy and get no pensions beyond their own savings. What's more, the pension system for private-sector workers already runs $9 billion in the red each year. As for Brazil's 1.2 million civil servants, they still collect generous benefits and retire early. Yet the public system runs $10 billion deficits, and civil servants have thwarted attempts to scale back.

Argentina's experience also shows that privatized systems can leave the elderly at the margin in a mismanaged economy. As part of its overhaul of the insolvent public pension system, Argentina in 1994 launched a scheme relying on funds managed by 11 private firms. Some 65% of Argentina's 14.5 million workers signed up for the new system. For many people, the 1990s were like "springtime—a time of great hope," says Maria Rosa Febrero, 49, a day-care center manager who is thankful she didn't invest in the private system. As a ceiling fan rustles piles of paperwork in her spartan, humid office, Febrero gazes at tourist posters of Patagonia's idyllic snow-capped peaks. "The funds were promising huge pensions and a perfect retirement. A lot of people bought into the dream." Unfortunately, the government obliged funds to invest two-thirds of their assets in government bonds. Their value plunged after the 2001 financial crisis, when Buenos Aires forced funds to swap the bonds for new, discounted paper and then defaulted altogether. The government also cut its contributions to pension plans.

Urgent Needs

Now, Argentina is trying to encourage higher contributions to private funds by offering another debt swap that would restore part of the funds' assets. Needless to say, Argentinians are dubious. "The whole system is poorly managed and totally corrupt," says Marina Amor, 79, who makes ends meet on the same monthly $104 stipend she has received since her late husband retired in 1989 after paying into the public pension for 40 years. "No one believes them anymore. I don't think there are many people left who believe they will ever be able to retire."

The challenge of providing for the elderly is especially urgent in the world's two biggest nations—India and China. Only 11% of Indians have pensions, and they tend to be civil servants and the affluent. With a young population and relatively big families, many of the elderly can still count on their children for support. That's not the case in China. By 2030, there will be only two working-age people to support every retiree. Yet only 20% of workers have government- or company-funded pensions or medical coverage.

Pension and medical reform. Later retirement. Higher productivity. More liberal immigration. Around the world, governments and businesses are searching for creative policies in each of these areas as they come to grips with one of the most profound social transformations in history. "Right now all of these issues are being dealt with piecemeal," says Ladan Manteghi, international affairs director for the Association for the Advancement of Retired Persons' global aging center. It all adds up to a big agenda—one that will determine whether the global economy that achieved such astounding progress in the youthful 20th century will continue to prosper as it matures in the 21st.

➡ **NO**

Population Implosion?

Across Europe, birth rates are falling and family sizes are shrinking. The total fertility rate is now less than two children per woman in every member nation in the European Union. As a result, European populations are either growing very slowly or beginning to decrease.

At the same time, low fertility is accelerating the ageing of European populations. As a region, Europe in 2000 had the highest percentage of people age 65 or older—15 percent. According to data from the U.S. Bureau of the Census, this percentage is expected to nearly double by 2050.[1]

These demographic trends portend difficult times ahead for European economies. For example, a shrinking workforce can reduce productivity. At the same time, the growing proportion of elderly individuals threatens the solvency of pension and social insurance systems. As household sizes decrease, the ability to care for the elderly diminishes. Meanwhile, elderly people face growing health care needs and costs. Taken together, these developments could pose significant barriers to achieving the European Union (EU) goals of full employment, economic growth, and social cohesion.

Concern over these trends has sparked intense debate over the most effective policies to reverse them or mitigate their impact. The policy debate has focused on three approaches: (1) promoting increased immigration of working-age people; (2) encouraging more childbearing, especially among younger couples; and (3) reforming social policy to manage the negative consequences of these trends—including measures that could raise the retirement age or encourage more women to join the workforce. To date, this debate has produced more heat than light, and solid research-based evidence to inform the debate remains sketchy. Many aspects of the relationship between national policies and demographic trends are either disputed or not well understood, and it remains difficult to disentangle the effects of specific policy initiatives from the effects of broader social, political, and economic conditions.

To help inform EU policy deliberations, analysts from RAND Europe and RAND U.S. examined the relationships between policy and demographic change. The RAND team analysed the interrelationships between European government policies and demographic trends and behaviour,

and assessed which policies can prevent or mitigate the adverse consequences of current low fertility and population ageing. The monograph,
Low Fertility and Population Ageing: Causes, Consequences, and Policy Options,
documents the study's findings.

The study carried out three tasks: It analysed European demographic
trends; it examined the relationship between national-level policies on the
one hand and demographic trends and household behaviours on the other
hand; and it conducted case studies of five countries—France, Germany,
Poland, Spain, and Sweden—which represent a mix of original and new
member states, with varying levels of fertility and net immigration, and
with different policy approaches.

The study found that:

- Immigration is not a feasible way of reversing population ageing or
  its consequences.
- National policies can slow fertility declines under the right circumstances.
- However, no single policy intervention necessarily works.
- And, what works in one country may not work in another. Social,
  economic, and political contexts influence the effect of policies.
- Policies designed to improve broader social and economic conditions may affect fertility, indirectly.
- Population policies take a long time to pay dividends—increases in
  fertility taking a generation to translate into an increased number
  of workers—making such policies politically unattractive.

Increased Immigration Will Not Reverse Population Ageing

Allowing large numbers of working-age immigrants to enter EU countries is
not a feasible solution to the problem of population ageing. The sheer numbers of immigrants needed to offset population ageing in the EU states would
be unacceptable in Europe's current sociopolitical climate. Furthermore, over
the longer term, these immigrants would themselves age. The study concluded that the debate should focus on using immigration as a potential tool
for slowing—as opposed to overcoming—population ageing.

Government Policies Can Slow Fertility Declines

Government policies can have an impact on fertility. For example, Spain
and France present an instructive contrast. Currently, Spain has the
second-lowest rate of fertility among the original 15 EU member states.
However, a generation ago (in 1971), Spain's fertility was among the highest in Europe. The dramatic decline in fertility since then is associated with
a shift from the pronatalist Franco regime—which banned contraception
and encouraged large families—to a democratic regime that has no explicit
population policy.

In contrast, France, which was the first European nation to experience a decline in its fertility rate and which has had an aggressive set of pronatalist policies in place for many decades, now has the second-highest fertility rate in Europe (behind Ireland). The fertility rate in France has not declined as much as that in other countries, and it actually increased between 1993 and 2002.

Reversing Fertility Decline Has Involved a Mix of Policies

No single policy intervention has worked to reverse low fertility. Historically, governments have attempted to boost fertility through a mix of policies and programmes. For example, France in recent decades has employed a suite of policies intended to achieve two goals: reconciling family life with work and reversing declining fertility. To accomplish the first goal, for example, France instituted generous child-care subsidies. To accomplish the second, families have been rewarded for having at least three children.

Sweden, by contrast, reversed the fertility declines it experienced in the 1970s through a different mix of policies, none of which specifically had the objective of raising fertility. Its parental work policies during the 1980s allowed many women to raise children while remaining in the workforce. The mechanisms for doing so were flexible work schedules, quality child care, and extensive parental leave on reasonable economic terms.

Political, Economic, and Social Contexts Influence Policy Impacts

Designing successful interventions is complicated by the fact that policies that work in one country may not work in another. Different interventions have varying effects because of the diverse, complex, and shifting political, economic, and social contexts in which they are implemented. The impact of these contexts appears in some of the sweeping political transitions Europe has witnessed over the past two decades.

For example, fertility declines in the former East Germany after unification appear to owe more to a shifting social environment than to policy change. Women who faced the unification with concerns about their economic situations were less likely to have children in the following year or two. The contrast between the former East Germany and West Germany is instructive. After reunification, the former West Germany's fertility rate remained relatively stable, whereas the former East Germany saw a precipitous decline over the next three years. Similarly, the transition to a free-market economy in Poland changed the economic environment and incentives for childbearing. Since 1989, Poland has experienced a sharp decrease in fertility.

Sweden provides a different kind of example. Although Sweden did not undergo political or economic transformation, its economic conditions nonetheless have affected fertility. Unlike in most other countries, fertility rates in Sweden are positively related to the earnings of women—likely because women's earnings in Sweden constitute a substantial proportion of dual-earner household income. Since parental-leave benefits are proportional to earnings, improvements in economic conditions lead to higher parental benefits, which can help promote increased fertility. Part of the decrease in fertility in Sweden during the 1990s is likely related to the decline in economic conditions.

Population Change Is Slow

Government policies intended to reverse fertility declines typically have a long-term focus and require many years to bear fruit. A few population policies may have an immediate effect (for example, those restricting/allowing abortion), but they are exceptions, and their effects tend to be on the timing of births rather than on completed fertility. Population policies to increase fertility take at least one generation before they ultimately increase the number of new entrants to the labour force.

As a result, there is a disconnect between electoral cycles (typically, 4–5 years) and the longer cycle of population policy. Politicians have limited incentives to advocate such policies, especially when doing so might entail the expenditure of political capital in entering a contentious policy domain. Therefore, population policies tend to lack both political appeal and political champions.

Instead, politicians tend to focus on policies for mitigating the effects of population ageing, which have shorter time horizons. One policy for doing so is encouraging participation in the workforce. This can mean promoting a longer working life and encouraging new entrants, such as women, into the workforce. Related to this are policies that seek to enhance the productivity of older workers.

Conclusion

This study showed that, under certain conditions, European governments can successfully confront the looming economic threats of declining fertility rates and ageing populations. Policies that remove workplace and career impediments to childrearing are a critical part of any solution. However, reversing long-term ageing and low fertility remains problematic, given that policies for doing so may not pay dividends until the next generation reaches working age. Prior to that time, millions of baby boomers will have retired. Hence, a solution will require long-term vision and political courage.

Note

1. Kevin Kinsella and Victoria A. Velkoff, *An Aging World: 2001*, Washington, D.C.: U.S. Census Bureau, Series P95/01-1, 2001, p. 9.

POSTSCRIPT

Is Global Aging in the Developed World a Major Problem?

The issue of the changing age composition in the developed world was foreseen a few decades ago but its heightened visibility is relatively recent. This visibility culminated in an UN-sponsored conference on aging in Madrid in April 2002. Its plan of action commits governments to address the problem of aging and provided them with a set of 117 specific recommendations covering three basic areas: older individuals and development, advancing health and well-being into old age, and ensuring enabling and supportive environments.

With the successful demographic transition in the industrial world, the percentage of those above the age of 60 is on the rise, while the labor force percentage is decreasing. In 1998, 19 percent of the first world fell into the post-60 category (10 percent worldwide). Children under age 15 also make up 19 percent of the developed world's population while the labor force is at 62 percent. With birth rates hovering around 1 percent or less, and life expectancy increasing, the percentages will likely continue to grow toward the upper end of the scale.

Paul Peterson has argued that the costs of global aging will not only outweigh the benefits, the capacity of the developed world to pay for these costs is questionable at best. The economic burden on the labor force will be "unprecedented," he suggests, and he offers a number of solutions ("Gray Dawn: The Global Aging Crisis" in *Foreign Affairs*, January/February 1999).

A particularly outspoken opponent of the "gloom" viewpoint is Phil Mullan. His book, *The Imaginary Time Bomb; Why an Ageing Population Is Not a Social Problem* (I. B. Tauris, New York, 2000), criticizes how the idea of an aging developed world has become "a kind of mantra for opponents of the welfare state and for a collection of alarmists." Mullan is joined by Phillip Longman, author of *The Empty Cradle* (Basic Books, 2004), who suggests in a *Foreign Affairs* article ("The Global Baby Bust," May/June 2004) that the coming "baby bust" will yield a variety of positive consequences as well as negative ones.

An excellent overview of the issues to be addressed in an era of global aging is *Global Aging: The Challenge of Success* by Kevin Kinsella and David R. Phillips (Population Reference Bureau, *Population Bulletin*, vol. 60, no 1, 2005; see also the Population Reference Bureau's March 2007 report, *Cross-National Research on Aging*).

A good introduction to global aging is found in "Aging of Population" by Leonid A. Gavrilov and Patrick Heuveline (*The Encyclopedia of Population*, Macmillan Reference, 2003). An excellent discussion of global aging is found in the U.S. Department of State's report "Why Population Aging Matters: A Global Perspective" (March 2007). See also Toshiko Kaneda's *A Critical Window for Policymaking on Population Aging in Developing Countries* (Population Reference Bureau, 2006) for an assessment of the problem in the world's poor sectors. The most succinct presentation of the effects of global aging can be found in John Hawksworth's "Seven Key Effects of Global Aging" (PricewaterhouseCoopers' web site, www.pwcglobal.com). This is "must reading" for those who want a concise, objective description of the potential consequence of the changing demographics associated with age distribution. His presentation focuses on the effects on economic growth, pensions systems, working lives, equity and bond markets, international capital flows, migration, and business strategies. A good source for the effect of declining population in Europe is "Population Policy Dilemmas in Europe at the Dawn of the Twenty-First Century" (*Population and Development Review*, The Population Council, Inc., March 2003). See also Jacques Vallin's "The End of the Demographic Transition: Relief or Concern?" (*Population and Development Review*, March 2002).

For some, such as Leon F. Bouvier and Jane T. Bertrand (*World Population: Challenges for the 21st Century*, Seven Locks Press, 1999), there seems to be a potential silver lining on the horizon. Although future increases in immigration will counterbalance the decline of the indigenous population, they assert, the real advance will be the decoupling of productivity expansion and work-force increases. The information age is knowledge-intensive, and becoming more so, not labor-intensive.

One author who accepts Bouvier and Bertrand's thesis is the noted scholar of management, Peter Drucker. In "The Future That Has Already Happened", *The Futurist* (November 1998), Drucker predicts that retirement age in the developed world will soon rise to 75, primarily because the greatest skill of this age group—knowledge—will become even more of an asset. He maintains that knowledge resources will become the most important commodity.

An important book on the fiscal problems facing the developed world because of aging can be found in Robert Stowe England's *The Fiscal Challenge of an Aging Industrial World* (CSIS *Significant Issues* Series, November 2001). An earlier report from CSIS is *Global Aging: The Challenge of the New Millennium* (CSIS and Watson Wyatt Worldwide). This document's presentation of the raw data is particularly useful. See also Ronald D. Lee's *Global Population Aging and Its Economic Consequences* (AEI Press, 2007); *Aging, Globalization and Inequality: The New Critical Gerontology* (Jan Baars et al., eds., Baywood Publishing Co., 2006); *Issues in Global Aging* (Frederick L. Ahearn, ed., Haworth Press, 2002); and *Global Health and Global Aging* (Mary Robinson, et al., eds., Jossey-Boss, 2007).

The Center for Strategic and International Studies (CSIS) in Washington is at the forefront of research and policy advocacy on the issue of global aging in the developed world. Its Global Aging Initiative (GAI) explores the international economic, financial, political, and security implications of aging and depopulation. Its report, *Meeting the Challenge of Global Aging: A Report to World Leaders from the CSIS Commission on Global Aging* (CSIS Press, 2002), suggests that the wide range of changes brought on by global aging poses significant challenges to the ability of countries to address problems associated with the elderly directly and to the national economy as a whole. Two other reports include *Meeting the Challenge of Global Aging* by Walter F. Mondale, et al. (2002) and *Macroeconomic Impact of Global Aging: A New Era of Economic Frailty?* (2002). See its web site: www.csis.org.

Other web sites include LinkAge 2000: Policy Implications of Global Aging (library.thinkquest.org/), The International Center on Global Aging (www.globalaging.org/resources), and The Environmental Literacy Council (www.enviroliteracy.org). See also the web site of the Program on the Global Demography of Aging at Harvard University (http://www.hsph.harvard.edu/pgda/).

Finally, the Second World Assembly on Aging in Madrid in April 2002 produced a huge number of documents. Its Plan of Action and other reports can be found at www.un.org/ageing/coverage.

ISSUE 4

Does Global Urbanization Lead Primarily to Undesirable Consequences?

YES: Divya Abhat, Shauna Dineen, Tamsyn Jones, Jim Motavilli, Rebecca Sanborn, and **Kate Slomkowski,** from "Today's 'Mega-Cities' Are Overcrowded and Environmentally Stressed," http://www.emagazine.com (September/October 2005)

NO: Robert M. McDonald, from "A World of the City, by the City, for the City," ZNet/Activism, http://www.zmag.org (December 20, 2005)

ISSUE SUMMARY

YES: Jim Motavalli, editor of *E/The Environmental Magazine,* suggests that the world's cities suffer from environmental ills, among them pollution, poverty, fresh water shortages, and disease.

NO: Robert McDonald, a postdoctoral fellow at Harvard University, suggests that global urbanization presents a great opportunity for the world to achieve international peace. It creates new possibilities for democracy and a sharing of common interests.

The year 2007 witnessed a turning point in the history of the world's cities. For the first time, the world's urban and rural populations were equal. Percentages are different for the developed and developing worlds, however. In 1950, 55 percent of the population of the developed world resided in urban areas, compared to only 18 percent in the developing world. By 2000, 76 percent of those in the developed world were urbanized, and it is expected, according to U.N. projections, to reach 82 percent by 2025. But because there will be low population growth throughout the developed world in the coming decades, the impact will not be substantial.

The story is different in the developing world. In 2000, the level of urbanization had risen to almost 40 percent, and is projected to be

54 percent in 2025. The percentages tell only part of the story, however, as they are not based on a stable national population level, but will occur in the context of substantial increases in the national population level. To illustrate the dual implication of urban growth as the consequence of both migration to the cities and increased births to those already living in urban areas, the U.N. projects that the urban population in the developing world will more than double in size between 2000 and 2030, from just under 2 billion to almost 5 billion or nearly two-thirds of the world's population (*State of the World's Cities 2006/07*, UN-Habitat, Earthscan, 2007).

Tremendous inequality will exist in cities. One out of three city dwellers reside in an urban environment that qualifies as slum conditions. The latter is defined as a lack of durable housing, lack of sufficient living area, lack of access to improved water, lack of access to improved sanitation, and lack of secure land tenure.

There are two ways to examine rapid urbanization. One can study the ability of society to provide services to the urban population. A second approach is to examine the adverse impacts of the urbanized area on the environment. The best place to begin a discussion of urbanization's effects is found in "An Urbanizing World" (Martin P. Brockerhoff, *Population Bulletin*, Population Reference Bureau, 2000). To Brockerhoff, increasing urbanization in the poor countries can be seen "as a welcome or as an alarming trend." He suggests that cities have been the "engines of economic development and the centers of industry and commerce." The diffusion of ideas is best found in cities around the world. And Brockerhoff observes the governmental cost savings of delivering goods and services to those in more densely populated environments.

The current problem is not that cities of the developing world are growing, but that they are expanding at a rapid pace. This calls into question the ability of both government and the private sector to determine what is necessary for urbanites to not only survive but to thrive. Many researchers believe that poverty and health problems (both physical and mental) are consequences of urbanization.

There is a more recent concern emerging among researchers about urbanization's impact—this time on biodiversity. One source has coined the phrase "heavy ecological footprints" ("Impact on the Environment," *Population Reports*, 2002) to describe the adverse effects. One study concludes, for example, that urban sprawl in the U.S. endangers more species than any other human behavior (Michael L. McKinney, "Urbanization, Biodiversity, and Conservation," *Bioscience*, 2002).

In the first selection, Jim Motavalli argues that most urban dwellers in the developing world are already confronted by severe environmental problems that will only increase in nature as population continues to grow. In the second selection, Robert McDonald suggests that global urbanization presents a great opportunity for the world to achieve international peace. It creates new possibilities for democracy and a sharing of common interests across national boundaries.

YES ↵

Divya Abhat et al.

Cities of the Future: Today's "Mega-Cities" Are Overcrowded and Environmentally Stressed

We take big cities for granted today, but they are a relatively recent phenomenon. Most of human history concerns rural people making a living from the land. But the world is rapidly urbanizing, and it's not at all clear that our planet has the resources to cope with this relentless trend. And, unfortunately, most of the growth is occurring in urban centers ill-equipped for the pace of change. You've heard of the "birth dearth"? It's bypassing Dhaka, Mumbai, Mexico City and Lagos, cities that are adding population as many of their western counterparts contract.

The world's first cities grew up in what is now Iraq, on the plains of Mesopotamia near the banks of the Tigris and Euphrates Rivers. The first city in the world to have more than one million people was Rome at the height of its Empire in 5 A.D. At that time, world population was only 170 million. But Rome was something new in the world. It had developed its own sophisticated sanitation and traffic management systems, as well as aqueducts, multi-story low-income housing and even suburbs, but after it fell in 410 A.D. it would be 17 centuries before any metropolitan area had that many people.

The first large city in the modern era was Beijing, which surpassed one million population around 1800, followed soon after by New York and London. But at that time city life was the exception; only three percent of the world's population lived in urban areas in 1800.

The rise of manufacturing spurred relocation to urban centers from the 19th through the early 20th century. The cities had the jobs, and new arrivals from the countryside provided the factories with cheap, plentiful labor. But the cities were also unhealthy places to live because of crowded conditions, poor sanitation and the rapid transmission of infectious disease. As the Population Reference Bureau reports, deaths exceeded births in many large European cities until the middle of the 19th century. Populations grew, then, by continuing waves of migration from the countryside and from abroad.

From First World to Third

In the first half of the 20th century, the fastest urban growth was in western cities. New York, London and other First World capitals were magnets for immigration and job opportunity. In 1950, New York, London, Tokyo and Paris boasted of having the world's largest metropolitan populations. (Also in the top 10 were Moscow, Chicago, and the German city of Essen.) By then, New York had already become the first "mega-city," with more than 10 million people. It would not hold on to such exclusivity for long.

In the postwar period, many large American cities lost population as manufacturing fled overseas and returning soldiers taking advantage of the GI Bill fueled the process of suburbanization. Crime was also a factor. As an example, riot-torn Detroit lost 800,000 people between 1950 and 1996, and its population declined 33.9 percent between 1970 and 1996. Midwestern cities were particularly hard-hit. St. Louis, for instance, lost more than half its population in the same period, as did Pittsburgh. Cleveland precipitously declined, as did Buffalo, Cincinnati, Minneapolis and many other large cities, emerging as regional players rather than world leaders.

Meanwhile, while many American cities shrank, population around the world was growing dramatically. In the 20th century, world population increased from 1.65 billion to six billion. The highest rate of growth was in the late 1960s, when 80 million people were added every year.

According to the "World Population Data Sheet," global population will rise 46 percent between now and 2050 to about nine billion. While developed countries are losing population because of falling birth rates and carefully controlled immigration rates (only the U.S. reverses this trend, with 45 percent growth to 422 million predicted by 2050), population is exploding in the developing world.

India's population will likely grow 52 percent to 1.6 billion by 2050, when it will surpass China as the world's most populous country. The population in neighboring Pakistan will grow to 349 million, up 134 percent in 2050. Triple-digit growth rates also are forecast for Iraq, Afghanistan and Nepal.

Africa could double in population to 1.9 billion by 2050. These growth rates hold despite the world's highest rates of AIDS infection, and despite civil wars, famines and other factors. Despite strife in the Congo, it could triple to 181 million by 2050, while Nigeria doubles to 307 million.

Big Cities Get Bigger—and Poorer

According to a 1994 U.N. report, 1.7 billion of the world's 2.5 billion urban dwellers were then living in less-developed nations, which were also home to two thirds of the world's mega-cities. The trend is rapidly accelerating.

People and the Planet reports that by 2007, 3.2 billion people—a number larger than the entire global population of 1967—will live in cities. Developing countries will absorb nearly all of the world's population increases between today and 2030. The estimated urban growth rate of 1.8 percent for the period between 2000 and 2030 will double the number of city dwellers. Meanwhile, rural populations are growing scarcely at all.

Also by 2030, more than half of all Asians and Africans will live in urban areas. Latin America and the Caribbean will at that time be 84 percent urban, a level comparable to the U.S. As urban population grows, rural populations will shrink. Asia is projected to lose 26 million rural dwellers between 2000 and 2030.

For many internal migrants, cities offer more hope of a job and better health care and educational opportunities. In many cases, they are home to an overwhelming percentage of a country's wealth. (Mexico City, for example, produces about 30 percent of Mexico's total Gross Domestic Product.) Marina Lupina, a Manila, Philippines resident, told *People and the Planet* that she and her two children endure the conditions of city living (inhabiting a shack made from discarded wood and cardboard next to a fetid, refuse-choked canal) because she can earn $2 to $3 a day selling recycled cloth, compared to 50 cents as a farm laborer in the rural areas. "My girls will have a better life than I had," she says. "That's the main reason I came to Manila. We will stay no matter what."

Movement like this will lead to rapidly changing population levels in the world's cities, and emerging giants whose future preeminence can now only be guessed. "By 2050, an estimated two-thirds of the world's population will live in urban areas, imposing even more pressure on the space infrastructure and resources of cities, leading to social disintegration and horrific urban poverty," says Werner Fornos, president of the Washington-based Population Institute.

Today, the most populous city is Tokyo (26.5 million people in 2001), followed by Sao Paulo (18.3 million), Mexico City (18.3 million), New York (16.8 million) and Bombay/Mumbai (16.5 million). But by 2015 this list will change, with Tokyo remaining the largest city (then with 27.2 million), followed by Dhaka (Bangladesh), Mumbai, Sao Paulo, New Delhi and Mexico City (each with more than 20 million). New York will have moved down to seventh place, followed by Jakarta, Calcutta, Karachi and Lagos (all with more than 16 million).

The speed by which some mega-cities are growing has slowed. Thirty years ago, for instance, the U.N. projected Mexico City's population would grow beyond 30 million by 2000, but the actual figures are much lower. Other cities not growing as much as earlier seen are Rio de Janeiro, Calcutta, Cairo, and Seoul, Korea. But against this development is the very rapid growth of many other cities (in some cases, tenfold in 40 years) such as Amman (Jordan), Dar es Salaam (Tanzania), Lagos, and Nairobi.

The rise of mega-cities, comments the *Washington Post,* "poses formidable challenges in health care and the environment, in both the developed and developing world. The urban poor in developing countries live in squalor unlike anything they left behind . . . In Caracas, more than half the total housing stock is squatter housing. In Bangkok, the regional economy is 2.1 percent smaller than it otherwise would be because of time lost in traffic jams. The mega-cities of the future pose huge problems for waste management, water use and climate change."

In Cairo, Egypt, the rooftops of countless buildings are crowded with makeshift tents, shacks and mud shelters. It's not uncommon to see a family cooking their breakfast over an open fire while businesspeople work in their cubicles below. The city's housing shortage is so severe that thousands of Egyptians have moved into the massive historic cemetery known as the City of the Dead, where they hang clotheslines between tombs and sleep in mausoleums.

By 2015, there will be 33 mega-cities, 27 of them in the developing world. Although cities themselves occupy only two percent of the world's land, they have a major environmental impact on a much wider area. London, for example, requires roughly 60 times its own area to supply its nine million inhabitants with food and forest products. Mega-cities are likely to be a drain on the Earth's dwindling resources, while contributing mightily to environmental degradation themselves.

The Mega-City Environment

Mega-cities suffer from a catalog of environmental ills. A World Health Organization (WHO)/United Nations Environment Programme (UNEP) study found that seven of the cities—Mexico City, Beijing, Cairo, Jakarta, Los Angeles, Sao Paulo and Moscow—had three or more pollutants that exceeded the WHO health protection guidelines. All 20 of the cities studied by WHO/UNEP had at least one major pollutant that exceeded established health limits.

According to the World Resources Institute, "Millions of children living in the world's largest cities, particularly in developing countries, are exposed to life-threatening air pollution two to eight times above the maximum WHO guidelines. Indeed, more than 80 percent of all deaths in developing countries attributable to air pollution-induced lung infections are among children under five." In the big Asian mega-cities such as New Delhi, Beijing and Jakarta, approximately 20 to 30 percent of all respiratory disease stems from air pollution.

Almost all of the mega-cities face major fresh water challenges. Johannesburg, South Africa is forced to draw water from highlands 370 miles away. In Bangkok, saltwater is making incursions into aquifers. Mexico City has a serious sinking problem because of excessive groundwater withdrawal.

More than a billion people, 20 percent of the world's population, live without regular access to clean running water. While poor people are forced to pay exorbitant fees for private water, many cities squander their resources through leakages and illegal drainage. "With the population of cities expected to increase to five billion by 2025," says Klaus Toepfer, executive director of the UNEP, "the urban demand for water is set to increase exponentially. This means that any solution to the water crisis is closely linked to the governance of cities."

Mega-city residents, crowded into unsanitary slums, are also subject to serious disease outbreaks. Lima, Peru (with population estimated at 9.4 million by 2015) suffered a cholera outbreak in the late 1990s partly because, as the *New York Times* reported, "Rural people new to Lima . . . live in houses without running water and use the outhouses that dot the hillsides above." Consumption of unsafe food and water subjects these people to life-threatening diarrhea and dehydration.

It's worth looking at some of these emerging mega-cities in detail, because daily life there is likely to be the pattern for a majority of the world's population. Most are already experiencing severe environmental problems that will only be exacerbated by rapid population increases. Our space-compromised list leaves out the largest European and American cities. These urban centers obviously face different challenges, among them high immigration rates.

Jakarta, Indonesia

A Yale University graduate student, who served as a college intern at the U.S. Embassy in Jakarta, brought back this account: "Directly adjacent to the Embassy's high-rise office building was a muddy, trash-filled canal that children bathed in every morning. The view from the top floors was unforgettable: a layer of brown sky rising up to meet the blue—a veritable pollution horizon. In the distance the tips of skyscrapers stretched up out of the atmospheric cesspool below, like giant corporate snorkels. Without fresh air to breathe, my days were characterized by nausea and constant low-grade headaches. I went to Indonesia wanting a career in government, and left determined to start a career working with the environment."

Jakarta is one of the world's fastest-growing cities. United Nations estimates put the city's 1995 population at 11.5 million, a dramatic increase from only 530,000 in 1930. Mohammad Dannisworo of the Bandung Institute of Technology (ITB) says 8.5 million people live within the city's boundaries at night and an additional 5.5 million migrate via 2.5 million private cars, 3.8 million motorcycles and 255,000 public transportation vehicles into the city during the day. This daily parade of combustion engines clogs the city streets and thickens the air, making Jakarta the world's third-most-polluted city after Bangkok and Mexico City.

Rapid growth has become one of the capital city's greatest challenges, as migrants continue to pour into Jakarta from the surrounding countryside in search of higher-paying jobs. An estimated 200,000 people come to the city looking for employment every year. In the face of such growth, the city has been unable to provide adequate housing, despite repeated attempts to launch urban improvement programs. The Kampung Improvement Program (KIP), established in the 1980s, was initially highly successful in boosting living conditions for more than 3.5 million established migrants, but it has been unable to accommodate the persistent migrant influx. There is an acute housing shortage, with a demand for 200,000 new units a year unfulfilled.

As Encarta describes it, "In the 1970s, efforts failed to control growth by prohibiting the entry of unemployed migrants. The current strategy emphasizes family planning, dispersing the population throughout the greater [metropolitan] region, and promoting transmigration (the voluntary movement of families to Indonesia's less-populated islands). Jakarta is a magnet for migrants . . . [During the late 1980s] most were between the ages of 15 and 39 years, many with six years of education or less."

The U.N. reports that the city's drinking water system is ineffective, leading 80 percent of Jakarta inhabitants to use underground water, which has become steadily depleted. In lowlying North Jakarta, groundwater depletion has caused serious land subsidence, making the area more vulnerable to flooding and allowing seawater from the Java Sea to seep into the coastal aquifers. According to Suyono Dikun, Deputy Minister for Infrastructure at the National Development Planning Board, more than 100 million people in Indonesia are living without proper access to clean water.

Jakarta's environment has been deteriorating rapidly, with serious air pollution and the lack of a waterborne sewer. Jakarta officials have only recently begun to acknowledge the source of over half of the city's air pollution, and have begun to take action against automobile congestion. The Blue Skies Program, founded in 1996, is dedicated to updating the city's public and private transportation technology. The project's successes to date include an increase in the percentage of vehicles meeting pollution standards, a near-complete phasing out of leaded gasoline, and an increase in the number of natural gas-fueled vehicles to 3,000 taxis, 500 passenger cars and 50 public buses.

The Blue Skies Project is pushing Jakarta toward a complete natural gas conversion and is working toward the installation of dedicated filling stations, establishing a fleet of natural gasfueled passenger buses, supplying conversion kits for gasoline-fueled cars, and creating adequate inspection and maintenance facilities.

Jakarta has acknowledged its traffic problems and undertaken both small and large scale projects to alleviate the stresses of pollution and congestion. The city has launched a "three-in-one" policy to encourage carpooling, demanding that every car on major thruways carry at least three passengers when passing through special zones from 4:30 p.m. to 7:30 p.m. The city has also undertaken the construction of a nearly 17-mile monorail system.

But if Jakarta really wants to alleviate its infrastructure problems, it has to work from within, says Gordon Feller of the California-based Urban Age Institute. "The mayor needs to create a partnership between the three sectors—the government, the local communities and the nongovernmental agencies. The job of the mayor is to empower the independent innovators, not to co-opt or block them."

Dhaka, Bangladesh

Dhaka had only 3.5 million people in 1951; now it has more than 13 million. The city has been gaining population at a rate of nearly seven percent a year since 1975, and it will be the world's second-largest city (after Tokyo) by 2015. According to a recent Japanese environmental report, "Dhaka city is beset with a number of socio-environmental problems. Traffic congestion, flooding, solid waste disposal, black smoke from vehicular and industrial emissions, air and noise pollution, and pollution of water bodies by industrial discharge. . . .

Black smoke coming out from the discharge is intolerable to breathe, burning eyes and throats. The city dwellers are being slowly poisoned by lead concentration in the city air 10 times higher than the government safety limit."

Because of a heavy concentration of cars burning leaded gasoline, Dhaka's children have one of the highest blood lead levels in the world. Almost 90 percent of primary school children tested had levels high enough to impair their developmental and learning abilities, according to a scientific study.

Water pollution is already rampant. According to the Japanese report, "The river Buriganga flows by the side of the densely populated area of the old city. Dumping of waste to the river by . . . industries is rather indiscriminate. . . . The indiscriminate discharge of domestic sewage, industrial effluents and open dumping of solid wastes are becoming a great concern from the point of water-environment degradation."

Nearly half of all Bangladeshis live below the poverty line, able only to glance at the gleaming new malls built in Dhaka. Urbanization and the pressures of poverty are severely stressing the country's once-abundant natural resources. According to U.S. Aid for International Development (USAID), "Pressures on Bangladesh's biological resources are intense and growing."

They include:

- Poor management of aquatic and terrestrial resources;
- Population growth;
- Overuse of resources;
- Unplanned building projects; and
- Expansion of agriculture onto less-productive lands, creating erosion and runoff, among other by-products.

Bangladesh's expanding population destroys critical habitats, reports USAID, causing a decrease in biodiversity. Most of Bangladesh's tropical forests and almost all of the freshwater floodplains have been negatively affected by human activities.

But despite all the negatives, there is a growing environmental movement in Bangladesh that is working to save Dhaka's natural resources. The Bangladesh Environmental Network (BEN), for instance, works on reducing the high level of arsenic in Bangladesh's water supply (more than 500 percent higher than World Health Organization standards), combats the country's severe flooding problem and tries to defeat India's River Linking Project, which could divert an estimated 10 to 20 percent of Bangladesh's water flow. Bangladesh Poribesh Andolon holds demonstrations and international action days to increase citizen awareness of endangered rivers.

International development projects are also addressing some of the country's environmental woes, including a $44 million arsenic mitigation project launched in 1998 and jointly financed by the World Bank and the Swiss Development and Cooperation Agency. The project is installing deep wells, installing hardware to capture rainwater, building sanitation plants, and expanding distribution systems. A $177 million World Bank project works with the government of Bangladesh to improve urban transportation in Dhaka. Private companies from Bangladesh and Pakistan recently announced a joint venture to construct a waste management plant that could handle 3,200 metric tons of solid waste per day, turning it into organic fertilizer.

Mexico City

Mexico City is like an anxious teenager, growing up faster than it probably should. That phenomenon manifests itself in awkward contrasts: Sports cars zipping down crowded streets, choked with air pollution; a Wal-Mart rising against a skyline of the ancient ruins of Teotihuacan; and trendy designer knock-off bags lining the walls of a grungy street stall.

The locale has long been a cultural hub—the ancient Aztec capital of Tenochtitlán, where Mexico City now stands, was the largest city in the Americas in the 14th century with a population of about 300,000. When the Spanish razed Tenochtitlán they erected Mexico City in its place, though a smallpox epidemic knocked the population back to 30,000. Mexico City served as the center of Spain's colonial empire during the 1500s, but the modern-day metropolis only began to materialize in the late 1930s when a combination of rapid economic growth, population growth, and a considerable rural migration filled the city with people.

The larger metropolitan area now engulfs once-distinct villages and population estimates range from 16 million to 30 million, depending on how the city's boundaries are drawn. Regardless, Mexico City is now widely considered the world's third-largest city, and still growing; birth rates are high and 1,100 new residents migrate to the capital each day.

With so many people crammed into a closed mountain valley, many environmental and social problems are bound to arise. Mexico City's air was ranked by WHO as the most contaminated in the world in 1992. By 1998, the Mexican capital had added the distinction of being "the world's most dangerous city for children." Twenty percent of the city's population lives in utter poverty, the Mega-Cities Project reports, 40 percent of the population lives in "informal settlements," and wealth is concentrated in very few hands.

A combination of population, geography and geology render air pollution one of the city's greatest problems. WHO studies have reported that it is unhealthy to breathe air with over 120 parts per billion of ozone contaminants more than one day a year, but residents breathe it more than 300 days a year. More than one million of the city's more than 18 million people suffer from permanent breathing problems.

According to the U.S. Energy Information Administration, "Exhaust fumes from Mexico City's approximately three million cars are the main source of air pollutants. Problems resulting from the high levels of exhaust are exacerbated by the fact that Mexico City is situated in a basin. The geography prevents winds from blowing away the pollution, trapping it above the city."

The International Development Research Center has observed that "despite more than a decade of stringent pollution control measures, a haze hangs over Mexico City most days, obscuring the surrounding snow-capped mountains and endangering the health of its inhabitants. Many factors have contributed to this situation: industrial growth, a population boom and the proliferation of vehicles." More than 30 percent of the city's vehicles are more than 20 years old.

Solid waste creates another major problem, and officials estimate that, of the 10,000 tons of waste generated each day, at least one quarter is dumped illegally. The city also lacks an effective sanitation and water distribution system. According to the United Nations, "Urbanization has had a serious negative effect on the ecosystem of Mexico City. Although 80 percent of the population has piped inside plumbing, residents in the peripheral areas cannot access the sewage network and a great percentage of wastewater remains untreated as it passes to the north for use as irrigation water."

Perhaps three million residents at the edge of the city do not have access to sewers, says the Mega-Cities Project. Untreated waste from these locations is discharged directly into water bodies or into the ground, where it can contaminate ground water. Only 50 percent of residents in squatter settlements have access to plumbing, and these residents are more likely to suffer from health effects linked to inadequate sanitation. Furthermore, Mexico City is now relying on water pumped from lower elevations to quench an ever-deepening thirst; as the city continues to grow, the need for water and the politics surrounding that need are likely only to intensify.

Mexican industry is centered within the city and is primarily responsible for many of the city's environmental problems as well as for the prosperity that certain areas have achieved. Mexico City houses 80 percent of all the firms in the country, and 2.6 million cars and buses bring people to work and shop in them. Sandwiched in between slums and sewers are glitzy, luxurious neighborhoods and shopping centers, as chic as any in New York or Los Angeles.

The streets of the Zócalo, a central city plaza modeled after Spanish cities, serve as Mexico City's cultural hub. Unwittingly, the plaza has become one of the economic centers as well. Most job growth in Mexico occurs in the underground sector—in street stalls that cover every square inch of sidewalk space, women flipping tortillas curbside, and kids hawking phone cards or pirated CDs to passersby. Despite efforts to clean up activities that are illegal or considered eyesores, street vendors make up an enormous part of Mexico's job force and, according to the *Los Angeles Times,* are primarily responsible for keeping the official unemployment rate below that of the United States. . . .

Robert M. McDonald  **NO**

A World of the City, by the City, for the City

Rip Van Winkle took his famous nap on the outskirts of Palenville in the Catskill Mountains. In Washington Irving's original story, Rip slept for only 20 years, managing to miss the entire American Revolution in the process. Let us imagine that Rip, being incredibly long-lived due to his many hours of restorative sleep, is still wandering around the Hudson Valley. How different it must look to him! The New York City megalopolis alone now holds more Americans than the Empire State and all of New England did in 1900. Rip has just been the witness to one of the most dramatic transformations of the last century, the shift from a rural to urban existence for the vast majority of Americans. In 1900, 60% of the U.S. population was rural. Today, less than 25% of the population is. It was a transformation that changed the very character of life for Americans, and drove a series of political and cultural changes that continue today.

I've heard that Rip Van Winkle has grown tired again. This time, however, in his quest to find a quiet place to rest his head, he's ventured to a calm spot along the China coast. What can Rip expect to see when he awakens, another 50 or 100 years hence?

The United Nations Population Division is making plans to celebrate the day, sometime in the next couple of years, when, for the first time in the history of the world, a majority of humanity will live in cities. Most of this growth will occur in developing countries, particularly India and China. In all likelihood, Rip will awaken from another long slumber to find a landscape far more modified than that of upstate New York. He will be witness to a momentous, qualitative change in the lived experience of humanity, one that poses a grave challenge to the goal of sustainable development, and yet offers hope of achieving the dream of international peace.

Sustainable Urbanization

This massive urbanization occurring worldwide creates new possibilities for environmental problems. An increase in urban population necessarily requires an increase in urban land area, on a grand scale: by one estimate, there will be more housing units built in the 21st century than in the rest of recorded human history. And as urban land increases, there will be a host of impacts on the environment. Many of the negative impacts will be clustered in poor neighborhoods in fast growing cities in developing countries: the fast growing *favelas* of Rio de Janeiro, the shantytowns of Mumbai. Understanding and managing this array of environmental impacts is thus crucial not just for environmentalists, but for anyone interested in reducing poverty and human misery.

Foremost among the problems that the megacities of the 21st century will face is the pollution of drinking water by industrial waste. The Chinese city of Harbin, for example, just had to shut off its public water supply after a petrochemical plant upstream exploded. Its three million residents had to survive without easily available water for several days. Even more common in cities in poorer countries that lack sewer systems are frequent outbreaks of cholera and other water borne diseases. The U.N. estimates that more than a billion people live in slums, the vast majority without clean drinking water, and this number will likely continue to grow unless there are substantial increases in infrastructure investment.

If Harbin is a warning of the water crises that may become common in the near future, then Lanshou is an example of the worst kind of air pollution that can occur with poorly planned development. This West China city has arguably the world's worst levels of total suspended particulates, which can cause bronchitis and asthma when inhaled, some 8 times more than recommended levels. This kind of air pollution problem is now common to virtually all big cities in developing countries. However, there's some evidence that as countries become wealthier they can clean up their air. A whole field of economics has sprung up investigating the relationship between a country's development and the emissions of different pollutants. For some pollutants such as suspended particulates, any increase in per capita income beyond a certain point is correlated with reductions in pollution levels. In effect, these pollutants can be reduced or eliminated—it just takes money and expertise that many rapidly growing cities in developing countries do not have. Increases in literacy levels and political rights are further correlated with reduction in these pollutants, suggesting that further democratization in the developing world will be good for the environment.

One of the most common mistakes environmentalists and progressives from developed countries often make is to assume that urbanization is always bad for the environment. This viewpoint focuses on urbanization without having a proper baseline—what would happen if all these people didn't move to cities? What would the world look like? People would be more dispersed across the landscape, multiplying the impact on the environment many times. One example is energy use, which is markedly more efficient in cities than in rural areas in many countries. Most major uses of energy, like heating and transportation, are more efficient at higher densities. For instance, 53% of New York City residents take public transit to work, far above the United States overall average of 5%, a gain that is possible in large part because of the increased population density of that city. This substantially reduces the energy required to transport people and goods: on average, European cities are 5 times denser than American cities and consume 3.6 times less transport energy per capita. In this sense, the massive migration to urban regions in the developing world provides an opportunity for energy savings, if planned properly. In effect, the world faces the largest urban planning challenge in the history of the human race. The question is, are we ready for it?

Convergence of Needs

If urbanization is a great challenge for sustainable development, it is also a great opportunity for progressives to build a more peaceful world. Urbanization involves a move away from rural areas, which often are isolated, without adequate education or political representation, toward an urban lifestyle. Despite the many problems of the slums, its residents often enjoy better education than their rural counterparts, and the sheer proximity of poor citizens to one another can greatly facilitate political organizing. The slum dwellers in El Alto in Bolivia, for example, through a series of protests, succeeded in forcing the state to take back control of water and sewer service from the private consortium that had failed to provide the slum dwellers with affordable service. In short, urbanization creates new potentialities for democracy.

City dwellers have much in common with one another, even if they are in different regions or nations. The slum dwellers in El Alto in Bolivia have more in common with the slum dwellers in Khan in Mumbai, India, than they do with those living in rural regions of Bolivia. While this commonality is often obscured by cultural differences and nationalist sentiment, it is a powerful political force that will be ascendant in the 21st century. Urban dwellers have a convergence of needs and desires that makes them a class with shared interests.

The increased mobility of many city dwellers heightens this sense of commonality among urban populations. It is worthwhile to note, for example, that much *international* migration is not rural to urban but interurban. In the developed world, the European Union provides a good example of what the future probably looks like: younger workers willing to move to find jobs will bounce between cities frequently. One acquaintance of mine, for example, moved from Barcelona to Paris to London in the space of 3 years, all in a quest of a better, more stable job. This kind of cross-cultural movement reduces the sense that this or that city seems foreign. Indeed, what seems foreign to many EU youth is a more rural lifestyle, even if it is in their native country.

This is not to sound sanguine about the political effects of this convergence of needs caused by the ongoing global urbanization. Significant resistance to a sense of commonality remains a political fact. Internally, cultural ties may bind urban dwellers to a rural culture long after that rural culture has ceased to exist. The United States political scene is a prime example of this, with the family farmer being seen as decent and the urban dweller seen as corrupt—never mind the fact that the net flow of tax dollars is from productive cities to stagnant rural areas, or that almost 80% of Americans are urbanites. That isn't to say that the good rural traits—hard work, honesty, and simplicity—should disappear, but rather that politically we must re-envision these ideals in an urban context.

Among countries, nationalism may prevent an acknowledgement of how similar the urban realities are. Still, progressives must be aware of the great opportunity this convergence of needs presents, and seize the opening to push for real improvements in the lives of urban dwellers. Progressives must also avoid any blanket condemnation of urbanization in the developing world, recognizing that any such condemnation is pointless and highly offensive to many Third World residents.

POSTSCRIPT

Does Global Urbanization Lead Primarily to Undesirable Consequences?

It appears self-evident that rapidly growing urbanized areas, particularly in the developing world, create special circumstances. Our visual image of such places accents this fact. First-world travelers, particularly to the developing world, are likely to take away from that experience a litany of pictures that paint a bleak image of life there. The critical question, though, is whether such environments really do create major problems for those who live within such areas and policy makers who must provide goods and services. Conventional wisdom that such problems must exist is found everywhere throughout the urbanization literature. We easily could have selected any one of a dozen or more articles that asserted this situation with much conviction.

Perhaps, however, those problems observed by urban visitors might, in fact, be a consequence of some other situation unrelated to urbanization. Moreover, others allude to the advantages of urbanization for modernization. These individuals tend to bring a historical perspective to their analysis, but therein lies a potential fatal flaw. Urbanization occurred first in the current developed world, where cities grew more slowly and where governments had the capacity and the inclination to provide a better quality of life for urban dwellers.

The most definite source of information about urbanization is UN-Habitat's *State of the World's Cities 2006/07* (Earthscan, 2007). UN-Habitat had sponsored a global conference called the Third World Urban Forum (WUF3) in Vancouver in Summer 2006. Among the 2007 publication's major findings is that 95 percent of urban growth in the next two decades will occur in the developing world, which will house 4 billion people or 80 percent of the world's urban population by 2030 (others indicate a figure closer to 5 billion). This report focuses on urban problems in the context of the U.N. Millennium goals for development.

George Martine's *The State of World Population 2007: Unleashing the Potential of Urban Growth* (United Nations, UNFPA, 2007) analyzes why such growth is occurring and what preparations need to take place to address the dramatic increases in urban growth forecasted for the first third of the twenty-first century.

Another important source of information about urbanization is found in the United Nations' *2005 Revision of World Urbanization Prospects* (U.N., 2006). Another important work is the National Research Council's

Cities Transformed: Demographic Change and Its Implications in the Developing World (National Academies Press, 2003). The Population Reference Bureau has produced a comprehensive monogram called "An Urbanizing World" by Martin P. Brockerhoff (*Population Bulletin*, September 2004). An interesting approach to the subject is found in Mike Davis' "Planet of Slums" (*Harper's*, June 2004). A sophisticated analysis is found in a 2003 article in *Sociological Perspectives* by John M. Shandra, Bruce London and John B. Williamson ("Environmental Degradation, Environmental Sustainability, and Overurbanization in the Developing World: A Quantitative, Cross-National Analysis," 2003). Klaus Toepler, Executive Director of the United Nations Environment Programme at the time, provides a thoughtful discussion of challenges facing megacities of the world.

Two articles with differing viewpoints are useful sources. Barbara Boyle Torrey, a member of the Population Reference Bureau's Board of Trustees and a writer/consultant, argues that extremely high urban growth rates are resulting in the developing world and will continue to create a range of negative environmental problems ("Urbanization: An Environmental Force to Be Reckoned With," Population Reference Bureau, April 2004). Gordon McGranahan and David Satterthwaite, members of London's International Institute for Environment and Development, suggest that there is little research about urban centers and their ability to provide sustainable development ("Urban Centers: An Assessment of Sustainability," *Annual Review of Energy and the Environment*, vol. 28, 2003). McGranahan and Satterthwaite do acknowledge that ecologically more sustainable patterns of urban development are needed. While they admit the existence of certain environmental impacts of urbanization, they are more concerned about how cities will handle these impacts in the future rather than concentrating on present deficiencies.

An article that focuses on megacities is Frauke Kraas' "Megacities and Global Change: Key Priorities" (*Geographical Journal*, March 2007).

A number of books address contemporary challenges posed by urbanization throughout the world: *Global Urbanization* by Albert J. Dauray (in HTML and PDF format); *Third World Cities in Global Perspective: The Political Economy of Uneven Urbanization* by David Smith (Westview Press, 1996); *Urban Environmentalism: Global Change and the Mediation of Local Conflict* by Peter Brand (Routledge, 2005); and *Financing Urban Shelter: Global Report on Human Settlements 2005* by the U.N. Human Settlements Program (Earthscan Publications, 2005).

Internet References . . .

UNEP World Conservation Monitoring Centre

The United Nations Environment Programme's World Conservation Monitoring Centre Web site contains information on conservation and sustainable use of the globe's natural resources. The center provides information to policymakers concerning global trends in conservation, biodiversity, loss of species and habitats, and more. This site includes a list of publications and environmental links.

http://www.unep-wcmc.org

The International Institute for Sustainable Development

This nonprofit organization based in Canada provides a number of reporting services on a range of environmental issues, with special emphasis on policy initiatives associated with sustainable development.

http://www.iisd.ca

The Hunger Project

The Hunger Project is a nonprofit organization that seeks to end global hunger. This organization asserts that society-wide actions are needed to eliminate hunger and that global security depends on ensuring that everyone's basic needs are fulfilled. Included on this site is an outline of principles that guide the organization, information on why ending hunger is so important, and a list of programs sponsored by the Hunger Project in 11 developing countries across South Asia, Latin America, and Africa.

http://www.thp.org

International Association for Environmental Hydrology

The International Association for Environmental Hydrology (IAEH) is a worldwide association of environmental hydrologists dedicated to the protection and cleanup of freshwater resources. The IAEH's mission is to provide a place to share technical information and exchange ideas and to provide a source of inexpensive tools for the environmental hydrologist, especially hydrologists and water resource engineers in developing countries.

http://www.hydroweb.com

United Nations Environment Programme (UNEP)

UNEP's general Web site provides a variety of information and links to other sources.

http://www.ourplanet.com

Global Resources and the Environment

*T*he availability of resources and the manner in which the planet's inhabitants use them characterize another major component of the global agenda. Many believe that environmentalists overstate their case because of ideology, not science. Many others state that renewable resources are being consumed at a pace that is too fast to allow for replenishment, while non-renewable resources are being consumed at a pace that is faster than our ability to find suitable replacements.

The production, distribution, and consumption of these resources also leave their marks on the planet. A basic set of issues relates to whether these impacts are permanent, too degrading to the planet, too damaging to one's quality of life, or simply beyond a threshold of acceptability.

- Do Environmentalists Overstate Their Case?

- Should the World Continue to Rely on Oil as the Major Source of Energy?

- Will the World Be Able to Feed Itself in the Foreseeable Future?

- Is the Threat of Global Warming Real?

- Is the Threat of a Global Water Shortage Real?

ISSUE 5

Do Environmentalists Overstate Their Case?

YES: Ronald Bailey, from "Debunking Green Myths," *Reason* (February 2002)

NO: David Pimentel, from "Skeptical of the Skeptical Environmentalist," *Skeptic* (vol. 9, no. 2, 2002)

ISSUE SUMMARY

YES: Environmental journalist Ronald Bailey in his review of the Bjørn Lomborg controversial book, *The Skeptical Environmentalist: Measuring the Real State of the World* (Cambridge University Press, 2001), argues that "An environmentalist gets it right," suggesting that finally someone has taken the environmental doomsdayers to task for their shoddy use of science.

NO: Bioscientist David Pimentel takes to task Bjørn Lomborg's findings, accusing him of selective use of data to support his conclusions.

In January 2007, the *Bulletin of Atomic Scientists* added to their "doomsday clock," originally created to forecast nuclear annihilation, the new threat of environmental catastrophe to its predictions. This was the latest in the war of words between the doomsdayers and the environmental skeptics. For a few decades, those skeptics of the claims of many environmentalists that the world was in danger of ecological collapse and in the not so distant future looked to Julian Simon for guidance. And Simon did not disappoint, as he constantly questioned these researchers' motives and methodology—their models, data, and data analysis techniques. Two seminal works, *The Ultimate Resource* and *The Ultimate Resource 2,* in particular, attempted to demonstrate that much research was really bad science. Simon's popularity reached its height when he took on the leading spokesperson of pending environmental catastrophe, Paul Ehrlich, in the late 1970s. Ehrlich, a professor at Stanford, along with his wife Anne (also a

Stanford professor), had been echoing "the sky is falling message" since the late 1960s. Simon challenged Ehrlich to a "forecasting duel," betting him $10,000 that the cost of five non-government raw materials (to be selected by Ehrlich) would fall by the end of the next decade (1990). Ehrlich won the bet. With Simons's death in 1998, the critics of environmental dooms-dayers lost their most effective voice and their central rallying cry.

Bjørn Lomborg, a young Danish political scientist, changed all of that with the 2001 publication of his *The Skeptical Environmentalist: Measuring the Real State of the World* (a take-off on the annual State of the World Series produced by Lester Brown and the Worldwatch Institute). Lomborg's central thesis is that statistical analyses of principal environmental indicators reveal that environmental problems have been overstated by most leading figures in the environmental movement.

What distinguished Simons' body of work that earned him the unofficial title of "doomsayer" from Lomborg's book was that the latter received much greater and more widespread attention, both by the popular media and by those in academic and scientific circles. In effect, it has become the most popular anti-environmental book ever, prompting a huge backlash by those vested in the scientific community. Because the popular press appeared to accept Lomberg's assertions with an uncritical eye, the scientific community began a comprehensive counter-attack against *The Skeptical Environmentalist.* *Scientific American,* in January 2002, published almost a dozen pages of critiques of the book by four experts and concluded that the book's purpose of showing the real state of the world was a failure.

The attention paid Lomborg's book by *Scientific American* was typical of the responses found in every far corner of the scientific community. Not only was Lomberg's analyses attacked, but his credentials were as well. Researchers scurried to discredit both him and his work, with a passion un-seen heretofore in the debate over the potential for global environmental catastrophe. The Danish Committees on Scientific Dishonesty was called upon to investigate the work. The Danish Ministry of Science, Technology and Innovation found serious flaws in Lomborg's critique. One reviewer concluded by observing that he wished he could find that the book had some scientific merit but he could not. The British Broadcasting Company (BBC) devoted a three-part series to Lomborg's claims. One critique was titled "No Friend of the Earth."

These examples illustrate the debate put forth in this issue, namely, do environmentalists overstate the case for environmental decay and potential catastrophe? Ronald Bailey, provides one of the few positive critiques of *The Skeptical Environmentalist.* His initial statement places the genesis of modern environmentalism in the radical movements of the 1960s, suggesting that their aim is to demonstrate that "the world is going to hell in a handbasket." Calling environmentalism an ideology, Bailey argues that like Marxists, environmentalists "have had to force the facts to fit their ideology." David Pimentel, a professor of insect ecology and agricultural sciences, argues that those who contend that the environment is not threatened are using data selectively while ignoring much evidence to the contrary.

YES ⤶   Ronald Bailey

Debunking Green Myths:
An Environmentalist
Gets It Right

Modern environmentalism, born of the radical movements of the 1960s, has often made recourse to science to press its claims that the world is going to hell in a handbasket. But this environmentalism has never really been a matter of objectively describing the world and calling for the particular social policies that the description implies.

Environmentalism is an ideology, very much like Marxism, which pretended to base its social critique on a "scientific" theory of economic relations. Like Marxists, environmentalists have had to force the facts to fit their theory. Environmentalism is an ideology in crisis: The massive, accumulating contradictions between its pretensions and the actual state of the world can no longer be easily explained away.

The publication of *The Skeptical Environmentalist,* a magnificent and important book by a former member of Greenpeace, deals a major blow to that ideology by superbly documenting a response to environmental doomsaying. The author, Bjorn Lomborg, is an associate professor of statistics at the University of Aarhus in Denmark. On a trip to the United States a few years ago, Lomborg picked up a copy of Wired that included an article about the late "doomslayer" Julian Simon.

Simon, a professor of business administration at the University of Maryland, claimed that by most measures, the lot of humanity is improving and the world's natural environment was not critically imperiled. Lomborg, thinking it would be an amusing and instructive exercise to debunk a "right-wing" anti-environmentalist American, assigned his students the project of finding the "real" data that would contradict Simon's outrageous claims.

Lomborg and his students discovered that Simon was essentially right, and that the most famous environmental alarmists (Stanford biologist Paul Ehrlich, Worldwatch Institute founder Lester Brown, former Vice President Al Gore, Silent Spring author Rachel Carson) and the leading environmentalist lobbying groups (Greenpeace, the World Wildlife Fund,

From *Reason* by Ronald Bailey, February 2002, pp. 396–403, 406–409, 416–420. Copyright © 2002 by Reason Foundation. Reprinted by permission.

Friends of the Earth) were wrong. It turns out that the natural environment is in good shape, and the prospects of humanity are actually quite good.

Lomborg begins with "the Litany" of environmentalist doom, writing: "We are all familiar with the Litany. . . . Our resources are running out. The population is ever growing, leaving less and less to eat. The air and water are becoming ever more polluted. The planet's species are becoming extinct in vast numbers. . . . The world's ecosystem is breaking down. . . . We all know the Litany and have heard it so often that yet another repetition is, well, almost reassuring." Lomborg notes that there is just one problem with the Litany: "It does not seem to be backed up by the available evidence."

Lomborg then proceeds to demolish the Litany. He shows how, time and again, ideological environmentalists misuse, distort, and ignore the vast reams of data that contradict their dour visions. In the course of The Skeptical Environmentalist, Lomborg demonstrates that the environmentalist lobby is just that, a collection of interest groups that must hype doom in order to survive monetarily and politically.

Lomborg notes, "As the industry and farming organizations have an obvious interest in portraying the environment as just-fine and no-need-to-do-anything, the environmental organizations also have a clear interest in telling us that the environment is in a bad state, and that we need to act now. And the worse they can make this state appear, the easier it is for them to convince us we need to spend more money on the environment rather than on hospitals, kindergartens, etc. Of course, if we were equally skeptical of both sorts of organization there would be less of a problem. But since we tend to treat environmental organizations with much less skepticism, this might cause a grave bias in our understanding of the state of the world." Lomborg's book amply shows that our understanding of the state of the world is indeed biased.

So what is the real state of humanity and the planet?

Human life expectancy in the developing world has more than doubled in the past century, from 31 years to 65. Since 1960, the average amount of food per person in the developing countries has increased by 38 percent, and although world population has doubled, the percentage of malnourished poor people has fallen globally from 35 percent to 18 percent, and will likely fall further over the next decade, to 12 percent. In real terms, food costs a third of what it did in the 1960s. Lomborg points out that increasing food production trends show no sign of slackening in the future.

What about air pollution? Completely uncontroversial data show that concentrations of sulfur dioxide are down 80 percent in the U.S. since 1962, carbon monoxide levels are down 75 percent since 1970, nitrogen oxides are down 38 percent since 1975, and ground level ozone is down 30 percent since 1977. These trends are mirrored in all developed countries.

Lomborg shows that claims of rapid deforestation are vastly exaggerated. One United Nations Food and Agriculture survey found that globally, forest cover has been reduced by a minuscule 0.44 percent since 1961. The World Wildlife Fund claims that two-thirds of the world's forests have been lost since the dawn of agriculture; the reality is that the world still has

80 percent of its forests. What about the Brazilian rainforests? Eighty-six percent remain uncut, and the rate of clearing is falling. Lomborg also debunks the widely circulated claim that the world will soon lose up to half of its species. In fact, the best evidence indicates that 0.7 percent of species might be lost in the next 50 years if nothing is done. And of course, it is unlikely that nothing will be done.

Finally, Lomborg shows that global warming caused by burning fossil fuels is unlikely to be a catastrophe. Why? First, because actual measured temperatures aren't increasing nearly as fast as the computer climate models say they should be—in fact, any increase is likely to be at the low end of the predictions, and no one thinks that would be a disaster. Second, even in the unlikely event that temperatures were to increase substantially, it will be far less costly and more environmentally sound to adapt to the changes rather than institute draconian cuts in fossil fuel use.

The best calculations show that adapting to global warming would cost $5 trillion over the next century. By comparison, substantially cutting back on fossil fuel emissions in the manner suggested by the Kyoto Protocol would cost between $107 and $274 trillion over the same period. (Keep in mind that the current yearly U.S. gross domestic product is $10 trillion.) Such costs would mean that people living in developing countries would lose over 75 percent of their expected increases in income over the next century. That would be not only a human tragedy, but an environmental one as well, since poor people generally have little time for environmental concerns.

Where does Lomborg fall short? He clearly understands that increasing prosperity is the key to improving human and environmental health, but he often takes for granted the institutions of property and markets that make progress and prosperity possible. His analysis, as good as it is, fails to identify the chief cause of most environmental problems. In most cases, imperiled resources such as fisheries and airsheds are in open-access commons where the incentive is for people to take as much as possible of the resource before someone else beats them to it. Since they don't own the resource, they have no incentive to protect and conserve it.

Clearly, regulation has worked to improve the state of many open-access commons in developed countries such as the U.S. Our air and streams are much cleaner than they were 30 years ago, in large part due to things like installing catalytic converters on automobiles and building more municipal sewage treatment plants. Yet there is good evidence that assigning private property rights to these resources would have resulted in a faster and cheaper cleanup. Lomborg's analysis would have been even stronger had he more directly taken on ideological environmentalism's bias against markets. But perhaps that is asking for too much in an already superb book.

"Things are better now," writes Lomborg, "but they are still not good enough." He's right. Only continued economic growth will enable the 800 million people who are still malnourished to get the food they need; only continued economic growth will let the 1.2 billion who don't have access to clean water and sanitation obtain those amenities. It turns out that ideological environmentalism, with its hostility to economic growth and technological progress, is the biggest threat to the natural environment and to the hopes of the poorest people in the world for achieving better lives.

"The very message of the book," Lomborg concludes, is that "children born today—in both the industrialized world and the developing countries—will live longer and be healthier, they will get more food, a better education, a higher standard of living, more leisure time and far more possibilities—without the global environment being destroyed. And that is a beautiful world."

David Pimentel  **NO**

Skeptical of the Skeptical Environmentalist

Bjørn Lomborg discusses a wide range of topics in his book and implies, through his title, that he will inform readers exactly what the real state of world is. In this effort, he criticizes countless world economists, agriculturists, water specialists, and environmentalists, and furthermore, accuses them of misquoting and/or organizing published data to mislead the public concerning the status of world population, food supplies, malnutrition, disease, and pollution. Lomborg bases his optimistic opinion on his selective use of data. Some of Lomborg's assertions will be examined in this review, and where differing information is presented, extensive documentation will be provided.

Lomborg reports that "we now have more food per person than we used to."[1] In contrast, the Food and Agricultural Organization (FAO) of the United Nations reports that food per capita has been declining since 1984, based on available cereal grains.[2] Cereal grains make up about 80% of the world's food. Although grain yields per hectare (abbreviated ha) in both developed and developing countries are still increasing, these increases are slowing while the world population continues to escalate.[3] Specifically from 1950 to 1980, U.S. grains yields increased at about 3% per year, but after 1980 the rate of increase for corn and other grains has declined to only about 1%.

Obviously fertile cropland is an essential resource for the production of foods but Lomborg has chosen not to address this subject directly. Currently, the U.S. has available nearly 0.5 ha of prime cropland per capita, but it will not have this much land if the population continues to grow at its current rapid rate.[4] Worldwide the average cropland available for food production is only 0.25 ha per person.[5] Each person added to the U.S. population requires nearly 0.4 ha (1 acre) of land for urbanization and transportation.[6] One example of the impact of population growth and development is occurring in California where an average of 156,000 ha of agricultural land is being lost each year.[7] At this rate it will not be long before California ceases to be the number one state in U.S. agricultural production.

In addition to the quantity of agricultural land, soil quality and fertility is vital for food production. The productivity of the soil is reduced

From *Skeptic* by David Pimentel, vol. 9 no. 2, 2002, pp. 90–93. Copyright © 2002 by David Pimentel. Reprinted by permission of the author.

when it is eroded by rainfall and wind.[8] Soil erosion is not a problem, according to Lomborg, especially in the U.S. where soil erosion has declined during the past decade. Yes, as Lomborg states, instead of losing an average of 17 metric tons per hectare per year on cropland, the U.S. cropland is now losing an average of 13 t/ha/yr.[9] However, this average loss is 13 times the sustainability rate of soil replacement.[10] Exceptions occur, as during the 1995–96 winter in Kansas, when it was relatively dry and windy, and some agricultural lands lost as much as 65 t/ha of productive soil. This loss is 65 times the natural soil replacement in agriculture.[11]

Worldwide soil erosion is more damaging than in the United States. For instance, in India soil is being lost at 30 to 40 times its sustainability.[12] Rate of soil loss in Africa is increasing not only because of livestock over-grazing but also because of the burning of crop residues due to the short-ages of wood fuel.[13] During the summer of 2000, NASA published a satellite image of a cloud of soil from Africa being blown across the Atlantic Ocean, further attesting to the massive soil erosion problem in Africa. Worldwide evidence concerning soil loss is substantiated and it is difficult to ignore its effect on sustainable agricultural production.

Contrary to Lomborg's belief, crop yields cannot continue to increase in response to the increased applications of more fertilizers and pesticides. In fact, field tests have demonstrated that applying excessive amounts of nitrogen fertilizer stresses the crop plants, resulting in declining yields.[14] The optimum amount of nitrogen for corn, one of the crops that require heavy use of nitrogen, is approximately 120 kg/ha.[15]

Although U.S. farmers frequently apply significantly more nitrogen fertilizer than 120 kg/ha, the extra is a waste and pollutant. The corn crop can only utilize about one-third of the nitrogen applied, while the remainder leaches either into the ground or surface waters.[16] This pollution of aquatic ecosystems in agricultural areas results in the high levels of nitrogen and pesticides occurring in many U.S. water bodies.[17] For example, nitrogen fertilizer has found its way into 97% of the well-water supplies in some regions, like North Carolina.[18] The concentrations of nitrate are above the U.S. Environmental Protection Agency drinking-water standard of 10 milligrams per liter (nitrogen) and are a toxic threat to young children and young livestock.[19] In the last 30 years, the nitrate content has tripled in the Gulf of Mexico,[20] where it is reducing the Gulf fishery.[21]

In an undocumented statement Lomborg reports that pesticides cause very little cancer.[22] Further, he provides no explanation as to why human and other nontarget species are not exposed to pesticides when crops are treated. There is abundant medical and scientific evidence that confirms that pesticides cause significant numbers of cancers in the U.S. and throughout the world.[23] Lomborg also neglects to report that some herbicides stimulate the production of toxic chemicals in some plants, and that these toxicants can cause cancer.[24]

In keeping with Lomborg's view that agriculture and the food supply are improving, he states that "fewer people are starving."[25] Lomborg criticizes the validity of the two World Health Organization reports that confirm more than 3 billion people are malnourished.[26] This is the largest number and proportion of malnourished people ever in history! Apparently Lomborg rejects the WHO data because they do not support his basic thesis. Instead, Lomborg argues that only people who suffer from calorie shortages are malnourished, and ignores the fact that humans die from deficiencies of protein, iron, iodine, and vitamin A, B, C, and D.[27]

Further confirming a decline in food supply, the FAO reports that there has been a three-fold decline in the consumption of fish in the human diet during the past seven years.[28] This decline in fish per capita is caused by overfishing, pollution, and the impact of a rapidly growing world population that must share the diminishing fish supply.

In discussing the status of water supply and sanitation services, Lomborg is correct in stating that these services were improved in the developed world during the 19th century, but he ignores the available scientific data when he suggests that these trends have been "replicated in the developing world" during the 20th century. Countless reports confirm that developing countries discharge most of their untreated urban sewage directly into surface waters.[29] For example, of India's 3,119 towns and cities, only eight have full waste water treatment facilities.[30] Furthermore, 114 Indian cities dump untreated sewage and partially cremated bodies directly into the sacred Ganges River. Downstream the untreated water is used for drinking, bathing, and washing.[31] In view of the poor sanitation, it is no wonder that water borne infectious diseases account for 80% of all infections worldwide and 90% of all infections in developing countries.[32]

Contrary to Lomborg's view, most infectious diseases are increasing worldwide.[33] The increase is due not only to population growth but also because of increasing environmental pollution.[34] Food-borne infections are increasing rapidly worldwide and in the United States. For example, during 2000 in the U.S. there were 76 million human food-borne infections with 5,000 associated deaths.[35] Many of these infections are associated with the increasing contamination of food and water by livestock wastes in the United States.[36]

In addition, a large number of malnourished people are highly susceptible to infectious diseases, like tuberculosis (TB), malaria, schistosomiasis, and AIDS.[37] For example, the number of people infected with tuberculosis in the U.S. and the world is escalating, in part because medicine has not kept up with the new forms of TB. Currently, according to the World Health Organization,[38] more than 2 billion people in the world are infected with TB,[39] with nearly 2 million people dying each year from it.[40]

Consistent with Lomborg's thesis that world natural resources are abundant, he reports that the U.S. Energy Information Agency for the period 2000 to 2020 projects an almost steady oil price over the next two decades at about $22 per barrel. This optimistic projection was crossed late in 2000 when oil rose to $30 or more per barrel in the United States and the world.[41] The best estimates today project that world oil reserves will last approximately 50 years, based on current production rates.[42]

Lomborg takes the World Wildlife Fund (WWF) to task for their estimates on the loss of world forests during the past decade and their emphasis on resulting ecological impacts and loss of biodiversity. Whether the loss of forests is slow, as Lomborg suggests, or rapid as WWF reports, there is no question that forests are disappearing worldwide. Forests not only provide valuable products but they harbor a vast diversity of species of plants, animals and microbes. Progress in medicine, agriculture, genetic engineering, and environmental quality depend on maintaining the species diversity in the world.[43]

This reviewer takes issue with Lomborg's underlying thesis that the size and growth of the human population is not a major problem. The difference between Lomborg's figure that 76 million humans were added to the world population in 2000, or the 80 million reported by the Population Reference Bureau,[44] is not the issue, though the magnitude of both projections is of serious concern. Lomborg neglects to explain that the major problem with world population growth is the young age structure that now exists. Even if the world adopted a policy of only two children per couple tomorrow, the world population would continue to increase for more than 70 years before stabilizing at more than 12 billion people.[45] As an agricultural scientist and ecologist, I wish I could share Lomborg's optimistic views, but my investigations and those of countless scientists lead me to a more conservative outlook. The supply of basic resources, like fertile cropland, water, energy, and an unpolluted atmosphere that support human life is declining rapidly, as nearly a quarter million people are daily added to the Earth. We all desire a high standard of living for each person on Earth, but with every person added, the supply of resources must be divided and shared. Current losses and degradation of natural resources suggest concern and a need for planning for future generations of humans. Based on our current understanding of the real state of the world and environment, there is need for conservation and protection of vital world resources.

References

1. Lomborg, B. 2001. *The Skeptical Environmentalist.* Cambridge University Press, 61.
2. FAO, 1961–1999. *Quarterly Bulletin of Statistics.* Food and Agriculture Organization of the United Nations.
3. Ibid.; PRB 2000. *World Population Data Sheet.* Washington, DC: Population Reference Bureau.
4. USBC, 2000. *Statistical Abstract of the United States 2000.* Washington, DC: U.S. Bureau of the Census, U.S. Government Printing Office.
5. PRB, 2000; WRI 1994. *World Resources 1994–95.* Washington, DC: World Resources Institute.
6. Helmlich, R. 2001. Economic Research Service, USDA, Washington, DC, personal communication.

7. UCBC, 2000, op. cit.

8. Lal, R., and Stewart, B. A. 1990. *Soil Degradation.* New York: Springer-Verlag: Troeh, F. R., Hobbs, J. A., & Donahue, R. L. 1991. *Soil and Water Conservation* (2nd ed.). Englewood Cliffs, NJ: Prentice Hall.

9. USDA, 1994. *Summary Report 1992 National Resources Inventory.* Washington, DC: Soil Conservation Service, U.S. Department of Agriculture.

10. Pimentel, D., and Kounang, N. 1998. "Ecology of Soil Erosion in Ecosystems," *Ecosystems,* 1, 416–426.

11. Lal and Stewart, 1990; Troeh et al., 1991, op. cit.

12. Khoshoo, T. N. & Tejwani, K. G. 1993. "Soil Erosion and Conservation in India (status and policies)." In Pimentel, D. (Ed.) *World Soil Erosion and Conservation.* pp. 109–146. Cambridge: Cambridge University Press.

13. Tolba, M. K. 1989. "Our Biological Heritage Under Siege." *BioScience,* 39: 725–728.

14. Romanova, A. K., Kuznetsova, L. G., Golovina, E. V., Novichkova, N. S., Karpilova, I. F., & Ivanov, B. N. 1987. *Proceedings of the Indian National Science Academy, B (Biological Sciences),* 53(5–6): 505–512.

15. Troeh, F. R., & Thompson, L. M. 1993. *Soils and Soil Fertility* (5th ed.). New York: Oxford University Press.

16. Robertson, G. P. 2000. "Dinitrification." In *Handbook of Soil Science.* M. E. Summer (Ed.), pp. C181–190. Boca Raton, FL: CRC Press.

17. Ibid.; Mapp, H. P. 1999. "Impact of Production Changes on Income and Environmental Risk in the Southern High Plains." *Journal of Agricultural and Applied Economics,* 31(2): 263–273; Gentry, L. E., David, M. B., Smith-Starks, K. M., and Kovacics, D. A. 2000. "Nitrogen Fertilizer and Herbicide Transport from Tile Drained Fields." *Journal of Environmental Quality,* 29(1): 232–240.

18. Smith, V. H., Tilman, G. D. and Nekola, J. C. 1999. "Eutrophication: Impacts of Excess Nutrient Inputs on Freshwater, Marine, and Terrestrial Ecosystems." *Environment and Pollution,* 100(1/3): 179–196.

19. Ibid.

20. Goolsby, D. A., Battaglin, W. A., Aulenbach, B. T. and Hooper, R. P. 2000. "Nitrogen Flux and Sources in the Mississippi River Basin." *Science and the Total Environment,* 248(2–3): 75–86.

21. NAS, 2000. *Clean Coastal Waters: Understanding and Reducing the Effects of Nutrient Pollution.* Washington, DC: National Academy of Sciences Press.

22. Lomborg, 2001, op. cit., 10.

23. WHO, 1992. *Our Planet, Our Health: Report of the WHO Commission on Health and Environment.* Geneva: World Health Organization: Ferguson, L. R. 1999. "Natural and Man-Made Mutagens and Carcinogens in the Human Diet." *Mutation Research, Genetic Toxicology and Environmental Mutagenesis,* 443(1/2): 1–10; NAS, 2000. *The Future Role of Pesticides in Agriculture.* Washington, DC: National Academy of Sciences Press.

24. Culliney, T. W., Pimentel, D., & Pimentel, M. H. 1992. "Pesticides and Natural Toxicants in Foods." *Agriculture, Eco-systems and Environment,* 41, 297–320.

25. Lomborg, 2001, op. cit., 328.

26. WHO, 1996. *Micronutrient Malnutrition—Half of the World's Population Affected* (Pages 1–4 No. Press Release WHO No. 78). World Health Organization; WHO, 2000a. *Malnutrition Worldwide* http://www.who.int/nut/malnutrition_worldwide.htm, July 27, 2000.

27. Sommer, A. and K. P. West, 1996. *Vitamin A Deficiency: Health, Survival and Vision.* New York: Oxford University Press; Tomashek, K. M., Woodruff, B. A., Gotway, C. A., Bloand, P. & Mbaruku, G. 2001. "Randomized Intervention Study Comparing Several Regimens for the Treatment of Moderate Anemia Refugee Children in Kigoma Region, Tanzania." *American Journal of Tropical Medicine and Hygiene,* 64(3/4): 164–171.

28. FAO, 1991. *Food Balance Sheets.* Rome: Food and Agriculture Organization of the United Nations; FAO, 1998. *Food Balance Sheets.* http://armanncorn: 98ivysub@ faostat.fao.org/lim . . . ap.pl?

29. WHO, 1993. "Global Health Situation." *Weekly Epidemiological Record,* World Health Organization 68 (12 February): 43–44; Wouters, A. V. 1993. "Health Care Utilization Patterns in Developing Countries: Role of the Technology Environment in 'Deriving' the Demand for Health Care." *Boletin de la Oficina Sanitaria Panamericana,* 115(2): 128–139; Biswas, M. R. 1999. "Nutrition, Food, and Water Security." *Food and Nutrition Bulletin,* 20(4): 454–457.

30. WHO, 1992, op. cit.

31. NGS, 1995, *Water: A Story of Hope.* Washington, DC: National Geographic Society.

32. WHO, 1992, op. cit.

33. Ibid.

34. Pimentel, D., Tort, M., D'Anna, L., Krawic, A., Berger, J., Rossman, J., Mugo, F., Doon, N., Shriberg, M., Howard, E. S., Lee, S., & Talbot, J. 1998. "Ecology of Increasing Disease: Population Growth and Environmental Degradation." *BioScience,* 48, 817–826.

35. Taylor, M. R. & Hoffman, S. A. 2001. "Redesigning Food Safety: Using Risk Analysis to Build a Better Food Safety System." *Resources.* Summer, 144: 13–16.

36. DeWaal, C. S., Alderton, L., and Jacobson, M. J. 2000. *Outbreak Alert! Closing the Gaps in Our Federal Food-Safety Net.* Washington, DC: Center for Science in the Public Interest.

37. Chandra, R. K. 1979. "Nutritional Deficiency and Susceptibility to Infection." *Bulletin of the World Health Organization,* 57(2): 167–177; Stephenson, L. S., Latham, M. C. & Ottesen, E. A. 2000a. "Global Malnutrition." *Parasitology.* 121: S5–S22; Stephenson, L. S., Latham, M. C. & Ottesen, E. A. 2000b. "Malnutrition and Parasitic Helminth Infections." *Parastiology.* S23–S38.

38. WHO, 2001. "World Health Organization. Global Tuberculosis Control." *WHO Report 2001.* Geneva, Switzerland, WHO/CDS/TB/2001. 287 (May 30, 2001).

39. WHO, 2000b. "World Health Organization. Tuberculosis." *WHO Fact Sheet 2000 No104.* Geneva, Switzerland, www.who.int/gtb (May 30, 2001).

40. WHO, 2001, op. cit.

41. BP, 2000. *British Petroleum Statistical Review of World Energy.* London: British Petroleum Corporate Communications Services; Duncan, R. C. 2001. "World Energy Production, Population Growth, and the Road to the Olduvai Gorge." *Population and Environment,* 22(5), 503–522.

42. Youngquist, W. 1997. *Geodestinies: The Inevitable Control of Earth Resources Over Nations and Individuals.* Portland, OR: National Book Company; Duncan, 2001, op. cit.

43. Myers, N. 1996. "The World's Forests and Their Ecosystem Services." In G. C. Dailey (Ed.), *Ecosystem Services: Their Nature and Value* (pp. 1–19 in press). Washington, DC: Island Press.

44. PRB, 2000, op. cit.

45. Population Action International, 1993. *Challenging the Planet: Connections Between Population and the Environment.* Washington, DC: Population Action International.

POSTSCRIPT

Do Environmentalists Overstate Their Case?

The issue of whether science or ideology is at the heart of the environmental debate is a vexing one. The issue is framed by the juxtaposition of three groups. The first are those individuals, commonly called political or environmental activists, who emerged in the late 1960s and early 1970s following the success of the early civil rights movement. Taking its inspiration from the 1962 publication of Rachel Carson's *The Silent Spring,* which exposed the dangers of the pesticide DDT, many politically active individuals found a new cause. When the book received legitimacy because of President John Kennedy's order that his Science Advisory Committee address the issues raised therein, the environmental movement was under way. The second group, government policy makers were then a part of the mix and the third group, scientists, were soon to come on board. The first global environmental conference sponsored by the United Nations was held in Stockholm in 1972 to address atmospheric pollution on Scandinavian lakes. Emerging from the conference was a commitment of the international policy making community to put environmental issues on the new global agenda. Environmentalism was now globalized.

Since the early 1970s, through a variety of forums and arenas, the issue has been on the forefront of this global agenda. As with any issue where debates focus not only on how to address problems but whether, in fact, the problems really exist in the first place, many disparate formal and informal interest groups have become involved in all aspects of the debate—from trying to make the case that a problem exists and will ultimately have dire consequences if left unsolved, to specific prescriptions for solving the issue. The intersection of science, public policy, and political activism then becomes like the center ring at a boxing match, where contenders vie for success. Objectivity clashes with passion as well intentioned and not so well intentioned individuals attempt to influence the debate and the ultimate outcome. In many cases, the doomsdayers gain the upper hand as their commitment to change seems greater than those who urge caution until all the scientific evidence is in.

The reaction to Lomborg illustrates this point perfectly. He has become the arch villain to environmentalists. One such Web site proclaims in headline, "Something is Rotten in Denmark" and then proceeds to "fight fire with fire" in attacking him (www.gristmagazine.com). *Grist Magazine* devoted a special issue (December 12, 2001) to the debate where experts in specific environmental fields took issue with Lomborg's conclusions.

Another source provides a variety of link to the debate fueled by *The Skeptical Scientist*. The journal *Scientific American* launched an extreme attack against Lomborg, while *The Economist* came to his defense. Google. com shows 247,000 references to the young Danish political scientist at last count. Amazon.com provides an array of related books that fall into the same genre.

In sum, one is struck by both the forcefulness with which Lomborg makes his case and the even greater passion with which the scientific community responds. While the latter may be more accurate with respect to the true state of the world, to paraphrase the essence of the debate, Lomborg does provide a valuable service by reminding us that at the heart of any meaningful prescription for effective public policy is an accurate assessment of the nature of the problem. Science, not ideology, provides the instruments for such an assessment.

One principal source that consistently sounds the alarm on environment issues is the Worldwatch Institute. Its web site, worldwatch@worldwatch. org, yields an extraordinary amount of resources on environmental issues.

In the first few decades after environment was placed on the global agenda, Julian Simon was one of the few, and certainly the most read, critic of environmentalists for their ideological approach to environmental problems, causing them, in Simon's view, to ignore science when science yielded an answer different from the one sought by the environmentalists. His *The Ultimate Resource* and *The Ultimate Resource 2* represented two harshly critical books that sought to show how science had taken a back seat to ideology. Since his death in 1998, his role as principal vocal critic of extremists in the environmental movement has been assumed by Ronald Bailey, science correspondent for the monthly magazine *Reason*. His *Global Warming and Other Eco-Myths* (Forum, 2002) charges the environmentalists with using "False Science to Scare Us to Death" (part of the book's subtitle). The titles of earlier books also suggest his basic message: *Earth Report 2000: Revisiting the True State of the Planet* (McGraw-Hill, 1999); *ECOSCAM: The False Prophets of Ecological Apocalypse* (St. Martin's Press, 1993); and *The True State of the Planet* (The Free Press, 1995).

Another early critic of the environmental "eco-extremists" was Martin W. Lewis (*Green Delusions: An Environmentalist Critique of Radical Environmentalism*, Duke University Press, 1994). A more recent critical book is John Berlau's *Eco-Freaks: Environmentalism Is Hazardous to Your Health!* (Thomas Nelson, 2006). See also Jacqueline R. Kasun's "Doomsday Every Day: Sustainable Economics, Sustainable Tyranny" (*The Independent Review*, Summer 1999).

Perhaps the most helpful Web site for gathering information about the debate as it relates to Lomborg is www.anti-lomborg.com. The Web site's name is misleading as it provides a list of pro-Lomborg sources in addition to those that attack him.

ISSUE 6

Should the World Continue to Rely on Oil as the Major Source of Energy?

YES: **Red Cavaney,** from "Global Oil Production about to Peak? A Recurring Myth," *World Watch* (January/February 2006)

NO: **James Howard Kunstler,** from *The Long Emergency* (Grove/ Atlantic, 2005)

ISSUE SUMMARY

YES: Red Cavaney, president and chief executive officer of the American Petroleum Institute, argues that recent revolutionary advances in technology will yield sufficient quantities of available oil for the foreseeable future.

NO: James Howard Kunster, author of *The Long Emergency* (2005), suggests that simply passing the all-time production peak of oil and heading toward its steady depletion will result in a global energy predicament that will substantially change our lives.

As 2008 arrived, gas prices passed the $3-a-gallon level, with no end in sight. This was not the first crisis in recent times, however, as the beginning of the new millennium had witnessed an oil crisis almost immediately, the third major crisis in the last 30 years (1972–1973 and 1979 were the dates of earlier problems). The crisis of 2000 manifested itself in the United States via much higher gasoline prices and in Europe via both rising prices and shortages at the pump. Both were caused by the inability of national distribution systems to adjust to the Organization of Petroleum Exporting Countries' (OPEC's) changing production levels. The 2000 panic eventually subsided but reappeared in 2005 in the wake of the uncertainty surrounding the Iraq war.

These four major fuel crises are discrete episodes in a much larger problem facing the human race, particularly the industrial world. That is, oil, the earth's current principal source of energy, is a finite resource that ultimately will be totally exhausted. And unlike earlier energy transitions, where a more attractive source invited a change (such as from wood to coal and from coal to oil), the next energy transition is being forced upon the human race in the absence of an attractive alternative. In short, we are being pushed out of our almost total reliance on oil toward a new system with a host of unknowns. What will the new fuel be? Will it be from a single source or some combination? Will it be a more attractive source? Will the source be readily available at a reasonable price, or will a new cartel emerge that controls much of the supply? Will its production and consumption lead to major new environmental consequences? Will it require major changes to our lifestyles and standards of living? When will we be forced to jump into using this new source?

Before considering new sources of fuel, other questions need to be asked. Are the calls for a viable alternative to oil premature? Are we simply running scared without cause? Did we learn the wrong lessons from the earlier energy crises? More specifically, were these crises artificially created or a consequence of the actual physical unavailability of the energy source? Have these crises really been about running out of oil globally, or were they due to other phenomena at work, such as poor distribution planning by oil companies or the use of oil as a political weapon by oil-exporting countries?

For well over half a century now, Western oil-consuming countries have been predicting the end of oil. Using a model known as Hubbert's Curve (named after a U.S. geologist who designed it in the 1930s), policymakers have predicted that the world would run out of oil at various times; the most recent prediction is that oil will run out a couple of decades from now. Simply put, the model visualizes all known available resources and the patterns of consumption on a time line until the wells run dry. Despite such prognostication, it was not until the crisis of the early 1970s that national governments began to consider ways of both prolonging the oil system and finding a suitable replacement. Prior to that time, governments, as well as the private sector, encouraged energy consumption. "The more, the merrier" was an oft-heard refrain. Increases in energy consumption were associated with economic growth.

But today the search for an alternative to oil still continues. Nuclear energy, once thought to be the answer, may play a future role, but at a reduced level. Both water power and wind power remain possibilities, as do biomass, geothermal, and solar energy. Many also believe that the developed world is about to enter the hydrogen age in order to meet future energy needs. The question before us, therefore, is whether the international community has the luxury of some time before all deposits of oil are exhausted.

The two selections for this issue suggest different answers to this last question. Red Cavaney argues that oil should and will define the energy future for some time to come. He argues that despite forecasts of gloom, we have found more oil nearly every year than we have used and reserves continue to grow. The answer is technology. James Howard Kunster suggests that we are facing the end of cheap fossil fuels as we have passed the all-time production peak of oil and are witnessing its steady depletion.

YES

Red Cavaney

Global Oil Production about to Peak? A Recurring Myth

Once again, we are hearing that world oil production is "peaking," and that we will face a steadily diminishing oil supply to fuel the global economy. These concerns have been expressed periodically over the years, but have always been at odds with energy and economic realities. Such is the case today.

Let's look at some history: In 1874, the chief geologist of Pennsylvania predicted we would run out of oil in four years—just using it for kerosene. Thirty years ago, groups such as the Club of Rome predicted an end of oil long before the current day. These forecasts were wrong because, nearly every year, we have found more oil than we have used, and oil reserves have continued to grow.

The world consumes approximately 80 million barrels of oil a day. By 2030, world oil demand is estimated to grow about 50 percent, to 121 million barrels a day, even allowing for significant improvements in energy efficiency. The International Energy Agency says there are sufficient oil resources to meet demand for at least the next 30 years.

The key factor here is technology. Revolutionary advances in technology in recent years have dramatically increased the ability of companies to find and extract oil—and, of particular importance, recover more oil from existing reservoirs. Rather than production peaking, existing fields are yielding markedly more oil than in the past. Advances in technology include the following:

Directional Drilling. It used to be that wellbores were basically vertical holes. This made it necessary to drill virtually on top of a potential oil deposit. However, the advent of miniaturized computers and advanced sensors that can be attached to the drill bit now allows companies to drill directional holes with great accuracy because they can get real-time information on the subsurface location throughout the drilling process.

From *World Watch Magazine,* January/February 2006, pp. 13–15. Copyright © 2006 by Worldwatch Institute. Reprinted by permission. www.worldwatch.org

Horizontal Drilling. Horizontal drilling is similar to directional drilling, but the well is designed to cut horizontally through the middle of the oil or natural gas deposit. Early horizontal wells penetrated only 500 to 800 feet of reservoir laterally, but technology advances recently allowed a North Slope operator to penetrate 8,000 feet of reservoir horizontally. Moreover, horizontal wells can operate up to 10 times more productively than conventional wells.

3-D Seismic Technology. Substantial enhancements in computing power during the past two decades have allowed the industry to gain a much clearer picture of what lies beneath the surface. The ability to process huge amounts of data to produce three-dimensional seismic images has significantly improved the drilling success rate of the industry.

Primarily due to these advances, the U.S. Geological Survey (USGS), in its 2000 *World Petroleum Assessment,* increased by 20 percent its estimate of undiscovered, technically recoverable oil. USGS noted that, since oil became a major energy source about 100 years ago, 539 billion barrels of oil have been produced outside the United States. USGS estimates there are 649 billion barrels of undiscovered, technically recoverable oil outside the United States. But, importantly, USGS also estimates that there will be an *additional* 612 billion barrels from "reserve growth"—nearly equaling the undiscovered resources. Reserve growth results from a variety of sources, including technological advancement in exploration and production, increases over initially conservative estimates of reserves, and economic changes.

The USGS estimates reflected several factors:

- As drilling and production within discovered fields progresses, new pools or reservoirs are found that were not previously known.
- Advances in exploration technology make it possible to identify new targets within existing fields.
- Advances in drilling technology make it possible to recover oil and gas not previously considered recoverable in the initial reserve estimates.
- Enhanced oil recovery techniques increase the recovery factor for oil and thereby increase the reserves within existing fields.

Here in the United States, rather than "running out of oil," potentially vast oil and natural gas reserves remain to be developed. According to the latest published government estimates, there are more than 131 billion barrels of oil and more than 1,000 trillion cubic feet of natural gas remaining to be discovered in the United States. However, 78 percent of this oil and 62 percent of this gas are expected to be found beneath federal lands—much of which are non-park and non-wilderness lands—and coastal waters. While there is plenty of oil in the ground, oil companies need to be allowed to make major investments to find and produce it.

The U.S. Energy Information Administration has projected that fossil fuels will continue to dominate U.S. energy consumption, with oil and natural gas providing almost two-thirds of that consumption in the year 2025, even though energy efficiency and renewables will grow faster than their historical rates. However, renewables in particular start from a very small base; and the major shares provided by oil, natural gas, and coal in 2025 are projected to be nearly identical to those in 2003.

Those who block oil and natural gas development here in the United States and elsewhere only make it much more difficult to meet the demand for oil, natural gas, and petroleum products. Indeed, it is not surprising that some of the end-of-oil advocates are the same people who oppose oil and natural gas development everywhere.

Failure to develop the potentially vast oil and natural gas resources that remain in the world will have a high economic cost. We must recognize that we live in a global economy, and that there is a strong link between energy and economic growth. If we are to continue to grow economically, here in the United States, in Europe, and the developing world, we must be cost-competitive in our use of energy. We need *all* sources of energy. We do not have the luxury of limiting ourselves to one source to the exclusion of others. Nor can we afford to write off our leading source of energy before we have found cost-competitive and readily available alternatives.

Consider how oil enhances our quality of life—fueling growth and jobs in industry and commerce, cooling and warming our homes, and getting us where we need to go. Here in the United States, oil provides about 97 percent of transportation fuels, which power nearly all of the cars and trucks traveling on our nation's highways. And plastics, medicines, fertilizers, and countless other products that extend and enhance our quality of life are derived from oil.

In considering our future energy needs, we also need to understand that gasoline-powered automobiles have been the dominant mode of transport for the past century—and the overwhelming preference of hundreds of millions of people throughout the world. Regardless of fuel, the automobile—likely to be configured far differently from today—will remain the consumer's choice for personal transport for decades to come. The freedom of mobility and the independence it affords consumers is highly valued.

The United States—and the world—cannot afford to leave the Age of Oil before realistic substitutes are fully in place. It is important to remember that man left the Stone Age not because he ran out of stones—and we will not leave the Age of Oil because we will run out. Yes, someday oil will be replaced, but clearly not until substitutes are found—substitutes that are proven more reliable, more versatile, and more cost-competitive than oil. We can rely on the energy marketplace to determine what the most efficient substitutes will be.

As we plan for our energy future, we also cannot afford to ignore the lessons of recent history. In the early 1970s, many energy policymakers were sure that oil and natural gas would soon be exhausted, and government policy was explicitly aimed at "guiding" the market in a smooth transition away from these fuels to new, more sustainable alternatives. Price controls, allocation schemes, limitations on natural gas, massive subsidies to synthetic fuels, and other measures were funded heavily and implemented.

Unfortunately, the key premises on which these programs were based, namely that oil was nearing exhaustion and that government guidance was desirable to safely transition to new energy sources, are now recognized as having been clearly wrong—and to have resulted in enormously expensive mistakes.

Looking into the distant future, there will be a day when oil is no longer the world's dominant energy source. We can only speculate as to when and how that day will come about. For example, there is an even bigger hydrocarbon resource that can be developed to provide nearly endless amounts of energy: methane hydrates (methane frozen in ice crystals). The deposits of methane hydrates are so vast that when we develop the technology to bring them to market, we will have clean-burning energy for 2,000 years. It's just one of the exciting scenarios we may see in the far-off future. But we won't be getting there anytime soon, and until we do, the Age of Oil will continue.

James Howard Kunstler   ➡ **NO**

The Long Emergency

$\mathbf{A}$ few weeks ago, the price of oil ratcheted above fifty-five dollars a barrel, which is about twenty dollars a barrel more than a year ago. The next
day, the oil story was buried on page six of the *New York Times* business section. Apparently, the price of oil is not considered significant news, even
when it goes up five bucks a barrel in the span of ten days. That same day,
the stock market shot up more than a hundred points because, CNN said,
government data showed no signs of inflation. Note to clueless nation:
Call planet Earth.

Carl Jung, one of the fathers of psychology, famously remarked that
"people cannot stand too much reality." What you're about to read may
challenge your assumptions about the kind of world we live in, and especially the kind of world into which events are propelling us. We are in for
a rough ride through uncharted territory.

It has been very hard for Americans—lost in dark raptures of nonstop
infotainment, recreational shopping and compulsive motoring—to make
sense of the gathering forces that will fundamentally alter the terms of
everyday life in our technological society. Even after the terrorist attacks of
9/11, America is still sleepwalking into the future. I call this coming time
the Long Emergency.

Most immediately we face the end of the cheap-fossil-fuel era. It is
no exaggeration to state that reliable supplies of cheap oil and natural gas
underlie everything we identify as the necessities of modern life—not to
mention all of its comforts and luxuries: central heating, air conditioning,
cars, airplanes, electric lights, inexpensive clothing, recorded music,
movies, hip-replacement surgery, national defense—you name it.

The few Americans who are even aware that there is a gathering
global-energy predicament usually misunderstand the core of the argument. That argument states that we don't have to run out of oil to start
having severe problems with industrial civilization and its dependent systems. We only have to slip over the all-time production peak and begin a
slide down the arc of steady depletion.

The term "global oil-production peak" means that a turning point will
come when the world produces the most oil it will ever produce in a given

year and, after that, yearly production will inexorably decline. It is usually represented graphically in a bell curve. The peak is the top of the curve, the halfway point of the world's all-time total endowment, meaning half the world's oil will be left. That seems like a lot of oil, and it is, but there's a big catch: It's the half that is much more difficult to extract, far more costly to get, of much poorer quality and located mostly in places where the people hate us. A substantial amount of it will never be extracted.

The United States passed its own oil peak—about 11 million barrels a day—in 1970, and since then production has dropped steadily. In 2004 it ran just above 5 million barrels a day (we get a tad more from natural-gas condensates). Yet we consume roughly 20 million barrels a day now. That means we have to import about two-thirds of our oil, and the ratio will continue to worsen.

The U.S. peak in 1970 brought on a portentous change in geoeconomic power. Within a few years, foreign producers, chiefly OPEC, were setting the price of oil, and this in turn led to the oil crises of the 1970s. In response, frantic development of non-OPEC oil, especially the North Sea fields of England and Norway, essentially saved the West's ass for about two decades. Since 1999, these fields have entered depletion. Meanwhile, worldwide discovery of new oil has steadily declined to insignificant levels in 2003 and 2004.

Some "cornucopians" claim that the Earth has something like a creamy nougat center of "abiotic" oil that will naturally replenish the great oil fields of the world. The facts speak differently. There has been no replacement whatsoever of oil already extracted from the fields of America or any other place.

Now we are faced with the global oil-production peak. The best estimates of when this will actually happen have been somewhere between now and 2010. In 2004, however, after demand from burgeoning China and India shot up, and revelations that Shell Oil wildly misstated its reserves, and Saudi Arabia proved incapable of goosing up its production despite promises to do so, the most knowledgeable experts revised their predictions and now concur that 2005 is apt to be the year of all-time global peak production.

It will change everything about how we live.

To aggravate matters, American natural-gas production is also declining, at five percent a year, despite frenetic new drilling, and with the potential of much steeper declines ahead. Because of the oil crises of the 1970s, the nuclear-plant disasters at Three Mile Island and Chernobyl and the acid-rain problem, the U.S. chose to make gas its first choice for electric-power generation. The result was that just about every power plant built after 1980 has to run on gas. Half the homes in America are heated with gas. To further complicate matters, gas isn't easy to import. Here in North America, it is distributed through a vast pipeline network. Gas imported from overseas would have to be compressed at minus-260 degrees Fahrenheit in pressurized tanker ships and unloaded (re-gasified) at special terminals, of which few exist in America. Moreover, the first attempts to site new terminals have met furious opposition because they are such ripe targets for terrorism.

Some other things about the global energy predicament are poorly understood by the public and even our leaders. This is going to be a permanent energy crisis, and these energy problems will synergize with the disruptions of climate change, epidemic disease and population overshoot to produce higher orders of trouble.

We will have to accommodate ourselves to fundamentally changed conditions.

No combination of alternative fuels will allow us to run American life the way we have been used to running it, or even a substantial fraction of it. The wonders of steady technological progress achieved through the reign of cheap oil have lulled us into a kind of Jiminy Cricket syndrome, leading many Americans to believe that anything we wish for hard enough will come true. These days, even people who ought to know better are wishing ardently for a seamless transition from fossil fuels to their putative replacements.

The widely touted "hydrogen economy" is a particularly cruel hoax. We are not going to replace the U.S. automobile and truck fleet with vehicles run on fuel cells. For one thing, the current generation of fuel cells is largely designed to run on hydrogen obtained from natural gas. The other way to get hydrogen in the quantities wished for would be electrolysis of water using power from hundreds of nuclear plants. Apart from the dim prospect of our building that many nuclear plants soon enough, there are also numerous severe problems with hydrogen's nature as an element that present forbidding obstacles to its use as a replacement for oil and gas, especially in storage and transport.

Wishful notions about rescuing our way of life with "renewables" are also unrealistic. Solar-electric systems and wind turbines face not only the enormous problem of scale but the fact that the components require substantial amounts of energy to manufacture and the probability that they can't be manufactured at all without the underlying support platform of a fossil-fuel economy. We will surely use solar and wind technology to generate some electricity for a period ahead but probably at a very local and small scale.

Virtually all "biomass" schemes for using plants to create liquid fuels cannot be scaled up to even a fraction of the level at which things are currently run. What's more, these schemes are predicated on using oil and gas "inputs" (fertilizers, weed-killers) to grow the biomass crops that would be converted into ethanol or bio-diesel fuels. This is a net energy loser—you might as well just burn the inputs and not bother with the biomass products. Proposals to distill trash and waste into oil by means of thermal depolymerization depend on the huge waste stream produced by a cheap oil and gas economy in the first place.

Coal is far less versatile than oil and gas, extant in less abundant supplies than many people assume and fraught with huge ecological drawbacks—as a contributor to greenhouse "global warming" gases and many health and toxicity issues ranging from widespread mercury poisoning to acid rain. You can make synthetic oil from coal, but the only time this was tried on a large scale was by the Nazis under wartime conditions, using impressive amounts of slave labor.

If we wish to keep the lights on in America after 2020, we may indeed have to resort to nuclear power, with all its practical problems and eco-conundrums. Under optimal conditions, it could take ten years to get a new generation of nuclear power plants into operation, and the price may be beyond our means. Uranium is also a resource in finite supply. We are no closer to the more difficult project of atomic fusion, by the way, than we were in the 1970s.

The Long Emergency is going to be a tremendous trauma for the human race. We will not believe that this is happening to us, that 200 years of modernity can be brought to its knees by a world-wide power shortage. The survivors will have to cultivate a religion of hope—that is, a deep and comprehensive belief that humanity is worth carrying on. If there is any positive side to stark changes coming our way, it may be in the benefits of close communal relations, of having to really work intimately (and physically) with our neighbors, to be part of an enterprise that really matters and to be fully engaged in meaningful social enactments instead of being merely entertained to avoid boredom. Years from now, when we hear singing at all, we will hear ourselves, and we will sing with our whole hearts.

POSTSCRIPT

Should the World Continue to Rely on Oil as the Major Source of Energy?

The twenty-first century ushered in another in a series of energy crises that have plagued the developed world since 1972. Gas prices jumped to record heights, and then rose even higher in 2006–2008, and the prospects of a return to $2.00-a-gallon levels (or even $3.00-a-gallon) seem increasingly remote.

Yet when one reads the UN assessment of foreseeable world energy supplies (Hisham Khatib et al., *World Energy Assessment: Energy and the Challenge of Sustainability,* United Nations Development Programme, 2002), a sobering message appears. Don't panic just yet. The study reveals no serious energy shortage during the first half of the twenty-first century. In fact, the report suggests that oil supply conditions have actually improved since the crises of the 1970s and early 1980s. The report goes further in its assessment, concluding that fossil fuel reserves are "sufficient to cover global requirements throughout this century, even with a high-growth scenario."

Francis R. Stabler argues in "The Pump Will Never Run Dry," (*The Futurist,* November 1998) that technology and free enterprise will combine to allow the human race to continue its reliance on oil far into the future. For Stabler, the title of his article tells the reader everything. The pump will not run dry!

To be sure, his view of the future availability of gas is a minority one. One supporter is Julian L. Simon who argues in his *The Ultimate Resource 2* (1996) that even God may not know exactly how much oil and gas are "out there." Chapter 11 of Simon's book is entitled "When Will We Run Out of Oil? Never!." Another Stabler supporter is Bjørn Lomborg in *The Skeptical Environment: Measuring the Real State of the World* (Cambridge University Press, 2001). Arguing that the world seems to find more fossil energy than it consumes, he concludes that "we have oil for at least 40 years at present consumption, at least 60 years' worth of gas, and 230 years' worth of coal."

Simon and Lomborg are joined by Michael C. Lynch in a published article on the Web under global oil supply (msn.com) entitled "Crying Wolf: Warnings about Oil Supply."

Seth Dunn, on the other hand, follows conventional wisdom in his article. That is, because oil is a finite resource, its supply will end some day, and that day will be sooner rather than later. Dunn has argued elsewhere (Christopher Flavin and Seth Dunn, "Reinventing the Energy

System," *State of the World 1999*, Worldwatch Institute, 1999) that the global economy has been built on the rapid depletion of non-renewable resources, and such consumption levels cannot possibly be maintained throughout the twenty-first century, as they were the previous century. Although Flavin and Dunn's arguments probably have received a receptive audience among most scholars who are concerned with the increasing scarcity of nonrenewable resources, they require the reader to accept a set of assumptions about the acceleration of future energy consumption. But one can easily be seduced by the logic of their argument, because it "just seems to make sense."

An excellent report is the Worldwatch Institute's "Energy for Development: The Potential Role of Renewable Energy in Meeting the Millennium Goals" (September 15, 2005). The report identifies those renewable energy options currently in wide use somewhere in the world. Another Worldwatch Institute report, "Biofuels for Transportation: Global Potential and Implications for Sustainable Agriculture and Energy in the 21st Century" (June 7, 2006), address one particular alternative to oil.

Lester R. Brown, et al. in *Beyond Malthus* (1999) suggest that most writers point to between the years 2010 and 2025 as the time when world oil production will peak. The consequence, if that is accurate, is a need for alternative sources. The student of energy politics, however, must be careful not to ignore how advances in energy source exploration and extraction have tended to expand known reserves. Is the future lesson that the tide has finally turned and no significant reserves remain to be discovered? Or is the lesson that history will repeat itself and modern science will yield more oil and gas deposits, as well as make their extraction cost effective?

James J. MacKensie has provided a comprehensive yet succinct article on the peaking of oil in "Oil as a Finite Resource: When Is Global Production Likely to Peak?" (World Resources Institute). Seth Dunn of the Worldwatch Institute in *State of the World 2001* suggests that a new energy system is fast approaching because of a series of revolutionary new technologies and approaches. David R. Francis provides a balanced assessment of the peaking debate in "Has Global Oil Production Peaked?" (*Christian Science Monitor*, January 29, 2004).

A number of books present a dire picture of the oil crisis: *Oil Addiction: The World in Peril* (Pierre Chomat, Universal Publishers, 2004); *The Collapsing Bubble: Growth and Fossil Energy* (Lindsay Grant, Seven Locks Press, 2005); *The Future of Global Oil Production: Facts, Figures, Trends and Projections, by Region* (Roger D. Blanchard, McFarland & Company, 2005); and two books by C. J. Campbell (*The Coming Oil Crisis*, Multi-Science Publishing Co., 2004; *Oil Crisis*, Multi-Science Publishing Co., 2005). Finally, the most recent book to address the end of the oil-based economy is *Profit from the Peak: The End of Oil and the Greatest Investment Event of the Century* (Brian Hicks, Wiley, 2008).

A much more optimistic picture of the future energy situation is Bill Paul's *Future Energy: How the New Oil Industry Will Change People, Politics and Portfolios* (Wiley, 2007). Finally, a book that charts a path to renewable energy is Hermann Scheer's *The Solar Economy: Renewable Energy for a Sustainable Global Future* (Earthscan Publications, 2004). Finally, a September 2006 special issue of *Scientific American* presented nine articles addressing various alternatives to oil.

The msn.com Web site provides numerous citations of articles on both sides of the issue.

ISSUE 7

Will the World Be Able to Feed Itself in the Foreseeable Future?

YES: Food and Agriculture Organization of the United Nations, from "The State of Food Insecurity in the World 2006" (2006)

NO: Janet Raloff, from "Global Food Trends," *Science News Online* (May 31, 2003)

ISSUE SUMMARY

YES: The 2006 FAO report argues that despite problems at some local and national levels, global food production "can grow in line with demand" for the foreseeable future as long as national governments and international organizations adopt appropriate policies.

NO: Janet Raloff, a writer for *Science News,* looks at a number of factors—declining per capita grain harvests, the world's growing appetite for meat, declining availability of fish for the developing world, and continuing individual poverty.

The lead editorial in *The New York Times* on March 3, 2008, began with the sentence: "The world's food situation is bleak. . . ." The primary culprit, according to the editorial, is the rising cost of wheat. The blame, in turn, was placed on the growing impact of biofuels. Others echoed the same message, adding climate change and the rising cost of shipping to the list of culprits. The UN Food and Agricultural Organization also issued a series of warnings in late 2007 and early 2008 about the growing food crisis.

Visualize two pictures. A group of people in Africa, including a significant number of small children, who show dramatic signs of advanced malnutrition and even starvation. The second picture shows an apparently wealthy couple finishing a meal at a rather expensive restaurant. The waiter removes their plates still half-full of food, and deposits them in the kitchen garbage can. The implication was quite clear. If only the wealthy would share their food with the poor, no one would go hungry. Today the simplicity of this image is obvious.

This issue addresses the question of whether or not the world will be able to feed itself by the middle of the twenty-first century. A prior question, of course, is whether or not enough food is grown throughout the world today to handle the needs of all the planet's citizens. News accounts of chronic food shortages somewhere in the world seem to have been appearing with regularly consistency for about 30 years. This time has witnessed graphic accounts in news specials about the consequences of insufficient food, usually somewhere in sub-Saharan Africa. Also, several national and international studies have been commissioned to address world hunger.

One might deduce from all of this activity that population growth had outpaced food production and that the planet's agricultural capabilities are no longer sufficient, or that the poor have been priced out of the marketplace. Yet, the ability of most countries to grow enough food has not yet been challenged. During the 1970–2000 period, only one region of the globe, sub-Saharan Africa, was unable to have its own food production keep pace with population growth.

This is instructive because, beginning in the early 1970s, a number of factors conspired to lessen the likelihood that all humans would go to bed each night adequately nourished. Weather in major food-producing countries turned bad; a number of countries, most notably Japan and the Soviet Union, entered the world grain importing business with a vengeance; the cost of energy used to enhance agricultural output rose dramatically; and less capital was available to poorer countries as loans or grants for purchasing agricultural inputs or the finished product (food) itself. Yet the world has had little difficulty growing sufficient food, enough to provide every person with two loaves of bread per day as well as other commodities.

Why then did famine and other food-related maladies appear with increasing frequency? The simple answer is that food is treated as a commodity, not a nutrient. Those who can afford to buy food or grow their own do not go hungry. However, the world's poor became increasingly unable to afford either to create their own successful agricultural ventures or to buy enough food.

Can the planet physically sustain increases in food production equal to or greater than the ability of the human race to reproduce itself? This question can only be answered by examining both factors in the comparison— likely future food production levels and future fertility scenarios. A second question relates to the economic dimension—will those poorer countries of the globe that are unable to grow their own food have sufficient assets to purchase it, or will the international community create a global distribution network that ignores a country's ability to pay? And third, will countries that want to grow their own food be given the opportunity to do so?

The selections for this issue address the specific question of the planet's continuing ability to grow sufficient food for its growing population. The FAO report suggests that lower growth rates in food production are a function of decreasing demand, in large part because population growth is slowing and per capita food consumption levels are maxing out in many countries. Janet Raloff suggests that a number of factors—declining per capita grain harvests, the world's growing appetite for meat, and declining availability of fish for the developing world, and continuing individual poverty.

YES

World Agriculture: Towards 2015/2030: Executive Summary of Report of Economic and Social Department

Executive Summary

In recent years the growth rates of world agricultural production and crop yields have slowed. This has raised fears that the world may not be able to grow enough food and other commodities to ensure that future populations are adequately fed.

However, the slowdown has occurred not because of shortages of land or water but rather because demand for agricultural products has also slowed. This is mainly because world population growth rates have been declining since the late 1960s, and fairly high levels of food consumption per person are now being reached in many countries, beyond which further rises will be limited. But it is also the case that a stubbornly high share of the world's population remains in absolute poverty and so lacks the necessary income to translate its needs into effective demand.

As a result, the growth in world demand for agricultural products is expected to fall from an average 2.2 percent a year over the past 30 years to 1.5 percent a year for the next 30. In developing countries the slowdown will be more dramatic, from 3.7 percent to 2 percent, partly as a result of China having passed the phase of rapid growth in its demand for food.

This study suggests that world agricultural production can grow in line with demand, provided that the necessary national and international policies to promote agriculture are put in place. Global shortages are unlikely, but serious problems already exist at national and local levels and may worsen unless focused efforts are made.

Food and Nutrition

Massive strides have been made in improving food security. The proportion of people living in developing countries with average food intakes below 2,200 kcal per day fell from 57 percent in 1964–66 to just 10 percent in 1997–99. Yet 776 million people in developing countries remain undernourished—about one person in six.

Global progress in nutrition is expected to continue, in parallel with a reduction in poverty as projected by the World Bank. The incidence of under nourishment should fall from 17 percent of the population of developing countries at present to 11 percent in 2015 and just 6 percent in 2030. By 2030, three-quarters of the population of the developing world could be living in countries where less than 5 percent of people are undernourished. Less than 8 percent live in such countries at present.

Despite impressive reductions in the *proportion* of undernourished, continuing population growth means that progress in reducing the total *number* will be slower. The World Food Summit of 1996 set a target of halving the number of undernourished people to about 410 million by 2015. This study's projections suggest that this may be difficult to achieve: some 610 million people could still be undernourished in that year, and even by 2030 about 440 million undernourished may remain. Priority for local food production and reduced inequality of access to food could improve this performance. The problem of undernourishment will tend to become more tractable and easier to address through policy interventions, both national and international, as the number of countries with high incidence declines.

Agriculture, Poverty and International Trade

Undernourishment is a central manifestation of poverty. It also deepens other aspects of poverty, by reducing the capacity for work and resistance to disease, and by affecting children's mental development and educational achievements.

Currently, one in four people in developing countries are living in extreme poverty, subsisting on less than US$1 a day. This proportion is down from almost one-third in 1990. But because of population growth the fall in numbers has been slower, from 1269 million to 1134 million. The latest World Bank assessment to 2015 suggests that such reductions in global poverty could continue. Sub-Saharan Africa is the exception, however. Here the numbers of poor rose steeply during the 1990s and seem likely to continue to do so. Seven out of ten of the world's poor still live in rural areas. Growth in the agricultural sector has a crucial role to play in improving the incomes of poor people, by providing farm jobs and stimulating off-farm employment. Some direct nutritional interventions may also be needed—such as vitamin and mineral supplementation of basic foods—while health, water and sanitation measures to reduce the effects of illness on food absorption will also be important.

Trade has an important role to play in improving food security and fostering agriculture. Some estimates put the potential annual increase in global welfare from freer trade in agriculture as high as US$165 billion. But the progress made in the current round of trade negotiations has been limited and the benefits so far remain modest. If future reforms focus too narrowly on the removal of subsidies in the countries of the Organisation for Economic Co-operation and Development (OECD), most of the gains will probably be reaped by consumers in developed countries. Developing countries should benefit more from the removal of trade barriers for products in which they have a comparative advantage (such as sugar, fruits and vegetables), from reduced tariffs for processed agricultural commodities, and from deeper preferential access to markets for the least developed countries.

Internal reforms are also needed within developing countries if free trade is to contribute to poverty reduction. Such reforms include: a reduction of the bias against agriculture in national policy making; the opening of borders for long-term foreign investments; the introduction of schemes to improve food quality and safety; investments in roads, irrigation, seeds, and skills; improved quality standards; and safety nets for the poor who face higher food prices.

Globalization in food and agriculture holds promise as well as presenting problems. It has generally led to progress in reducing poverty in Asia. But it has also led to the rise of multinational food companies with the potential to disempower farmers in many countries. Developing countries need the legal and administrative frameworks to ward off the threats while reaping the benefits.

Crop Production

The annual growth rate of world demand for cereals has declined from 2.5 percent a year in the 1970s and 1.9 percent a year in the 1980s to only 1 percent a year in the 1990s. Annual cereal use per person (including animal feeds) peaked in the mid-1980s at 334 kg and has since fallen to 317 kg.

The decline is not cause for alarm: it was above all the natural result of slower population growth and shifts in human diets and animal feeds. However, in the 1990s it was accentuated by a number of temporary factors, including serious recessions in the transition countries and some East and Southeast Asian countries.

The growth rate of demand for cereals is expected to rise again to 1.4 percent a year to 2015, slowing to 1.2 percent per year thereafter. In developing countries overall, cereal production is not expected to keep pace with demand. The net cereal deficits of these countries, which amounted to 103 million tonnes or 9 percent of consumption in 1997–99, could rise to 265 million tonnes by 2030, when they will be 14 percent of consumption. This gap can be bridged by increased surpluses from traditional grain exporters, and by new exports from the transition countries, which are expected to shift from being net importers to being net exporters.

Oilcrops have seen the fastest increase in area of any crop sector, expanding by 75 million ha from the mid-1970s until the end of the 1990s, while cereal area fell by 28 million ha over the same period. Future per capita consumption of oilcrops is expected to rise more rapidly than that of cereals. These crops will account for 45 out of every 100 extra kilocalories added to average diets in developing countries between now and 2030.

Sources of Growth in Crop Production

There are three main sources of growth in crop production: expanding the land area, increasing the frequency with which it is cropped (often through irrigation), and boosting yields. It has been suggested that we may be approaching the ceiling of what is possible for all three sources.

A detailed examination of production potentials does not support this view at the global level, although in some countries, and even in whole regions, serious problems already exist and could deepen.

Land. Less new agricultural land will be opened up than in the past. In the coming 30 years, developing countries will need an extra 120 million ha for crops, an overall increase of 12.5 percent. This is only half the rate of increase observed between 1961–63 and 1997–99.

At global level there is adequate unused potential farmland. A comparison of soils, terrains and climates with the needs of major crops suggests that an extra 2.8 billion ha are suitable in varying degrees for the rainfed production of arable and permanent crops. This is almost twice as much as is currently farmed. However, only a fraction of this extra land is realistically available for agricultural expansion in the foreseeable future, as much is needed to preserve forest cover and to support infrastructural development. Accessibility and other constraints also stand in the way of any substantial expansion.

More than half the land that could be opened up is in just seven countries of tropical Latin America and sub-Saharan Africa, whereas other regions and countries face a shortage of suitable land. In the Near East and North Africa, 87 percent of suitable land was already being farmed in 1997–99, while in South Asia the figure is no less than 94 percent. In these regions, intensification through improved management and technologies will be the main, indeed virtually the only, source of production growth. In many places land degradation threatens the productivity of existing farmland and pasture.

Water. Irrigation is crucial to the world's food supplies. In 1997–99, irrigated land made up only about one-fifth of the total arable area in developing countries but produced two-fifths of all crops and close to three-fifths of cereal production.

The role of irrigation is expected to increase still further. The developing countries as a whole are likely to expand their irrigated area from 202 million ha in 1997–99 to 242 million ha by 2030. Most of this expansion will occur in land-scarce areas where irrigation is already crucial.

The net increase in irrigated land is predicted to be less than 40 percent of that achieved since the early 1960s. There appears to be enough unused irrigable land to meet future needs: FAO studies suggest a total irrigation potential of some 402 million ha in developing countries, of which only half is currently in use. However, water resources will be a major factor constraining expansion in South Asia, which will be using 41 percent of its renewable freshwater resources by 2030, and in the Near East and North Africa, which will be using 58 percent. These regions will need to achieve greater efficiency in water use.

Yields. In the past four decades, rising yields accounted for about 70 percent of the increase in crop production in the developing countries. The 1990s saw a slowdown in the growth of yields. Wheat yields, for example, grew at an average 3.8 percent a year between 1961 and 1989, but at only 2 percent a year between 1989 and 1999. For rice the respective rates fell by more than half, from 2.3 percent to 1.1 percent.

Yield growth will continue to be the dominant factor underlying increases in crop production in the future. In developing countries, it will account for about 70 percent of growth in crop production to 2030. To meet production projections, future yield growth will not need to be as rapid as in the past. For wheat yields, an annual rise of only 1.2 percent a year is needed over the next 30 years. The picture for other crops is similar. Growth in fertilizer use in developing countries is expected to slow to 1.1 percent per year over the next three decades, a continuation of the slowdown already under way.

Overall, it is estimated that some 80 percent of future increases in crop production in developing countries will have to come from intensification: higher yields, increased multiple cropping and shorter fallow periods.

Improved Technology

New technology is needed for areas with shortages of land or water, or with particular problems of soil or climate. These are frequently areas with a high concentration of poor people, where such technology could play a key role in improving food security.

Agricultural production could probably meet expected demand over the period to 2030 even without major advances in modern biotechnology. However, the new techniques of molecular analysis could give a welcome boost to productivity, particularly in areas with special difficulties, thereby improving the incomes of the poor, just as the green revolution did in large parts of Asia during the 1960s to 1980s.

Needed for the twenty-first century is a second, doubly green revolution in agricultural technology. Productivity increases are still vital, but must be combined with environmental protection or restoration, while new technologies must be both affordable by, and geared to the needs of, the poor and undernourished.

Biotechnology offers promise as a means of improving food security and reducing pressures on the environment, provided the perceived environmental threats from biotechnology itself are addressed. Genetically modified crop varieties—resistant to drought, water-logging, soil acidity, salinity and extreme temperatures—could help to sustain farming in marginal areas and to restore degraded lands to production. Pest-resistant varieties can reduce the need for pesticides.

However, the widespread use of genetically modified varieties will depend on whether or not food safety and environmental concerns can be adequately addressed. Indeed, the spread of these varieties, in the developed countries at least, has recently slowed somewhat in response to these concerns, which must be addressed through improved testing and safety protocols if progress is to resume.

Meanwhile, other promising technologies have emerged that combine increased production with improved environmental protection. These include no-till or conservation agriculture, and the lower-input approaches of integrated pest or nutrient management and organic agriculture.

Livestock

Diets in developing countries are changing as incomes rise. The share of staples, such as cereals, roots and tubers, is declining, while that of meat, dairy products and oil crops is rising.

Between 1964–66 and 1997–99, per capita meat consumption in developing countries rose by 150 percent, and that of milk and dairy products by 60 percent. By 2030, per capita consumption of livestock products could rise by a further 44 percent. As in the past, poultry consumption will grow fastest.

Productivity improvements are likely to be a major source of growth. Milk yields should improve, while breeding and improved management will increase average carcass weights and off-take rates. This will allow increased production with lower growth in animal numbers, and a corresponding slowdown in the growth of environmental damage from grazing or wastes.

In developing countries, demand will grow faster than production, producing a growing trade deficit. In meat products this will rise steeply, from 1.2 million tonnes a year in 1997–99 to 5.9 million tonnes in 2030 (despite growing meat exports from Latin America), while in milk and dairy products the rise will be less steep but still considerable, from 20 million to 39 million tonnes a year.

An increasing share of livestock production will probably come from industrial enterprises. In recent years production from this sector has grown twice as fast as that from more traditional mixed farming systems and more than six times faster than from grazing systems.

Forestry

During the 1990s the world's total forest area shrank by 9.4 million ha—about three times the size of Belgium—each year. However, the rate of deforestation was slower in the 1990s than in the 1980s. Industrial and transition countries expanded their forest areas, and many developing countries—including Bangladesh, China, India, Turkey and Viet Nam—are now planting more forest area than they cut.

The crop projections suggest that cropland will need to expand by an extra 120 million ha by 2030, while urban land areas will continue to grow by a considerable amount. Much of this extra land will have to come from forest clearance. In addition, by 2030 annual world consumption of industrial round-wood is expected to rise by 60 percent over current levels, to around 2,400 million m^3.

Even so, deforestation is expected to slow further in the coming decades and the world is unlikely to face a wood supply crisis. Production of wood-based materials is continually increasing in efficiency. The area of plantations is also growing rapidly: production of industrial round-wood from plantations is expected to double by 2030, from 400 million m^3 today, to around 800 million m^3. In addition, a big increase in tree-growing outside forests and plantations—along roads, in towns, around homes and on farms—will boost the supply of wood and other tree products.

The central challenges for the forestry sector are to find ways of managing natural and cultivated tree resources so as to increase production, improve the food security and energy supply of the poor, and safeguard the environmental services and biodiversity provided by forests.

Fisheries

World fisheries production has kept ahead of population growth over the past three decades. Total fish production almost doubled, from 65 million tonnes in 1970 to 125 million tonnes in 1999, when world average intake of fish, crustaceans and molluscs reached 16.3 kg per person. By 2030, annual fish consumption is likely to rise to some 150 to 160 million tonnes, or between 19 and 20 kg per person.

This amount is significantly lower than the potential demand, because environmental factors are expected to limit supply. By the turn of the century, three-quarters of ocean fish stocks were overfished, depleted or exploited up to their maximum sustainable yield. Further growth in the marine catch can be only modest. During the 1990s the marine catch levelled out at 80 to 85 million tonnes a year, not far from its maximum sustainable yield.

Aquaculture compensated for this marine slowdown, doubling its share of world fish production during the 1990s. It will continue to grow rapidly, at rates of 5 to 7 percent a year up to 2015. In all sectors of fishing it will be essential to pursue forms of management conducive to sustainable exploitation, especially for resources under common ownership or no ownership.

Environment and Climate

Over the next 30 years, many of the environmental problems associated with agriculture will remain serious. Loss of biodiversity caused by the expansion and intensification of production often continues unabated even in the developed countries, where nature is highly valued and, supposedly, protected.

Nitrogen fertilizers are a major source of water and air pollution. The crop projections imply slower growth in the use of these fertilizers than in the past, but the increase could still be significant for pollution. Projections also suggest a 60 percent increase in emissions of ammonia and methane from the livestock sector. Comprehensive measures will be needed to control and reduce air and water pollution from these sources.

Global warming is not expected to depress food availability at the global level, but at the regional and local levels there may be significant impacts. Current projections suggest that the potential for crop production will increase in temperate and northerly latitudes, while in parts of the tropics and subtropics it may decline. This may further deepen the dependence of developing countries on food imports, though at the same time it may improve the ability of temperate exporters to fill the gap. Rising sea levels will threaten crop production and livelihoods in countries with large areas of low-lying land, such as Bangladesh and Egypt.

Food insecurity for some vulnerable rural groups in developing countries may well worsen. By 2030, climate change is projected to depress cereal production in Africa by 2 to 3 percent. Improved seeds and increased fertilizer use should more than compensate, but this factor will still weigh heavily on efforts to make progress.

Forestry and agriculture both contribute to human impact on climate. The burning of biomass—in deforestation, savannah fires, the disposal of crop residues and cooking with firewood or dung—is a major source of atmospheric carbon dioxide, while fertilizers and animal wastes create large emissions of nitrous oxide and ammonia.

Forestry can help to soak up some of the carbon released by human activities. Between 1995 and 2050, slower deforestation, together with regeneration and plantation development, could reduce carbon dioxide emissions by the equivalent of 12 to 15 percent of all fossil fuel emissions.

Farming also has a positive role to play. By 2030 the amount of carbon locked up in cropland soils, as soil organic matter from crop residues and manure, could rise by 50 percent if better management practices are introduced.

Janet Raloff   ➥ **NO**

Global Food Trends

Last year, for the third year in four, world per-capita grain production fell. Even more disturbing in a world where people still go hungry, at 294 kilograms, last year's per capita grain yield was the lowest in more than 30 years. Indeed, the global grain harvest has not met demand for 4 years, causing governments and food companies to mine stocks of these commodities that they were holding in reserve.

This is just one of the sobering observations about world food trends offered by researchers with the Worldwatch Institute, an Earth-resources think tank in Washington, D.C.

Each year, Worldwatch reads several key indicators of our planet's environmental health. The organization's latest 153-page almanac, *Vital Signs 2003,* issued May 22 in cooperation with the United Nations Environment Programme, notes that production of the world's three major cereals fell in absolute terms in 2002: wheat by 3 percent, to 562 million metric tons (Mt); corn by almost 2 percent, to 598 Mt; and rice by 2 percent, to 391 Mt. Together, these three crops make up 85 percent of the world's grain harvest, notes Worldwatch's Brian Halweil.

Throughout the early 1960s, world grain reserves were equal to at least 1 year's global demand for these commodities. By last year, that excess had fallen to just 20 percent of what's now consumed annually.

What makes these trends so dangerous, Halweil reports, is that despite increasing dietary diversity, most people around the world "still primarily eat foods made from grain." Globally, people derive 48 percent of their calories from grain-based foods. Moreover, Halweil points out, grains—especially corn—serve as "the primary feedstock for industrial livestock production."

Indeed, he told *Science News Online,* "livestock consume 35 percent of the world's grain, over 90 percent of the soybeans, and millions of tons of other oilseeds, roots, and tubers each year." In the United States, the share of these plant-based foods going to livestock is even higher: 50 percent of all grains (including 60 percent of corn) and virtually all soy.

Parched Bread Baskets

Drought in Australia and the United States last year explains much of the drop in world cereal harvests, Halweil says.

From *Science News,* vol. 163, no. 22, May 31, 2003. Copyright © 2003 by Science Service, Inc. Reprinted by permission via Copyright Clearance Center.

New data issued by the U.S. Department of Agriculture flesh out the picture. They show that record or near-record droughts last year throughout much of the western and midwestern United States—the nation's breadbasket and corn belt, respectively—accounted for shortfalls in wheat and corn. It was so bad throughout much of the West that earlier this month the USDA announced a new $53 million program to help farmers and ranchers mitigate the effect of drought. The initiative will provide money for implementing new water-conserving technologies and farming practices.

Agricultural economists see no sign that U.S. grain production will recover soon. A map in the USDA's May 20 *Weekly Weather and Crop Bulletin* depicts much of the intermountain West in the throes of "extreme drought" with large surrounding areas—spanning from Mexico to Canada and from Nevada through middle-Nebraska—in only a slightly better situation: suffering merely a "severe drought."

Data reported in a May 1 water forecast by the National Drought Mitigation Center in Lincoln, Neb., show "spring and summer stream flows [at] less than 50 percent of average in parts of the Intermountain West." Water reservoirs mirror the problem. Despite a cool, wet spring throughout much of the West, fall and winter drought conditions have left water supplies well below average—in some cases at half of average amounts—in many Western basins.

The bottom line: No one expects bumper grain crops even in the United States. Attaining just average yields may prove difficult.

Feed's Growing Demand on Grains

In a second *Vital Signs 2003* report, Danielle Nierenberg highlights a related food trend, the world's growing appetite for meat. Last year, livestock growers raised some 242 million metric tons of meat. That's five times what was produced in 1950 and double the yield in 1977.

Because meat production is relatively expensive—it requires 11 to 17 calories of feed to produce each calorie of beef, pork, or chicken—wealthy industrialized countries have led in demand for these foods. But Nierenberg reports that "two-thirds of the gains in meat consumption in 2002 occurred in developing countries, where urbanization, rising incomes, and the globalization of trade are changing diets." In fact, she finds, developing countries have recently surpassed industrialized ones as producers of meat by total weight.

Still, there's a huge disparity in the amounts of meat consumed per capita in rich and poor countries. In industrial nations, the average person eats some 80 kilograms per year—or 2.8 times that in the developing world. Most people eat pork, which accounts for 38 percent of world meat production, followed by poultry at 30 percent and beef at 25 percent.

To help raise some 5 billion hoofed and 16 billion winged animals for meat, farmers have increasingly turned to raising animals in factory-like conditions. Today, industrial feedlots account for 43 percent of the world's beef and more than 50 percent of all pork and poultry. These confined setups also concentrate the noise, stink, and wastes associated with livestock into industrial operations. As unpopular as these are, they will probably dominate world meat production if it continues to grow. And the United Nations projects that it will grow, to 300 Mt by 2020.

Nevertheless, many people of the world won't have the luxury of choosing between grains or meats, even by 2020. Today, Halweil notes, more than 800 million people regularly go to bed hungry—a number that's greater than 2.5 times the combined population of the United States, Canada, and Mexico. It's tempting to speculate that if humanity ate less meat, there would be more grain available to feed these people, Halweil says. However, he says, "you can't necessarily make that leap," since most hunger today stems not from a shortage of food as much as a shortage of funds to pay for it.

On the other hand, Halweil notes that there is one food for which the industrialized world's consumption directly robs the developing world: fish. Recent reports have chronicled how overfishing by commercial fleets are decimating fish stocks around the world. "Because fishing is really a global industry—that is, you have American, Japanese, and Norwegian ships crisscrossing the globe and plucking fish from all over the planet," Halweil says, "meeting the demands of diners in New York or Tokyo can mean there's less available for someone in Bangkok or Bombay."

"I think the take-home message" on worldwide production and consumption patterns for grain and meat, Nierenberg says, is that people in the industrial world "are overconsuming and setting a bad example."

References

2003. USDA provides $53 million to farmers and ranchers in 17 states to help with drought recovery. U.S. Department of Agriculture press release. May 9. Available at http://www.usda.gov/news/releases/2003/05/0148.htm.

Halweil, B. 2003. Grain production drops. In *Vital Signs 2003,* L. Starke, ed. New York: W.W. Norton. See http://www.worldwatch.org/pubs/vs/2003.

Nierenberg, D. 2003. Meat production and consumption grow. In *Vital Signs 2003,* L. Starke, ed. New York: W.W. Norton. See http://www.worldwatch.org/pubs/vs/2003.

U.S. Department of Agriculture. 2003. U.S. drought monitor. *Weekly Weather and Crop Bulletin* 90(May 20):5. Available at http://www.usda.gov/oce/waob/jawf/wwcb/p_5.pdf.

_____. 2003. Water supply forecast for the western United States. *Weekly Weather and Crop Bulletin* 90(May 20):2-3. Available at http://www.usda.gov/oce/waob/jawf/wwcb/p_2.pdf.

POSTSCRIPT

Will the World Be Able to Feed Itself in the Foreseeable Future?

Presumably, economist Thomas Robert Malthus was not the first to address the question of the planet's ability to feed its population. But his 1789 *Essay on the Principle of Population* is the most quoted of early writings on the subject. Malthus' basic proposition was that population, if left unchecked, would grow geometrically, while subsistence resources could grow only arithmetically. Malthus, who wrote his essay in response to an argument with his father about the ability of the human race to produce sufficient resources vital for life, created a stir back in the late eighteenth century. The same debate holds the public's attention today as the momentum of recent high population growth rates yields human increases unparalleled at any other time in human history.

The 2006 FAO report lays out an argument for a more optimistic scenario for the twenty-first century. It predicts that the growth in global demand for food will rise only 1.5 percent a year for the next 30 years, a drop from the 1.5 percent of the previous 30 years. And the growth in global demand for cereals will be cut in half, from 2.5 percent per year to 1.2 percent. The report suggests that future demand will be met in three ways: (1) tapping into adequate potential farmland; (2) increasing the rate of irrigation; and (3) acquiring higher yield levels due to improved technology. This optimistic view is shared by Sylvie Brunel in *The Geopolitics of Hunger, 2000–2001: Hunger and Power* (Lynne Rienner, 2001).

Janet Raloff, a writer for *Science News,* looks at a number of factors—declining per capita grain harvests, the world's growing appetite for meat, the declining availability of fish for the developing world, and continuing individual poverty. Lester R. Brown adds another dimension to the problem in *State of the World 2001* (W.W. Norton & Company, 2001). His pessimism about future food supplies arises from the belief that world leaders have not come forward with a comprehensive master plan to address the problem and are extremely unlikely to do so in the foreseeable future.

A balanced look at the planet's capacity to feed the UN's projected 2050 population is L.T. Evans' *Feeding the Ten Billion* (Cambridge University Press, 1998). In it, the author takes the reader through the ages, showing how the human race has addressed the agricultural needs of each succeeding billion people. The biggest challenge during the next half century, according to Evans, is to solve two problems: producing enough food for a 67 percent increase in the population, and eliminating the chronic undernutrition afflicting so many people. Solving the first problem requires a focus on the main components of increased food supply. For Evans, these include: "(1) increase in land under cultivation; (2) increase in yield per hectare per crop; (3) increase in the number of crops per hectare per year; (4) displacement of lower yielding crops by higher yielding ones; (5) reduction of post-harvest losses; and (6) reduced use as feed for animals."

The second problem brings into play many socioeconomic factors beyond those that are typically associated with agricultural production. Many studies have observed that the root cause of hunger is poverty. Addressing poverty, therefore, is a prerequisite for ensuring that the world's food supply is distributed such that the challenge of global hunger is met.

Three other sources are reports by the UN's Food and Agricultural Organization: *World Agriculture: Towards 2000; The State of Food and Agriculture 2002;* and *World Agriculture: Towards 2015/2030.* The central message of these studies is that the planet will be able to feed a growing population in the foreseeable future, if certain conditions are met. Another FAO report, *The State of Food Insecurity in the World 2005,* analyses the latest data on hunger in the context of the Millennium Development Goals.

Another optimistic viewpoint about future food prospects is *The World Food Outlook* by Donald Mitchell, Merlinda D. Ingco, and Ronald C. Duncan (Cambridge University Press, 1997). Their basic conclusion is that the world food situation has improved dramatically for most of the regions of the globe and will continue to do so. The only exception is sub-Saharan Africa.

For Julian L. Simon in "What Are the Limits on Food Production," *The Ultimate Resource 2* (Princeton University Press, 1996) the answer is simple. The world can produce vastly more food than it currently does, even in those places that rely on conventional methods. The essence of his argument is this. More people with higher incomes cause scarcity problems in the short run, which, in turn, results in raised prices. Into the picture then come inventors and entrepreneurs, some of whom will be successful in finding appropriate solutions.

David Pimentel et al., "Impact of Population Growth on Food Supplies and Environment," *Population and Environment* (1997) allude to the warnings of a number of impressive groups concerning the world's future food situation. They cite the Royal Society, the U.S. National Academy of Sciences, the UN Food and Agricultural Organization, numerous other international organizations, as well as scientific research to support their view of the pending danger. For them, two issues are significant. The first is the existence of enough agricultural inputs: water, land, energy, and the like. The second is the global economic system that treats food as a commodity rather than a nutrient. For these authors, the bottom line is that population must be curtailed.

Two other sources are worth mentioning. *Halving Global Hunger* (Sara Scherr, Background Paper of the Millennium Project's Task Force 2 on Hunger, April 18, 2003) provides an overview of existing knowledge relating to the reduction of hunger. Joachim von Braun and associates analyze two future policy scenarios for ensuring food security by 2050 (*New Risks and Opportunities for Food Security: Scenario Analyses for 2015 and 2050,* International Food Policy Research Institute, February 2005). See also von Braun's *The World Food Situation: New Driving Forces and Required Actions* (IFPRI, December 2007) and FAO's *The State of Food Insecurity in the World 2005.* Finally, a comprehensive look at the world food future is Richard Heinberg's "What Will We Eat as the Oil Runs Out?" (Global Public Media, December 2007).

ISSUE 8

Is the Threat of Global Warming Real?

YES: David Biello, from "State of the Science: Beyond the Worst Case Climate Change Scenario," *Scientific American* (November 26, 2007)

NO: Richard S. Lindzen, from "No Global Warming," *Environment News,* The Heartland Institute (August 2006)

ISSUE SUMMARY

YES: David Biello summarizes the 2007 report of the United Nations Intergovernmental Panel on Climate Change (IPCC), which concludes that climate change is unequivocal, almost certain to be caused by human activity.

NO: Richard S. Lindzen takes issue with those, who suggest that "the debate in the scientific community is over" regarding the existence of global warming, and argues that to believe in such warming requires one to "ignore the truly inconvenient facts."

In December 2007, the Intergovernmental Panel on Climate Change (IPCC), and former U.S. Vice President Al Gore, were jointly awarded the Nobel Peace Prize for their work "to build up and disseminate greater knowledge about man-made climate change, and to lay the foundations for measures" to counteract such change. This was the culmination of a story that began 15 years earlier at the UN-sponsored Earth Summit in Rio de Janeiro in 1992, when a Global Climate Treaty was signed. According to S. Fred Singer, in *Hot Talks, Cold Science: Global Warming's Unfinished Debate* (Independent Institute, 1998), the treaty rested on three basic assumptions. First, global warming has been detected in the records of climate of the last 100 years. Second, a substantial warming in the future will produce catastrophic consequences—droughts, floods, storms, a rapid and significant rise in sea level, agricultural collapse, and the spread of tropical disease. And third, the scientific and policy-making communities know: (1) which atmospheric concentrations of greenhouse gases are dangerous and which ones are not, (2) that drastic reductions of carbon dioxide (CO_2) emissions as well as energy use in general by industrialized countries will stabilize CO_2 concentrations at close to current levels, and (3) that such economically damaging measures can be justified politically despite no significant scientific support for global warming as a threat.

Since the Earth Summit, it appears that scientists have opted for placement into one of three camps. The first camp buys into the three assumptions outlined above. In late 1995, 2,500 leading climate scientists announced in the first Intergovernmental Panel on Climatic Change (IPCC) report that the planet was warming due to coal and gas emissions. Scientists in a second camp suggest that while global warming has occurred and continues at the present, the source of such temperature rise cannot be ascertained yet. The conclusions of the Earth Summit were misunderstood by many in the scientific community, the second camp would suggest.

A third group of scientists, representing a minority, argues that we cannot be certain that global warming is taking place, yet alone determine its cause. They present a number of arguments in support of their position. Among them is the contention that pre-satellite data (pre-1979) showing a century-long pattern of warming is an illusion because satellite data (post-1979) reveal no such warming. Scientists in the third camp are also skeptical of studying global warming in the laboratory. They suggest, moreover, that most of the scientists who have opted for one of the first two camps have done so as a consequence of laboratory experiments, rather than of evidence from the real world.

Despite what appear to be wide differences in scientific thinking about the existence of global warming and its origins, the global community has moved forward with attempts to achieve consensus among the nations of the world for taking appropriate action to curtail human activities thought to affect warming. A 1997 international meeting in Kyoto, Japan, concluded with an agreement for reaching goals established at the earlier Earth Summit. Thirty-eight industrialized countries, including the United States, agreed to reduction levels outlined in the treaty. However, the U.S. Senate never ratified the treaty, and the Bush administration decided not to support it. Nonetheless, the two basic criteria for going into effect—the required number of countries (55) with the required levels of carbon dioxide's emissions (55 percent of carbon dioxide emissions from developed countries) must sign the treaty—were met when Russia ratified the treaty on November 18, 2004. The treaty went into effect on February 19, 2005.

In the 2007 ICPP report (fourth in the series of IPCC reports), more than 2,500 scientists reaffirmed the existence of global warming. The first selection summarizes this most recent IPCC report. It suggests that among the risks are warming temperatures, heat waves, heavy rains, drought, stronger storms, decreased biodiversity, and sea-level rise. The second selection by Richard Lindzen, an MIT science professor, is one of the many writings by the author that attacks the basic thesis of the global warming advocates and the science on which it is based.

YES

David Biello

State of the Science: Beyond the Worst Case Climate Change Scenario

Climate change is "unequivocal" and it is 90 percent certain that the "net effect of human activities since 1750 has been one of warming," the Intergovernmental Panel on Climate Change (IPCC)—a panel of more than 2,500 scientists and other experts—wrote in its first report on the physical science of global warming earlier this year. In its second assessment, the IPCC stated that human-induced warming is having a discernible influence on the planet, from species migration to thawing permafrost. Despite these findings, emissions of the greenhouse gases driving this process continue to rise thanks to increased burning of fossil fuels while cost-effective options for decreasing them have not been adopted, the panel found in its third report.

The IPCC's fourth and final assessment of the climate change problem—known as the Synthesis Report—combines all of these reports and adds that "warming could lead to some impacts that are abrupt or irreversible, depending upon the rate and magnitude of the climate change." Although countries continue to debate the best way to address this finding, 130 nations, including the U.S., China, Australia, Canada, and even Saudi Arabia, have concurred with it.

"The governments now require, in fact, that the authors report on risks that are high and 'key' because of their potentially very high consequence," says economist Gary Yohe, a lead author on the IPCC Synthesis Report. "They have, perhaps, given the planet a chance to save itself."

Among those risks:

Warming temperatures. Continued global warming is virtually certain (or more than 99 percent likely to occur) at this point, leading to both good and bad impacts. On the positive side, fewer people will die from freezing temperatures and agricultural yield will increase in colder areas. The negatives include reduced crop production in the tropics and subtropics, increased insect outbreaks, diminished water supply caused by dwindling snowpack, and increasingly poor air quality in cities.

Heat waves. Scientists are more than 90 percent certain that episodes of extreme heat will increase worldwide, leading to increased danger of wildfires, human deaths and water quality issues such as algal blooms.

Heavy rains. Scientific estimates suggest that extreme precipitation events—from downpours to whiteouts—are more than 90 percent likely to become more common, resulting in diminished water quality and increased flooding, crop damage, soil erosion and disease risk.

Drought. Scientists estimate that there is a more than 66 percent chance that droughts will become more frequent and widespread, making water scarcer, upping the risk of starvation through failed crops and further increasing the risk of wildfires.

Stronger storms. Warming ocean waters will likely increase the power of tropical cyclones (variously known as hurricanes and typhoons), raising the risk of human death, injury, and disease as well as destroying coral reefs and property.

Biodiversity. As many as a third of the species known to science may be at risk of extinction if average temperatures rise by more than 1.5 degrees Celsius.

Sea level rise. The level of the world's oceans will rise, likely inundating low-lying land, turning freshwater brackish and potentially triggering widespread migration of human populations from affected areas.

"As temperatures rise, thermal expansion will lead to sea-level rise, independent of melting ice," says chemical engineer Lenny Bernstein, another lead author of the recent IPCC report. "The indications are that this factor alone could cause serious problems [and] ice-sheet melting would greatly accelerate [it]."

Such ice-sheet melting, which the IPCC explicitly did not include in its predictions of sea-level rise, has already been observed and may be speeding up, according to recent research that determined that the melting of Greenland's ice cap has accelerated to six times the average flow of the Colorado River. Research has also shown that the world has consistently emitted greenhouse gases at the highest projected levels examined and sea-level rise has also outpaced projections from the IPCC's last assessment in 2001.

"We are above the high scenario now," says climatologist Stephen Schneider of Stanford University, an IPCC lead author. "This is not a safe world."

Other recent findings include:

Carbon intensity increasing. The amount of carbon dioxide per car built, burger served or widget sold had been consistently declining until the turn of the century. But since 2000, CO_2 emissions have grown by more than 3 percent annually. This is largely due to the economic booms in China and India, which rely on polluting coal to power production. But emissions in the developed world have started to rise as well, increasing by 2.6 percent since 2000, according to reports made by those countries to the United Nations Framework Convention on Climate Change. Researchers at the Massachusetts Institute of Technology also recently argued that U.S. emissions may continue to increase as a result of growing energy demand.

Carbon sinks slowing.   The world's oceans and forests are absorbing less of the CO_2 released by human activity, resulting in a faster rise in atmospheric levels of greenhouse gases. All told, humanity released 9.9 billion metric tons (2.18×10^{13} pounds) of carbon in 2006 at the same time that the ability of the North Atlantic to take in such emissions, for example, dropped by 50 percent.

Impacts accelerating.   Warming temperatures have prompted earlier springs in the far north and have caused plant species to spread farther into formerly icy terrain. Meanwhile, sea ice in the Arctic reached a record low this year, covering just 1.59 million square miles and thus shattering the previous 2005 minimum of 2.05 million square miles.

"The observed rate of loss is faster than anything predicted," says senior research scientist Mark Serreze of the U.S. National Snow and Ice Data Center in Boulder, Colo. "We're already set up for another big loss next year. We've got so much open water in the Arctic now that has absorbed so much energy over the summer that the ocean has warmed. The ice that grows back this autumn will be thin."

The negative consequences of such reinforcing, positive feedbacks (white ice is replaced by dark water, which absorbs more energy and prevents the formation of more white ice) remain even when they seemingly work in our favor.

For example, scientists at the Leibniz Institute of Marine Sciences at the University of Kiel in Germany recently discovered that plankton consumes more carbon at higher atmospheric concentrations of CO_2. "The plankton were carbon-enriched," says marine biologist Ulf Riebesell, who conducted the study. "There weren't more of them, but each cell had more carbon."

This could mean that microscopic ocean plants may potentially absorb more of the carbon emitted into the atmosphere. Unfortunately, other research (from the Woods Hole Oceanographic Institution) has shown that such plankton does not make it to the seafloor in large enough amounts to sequester the carbon in the long term.

Further, such carbon-heavy plankton do not begin to appear until CO_2 concentrations reach twice present values—750 parts per million (ppm) in the atmosphere compared with roughly 380 ppm presently (a level at which catastrophic change may be a certainty)—and they are less nutritious to all the animals that rely on them for food. "This mechanism is both too small and too late," Riebesell says. "By becoming more carbon-rich, zooplankton have to eat more phytoplankton to achieve the same nutrition" and, therefore, "they grow and reproduce more slowly."

The IPCC notes that there are cost-effective solutions, such as retrofitting buildings for energy efficiency, but says they must be implemented in short order to stem further damage. "We are 25 years too late," Schneider says. "If the object is to avoid dangerous change, we've already had it. The object now is to avoid really dangerous change."

Richard S. Lindzen   → **NO**

No Global Warming

According to Al Gore's new film "An Inconvenient Truth," we're in for "a planetary emergency": melting ice sheets, huge increases in sea levels, more and stronger hurricanes, and invasions of tropical disease, among other cataclysms—unless we change the way we live now.

Bill Clinton has become the latest evangelist for Mr. Gore's proposal, proclaiming that current weather events show that he and Mr. Gore were right about global warming, and we are all suffering the consequences of President Bush's obtuseness on the matter. And why not? Mr. Gore assures us that "the debate in the scientific community is over."

That statement, which Mr. Gore made in an interview with George Stephanopoulos on ABC, ought to have been followed by an asterisk. What exactly is this debate that Mr. Gore is referring to? Is there really a scientific community that is debating all these issues and then somehow agreeing in unison? Far from such a thing being over, it has never been clear to me what this "debate" actually is in the first place.

The media rarely help, of course. When *Newsweek* featured global warming in a 1988 issue, it was claimed that all scientists agreed. Periodically thereafter it was revealed that although there had been lingering doubts beforehand, now all scientists did indeed agree. Even Mr. Gore qualified his statement on ABC only a few minutes after he made it, clarifying things in an important way. When Mr. Stephanopoulos confronted Mr. Gore with the fact that the best estimates of rising sea levels are far less dire than he suggests in his movie, Mr. Gore defended his claims by noting that scientists "don't have any models that give them a high level of confidence" one way or the other and went on to claim—*in his defense*—that scientists "don't know. . . . They just don't know."

So, presumably, those scientists do not belong to the "consensus." Yet their research is forced, whether the evidence supports it or not, into Mr. Gore's preferred global warming template—namely, shrill alarmism. To believe it requires that one ignore the truly inconvenient facts. To take the issue of rising sea levels, these include: that the Arctic was as warm or warmer in 1940; that icebergs have been known since time immemorial;

From *Environmental News*, August 2006; originally appeared in *The Wall Street Journal*, July 2, 2006. Copyright © 2006 by Dow Jones & Company, Inc. Reprinted by permission of Dow Jones & Company, Inc. via the Copyright Clearance Center.

that the evidence so far suggests that the Greenland ice sheet is actually growing on average. A likely result of all this is increased pressure pushing ice off the coastal perimeter of that country, which is depicted so ominously in Mr. Gore's movie. In the absence of factual context, these images are perhaps dire or alarming.

They are less so otherwise. Alpine glaciers have been retreating since the early 19th century, and were advancing for several centuries before that. Since about 1970, many of the glaciers have stopped retreating and some are now advancing again. And, frankly, we don't know why.

The other elements of the global-warming scare scenario are predicated on similar oversights. Malaria, claimed as a byproduct of warming, was once common in Michigan and Siberia and remains common in Siberia—mosquitoes don't require tropical warmth. Hurricanes, too, vary on multidecadal time scales; sea-surface temperature is likely to be an important factor. This temperature, itself, varies on multidecadal time scales. However, questions concerning the origin of the relevant sea-surface temperatures and the nature of trends in hurricane intensity are being hotly argued within the profession. Even among those arguing, there is general agreement that we can't attribute any particular hurricane to global warming. To be sure, there is one exception, Greg Holland of the National Center for Atmospheric Research in Boulder, Colo., who argues that it must be global warming because he can't think of anything else. While arguments like these, based on lassitude, are becoming rather common in climate assessments, such claims, given the primitive state of weather and climate science, are hardly compelling.

A general characteristic of Mr. Gore's approach is to assiduously ignore the fact that the Earth and its climate are dynamic; they are always changing even without any external forcing. To treat all change as something to fear is bad enough; to do so in order to exploit that fear is much worse. Regardless, these items are clearly not issues over which debate is ended—at least not in terms of the actual science.

A clearer claim as to what debate has ended is provided by the environmental journalist Gregg Easterbrook. He concludes that the scientific community now agrees that significant warming is occurring, and that there is clear evidence of human influences on the climate system. This is still a most peculiar claim. At some level, it has never been widely contested. Most of the climate community has agreed since 1988 that global mean temperatures have increased on the order of one degree Fahrenheit over the past century, having risen significantly from about 1919 to 1940, decreased between 1940 and the early '70s, increased again until the '90s, and remaining essentially flat since 1998.

There is also little disagreement that levels of carbon dioxide in the atmosphere have risen from about 280 parts per million by volume in the 19th century to about 387 ppmv today. Finally, there has been no question whatever that carbon dioxide is an infrared absorber (i.e., a greenhouse gas—albeit a minor one), and its increase should theoretically contribute to warming. Indeed, if all else were kept equal, the increase in carbon dioxide should have led to somewhat more warming than has been observed, assuming that the small observed increase was in fact due to increasing carbon dioxide rather than a natural fluctuation in the climate system. Although no cause for alarm rests on this issue, there has been an intense effort to claim that the theoretically expected contribution from additional carbon dioxide has actually been detected.

Given that we do not understand the natural internal variability of climate change, this task is currently impossible. Nevertheless there has been a persistent effort to suggest otherwise, and with surprising impact. Thus, although the conflicted state of the affair was accurately presented in the 1996 text of the Intergovernmental Panel on Climate Change, the infamous "summary for policy makers" reported ambiguously that "The balance of evidence suggests a discernible human influence on global climate." This sufficed as the smoking gun for Kyoto.

The next IPCC report again described the problems surrounding what has become known as the attribution issue: that is, to explain what mechanisms are responsible for observed changes in climate. Some deployed the lassitude argument—e.g., we can't think of an alternative—to support human attribution. But the "summary for policy makers" claimed in a manner largely unrelated to the actual text of the report that "In the light of new evidence and taking into account the remaining uncertainties, most of the observed warming over the last 50 years is likely to have been due to the increase in greenhouse gas concentrations."

In a similar vein, the National Academy of Sciences issued a brief (15-page) report responding to questions from the White House. It again enumerated the difficulties with attribution, but again the report was preceded by a front end that ambiguously claimed that "The changes observed over the last several decades are likely mostly due to human activities, but we cannot rule out that some significant part of these changes is also a reflection of natural variability." This was sufficient for CNN's Michelle Mitchell to presciently declare that the report represented a "unanimous decision that global warming is real, is getting worse and is due to man. There is no wiggle room." Well, no.

More recently, a study in the journal *Science* by the social scientist Nancy Oreskes claimed that a search of the ISI Web of Knowledge Database for the years 1993 to 2003 under the key words "global climate change" produced 928 articles, all of whose abstracts supported what she referred to as the consensus view. A British social scientist, Benny Peiser, checked her procedure and found that only 913 of the 928 articles had abstracts at all, and that only 13 of the remaining 913 explicitly endorsed the so-called consensus view. Several actually opposed it.

Even more recently, the Climate Change Science Program, the Bush administration's coordinating agency for global-warming research, declared it had found "clear evidence of human influences on the climate system." This, for Mr. Easterbrook, meant: "Case closed." What exactly was this evidence? The models imply that greenhouse warming should impact atmospheric temperatures more than surface temperatures, and yet satellite data showed no warming in the atmosphere since 1979. The report showed that selective corrections to the atmospheric data could lead to some warming, thus reducing the conflict between observations and models descriptions of what greenhouse warming should look like. That, to me, means the case is still very much open.

So what, then, is one to make of this alleged debate? I would suggest at least three points.

First, nonscientists generally do not want to bother with understanding the science. Claims of consensus relieve policy types, environmental advocates, and politicians of any need to do so. Such claims also serve to intimidate the public and even scientists—especially those outside the area of climate dynamics.

Secondly, given that the question of human attribution largely cannot be resolved, its use in promoting visions of disaster constitutes nothing so much as a bait-and-switch scam. That is an inauspicious beginning to what Mr. Gore claims is not a political issue but a "moral" crusade.

Lastly, there is a clear attempt to establish truth not by scientific methods but by perpetual repetition. An earlier attempt at this was accompanied by tragedy. Perhaps Marx was right. This time around we may have farce—if we're lucky.

POSTSCRIPT

Is the Threat of Global Warming Real?

T he issue of global warming is to the current era what acid rain was to the 1970s. Just as the blighted trees and polluted lakes of Scandinavia captured the hearts of the then newly emerging group of environmentalists, the issue of global warming has been front page news for over a decade and fodder for environmentalists and policymakers everywhere. Library citations abound, making it the most often written about global issue today. Web sites pop up, public interest groups emerge, and scientists and nonscientists pick up the rallying cry for one side or another. "Googling" the words "global warming" on the Internet yields over 44 million responses.

In a sense, the issue of global warming is a prototype of the contemporary issue making its way onto the global agenda. Recall that a global issue is characterized by disagreement over the extent of the condition, disagreement over the causes of the condition, disagreement over desirable future alternatives to the present condition, and disagreement over appropriate policies to reach desired end states.

All of these characteristics are present in global warming. Both sides of the issue can find a substantial number of scientists, measured in the thousands, to support their case that the Earth is or is not warming. Both sides can find hundreds of experts who will attest that the warming is either a cyclical phenomenon or the consequence of human behavior. Both sides can find a substantial number of policymakers and policy observers who will say that the Kyoto Treaty is humankind's best hope to reverse the global warming trend or that the treaty is seriously flawed with substantial negative consequences for the United States. It is an issue whose debate heats up on occasion as the international community grapples with answers to the various disagreements summarized above. Finally, it is an issue whose potential solutions will impact different sectors of the economy and different countries differently.

The IPCC 2001 report concludes the following. First, the global average surface temperature has risen over the twentieth century by about 0.6°C. Two, temperatures have risen during the past four decades in the lowest 8 kilometers of the atmosphere. Third, snow cover and ice extent have decreased. Fourth, global average sea level has risen, and ocean heat has increased. Fifth, changes have occurred in other important aspects of climate. Sixth, concentrations of atmospheric greenhouse gases have continued to increase as a result of human activity. Seventh, there is new and stronger evidence that most of the warming observed over the last 50 years is attributable to human activities. Eighth, human influences will continue to change atmospheric composition throughout the twenty-first century. Ninth, global average temperature and sea level are projected to rise under all IPCC scenarios. And tenth, climate change will persist for many centuries. The list is impressive.

The 2007 IPCC report suggested the following conclusions:. First, "warming of the climate system is unequivocal." Second, many natural systems around the world "are being affected by regional climate changes." Third, global greenhouse gases have grown 70 percent between 1970 and 2004. Fourth, global emissions of greenhouse gases "will continue to grow over the next few decades." And fifth, the consequences of these four conclusions will lead to the set of risks mentioned earlier.

Yet others argue the opposite position. In their comprehensive book on the subject (*Taken by Storm: The Troubled Science, Policy and Politics of Global Warming*, Key Porter Books, 2002), Christopher Essex and Ross McKitrick lay out a series of nine statements that comprise the "Doctrine" of global warming. In their analysis of these components, they conclude that the evidence simply does not warrant the global community's undertaking policy making at this time to address a problem that may not exist or may have been caused by some other phenomena.

Richard Lindzen has been an active critic of global warming advocates, testifying before the American Congress from time to time as well as publishing in the more popular media (see, for example, "Climate of Fear," *The Wall Street Journal*, April 12, 2006).

This view is a shared one. Brian Tucker's 1997 article in *The National Interest* ("Science Fiction: The Politics of Global Warming") suggests that science "does not support the conclusion that calamitous effects from global warming are nigh upon us." He continues: "There is no scientific justification for such a view." Tucker raises the stakes by asserting that the global warming controversy is much more than a debate about the causes and extent of the phenomenon. It is also about global development, power, and morality in the struggle between the rich and poor countries, with population "control" a central issue.

This view is echoed by John R. Christy in "The Global Warming Fiasco" (*Global Warming and Other Eco-Myths*, Ronald Bailey, Forum, 2002). He accuses those who suggest global warming is a major problem of adhering to the science of "calamitology" rather than the science of "climatology." His bottom line assessment is that "No global climate disaster is looming."

The Heartland Institute (www.heartland.org/studies/ieguide.htm) suggests "seven facts" to counteract observations such as those of the recent and earlier IPCC studies. First, "most scientists do not believe human activities threaten to disrupt the earth's climate." Second, "the most reliable temperature data show no global warming trend." Third, "global computer models are too crude to predict future climate changes." Fourth, "the IPCC did not prove that human activities are causing global warming" (a reference to the 1995 study). Fifth, "a modest amount of global warming, should it occur, would be beneficial to the natural world and to human civilization." Sixth, "reducing our greenhouse gas emissions would be costly and would not stop global warming." And seventh, "the best strategy to pursue is one of 'no regrets'." The latter refers to the idea that it is not better to be safe than sorry (suggested by the other side), as immediate action will not make us safer, just poorer. Another sharp critique of the 2001 IPCC report is a web-based book by Vincent Gray, *The Greenhouse Delusion: Critique of "Climate Change 2001": The Scientific Basis* (http://www.john-daly.com/tar-2000/summary.htm). Another oft-published critic is Bill McKibben (see, for example, "The Real News About Global Warming," *The New York Review of Books,* March 15, 2007).

The above references capture the extreme distance between the two sides in the debate. Other sources are equally certain of their position. Ross Gelbson in *The Heat Is On: The High Stakes Battle Over Earth's Threatened Climate* (Addison-Wesley, 1997) examines "the campaign of deception by big coal and big oil" that is keeping the global warming issue off the public policy agenda.

Three other studies make valuable reading, each one of which takes a different position (one each at the extreme ends of the debate and a third one that suggests moderate climate change.) S. Fred Singer's *Hot Talk; Cold Science: Global Warming's Unfinished Debate* (Independent Institute, 1998) enhances the author's reputation as one of the leading opponents of global warming's adverse consequences. At the other extreme, John Houghton in *Global Warming: The Complete Briefing,* 2d ed. (Cambridge University Press, 1997) accepts global warming as a significant concern and describes how it can be reversed in the future. S. George Philander, in *Is the Temperature Rising?* (1998), concludes that the global temperatures will rise 2°C over several decades, creating the prospect of some regional climate changes, with major consequences. Roy W. Spencer's "How Do We Know the Temperature of the Earth?" (Ronald Bailey, ed., *Earth Report 2000,* 2000), presents a basic argument with evidence that the popular perception of global warming as an environmental catastrophe cannot be supported with evidence. Finally, an objective analysis of the issue can be found in Chapter 5 ("Is the Earth Warming?") of Jack M. Hollander's *The Real Environmental Crisis* (University of California Press, 2003).

For an official U.S. government Web site on global warming, see http://www.epa.gov/climatechange/index.html. Another U.S. government site is www.usgcrp.gov. A relevant Web site for a worldwide network of over 430 nongovernmental organizations, termed the Climate Action Network (CAN), is http://www.climatenetwork.org. Another site is http://earthsave.org/globalwarming.htm (EarthSave).

A book that presents in layman's terms the story of global warming is *Time Magazine's Global Warming* (2007). Al Gore's documentary, *An Inconvenient Truth* (both in DVD and in print), has become the poster source for those who support the link between human behavior and rises in global temperature. A source arguing that global warming is a recurring phenomenon and is caused by the sun is *Unstoppable Global Warming: Every 1,500 Years* by Dennis T. Avery and S. Fred Singer (Roman & Littlefield, 2007). Other anti-global warming books are Christopher C. Horner's *The Politically*

Incorrect Guide to Global Warming and Environmentalism (Regnery Publishers, 2007), *Shattered Consensus: The True State of Global Warming* by Patrick J. Michaels (Rowan & Littlefield, 2005), *Meltdown: The Predictable Distortion of Global Warming by Scientists, Politicians and the Media* (CATO Institute, 2005), and S. Fred Singer's *Unstoppable Global Warming: Every 1,500 Years* (Rowan & Littlefield, 2008). A much more balanced book that lays out the conflicting claims in the debate is *The Science and Politics of Global Climate Change: A Guide to the Debate* by Andrew E. Dessler and Edward A. Parson (Cambridge University Press, 2006). An earlier readable and balanced account is Frances Drake's *Global Warming: The Science of Climate Change* (Hodder Arnold Publication, 2000).

What are we to make of all of this? Simply put, whether or not global warming exists and is caused by human behavior, the issue will remain on the front page until agreement can be reached on these two fundamental questions.

ISSUE 9

Is the Threat of a Global Water Shortage Real?

YES: Mark W. Rosegrant, Ximing Cai, and Sarah A. Cline, from "Global Water Outlook to 2025: Averting an Impending Crisis," A Report of the International Food Policy Research Institute and the International Water Management Institute (September 2002)

NO: Bjørn Lomborg, from *The Skeptical Environment: Measuring the Real State of the World* (Cambridge University Press, 2001)

ISSUE SUMMARY

YES: Rosegrant and colleagues conclude that if current water policies continue, farmers will find it difficult to grow sufficient food to meet the world's needs.

NO: Lomborg contends that water is not only plentiful but is a renewable resource that, if properly treated as valuable, should not pose a future problem.

Water shortages and other water problems are occurring with greater frequency, particularly in large cities. Some observers have speculated that the situation is reminiscent of the fate that befell ancient glorious cities like Rome. Recognition that the supply of water is a growing problem is not new. As early as 1964, the United Nations Environmental Programme (UNEP) revealed that close to a billion people were at risk from desertification. At the Earth Summit in Rio in 1992, world leaders reaffirmed that desertification was of serious concern.

Moreover, in conference after conference and study after study, increasing population growth and declining water supplies and quality are being linked together, as is the relationship between the planet's ability to meet its growing food needs and available water. Lester R. Brown, in "Water Deficits Growing in Many Countries: Water Shortages May Cause Food Shortages," *Eco-Economy Update 2002–11* (August 6, 2002), sums up the problem this way: "The world is incurring a vast water deficit. It is largely invisible, historically recent, and growing fast." The World Water Council's study, "World Water Actions Report, Third Draft" (October 31, 2002), describes the problem in much the same way: "Water is no longer taken for granted as a plentiful resource that will always be available when we need it." Some scholars are now arguing that water shortage is likely to become the twenty-first century's analog to the oil crisis of the last half of the previous century. The one major difference, as scholars are quick to point out, is that water is not like oil; there is no substitute.

Proclamations of impending water problems abound. Peter Gleick, in *The World's Water 1998–99: The Biennial Report on Freshwater Resources* (Island Press, 1998), reports that the demand for freshwater increased six-fold between 1900 and 1995, twice the rate of population growth. The UN study "United Nations Comprehensive Assessment of Freshwater Resources of the World" (1997) suggested that one-third of the world's population live in countries having medium to high water stress. One 2001 headline reporting the release of a new study proclaimed that "Global thirst 'will turn millions into water refugees'" (The Millennium Environment Debate). News reports released by the UN Food and Agricultural Organization in conjunction with World Food Day 2002 asserted that water scarcity could result in millions of people having inadequate access to clean water or sufficient food. And the World Meteorological Organization predicts that two out of every three people will live in water-stressed conditions by 2050 if consumption patterns remain the same.

Sandra Postel, in *Pillar of Sand: Can the Irrigation Miracle Last?* (W.W. Norton, 1999) suggests another variant of the water problem. For her, the time-tested method of maximizing water usage in the past, irrigation, may not be feasible as world population marches toward seven billion. She points to the inadequacy of surface water supplies, increasing depletion of groundwater supplies, the salinization of the land, and the conversion of traditional agricultural land to other uses as reasons for the likely inability of irrigation to be a continuing panacea. Yet the 1997 UN study concluded that annual irrigation use would need to increase 30 percent for annual food production to double, necessary for meeting food demands of 2025.

The issue of water quality is also in the news. The World Health Organization reports that in some parts of the world, up to 80 percent of all transmittable diseases are attributable to the consumption of contaminated water. Also, a UNEP-sponsored study, *Global Environment Outlook 2000,* reported that 200 scientists from 50 countries pointed to the shortage of clean water as one of the most pressing global issues.

Mark W. Rosegrant, Ximing Cai, and Sarah A. Cline project that by 2025, water scarcity will result in annual global losses of 350 million metric tons. In the second selection, Bjørn Lomborg takes issue with the prevailing wind in the global water debate. His argument can be summed up in his simple quote: "Basically we have sufficient water." Lomborg maintains that water supplies rose during the twentieth century and that we have gained access to more water through technology.

YES ↵

Mark W. Rosegrant, Ximing Cai, and Sarah A. Cline

Global Water Outlook to 2025: Averting an Impending Crisis

Introduction

Demand for the world's increasingly scarce water supply is rising rapidly, challenging its availability for food production and putting global food security at risk. Agriculture, upon which a burgeoning population depends for food, is competing with industrial, household, and environmental uses for this scarce water supply. Even as demand for water by all users grows, groundwater is being depleted, other water ecosystems are becoming polluted and degraded, and developing new sources of water is getting more costly.

A Thirsty World

Water development underpins food security, people's livelihoods, industrial growth, and environmental sustainability throughout the world. In 1995 the world withdrew 3,906 cubic kilometers (km^3) of water for these purposes (Figure 1). By 2025 water withdrawal for most uses (domestic, industrial, and livestock) is projected to increase by at least 50 percent. This will severely limit irrigation water withdrawal, which will increase by only 4 percent, constraining food production in turn.

About 250 million hectares are irrigated worldwide today, nearly five times more than at the beginning of the 20th century. Irrigation has helped boost agricultural yields and outputs and stabilize food production and prices. But growth in population and income will only increase the demand for irrigation water to meet food production requirements (Figure 2). Although the achievements of irrigation have been impressive, in many regions poor irrigation management has markedly lowered groundwater tables, damaged soils, and reduced water quality.

Water is also essential for drinking and household uses and for industrial production. Access to safe drinking water and sanitation is critical to maintain health, particularly for children. But more than 1 billion people

Excerpts from the *2020 Vision Food Policy Report*. Washington, DC, and Colombo, Sri Lanka: International Food Policy Research Institute and International Water Management Institute. Excerpted and reproduced with permission from the International Food Policy Research Institute www.ifpri.org and the International Water Management Institute www.iwmi.cgiar.org. The report from which these excerpts come can be found online at http://www.ifpri.org/pubs/fpr/ fprwater2025.pdf.

Figure 1

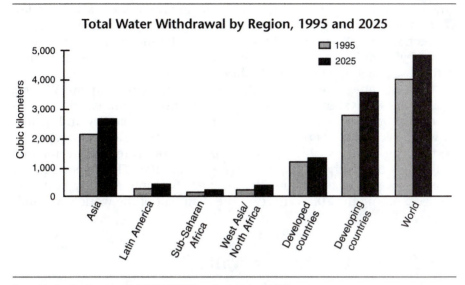

Total Water Withdrawal by Region, 1995 and 2025

Source: Authors' estimates and IMPACT-WATER projections, June 2002.
Note: Projections for 2025 are for the business as usual scenario.

Figure 2

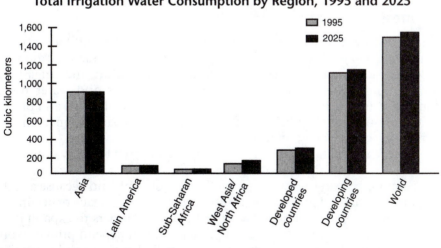

Total Irrigation Water Consumption by Region, 1995 and 2025

Source: Authors' estimates and IMPACT-WATER projections, June 2002.
Note: Projections for 2025 are for the business as usual scenario.

across the globe lack enough safe water to meet minimum levels of health and income. Although the domestic and industrial sectors use far less water than agriculture, the growth in water consumption in these sectors has been rapid. Globally, withdrawals for domestic and industrial uses quadrupled between 1950 and 1995, compared with agricultural uses, for which withdrawals slightly more than doubled.[1]

Water is integrally linked to the health of the environment. Water is vital to the survival of ecosystems and the plants and animals that live in them, and in turn ecosystems help to regulate the quantity and quality of water. Wetlands retain water during high rainfall, release it during dry periods, and purify it of many contaminants. Forests reduce erosion and sedimentation of rivers and recharge groundwater. The importance of reserving water for environmental purposes has only recently been recognized: during the 20th century, more than half of the world's wetlands were lost.[2]

Alternative Futures for Water

The future of water and food is highly uncertain. Some of this uncertainty is due to relatively uncontrollable factors such as weather. But other critical factors can be influenced by the choices made collectively by the world's people. These factors include income and population growth, investment in water infrastructure, allocation of water to various uses, reform in water management, and technological changes in agriculture. Policy decisions— and the actions of billions of individuals—determine these fundamental, long-term drivers of water and food supply and demand.

To show the very different outcomes that policy choices produce, we present three alternative futures for global water.[3] . . .

Business As Usual Scenario

In the business as usual scenario current trends in water and food policy, management, and investment remain as they are. International donors and national governments, complacent about agriculture and irrigation, cut their investments in these sectors. Governments and water users implement institutional and management reforms in a limited and piecemeal fashion. These conditions leave the world ill prepared to meet major challenges to the water and food sectors.

Over the coming decades the area of land devoted to cultivating food crops will grow slowly in most of the world because of urbanization, soil degradation, and slow growth in irrigation investment, and because a high proportion of arable land is already cultivated. Moreover, steady or declining real prices for cereals will make it unprofitable for farmers to expand harvested area. As a result, greater food production will depend primarily on increases in yield. Yet growth in crop yields will also diminish because of falling public investment in agricultural research and rural infrastructure. Moreover, many of the actions that produced yield gains in recent decades, such as increasing the density of crop planting, introducing strains that are more responsive to fertilizer, and improving management practices, cannot easily be repeated.

In the water sector, the management of river basin and irrigation water will become more efficient, but slowly. Governments will continue to transfer management of irrigation systems to farmer organizations and water-user associations. Such transfers will increase water efficiency when they are built upon existing patterns of cooperation and backed by a supportive policy and legal environment. But these conditions are often lacking.

In some regions farmers will adopt more efficient irrigation practices. Economic incentives to induce more efficient water management, however, will still face political opposition from those concerned about the impact of higher water prices on farmers' income and from entrenched interests that benefit from existing systems of allocating water. Water management will also improve slowly in rainfed agriculture as a result of small advances in water harvesting, better on-farm management techniques, and the development of crop varieties with shorter growing seasons.

Public investment in expanding irrigation systems and reservoir storage will decline as the financial, environmental, and social costs of building new irrigation systems escalate and the prices of cereals and other irrigated crops drop. Nevertheless, where benefits outweigh costs, many governments will construct dams, and reservoir water for irrigation will increase moderately.

With slow growth in irrigation from surface water, farmers will expand pumping from groundwater, which is subject to low prices and little regulation. Regions that currently pump groundwater faster than aquifers can recharge, such as the western United States, northern China, northern and western India, Egypt, and West Asia and North Africa, will continue to do so.

The cost of supplying water to domestic and industrial users will rise dramatically. Better delivery and more efficient home water use will lead to some increase in the proportion of households connected to piped water. Many households, however, will remain unconnected. Small price increases for industrial water, improvements in pollution control regulation and enforcement, and new industrial technologies will cut industrial water use intensity (water demand per $1,000 of gross domestic product). Yet industrial water prices will remain relatively low and pollution regulations will often be poorly enforced. Thus, significant potential gains will be lost.

Environmental and other interest groups will press to increase the amount of water allocated to preserving wetlands, diluting pollutants, maintaining riparian flora and other aquatic species, and supporting tourism and recreation. Yet because of competition for water for other uses, the share of water devoted to environmental uses will not increase.

The water situation   Almost all users will place heavy demands on the world's water supply under the business as usual scenario. Total global water withdrawals in 2025 are projected to increase by 22 percent above 1995 withdrawals, to 4,772 km^3 (see Figure 1).[4] Projected withdrawals in developing countries will increase 27 percent over the 30-year period, while developed-country withdrawals will increase by 11 percent.[5]

Together, consumption of water for domestic, industrial, and livestock uses—that is, all nonirrigation uses—will increase dramatically, rising by 62 percent from 1995 to 2025. Because of rapid population growth and rising per capita water use, total domestic consumption will increase by 71 percent, of which more than 90 percent will be in developing countries. Conservation and technological improvements will lower per capita domestic water use in developed countries with the highest per capita water consumption.

Industrial water use will grow much faster in developing countries than in developed countries. In 1995 industries in developed countries consumed much more water than industries in the developing world. By 2025, however, developing-world industrial water demand is projected to increase to 121 km^3, 7 km^3 greater than in the developed world. The intensity of industrial water use will decrease worldwide, especially in developing countries (where initial intensity levels are very high), thanks to improvements in water-saving technology and demand policy. Nonetheless, the sheer size of the increase in the world's industrial production will still lead to an increase in total industrial water demand.

Direct water consumption by livestock is very small compared with other sectors. But the rapid increase of livestock production, particularly in developing countries, means that livestock water demand is projected to increase 71 percent between 1995 and 2025. Whereas livestock water demand will increase only 19 percent in the developed world between 1995 and 2025, it is projected to more than double in the developing world, from 22 to 45 km^3.

Although irrigation is by far the largest user of the world's water, use of irrigation water is projected to rise much more slowly than other sectors. For irrigation water, we have computed both potential demand and actual consumption. Potential demand is the demand for irrigation water in the absence of any water supply constraints, whereas actual consumption of irrigation water is the realized water demand, given the limitations of water supply for irrigation. The proportion of potential demand that is realized in actual consumption is the irrigation water supply reliability index (IWSR).[6] An IWSR of 1.0 would mean that all potential demand is being met.

Potential irrigation demand will grow by 12 percent in developing countries, while it will actually decline in developed countries by 1.5 percent. The fastest growth in potential demand for irrigation water will occur in Sub-Saharan Africa, with an increase of 27 percent, and in Latin America, with an increase of 21 percent. Each of these regions has a high percentage increase in irrigated area from a relatively low 1995 level. India is projected to have the highest absolute growth in potential irrigation water demand, 66 km^3 (17 percent), owing to relatively rapid growth in irrigated area from an already high level in 1995. West Asia and North Africa will increase by 18 percent (28 km^3, mainly in Turkey), while China will experience a much smaller increase of 4 percent (12 km^3). In Asia as a region, potential irrigation water demand will increase by 8 percent (100 km^3).

Water scarcity for irrigation will intensify, with actual consumption of irrigation water worldwide projected to grow more slowly than potential consumption, increasing only 4 percent between 1995 and 2025. In developing countries a declining fraction of potential demand will be met over time. The IWSR for developing countries will decline from 0.81 in 1995 to 0.75 in 2025, and in dry river basins the decline will be steeper. For example, in the Haihe River Basin in China, which is an important wheat and maize producer and serves major metropolitan areas, the IWSR is projected to decline from 0.78 to 0.62, and in the Ganges of India, the IWSR will decline from 0.83 to 0.67.

In the developed world, the situation is the reverse: the supply of irrigation water is projected to grow faster than potential demand (although certain basins will face increasing water scarcity). Increases in river basin efficiency will more than offset the very small increase in irrigated area. As a result, after initially declining from 0.87 to 0.85 in 2010, the IWSR will improve to 0.90 in 2025, thanks to slowing growth of domestic and industrial demand (and actual declines in total domestic and industrial water use in the United States and Europe) and more efficient use of irrigation water. . . .

Water Crisis Scenario

A moderate worsening of many of the current trends in water and food policy and in investment could build to a genuine water crisis. In the water crisis scenario, government budget problems worsen. Governments further cut their spending on irrigation systems and accelerate the turnover of irrigation systems to farmers and farmer groups but without the necessary reforms in water rights. Attempts to fund operations and maintenance in the main water system, still operated by public agencies, cause water prices to irrigators to rise. Water users fight price increases, and conflict spills over to local management and cost-sharing arrangements. Spending on the operation and maintenance of secondary and tertiary systems falls dramatically, and deteriorating infrastructure and poor management lead to falling water use efficiency. Likewise, attempts to organize river basin organizations to coordinate water management fail because of inadequate funding and high levels of conflict among water stakeholders within the basin.

National governments and international donors will reduce their investments in crop breeding for rainfed agriculture in developing countries, especially for staple crops such as rice, wheat, maize, other coarse grains, potatoes, cassava, yams, and sweet potatoes. Private agricultural research will fail to fill the investment gap for these commodities. This loss of research funding will lead to further declines in productivity growth in rainfed crop areas, particularly in more marginal areas. In search of improved incomes, people will turn to slash-and-burn agriculture, thereby deforesting the upper watersheds of many basins. Erosion and sediment loads in rivers will rise, in turn causing faster sedimentation of reservoir storage. People will increasingly encroach on wetlands for both land and water, and the integrity and health of aquatic ecosystems will be compromised. The amount of water reserved for environmental purposes will decline as unregulated and illegal withdrawals increase.

The cost of building new dams will soar, discouraging new investment in many proposed dam sites. At other sites indigenous groups and nongovernmental organizations (NGOs) will mount opposition, often violent, over the environmental and human impacts of new dams. These protests and high costs will virtually halt new investment in medium and large dams and storage reservoirs. Net reservoir storage will decline in developing countries and remain constant in developed countries.

In the attempt to get enough water to grow their crops, farmers will extract increasing amounts of groundwater for several years, driving down water tables. But because of the accelerated pumping, after 2010 key aquifers in northern China, northern and northwestern India, and West Asia and North Africa will begin to fail. With declining water tables, farmers will find the cost of extracting water too high, and a big drop in groundwater extraction from these regions will further reduce water availability for all uses.

As in the business as usual scenario, the rapid increase in urban populations will quickly raise demand for domestic water. But governments will lack the funds to extend piped water and sewage disposal to newcomers. Governments will respond by privatizing urban water and sanitation services in a rushed and poorly planned fashion. The new private water and sanitation firms will be undercapitalized and able to do little to connect additional populations to piped water. An increasing number and percentage of the urban population must rely on high-priced water from vendors or spend many hours fetching often-dirty water from standpipes and wells.

The water situation   The developing world will pay the highest price for the water crisis scenario. Total worldwide water consumption in 2025 will be 261 km^3 higher than under the business as usual scenario—a 13 percent increase—but much of this water will be wasted, of no benefit to anyone. Virtually all of the increase will go to irrigation, mainly because farmers will use water less efficiently and withdraw more water to compensate for water losses. The supply of irrigation water will be less reliable, except in regions where so much water is diverted from environmental uses to irrigation that it compensates for the lower water use efficiency.

For most regions, per capita demand for domestic water will be significantly lower than under the business as usual scenario, in both rural and urban areas. The result is that people will not have access to the water they need for drinking and sanitation. The total domestic demand under the water crisis scenario will be 162 km^3 in developing countries, 28 percent less than under business as usual; 64 km^3 in developed countries, 7 percent less than under business as usual; and 226 km^3 in the world, 23 percent less than under business as usual.

Demand for industrial water, on the other hand, will increase, owing to failed technological improvements and economic measures. In 2025 the total industrial water demand worldwide will be 80 km^3 higher than under the business as usual scenario—a 33 percent rise—without generating additional industrial production.

With water diverted to make up for less efficient water use, the water crisis scenario will hit environmental uses particularly hard. Compared with business as usual, environmental flows will drop significantly by 2025, with 380 km^3 less environmental flow in the developing world, 80 km^3 less in the developed world, and 460 km^3 less globally. . . .

Sustainable Water Scenario

A sustainable water scenario would dramatically increase the amount of water allocated to environmental uses, connect all urban households to piped water, and achieve higher per capita domestic water consumption, while maintaining food production at the levels described in the business as usual scenario. It would achieve greater social equity and environmental protection through both careful reform in the water sector and sound government action.

Governments and international donors will increase their investments in crop research, technological change, and reform of water management to boost water productivity and the growth of crop yields in rainfed agriculture. Accumulating evidence shows that even drought-prone and high-temperature rainfed environments have the potential for dramatic increases in yield. Breeding strategies will directly target these rainfed areas. Improved policies and increased investment in rural infrastructure will help link remote farmers to markets and reduce the risks of rainfed farming.

To stimulate water conservation and free up agricultural water for environmental, domestic, and industrial uses, the effective price of water to the agricultural sector will be gradually increased. Agricultural water price increases will be implemented through incentive programs that provide farmers income for the water that they save, such as charge-subsidy schemes that pay farmers for reducing water use, and through the establishment, purchase, and trading of water use rights. By 2025 agricultural water prices will be twice as high in developed countries and three times as high in developing countries as in the business as usual scenario. The government will simultaneously transfer water rights and the responsibility for operation and management of irrigation systems to communities and water user associations in many countries and regions. The transfer of rights and systems will be facilitated with an improved legal and institutional environment for preventing and eliminating conflict and with technical and organizational training and support. As a result, farmers will increase their on-farm investments in irrigation and water management technology, and the efficiency of irrigation systems and basin water use will improve significantly.

River basin organizations will be established in many water-scarce basins to allocate mainstream water among stakeholder interests. Higher funding and reduced conflict over water, thanks to better water management, will facilitate effective stakeholder participation in these organizations.

Farmers will be able to make more effective use of rainfall in crop production, thanks to breakthroughs in water harvesting systems and the adoption of advanced farming techniques, like precision agriculture, contour plowing, precision land leveling, and minimum-till and no-till technologies. These technologies will increase the share of rainfall that goes to infiltration and evapotranspiration.

Spurred by the rapidly escalating costs of building new dams and the increasingly apparent environmental and human resettlement costs, developing and developed countries will reassess their reservoir construction plans, with comprehensive analysis of the costs and benefits, including environmental and social effects, of proposed projects. As a result, many planned storage projects will be canceled, but others will proceed with support from civil society groups. Yet new storage capacity will be less necessary because rapid growth in rainfed crop yields will help reduce rates of reservoir sedimentation from erosion due to slash-and-burn cultivation.

Policy toward groundwater extraction will change significantly. Market-based approaches will assign rights to groundwater based on both annual withdrawals and the renewable stock of groundwater. This step will be combined with stricter regulations and better enforcement of these regulations. Groundwater overdrafts will be phased out in countries and regions that previously pumped groundwater unsustainably.

Domestic and industrial water use will also be subject to reforms in pricing and regulation. Water prices for connected households will double, with targeted subsidies for low-income households. Revenues from price increases will be invested to reduce water losses in existing systems and to extend piped water to previously unconnected households. By 2025 all households will be connected. Industries will respond to higher prices, particularly in developing countries, by increasing in-plant recycling of water, which reduces consumption of water.

With strong societal pressure for improved environmental quality, allocations for environmental uses of water will increase. Moreover, the reforms in agricultural and nonagricultural water sectors will reduce pressure on wetlands and other environmental uses of water. Greater investments and better water management will improve the efficiency of water use, leaving more water instream for environmental purposes. All reductions in domestic and urban water use, due to higher water prices, will be allocated to instream environmental uses.

The water situation   In the sustainable water scenario the world consumes less water but reaps greater benefits than under business as usual, especially in developing countries. In 2025, total worldwide water consumption is 408 km^3, or 20 percent, lower under the sustainable scenario than under business as usual. This reduction in consumption frees up water for environmental uses. Higher water prices and higher water use efficiency reduces consumption of irrigation water by 296 km^3 compared with business as usual. The reliability of irrigation water supply is reduced slightly in the sustainable scenario compared with business as usual, because this scenario places a high priority on environmental flows. Over time, however, more efficient water use in this scenario counterbalances the transfer of water to the environment and results in an improvement in the reliability of supply of irrigation water by 2025.

This scenario will improve the domestic water supply through universal access to piped water for rural and urban households. Globally, potential domestic water demand under the sustainable water scenario will decrease 9 percent compared with business as usual, owing to higher water prices. However, potential per capita domestic demand for connected households in rural areas will be 12 percent higher than that under business as usual in the developing world, and 5 percent higher in the developed world. This increase is accomplished by expanding universal access to piped water in rural areas even with higher prices for water. And in urban areas, potential per capita water consumption for poor households sharply improves through connection to piped water, while the initially connected households reduce consumption in response to higher prices and improved water-saving technology.

Through technological improvements and effective economic incentives, the sustainable water scenario will reduce industrial water demand. In 2025 total industrial water demand worldwide under the sustainable scenario will be 85 km^3, or 35 percent, lower than under business as usual.

The environment is a major beneficiary of the sustainable water scenario, with large increases in the amount of water reserved for wetlands, instream flows, and other environmental purposes. Compared with the business as usual scenario, the sustainable scenario will also result in an increase in the environmental flow of 850 km^3 in the developing world, 180 km^3 in the developed world, and 1,030 km^3 globally. This is the equivalent of transferring 22 percent of global water withdrawals under business as usual to environmental purposes.

Notes

1. W. J. Cosgrove and F. Rijsberman, *World Water Vision: Making Water Everybody's Business* (London: World Water Council and World Water Vision and Earthscan, 2000); I. A. Shiklomanov, "Electronic Data Provided to the Scenario Development Panel, World Commission on Water for the 21st Century" (State Hydrological Institute, St. Petersburg, Russia, 1999), mimeo.

2. E. Bos and G. Bergkamp, "Water and the Environment," in *Overcoming Water Scarcity and Quality Constraints,* 2020 Focus 9, ed. R. S. Meinzen-Dick

and M. W. Rosegrant (Washington, D.C.: International Food Policy Research Institute, 2001).

3. The business as usual, crisis, and sustainable scenarios are compared using average 2025 results generated from 30 hydrologic scenarios. The other scenarios are compared with business as usual based on a single 30-year hydrologic sequence drawn from 1961–90, and results are shown as the average of the years 2021–25.

4. Water demand can be defined and measured in terms of withdrawals and actual consumption. While water withdrawal is the most commonly estimated figure, consumption best captures actual water use, and most of our analysis will utilize this concept.

5. The global projection is broadly consistent with other recent projections to 2025, including the 4,580 km^3 in the medium scenario of J. Alcamo, P. Döll, F. Kaspar, and S. Sieberg, *Global Change and Global Scenarios of Water Use and Availability: An Application of Water GAP 1.0* (Kassel, Germany: Center for Environmental System Research, University of Kassel, 1998), the 4,569 km^3 in the "business-as-usual" scenario of D. Seckler, U. Amarasinghe, D. Molden, S. Rhadika, and R. Barker, *World Water Demand and Supply, 1990 to 2025: Scenarios and Issues,* Research Report Number 19 (Colombo, Sri Lanka: International Water Management Institute, 1998), and the forecast of 4,966 km^3 (not including reservoir evaporation) of Shiklomanov, "Electronic Data."

6. Compared with other sectors, the growth of irrigation water potential demand is much lower, with 12 percent growth in potential demand between 1995 and 2025 in developing countries and a slight decline in potential demand in developed countries.

Bjørn Lomborg

Water

Thereis a resource which we often take for granted but which increasingly has been touted as a harbinger of future trouble. Water.

Ever more people live on Earth and they use ever more water. Our water consumption has almost quadrupled since 1940. The obvious argument runs that "this cannot go on." This has caused government agencies to worry that "a threatening water crisis awaits just around the corner." The UN environmental report *GEO 2000* claims that the water shortage constitutes a "full-scale emergency," where "the world water cycle seems unlikely to be able to cope with the demands that will be made of it in the coming decades. Severe water shortages already hamper development in many parts of the world, and the situation is deteriorating."

The same basic argument is invoked when WWF [World Wildlife Fund] states that "freshwater is essential to human health, agriculture, industry, and natural ecosystems, but is now running scarce in many regions of the world." *Population Reports* states unequivocally that "freshwater is emerging as one of the most critical natural resource issues facing humanity." Environmental discussions are replete with buzz words like "water crisis" and "time bomb: water shortages," and *Time* magazine summarizes the global water outlook with the title "Wells running dry." The UN organizations for meteorology and education simply refer to the problem as "a world running out of water."

The water shortages are also supposed to increase the likelihood of conflicts over the last drops—and scores of articles are written about the coming "water wars." Worldwatch Institute sums up the worries nicely, claiming that "water scarcity may be to the nineties what the oil price shocks were to the seventies—a source of international conflicts and major shifts in national economies."

But these headlines are misleading. True, there may be *regional* and *logistic* problems with water. We will need to get better at using it. But basically we have sufficient water.

How Much Water in the World?

Water is absolutely decisive for human survival, and the Earth is called the Blue Planet precisely because most of it is covered by water: 71 percent of

Excerpt from chapter 13 of *The Skeptical Environmentalist: Measuring the Real State of the World,* by Bjørn Lomborg, (2001) pp. 149–156. Copyright © 2001 by Bjørn Lomborg and David Pimental. Reprinted by permission of Cambridge University Press and David Pimental.

the Earth's surface is covered by water, and the total amount is estimated at the unfathomably large 13.6 billion cubic kilometers. Of all this water, oceans make up 97.2 percent and the polar ice contains 2.15 percent. Unfortunately sea water is too saline for direct human consumption, and while polar ice contains potable water it is hardly within easy reach. Consequently, humans are primarily dependent on the last 0.65 percent water, of which 0.62 percent is groundwater.

Fresh water in the groundwater often takes centuries or millennia to build up—it has been estimated that it would require 150 years to recharge all of the groundwater in the United States totally to a depth of 750 meters if it were all removed. Thus, thoughtlessly exploiting the groundwater could be compared to mining any other non-renewable natural resource. But groundwater is continuously replenished by the constant movement of water through oceans, air, soil, rivers, and lakes in the so-called hydrological cycle. The sun makes water from the oceans evaporate, the wind moves parts of the vapor as clouds over land, where the water is released as rain and snow. The precipitated water then either evaporates again, flows back into the sea through rivers and lakes, or finds its way into the groundwater.

The total amount of precipitation on land is about 113,000 km^3, and taking into account an evaporation of 72,000 km^3 we are left with a net fresh water influx of 41,000 km^3 each year or the equivalent of 30 cm (1 foot) of water across the entire land mass. Since part of this water falls in rather remote areas, such as the basins of the Amazon, the Congo, and the remote North American and Eurasian rivers, a more reasonable, geographically accessible estimate of water is 32,900 km^3. Moreover, a large part of this water comes within short periods of time. In Asia, typically 80 percent of the runoff occurs from May to October, and globally the flood runoff is estimated at about three-quarters of the total runoff. This leaves about 9,000 km^3 to be captured. Dams capture an additional 3,500 km^3 from floods, bringing the total accessible runoff to 12,500 km^3. This is equivalent to about 5,700 liters of water for every single person on Earth *every single day*. For comparison, the average citizen in the EU uses about 566 liters of water per day. This is about 10 percent of the global level of available water and some 5 percent of the available EU water. An American, however, uses about three times as much water, or 1,442 liters every day.

Looking at global water consumption, as seen in Figure 1, it is important to distinguish between water withdrawal and water use. Water withdrawal is the amount of water physically removed, but this concept is less useful in a discussion of limits on the total amount of water, since much of the withdrawn water is later returned to the water cycle. In the EU and the US, about 46 percent of the withdrawn water is used merely as cooling water for power generation and is immediately released for further use downstream. Likewise, most industrial uses return 80–90 percent of the water, and even in irrigation 30–70 percent of the water runs back into lakes and rivers or percolates into aquifers, whence it can be reused. Thus, a more useful measure of water consumption is the amount of water

Figure 1

Global, Annual Water Withdrawal and Use, in Thousand km³ and Percentage of Accessible Runoff, 1900–95, and Predictions for 2025

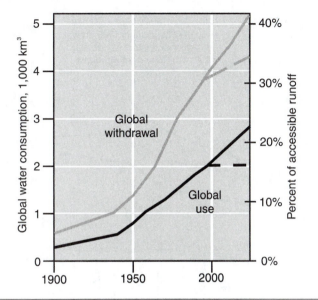

Source: Shiklomanov 2000:22 (high prediction), World Water Council 2006:26 (low prediction).

this consumption causes to be irretrievably lost through evaporation or transpiration from plants. This is called water use.

Over the twentieth century, Earth's water use has grown from about 330 km³ to about 2,100 km³. As can be seen from Figure 1 there is some uncertainty about the future use and withdrawal (mainly depending on the development of irrigation), but until now most predictions have tended to overestimate the actual water consumption by up to 100 percent. Nevertheless, total use is still less than 17 percent of the accessible water and even with the high prediction it will require just 22 percent of the readily accessible, annually renewed water in 2025.

At the same time, we have gained access to more and more water, as indicated in Figure 2. Per person we have gone from using about 1,000 liters per day to almost 2,000 liters over the past 100 years. Particularly, this is due to an approximately 50 percent increase in water use in agriculture, allowing irrigated farms to feed us better and to decrease the number of starving people. Agricultural water usage seems, however, to have stabilized below 2,000 liters per capita, mainly owing to higher efficiency and less water consumption in agriculture since 1980. This pattern is also found in the EU and the US, where consumption has increased dramatically over the twentieth century, but is now leveling off. At the same time, personal consumption (approximated by the municipal withdrawal) has

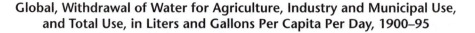

Figure 2

Global, Withdrawal of Water for Agriculture, Industry and Municipal Use, and Total Use, in Liters and Gallons Per Capita Per Day, 1900–95

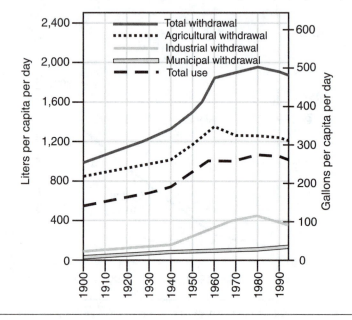

Source: Shiklomanov 2000:24.

more than quadrupled over the century, reflecting an increase in welfare with more easily accessible water. In developing countries, this is in large part a question of health—avoiding sickness through better access to clean drinking water and sanitation, whereas in developed countries higher water use is an indication of an increased number of domestic amenities such as dishwashers and better-looking lawns.

So, if the global use is less than 17 percent of the readily accessible and renewable water and the increased use has brought us more food, less starvation, more health and increased wealth, why do we worry?

The Three Central Problems

There are three decisive problems. First, precipitation is by no means equally distributed all over the globe. This means that not all have equal access to water resources and that some countries have much less accessible water than the global average would seem to indicate. The question is whether water shortages are already severe in some places today. Second, there will be more and more people on Earth. Since precipitation levels will remain more or less constant this will mean fewer water resources for each person. The question is whether we will see more severe shortages in the future. Third, many countries receive a large part of their water resources from rivers; 261 river systems, draining just less than half of the planet's land area, are shared by two or more countries, and at least ten rivers flow through half a dozen or more countries. Most Middle Eastern countries share aquifers. This means that the water question also has an international perspective and—if cooperation breaks down—an international conflict potential.

Beyond these three problems there are two other issues, which are often articulated in connection with the water shortage problem, but which are really conceptually quite separate. One is the worry about water pollution, particularly of potable water. While it is of course important to avoid water pollution in part because pollution restricts the presently available amount of freshwater, it is not related to the problem of water shortage *per se*. . . .

The second issue is about the shortage of *access* to water in the Third World. . . . This problem, while getting smaller, is still a major obstacle for global welfare. In discussing water shortage, reference to the lack of universal access to drinking water and sanitation is often thrown in for good measure, but of course this issue is entirely separate from the question of shortages. First, the cause is *not* lack of water (since human requirements constitute just 50–100 liters a day which any country but Kuwait can deliver, cf. Table 1) but rather a lack of investment in infrastructure. Second, the solution lies not in cutting back on existing consumption but actually in increasing future consumption.

Finally, we should just mention global warming . . . and its connection to water use. Intuitively, we might be tempted to think that a warmer world would mean more evaporation, less water, more problems. But more evaporation also means more precipitation. Essentially, global climate models seem to change *where* water shortages appear (pushing some countries above or below the threshold) but the total changes are small (1–5 percent) and go both ways.

Not Enough Water?

Precipitation is not distributed equally. Some countries such as Iceland have almost 2 million liters of water for each inhabitant every day, whereas Kuwait must make do with just 30 liters. The question, of course, is when does a country not have *enough* water.

It is estimated that a human being needs about 2 liters of water a day, so clearly this is not the restrictive requirement. The most common approach is to use the so-called *water stress index* proposed by the hydrologist Malin Falkenmark. This index tries to establish an approximate minimum level of water per capita to maintain an adequate quality of life in a moderately developed country in an arid zone. This approach has been used by many organizations including the World Bank, in the standard literature on environmental science, and in the water scarcity discussion in

World Resources. With this index, human beings are assessed to need about 100 liters per day for drinking, household needs and personal hygiene, and an additional 500–2,000 liters for agriculture, industry and energy production. Since water is often most needed in the dry season, the water stress level is then set even higher—if a country has less than 4,660 liters per person available it is expected to experience periodic or regular water stress. Should the accessible runoff drop to less than 2,740 liters the country is said to experience chronic water scarcity. Below 1,370 liters, the country experiences absolute water scarcity, outright shortages and acute scarcity.

Table 1 shows the 15 countries comprising 3.7 percent of humanity in 2000 suffering chronic water scarcity according to the above definition. Many of these countries probably come as no surprise. But the question is whether we are facing a serious problem.

How does Kuwait actually get by with just 30 liters per day? The point is, it doesn't. Kuwait, Libya and Saudi Arabia all cover a large part of their water demand by exploiting the largest water resource of all—through desalination of sea water. Kuwait in fact covers more than half its total use through desalination. Desalting requires a large amount of energy (through either freezing or evaporating water), but all of these countries also have great energy resources. The price today to desalt sea water is down to 50–80 ¢/m³ and just 20–35 ¢/m³ for brackish water, which makes desalted water a more expensive resource than fresh water, but definitely not out of reach.

This shows two things. First, we can have sufficient water, if we can pay for it. Once again, this underscores that *poverty* and not the environment is the primary limitation for solutions to our problems. Second, desalination puts an upper boundary on the degree of water problems in the world. In principle, we could produce the Earth's entire present water consumption with a single desalination facility in the Sahara, powered by solar cells. The total area needed for the solar cells would take up less than 0.3 percent of the Sahara.

Today, desalted water makes up just 0.2 percent of all water or 2.4 percent of municipal water. Making desalination cover the total municipal water withdrawal would cost about 0.5 percent of the global GDP. This would definitely be a waste of resources, since most areas have abundant water supplies and all areas have some access to water, but it underscores the upper boundary of the water problem.

Also, there's a fundamental problem when you only look at the total water resources and yet try to answer whether there are sufficient supplies of water. The trouble is that we do not necessarily know *how* and *how wisely* the water is used. Many countries get by just fine with very limited water resources because these resources are exploited very effectively. Israel is a prime example of efficient water use. It achieves a high degree of efficiency in its agriculture, partly because it uses the very efficient drip irrigation system to green the desert, and partly because it recycles household wastewater for irrigation. Nevertheless, with just 969 liters per person per day, Israel should according to the classification be experiencing absolute water

Table 1

Countries With Chronic Water Scarcity (Below 2,740 Liters Per Capita Per Day) in 2000, 2025, and 2050, Compared to a Number of Other Countries

Available water, liters per capita per day	2000	2025	2050
Kuwait	30	20	17
United Arab Emirates	174	129	116
Libya	275	136	92
Saudi Arabia	325	166	118
Jordan	381	203	145
Singapore	471	401	403
Yemen	665	304	197
Israel	969	738	644
Oman	1,077	448	268
Tunisia	1,147	834	709
Algeria	1,239	827	664
Burundi	1,496	845	616
Egypt	2,343	1,667	1,382
Rwanda	2,642	1,562	1,197
Kenya	2,725	1,647	1,252
Morocco	2,932	2,129	1,798
South Africa	2,959	1,911	1,497
Somalia	3,206	1,562	1,015
Lebanon	3,996	2,971	2,533
Haiti	3,997	2,497	1,783
Burkina Faso	4,202	2,160	1,430
Zimbabwe	4,408	2,830	2,199
Peru	4,416	3,191	2,680
Malawi	4,656	2,508	1,715
Ethiopia	4,849	2,354	1,508
Iran, Islamic Rep.	4,926	2,935	2,211
Nigeria	5,952	3,216	2,265
Eritrea	6,325	3,704	2,735
Lesotho	6,556	3,731	2,665
Togo	7,026	3,750	2,596
Uganda	8,046	4,017	2,725
Niger	8,235	3,975	2,573
Percent people with chronic scarcity	3.7%	8.6%	17.8%
United Kingdom	3,337	3,270	3,315
India	5,670	4,291	3,724
China	6,108	5,266	5,140
Italy	7,994	8,836	10,862
United States	24,420	20,405	19,521
Botswana	24,859	15,624	12,122
Indonesia	33,540	25,902	22,401
Bangladesh	50,293	35,855	29,576
Australia	50,913	40,077	37,930
Russian Federation	84,235	93,724	107,725
Iceland	1,660,502	1,393,635	1,289,976

Source: WRI 1998a.

scarcity. Consequently, one of the authors in a background report for the 1997 UN document on water points out that the 2,740 liters water benchmark is "misguidedly considered by some authorities as a critical minimum amount of water for the survival of a modern society."

Of course, the problem of faulty classification increases, the higher the limit is set. The European Environmental Agency (EEA) in its 1998 assessment somewhat incredibly suggested that countries below 13,690 liters per person per day should be classified as "low availability," making not only more than half the EU low on water but indeed more than 70 percent of the globe. Denmark receives 6,750 liters of fresh water per day and is one of the many countries well below this suggested limit and actually close to EEA's "very low" limit. Nevertheless, national withdrawal is just 11 percent of the available water, and it is estimated that the consumption could be almost doubled without negative environmental consequences. The director of the Danish EPA has stated that, "from the hand of nature, Denmark has access to good and clean groundwater far in excess of what we actually use."

By far the largest part of all water is used for agriculture—globally, agriculture uses 69 percent, compared to 23 percent for industry and 8 percent for households. Consequently, the greatest gains in water use come from cutting down on agricultural use. Many of the countries with low water availability therefore compensate by importing a large amount of their grain. Since a ton of grain uses about 1,000 tons of water, this is in effect a very efficient way of importing water. Israel imports about 87 percent of its grain consumption, Jordan 91 percent, Saudi Arabia 50 percent.

Summing up, more than 96 percent of all nations have at present sufficient water resources. On all continents, water accessibility has *increased* per person, and at the same time an ever higher proportion of people have gained access to clean drinking water and sanitation. While water accessibility has been getting *better* this is not to deny that there are still widespread shortages and limitations of basic services, such as access to clean drinking water, and that local and regional scarcities occur. But these problems are primarily related not to physical water scarcity but to a lack of proper water management and in the end often to lack of money— money to desalt sea water or to increase cereal imports, thereby freeing up domestic water resources.

Will It Get Worse in the Future?

The concerns for the water supply are very much concerns that the current problems will become worse over time. As world population grows, and as precipitation remains constant, there will be less water per person, and using Falkenmark's water stress criterion, there will be more nations experiencing water scarcity. In Figure 3 it is clear that the proportion of people in water stressed nations will increase from 3.7 percent in 2000 to 8.6 percent in 2025 and 17.8 percent in 2050.

It is typically pointed out that although more people by definition means more water stress, such "projections are neither forecasts nor

Figure 3

Share of Humanity With Maximum Water Availability in the Year 2000, 2025, and 2050, Using UN Medium Variant Population Data

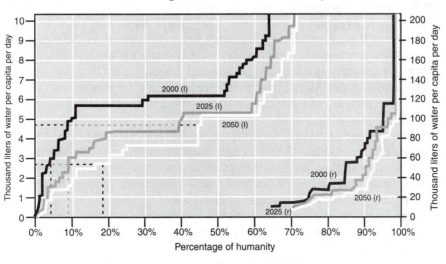

The left side uses the left axis, the right side the right axis.
Source: WRI 1998a.

predictions." Indeed, the projections merely mean that if we do not improve our handling of water resources, water will become more scarce. But it is unlikely that we will not become better at utilizing and distributing water. Since agriculture takes up the largest part of water consumption, it is also here that the largest opportunities for improving efficiency are to be found. It is estimated that many irrigation systems waste 60–80 percent of all water. Following the example of Israel, drip irrigation in countries as diverse as India, Jordan, Spain and the US has consistently been shown to cut water use by 30–70 percent while increasing yields by 20–90 percent. Several studies have also indicated that industry almost without additional costs could save anywhere from 30 to 90 percent of its water consumption. Even in domestic distribution there is great potential for water savings. EEA estimates that the leakage rates in Europe vary from 10 percent in Austria and Denmark up to 28 percent in the UK and 33 percent in the Czech Republic.

The problem of water waste occurs because water in many places is not well priced. The great majority of the world's irrigation systems are based on an annual flat rate, and not on charges according to the amount of water consumed. The obvious effect is that participants are not forced to consider whether all in all it pays to use the last liter of water—when you have first paid to be in, water is free. So even if there is only very little private utility from the last liter of water, it is still used because it is free. . . .

This is particularly a problem for the poor countries. The poorest countries use 90 percent of their water for irrigation compared to just 37 percent in the rich countries. Consequently, it will be necessary to redistribute water from agriculture to industry and households, and this will probably involve a minor decline in the potential agricultural production (i.e. a diminished increase in the actual production). The World Bank estimates that this reduction will be very limited and that water redistribution definitely will be profitable for the countries involved. Of course, this will mean increased imports of grain by the most water stressed countries, but a study from the International Water Management Institute indicates that it should be possible to cover these extra imports by extra production in the water abundant countries, particularly the US.

At the same time there are also large advantages to be reaped by focusing on more efficient household water consumption. In Manila 58 percent of all water disappears (lost in distribution or stolen), and in Latin America the figure is about 40 percent. And on average households in the Third World pay only 35 percent of the actual price of water. Naturally, this encourages overconsumption. We know that pricing and metering reduces demand, and that consumers use less water if they have to pay for each unit instead of just paying a flat rate.

Actually, it is likely that more sensible pricing will not only secure future water supplies but also increase the total social efficiency. When agriculture is given cheap or even free water, this often implies a hidden and very large subsidy—in the United States the water subsidy to farmers is estimated to be above 90 percent or $3.5 billion. For the developing countries this figure is even larger: it is estimated that the hidden water subsidy to cities is about $22 billion, and the hidden subsidy to agriculture around $20–25 billion.

Thus, although an increasing population will increase water demands and put extra water stress on almost 20 percent of humanity, it is likely that this scarcity can be solved. Part of the solution will come from higher water prices, which will cut down on inefficient water use. Increased cereal imports will form another part of the solution, freeing up agricultural water to be used in more valuable areas of industry or domestic consumption. Finally, desalting will again constitute a backstop process which can produce virtually unlimited amounts of drinking water given sufficient financial backing.

POSTSCRIPT

Is the Threat of a Global Water Shortage Real?

The authors of the two selections agree that something must be done—that is, major public policy making must occur—if the water future is going to be acceptable. They disagree, however, on the urgency of the task and the level of optimism (or pessimism) that they bring to their analysis of likely success. Rosegrant and his colleagues approach the global water problem from the perspective of its role in food production. They argue that water is among one of the main factors that will limit food production in the future. Competition for water comes from many quarters, and farmers find themselves in an increasingly competitive situation as they attempt to keep pace with agricultural needs.

Rosegrant and his colleagues' view of past water trends—whether for irrigation or for drinking and household uses—leads them to conclude that the future of water is "highly uncertain," at best. The authors' pessimism stems from the failure of governments to address the issue adequately to date. Their model used to analyze future trends posits three basic scenarios: business as usual, water crisis, and sustainable water scenarios.

In the business-as-usual scenario, farmers will be unable to grow food as quickly as in the past. The cost of supplying water to users will increase, as heavier demands are placed on the global water supply. Industrial water use in the developing world is expected to grow faster than in the developed world as the developing countries push toward industrialization. Water availability for irrigation in the poorer sectors of the globe will decline significantly. Sub-Saharan Africa will, as it has for three decades, be the region of the globe hardest hit by the business-as-usual scenario. The water crisis scenario posits that "increasing water scarcity, combined with poor water policies and inadequate investment in water, has the potential to generate sharp increases in cereal food prices over the coming decades." Finally, the sustainable water scenario would result in a dramatic increase in water availability, improve environmental uses, lead to higher per capita domestic water consumption, and maintain food production at the business-as-usual scenario levels.

Lomborg argues that our ability to find more water has resulted in a global usage rate of 17 percent of the readily accessible and renewable water. The consequence, according to Lomborg, is that the world has "more food, less starvation, more health and increased wealth [so] why do we worry?" He does suggest that there are significant problems and identifies three: (1) the unequal distribution of precipitation throughout the globe, (2) increasing global population, and (3) the fact that many countries receive their water through shared river systems. Additionally, water pollution and the shortage of access to water in the developing world are issues, but of a different sort.

Both readings point out the need for aggressive policy action on the part of governments and other actors in the global water regime. This is not to suggest, however, that the world's leaders have been idle. At least 10 major international conferences since 1977 have addressed water issues, resulting in significant action-oriented proposals. For example, the 1992 International Conference on Water and Environment in Dublin established four basic ideas (known as the Dublin Principles). The 1992 Earth Summit highlighted water as an integral part of the ecosystem.

The current cry is for aggressive global water management. Every major study related to water concludes with the observation that governments need to do much more if future water crises are to be avoided. The Web is replete with public (and private) interest groups urging more global action. The Third World Traveler site titles one such plea from the International Forum on Globalization "The Failure of Governments" in a discussion of the crisis. The World Water Council's recent draft of its *World Water Actions Report* presents an overview of global actions to improve water management and to spell out priorities for future efforts. The report centers on a new paradigm for looking at water. No longer to be viewed as a physical product, the paradigm calls for water to be seen as an ecological process "that connects the glass of water on the table with the upper reaches of the watershed." The key ideas are "scarcity, conservation, and awareness of water's life cycle from rain to capture, consumption, and disposal."

The good news for the World Water Council is that the international community has broad consensus, forged at the 10 conferences mentioned above, about the need for policy action. The creation of the World Water Council itself in 1996 and of the Global Water Partnership the same year is an example of such institutional action. But it was the Second World Water Forum, held at The Hague in The Netherlands in March 2000, that was a landmark event in raising global water consciousness. Among the many research reports and documents that emerged from the conference, two stand out: *Vision for Water, Life, and the Environment in the 21st Century* and *Towards Water Security: Framework for Action.*

Vision proposed five key actions: "Involve all stakeholders in integrated management, move towards full-cost pricing of all water services, increase public funding for research and innovation in the public interest, increase cooperation in international water basins, (and) massively increase investments in water." The *Framework for Action* document addresses the question of where do we go from here, suggesting four basic steps: "generating water wisdom . . . , expanding and deepening dialogue among diverse stakeholders, strengthening the capabilities of the organizations involved in water management, and ensuring adequate financial resources to pay for the many actions required." A number of recent books echo the call for governmental action: *Troubled Water: Saints, Sinners, Truth and Lies About the Global Water Crisis* (Anita Roddick et al., Chelsea Green Publishing Company, 2004); *Water: Global Common and Global Problems* (Velma I. Grover, ed., Science Publishers, 2006); *Integrated Assessment of Water Resources and Global Change: A North–South Analysis* (Springer, 2007); and *Blue Covenant: The Global Water Crisis and the Coming battle for the Right to Water* (New Press, 2008). See also *Water: A Shared Responsibility* (The United Nations World Water Development Report 2, 2006).

The fourth volume in a series by Peter H. Gleick and his research team analyzes current worldwide water trends and also addresses a variety of related world water issues (*The World's Water 2004–2005: The Biennial Report on Freshwater Resources,* Island Press, 2004).

A final important source for understanding the global water problem, particularly its relationship to food and the environment, is *Dialogue on Water, Food and Environment* (2002), published by 10 important actors in the field (FAO, GWP, ICID, IFAP, IWMI, IUCN, UNEP, WHO, WWC, and WWF). Perhaps it is fitting to end this discussion with the quote from UN Secretary General Kofi Annan on the cover of this report: "We need a blue revolution in agriculture that focuses on increasing productivity per unit of water—more crop per drop."

Internet References . . .

United Nations Office on Drugs and Crime

Established in 1997, this UN organization assists members in their struggle against illicit drugs and human trafficking. It focuses on research, assistance with treaties, and field-based technical assistance. It is headquartered in Vienna with 21 field offices.

http://www.unodc.org

Beckley Foundation Drug Policy Programme (BFDPP)

This British foundation aims to promote objective debate about national and international drug policies. It lists many other Web sites as well.

http://www.internationaldrugpolicy.net

World Health Organization

This international organization's Web site provides substantial information about current and potential pandemics as well as other Web site links. See also http://www.globalhealthreporting.org and http://www.globalhealthfacts.org for additional information.

http://www.who.int/en/

Council of Europe

The Council of Europe established a campaign in 2006 to combat trafficking of human beings. It focuses on creating awareness among governments, NGOs, and civil society about the problem, as well as promoting global public policy to combat the problem.

http://www.coe.int

Globalization Guide.Org

This Web site lists around 40 pro- and anti-globalization Web sites as well as other sources on both globalization and cultural imperialism.

http://globalizationguide.org

Globalization: Threat or Opportunity?

This Web site contains the article "Globalization: Threat or Opportunity?" by the staff of the International Monetary Fund (IMF). This article discusses such aspects of globalization as current trends, positive and negative outcomes, and the role of institutions and organizations. "The Challenge of Globalization in Africa," by IMF acting managing director Stanley Fischer, and "Factors Driving Global Economic Integration," by Michael Mussa, IMF's director of research, are also included on this site.

http://www.imf.org/external/np/exr/ib/2000/041200.htm

Expanding Global Forces and Movements

*O*ur ability to travel from one part of the globe to another in a short amount of time has expanded dramatically since the Wright brothers first lifted an airplane off the sand dunes of North Carolina's Outer Banks. The decline of national borders has also been made possible by the explosion of global technology. This technological explosion has not only increased the speed of information dissemination but it has also expanded its reach and impact making any individual with internet access a global actor in every sense of the term.

Many consequences flow from this realization, including the expansion of the drug war and the global spread of health pandemics along with the trafficking in human beings against their will. In addition, flow of money, information and ideas that connect people around the world also creates fissures of conflict that heighten anxieties and cause increased tensions between rich and poor, connected and disconnected, cultures and regimes. The impact of these new and emerging patterns of access has yet to be fully calculated or realized, but we do know that billions are feeling their impact, and the result is both exhilarating and frightening.

- Can the Global Community "Win" the Drug War?

- Is the International Community Adequately Prepared to Address Global Health Pandemics?

- Do Adequate Strategies Exist to Combat Human Trafficking?

- Is Globalization a Positive Development for the World Community?

- Is the World a Victim of American Cultural Imperialism?

- Do MySpace and YouTube Make Globalization Democratized?

ISSUE 10

Can the Global Community "Win" the Drug War?

YES: **United Nations Office on Drugs and Crime**, from "2007 World Drug Report" (2007)

NO: **Ethan Nadelmann**, from "Drugs," *Foreign Policy* (September/October 2007)

ISSUE SUMMARY

YES: This 2007 report by the UN's Office on Drugs and Crime provides "robust evidence" that "drug control is working" and "the world drug problem is being contained."

NO: Ethan Nadelmann argues that prohibition has failed by not treating the "demand for drugs as a market, and addicts as patients," resulting in "boosting the profits of drug lords, and fostering narcostates that would frighten Al Capone."

In 1999, the United Nations pegged the world illicit drug trade at $400 billion, about the size of the Spanish economy. Such activity takes place as part of a global supply chain that "uses everything from passenger jets that can carry shipments of cocaine worth $500 million in a single trip to custom-built submarines that ply the waters between Colombia and Puerto Rico." *The UN 2007 World Drug Report* suggested the global drug problem was being contained, as there appeared to be "a leveling of growth in all of the main illegal drug markets." Opium production increased but was still much lower than any peak year. Cocaine and ATS (amphetamine-type stimulants) production remained stable, while cannabis production declined.

The report revealed that 5 percent of the world's population between the ages of 15 and 64 have used drugs at least once in the year under study (2005), compared to global tobacco use of 28 percent. Approximately 200 million people use drugs each year. At the global level, the opiates, particularly heroin, rank first in usage, followed by cocaine. Opiates remain the principal problem drug in Europe and Asia, while cocaine tops the list in South America and cannabis in Africa. Estimates suggest that in 2005, 42 percent of global cocaine production and 26 percent of global heroin production were intercepted by authorities. There were 1.5 million drug seizure cases, and large quantities of drugs were seized.

The report followed good news relating to government action in the 2004 report. Especially important was the emergence of a consensus among governments and global public opinion that the current levels of illegal drug use is unacceptable. In two drug-producing regions, declines in production actually occurred. In Southeast Asia, opium poppy cultivation continues to drop in Myanmar and Laos. In the Andean region, coca cultivation has declined for four straight years in the three leading producing countries (Colombia, Peru and Bolivia).

The illegal movement of drugs across national borders is accompanied by the same kind of movement for illegal weapons. They go hand in hand with one another. It was estimated by the UN in its 2004 report that only 3 percent of such weapons (18 million of a total of 550 million in circulation) are used by government, the military or police.

This increase in drug use has occurred despite a rather long history of government attempts to control the illegal international drug trade. Beginning in 1961, such efforts have been part of the social policies of governments' worldwide. Precisely because drug policy crosses over into social policy, policymakers and scholars have been at odds over how best to deal with this ever growing problem, whether talking about national policy or international policy. Simply stated, the debate has centered on legalization vs. prohibition, and treatment vs. prevention.

Policies of the United States have always had the goal of drug use reduction and punishment for abusers, resulting in less attention to treatment. This includes a number of important elements, as outlined in a Congressional Research Service Brief for Congress (2003): "(1) eradication of narcotic crops, (2) interdiction and law enforcement activities in drug-producing and drug-transmitting countries, (3) international cooperation, (4) sanctions/economic assistance, and (5) institution development." Many have charged the United States and those other countries that share its fundamental philosophy of drug wars of using the issue to expand its national power in other domains. On the other hand, other countries, particularly those in Western Europe, have been shifting attention for some time away from "repressive policies" and toward those associated with harm reduction and treatment.

The two selections in this section contribute to the debate over the proper approach to "winning" the drug war. The UN's 2007 report presents an optimistic picture of the effects of governmental action in the war on drugs, with strong language used to paint the picture. The second selection by Ethan Nadelmann suggests that, on the contrary, drug lords and narcostates are flourishing.

171

YES

**United Nations Office
on Drugs and Crime**

2007 World Drug Report

1. Trends in World Drug Markets

1.1 Overview

1.1.1 Evolution of the World Drug Problem

Continued containment of the drug problem

The global drug problem is being contained. The production and consumption of cannabis, cocaine, amphetamines and ecstasy have stabilized at the global level—with one exception. The exception is the continuing expansion of opium production in Afghanistan. This expansion continues to pose a threat—to the security of the country and to the global containment of opiates abuse. Even in Afghanistan, however, the large scale production of opium is concentrated and expanding in a few southern provinces where the authority of the central government is currently limited and insurgents continue to exploit the profits of the opium trade.

On the whole, most indications point to a levelling of growth in all of the main illegal drug markets. This is good news and may indicate an important juncture in long term drug control. A stable and contained problem is easier to address than one which is expanding chaotically, provided it is seen as an opportunity for renewed commitment rather than an excuse to decrease vigilance.

Most indications are, however, that Member States do have the will to re-commit to drug control. Although it is outside of the scope of this Report to assess policy, the estimates and trends which are provided in the following pages contain several examples of progress forged on the back of international collaboration. The extent of international collaboration, the sharing of intelligence, knowledge and experience, as well as the conviction that the global drug problem must be tackled on the basis of a 'shared responsibility' seem to be growing and bearing fruit.

From *World Drug Report, 2007,* UNODC Series No. E. 07.XI.5, pp. 25–27, 29–31. Copyright © 2007 by United Nations Publications. Reprinted by permission.

Following stabilization in 2005, opium production increased in 2006 . . .

The total area under opium cultivation was 201,000 ha in 2006. This is clearly higher than a year earlier (+33%) though still below the level in 1998 (238,000 ha) and some 29 percent lower than at the peak in 1991 (282,000 ha). Given higher opium yields in Afghanistan than in South-East Asia, global opium production is, however, higher than in the 1990s.

Following a small decline of global opium production in 2005 (−5%), global opium production increased again strongly in 2006 (+43%) to reach 6610 mt, basically reflecting the massive expansion of opium production in Afghanistan (+49%). Afghanistan accounted for 92 percent of global illicit opium production in 2006. As a result global heroin production is estimated to have increased to 606 mt in 2006. The bad news from Afghanistan also overshadows the good news from South-East Asia. Opium production in the Golden Triangle (mainly Myanmar and Laos) declined by 77 percent between 1998 and 2006 and by 84 percent since the peak in 1991.

. . . while cocaine production remained stable

If only the area under coca cultivation is considered, a small decline by 2 percent to 157,000 ha was reported for the year 2006. As compared to the year 2000, the area under coca cultivation in the Andean region declined by 29 percent; in Colombia, it fell by as much as 52 percent. This progress was, however, not translated into a decline of global cocaine production, due to improved yields and production techniques. Global cocaine production is estimated to have remained basically unchanged in 2006 as compared to a year earlier or two years earlier. Following a revision of yield estimates, global production is now estimated at 984 mt. A decline in Colombia (−5%) was compensated by increases reported from Bolivia (+18%) and Peru (+8%).

Cannabis production declined in 2005 . . .

Estimates for both cannabis herb and cannabis resin showed a decline for the year 2005. This decline follows several years of sustained growth. Global cannabis herb production is now estimated at 42,000 mt, down from 45,000 mt in 2004. Global cannabis resin production declined from 7,500 mt in 2004 to 6,600 mt in 2005, reflecting mainly the decline of cannabis resin production in Morocco.

. . . and ATS production stabilized

Global production of amphetamine-type stimulants seems to have stabilized at around 480 mt in 2005, slightly down from 500 mt in 2000. There has been a decline in ecstasy production (from 126 mt in 2004 to 113 mt in 2005), and a small decline in methampheta-mine production (from 291 to 278 mt) which was offset by an increase in global amphetamine production (from 63 to 88 mt).

Member States reported 1.5 million drug seizure cases to UNODC

Member States reported 1.5 million drug seizure cases to UNODC for the year 2005, 21 percent more than a year earlier. Some of the increase was

Figure 1

Breakdown of Seizure Cases in 2005 by Substance (N = 1.51 Million)

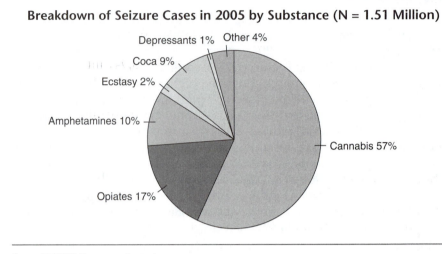

Source: UNODC, Government reports.

due to improved reporting. One hundred and twelve countries provided detailed statistics on seizure cases in 2005, up from 95 countries in 2004. If only the data of those countries that reported in both 2004 and 2005 is considered, the increase amounts to 10 percent.

More than half (57%) of all seizure cases involved cannabis (herb, resin, oil, plants and seeds). Opiates (opium, morphine, heroin, synthetic opiates and poppy seeds), accounted for 17 percent, with heroin alone accounting for 14 percent of the total. This is followed by seizures of the amphetamine-type stimulants (12%). About half of these seizures (or 5.5% of the total) is accounted for by methamphetamine, followed by amphetamine (2.5%) and ecstasy (2%); the rest (2%) includes 'Captagon' tablets (Near East) and 'Maxiton Forte' (Egypt), 'ephedrone' (methcathinone) and various undefined amphetamines. Coca products account for 9 percent of global seizure cases; the bulk of coca related seizure cases concern cocaine (8% of total).

Depressants account for 1 percent of global seizure cases and other drugs for 4 percent. This includes substances such as methaqualone, khat, various synthetic narcotics, LSD, ketamine, various non-specified psychotropic substances, and inhalants. Some of these substances (such as khat, ketamine and some of the psychotropic substances) are not under international control, but are under national control in several Member States.

Largest quantities of drugs seized are cannabis, cocaine and opiates

Information on the quantities of drugs seized was provided by 118 countries for the year 2005 in reply to UNODC's Annual Reports Questionnaire.

Supplementing ARQ data with information obtained from other sources,[1] UNODC has compiled data and information from 165 countries and territories. This forms the basis for the analysis which follows.

The largest seizures worldwide are for cannabis (herb and then resin), followed by cocaine, the opiates and ATS. All cannabis related seizures amounted to more than 9,700 mt in 2005, including 5,947 mt for cannabis end products (herb, resin and oil). Cocaine seizures amounted to 752 mt, opiate seizures, expressed in heroin equivalents, amounted to 125 mt and ATS seizures (methamphetamine, amphetamine, non-defined amphetamines and ecstasy) amounted to 43 mt.

Increases in 2005 were reported for coca leaf, cocaine, the amphetamines as well as GHB and LSD. As global cocaine production remained unchanged, the strong increase in cocaine seizures is likely to have been the exclusive result of effective and successful law enforcement. Though amphetamines seizures increased in 2005 they are still below the peak levels of 2000 and 2001. Global trafficking in amphetamines over the last five years has remained basically stable.

Opiates seizures as a whole remained stable in 2005—reflecting stable global opium production in that year. Rising seizures of opium offset declines in heroin and morphine seizures. For 2006, however, preliminary data indicate a strong increase in opiates seizures, in line with growing levels of opium production in Afghanistan.

In 2005, global seizures of cannabis herb, resin and oil declined. The decline in cannabis herb seizures seems to be linked to intensified eradication efforts in a number of countries across the globe. The decline in cannabis resin seizures can be linked to the decline of cannabis resin production in Morocco.

Drug seizures in unit terms decline in 2005

As the quantities of drugs seized are not directly comparable, it is difficult to draw general conclusions on overall drug trafficking patterns from them. Since the ratio of weight to psychoactive effects varies greatly from one drug to another (the use of one gram of heroin is not equivalent to the use of one gram of cannabis herb), the comparability of the data is improved if the weight of a seizure is converted into typical consumption units, or doses, taken by drug users. Typical doses tend, however, to vary across countries (and sometime across regions within the same country), across substances aggregated under one drug category (e.g. commercial cannabis herb and high-grade cannabis herb), across user groups and across time. There are no conversion rates which take all of these factors into account. Comparisons made here are based on global conversion rates, of milligrams per dose,[2] found in scientific literature or used among law enforcement agencies as basic rules of thumb. The resulting estimates should be interpreted with some caution.

Based on such calculations, global seizures were equivalent to 32.5 billion units in 2005, down from 35.8 billion units a year earlier (−9%). As the number of drug seizure cases increased in 2005, the decline of seizures in unit equivalents cannot be attributed to reduced law enforcement activity. It most likely reflects the first signs of stabilization in global drug trafficking flows parallel to the stabilization in global drug production and drug consumption.

In units terms, more than half of all seizures (59%) are cannabis, followed by coca related substances (24%), opiates (12%) and amphetamine-type stimulants (4%). While cannabis leads the table, irrespective of the measurement used, it may be interesting to note that in terms of drug units seized, cocaine ranks second. In terms of reported drug seizure cases, cocaine ranked fourth, behind the opiates and behind the ATS. This reflects the fact that, while there are many multi-ton seizures of cocaine every year, other drugs are usually trafficked in far smaller quantities.

A regional breakdown shows that 44 percent of all drugs, expressed in unit equivalents, were seized in the Americas, 29 percent in Europe, 18 percent in Asia, 9 percent in Africa and 0.2 percent in the Oceania region. Seizures declined in 2005 in Africa, in the Oceania region, in Europe and in North America but increased in South America and in Asia.

On a per capita basis, drug trafficking is most widespread in North America, reflecting higher abuse levels and/or the fact that law enforcement in North America is the most active in fighting drug trafficking. The largest amounts of drugs per inhabitant are seized in North America (19 doses per inhabitant), followed by South America (13 doses) and Europe (11 doses). The global average is 5 doses per inhabitant per year. Africa, Oceania and Asia are all below the global average. Within Asia, however, data differ among the various subregions. For the Near & Middle East/South-West Asia region, seizures amount to 11 doses per inhabitant, which is almost the same level as reported from Europe.

Overall stabilization in global drug use

The estimated level of drug use in the world has remained more or less unchanged for the third year in a row. Approximately 200 million people or 5 percent of the world's population aged between 15 and 64 years have used drugs at least once in the previous 12 months.

This continues to be a far lower level than tobacco use (28%). UNODC's estimate of the global number of problem drug users also remains unchanged at around 25 million people or 0.6% of the global population age 15–64.

With the exception of a small increase in cocaine use (based on prevalence estimates), use of all illicit drugs was either stable or declined slightly in 2005/6. The increases in cannabis and ecstasy use which were recorded in 2004/5 were not carried over into the 2005/6 period.

Consumed by almost 4 percent of the population or close to 160 million persons, cannabis continues to account for the vast majority of illegal drug use. Global cannabis use estimates are slightly lower than last year's estimates, due to ongoing declines in North America and—for the first time-some declines in the largest cannabis markets of Western Europe. Cannabis use in the Oceana region also continued to decline. In addition, a number of new household surveys found lower prevalence

Figure 2

Use of Illicit Drugs Compared to the Use of Tobacco (in % of World Population Age 15–64)

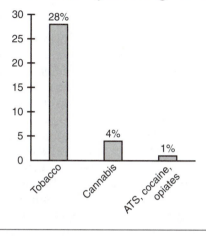

Source: UNODC, WHO.

Figure 3

Illegal Drug Use at the Global Level (2005/2006)

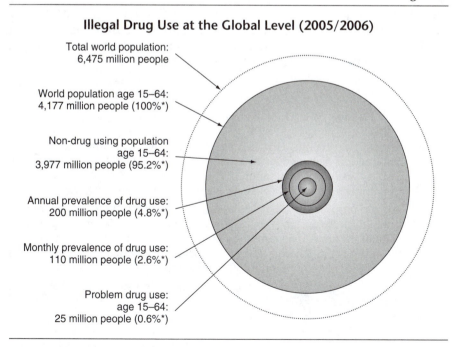

Total world population:
6,475 million people

World population age 15–64:
4,177 million people (100%*)

Non-drug using population
age 15–64:
3,977 million people (95.2%*)

Annual prevalence of drug use:
200 million people (4.8%*)

Monthly prevalence of drug use:
110 million people (2.6%*)

Problem drug use:
age 15–64:
25 million people (0.6%*)

*in percent of population age 15–64.

rates than UNODC had previously estimated for the countries concerned. Growth in cannabis use occurred in Africa, several parts of South America, some parts of Asia (South-West Asia, Central Asia and South Asia) and parts of Eastern and South-eastern Europe. Although it is too early to speak of general decline, signs of a stabilization of cannabis use at the global level are apparent.

Amphetamine-type stimulants (ATS), including amphetamines, methamphetamine and ecstasy, remain the second most widely consumed group of substances. Over the 2005/6 period 25 million people are estimated to have used amphetamines (including methamphetamine) at least once in the previous 12 months, about the same as a year earlier. An estimated 9 million people used ecstasy over the 2005/6 period, down from 10 million in 2004/5. Declines in ecstasy use occurred primarily in North America.

The number of opiates users remained stable at 2004/5 levels. As in that period, 16 million persons or 0.4 percent of the global population aged 15 to 64 consumed opiates. Out of these 16 million persons, 11 million or 0.3 percent of the population abuse heroin. Overall, consumption declined or stabilized in established markets, including those of Western Europe and North America, but increased in countries in the vicinity of Afghanistan as well as in new markets, such as Africa. In most of the countries of East and South-East Asia opiate abuse stabilized or declined.

UNODC's estimate of the global level of cocaine use increased slightly to 14 million persons or 0.3 percent of the global population. Continued increases in South America, Africa and Europe were partially offset by decreases reported from North America. UNODC also compiles data based on use trends as perceived by experts. Results from these data are not always identical to actual reported information.[3] Trend estimates provided by Member States to UNODC differ slightly, and indicate that global cocaine use declined slightly in 2005.

Notes

1. Government reports, HONLEA reports, UNODC Field Offices, Drug Abuse Information Network for Asia and the Pacific (DAINAP), ICPO/Interpol, World Customs Organisation (WCO), CICAD, EMCDDA, United States Department of State, *International Narcotics Control Strategy Report*, etc.

2. For the purposes of this calculation, the following typical consumption units (at street purity) were assumed: cannabis herb: 0.5 grams per joint; cannabis resin: 0.135 grams per joint; cocaine: 0.1 grams per line; ecstasy: 0.1 grams per pill; heroin: 0.03 grams per dose; amphetamines: 0.03 grams per pill; LSD: 0.00005 grams (50 micrograms).

3. A detailed explanation of this can be found in the Methodology section of this Report.

Ethan Nadelmann

➡ **NO**

Drugs

Prohibition has failed—again. Instead of treating the demand for illegal drugs as a market, and addicts as patients, policymakers the world over have boosted the profits of drug lords and fostered narcostates that would frighten Al Capone. Finally, a smarter drug control regime that values reality over rhetoric is rising to replace the "war" on drugs.

"The Global War on Drugs Can Be Won"

No, it can't. A "drug-free world," which the United Nations describes as a realistic goal, is no more attainable than an "alcohol-free world"—and no one has talked about that with a straight face since the repeal of Prohibition in the United States in 1933. Yet futile rhetoric about winning a "war on drugs" persists, despite mountains of evidence documenting its moral and ideological bankruptcy. When the U.N. General Assembly Special Session on drugs convened in 1998, it committed to "eliminating or significantly reducing the illicit cultivation of the coca bush, the cannabis plant and the opium poppy by the year 2008" and to "achieving significant and measurable results in the field of demand reduction." But today, global production and consumption of those drugs are roughly the same as they were a decade ago; meanwhile, many producers have become more efficient, and cocaine and heroin have become purer and cheaper.

It's always dangerous when rhetoric drives policy—and especially so when "war on drugs" rhetoric leads the public to accept collateral casualties that would never be permissible in civilian law enforcement, much less public health. Politicians still talk of eliminating drugs from the Earth as though their use is a plague on humanity. But drug control is not like disease control, for the simple reason that there's no popular demand for smallpox or polio. Cannabis and opium have been grown throughout much of the world for millennia. The same is true for coca in Latin America. Methamphetamine and other synthetic drugs can be produced anywhere. Demand for particular illicit drugs waxes and wanes, depending not just on availability but also fads, fashion, culture, and competition

From *Foreign Policy,* September/October 2007, pp. 24–26, 28–29. Copyright © 2007 by the Carnegie Endowment for International Peace. Reprinted with permission. www.foreignpolicy. com from alternative means of stimulation and distraction. The relative harshness of drug laws and the intensity of enforcement matter surprisingly little, except in totalitarian states. After all, rates of illegal drug use in the United States are the same as, or higher than, Europe, despite America's much more punitive policies.

"We Can Reduce the Demand for Drugs"

Good luck. Reducing the demand for illegal drugs seems to make sense. But the desire to alter one's state of consciousness, and to use psychoactive drugs to do so, is nearly universal—and mostly not a problem. There's virtually never been a drug-free society, and more drugs are discovered and devised every year. Demand-reduction efforts that rely on honest education and positive alternatives to drug use are helpful, but not when they devolve into unrealistic, "zero tolerance" policies.

As with sex, abstinence from drugs is the best way to avoid trouble, but one always needs a fallback strategy for those who can't or won't refrain. "Zero tolerance" policies deter some people, but they also dramatically increase the harms and costs for those who don't resist. Drugs become more potent, drug use becomes more hazardous, and people who use drugs are marginalized in ways that serve no one.

The better approach is not demand reduction but "harm reduction." Reducing drug use is fine, but it's not nearly as important as reducing the death, disease, crime, and suffering associated with both drug misuse and failed prohibitionist policies. With respect to legal drugs, such as alcohol and cigarettes, harm reduction means promoting responsible drinking and designated drivers, or persuading people to switch to nicotine patches, chewing gums, and smokeless tobacco. With respect to illegal drugs, it means reducing the transmission of infectious disease through syringe-exchange programs, reducing overdose fatalities by making antidotes readily available, and allowing people addicted to heroin and other illegal opiates to obtain methadone from doctors and even pharmaceutical heroin from clinics. Britain, Canada, Germany, the Netherlands, and Switzerland have already embraced this last option. There's no longer any question that these strategies decrease drug-related harms without increasing drug use. What blocks expansion of such programs is not cost; they typically save taxpayers' money that would otherwise go to criminal justice and healthcare. No, the roadblocks are abstinence-only ideologues and a cruel indifference to the lives and well-being of people who use drugs.

"Reducing the Supply of Drugs Is the Answer"

Not if history is any guide. Reducing supply makes as much sense as reducing demand; after all, if no one were planting cannabis, coca, and opium, there wouldn't be any heroin, cocaine, or marijuana to sell or consume. But the carrot and stick of crop eradication and substitution have been tried and failed, with rare exceptions, for half a century. These methods may succeed in targeted locales, but they usually simply shift production from one region to another: Opium production moves from Pakistan to Afghanistan; coca from Peru to Colombia; and cannabis from Mexico to the United States, while overall global production remains relatively constant or even increases.

The carrot, in the form of economic development and assistance in switching to legal crops, is typically both late and inadequate. The stick, often in the form of forced eradication, including aerial spraying, wipes out illegal and legal crops alike and can be hazardous to both people and local environments. The best thing to be said for emphasizing supply reduction is that it provides a rationale for wealthier nations to spend a little money on economic development in poorer countries. But, for the most part, crop eradication and substitution wreak havoc among impoverished farmers without diminishing overall global supply.

The global markets in cannabis, coca, and opium products operate essentially the same way that other global commodity markets do: If one source is compromised due to bad weather, rising production costs, or political difficulties, another emerges. If international drug control circles wanted to think strategically, the key question would no longer be how to reduce global supply, but rather: Where does illicit production cause the fewest problems (and the greatest benefits)? Think of it as a global vice control challenge. No one expects to eradicate vice, but it must be effectively zoned and regulated—even if it's illegal.

"U.S. Drug Policy Is the World's Drug Policy"

Sad, but true. Looking to the United States as a role model for drug control is like looking to apartheid-era South Africa for how to deal with race. The United States ranks first in the world in per capita incarceration—with less than 5 percent of the world's population, but almost 25 percent of the world's prisoners. The number of people locked up for U.S. drug-law violations has increased from roughly 50,000 in 1980 to almost 500,000 today; that's more than the number of people Western Europe locks up for everything. Even more deadly is U.S. resistance to syringe-exchange programs to reduce HIV/ AIDS both at home and abroad. Who knows how many people might not have contracted HIV if the United States had implemented at home, and supported abroad, the sorts of syringe-exchange and other harm-reduction programs that have kept HIV/AIDS rates so low in Australia, Britain, the Netherlands, and elsewhere. Perhaps millions.

And yet, despite this dismal record, the United States has succeeded in constructing an international drug prohibition regime modeled after its own highly punitive and moralistic approach. It has dominated the drug control agencies of the United Nations and other international organizations, and its federal drug enforcement agency was the first national police organization to go global. Rarely has one nation so successfully promoted its own failed policies to the rest of the world.

But now, for the first time, U.S. hegemony in drug control is being challenged. The European Union is demanding rigorous assessment of drug control strategies. Exhausted by decades of service to the U.S.-led war on drugs, Latin Americans are far less inclined to collaborate closely with U.S. drug enforcement efforts. Finally waking up to the deadly threat of HIV/AIDS, China, Indonesia, Vietnam, and even Malaysia and Iran are increasingly accepting of syringe-exchange and other harm-reduction programs. In 2005, the ayatollah in charge of Iran's Ministry of Justice issued a *fatwa* declaring methadone maintenance and syringe-exchange programs compatible with *sharia* (Islamic) law. One only wishes his American counterpart were comparably enlightened.

"Afghan Opium Production Must Be Curbed"

Be careful what you wish for. It's easy to believe that eliminating record-high opium production in Afghanistan—which today accounts for roughly 90 percent of global supply, up from 50 percent 10 years ago—would solve everything from heroin abuse in Europe and Asia to the resurgence of the Taliban.

But assume for a moment that the United States, NATO, and Hamid Karzai's government were somehow able to cut opium production in Afghanistan. Who would benefit? Only the Taliban, warlords, and other black-market entrepreneurs whose stockpiles of opium would skyrocket in value. Hundreds of thousands of Afghan peasants would flock to cities, ill-prepared to find work. And many Afghans would return to their farms the following year to plant another illegal harvest, utilizing guerrilla farming methods to escape intensified eradication efforts. Except now, they'd soon be competing with poor farmers elsewhere in Central Asia, Latin America, or even Africa. This is, after all, a global commodities market.

And outside Afghanistan? Higher heroin prices typically translate into higher crime rates by addicts. They also invite cheaper but more dangerous means of consumption, such as switching from smoking to injecting heroin, which results in higher HIV and hepatitis C rates. All things considered, wiping out opium in Afghanistan would yield far fewer benefits than is commonly assumed.

So what's the solution? Some recommend buying up all the opium in Afghanistan, which would cost a lot less than is now being spent trying to eradicate it. But, given that farmers somewhere will produce opium so long as the demand for heroin persists, maybe the world is better off, all things considered, with 90 percent of it coming from just one country. And if that heresy becomes the new gospel, it opens up all sorts of possibilities for pursuing a new policy in Afghanistan that reconciles the interests of the United States, NATO, and millions of Afghan citizens.

"Legalization Is the Best Approach"

It might be. Global drug prohibition is clearly a costly disaster. The United Nations has estimated the value of the global market in illicit drugs at $400 billion, or 6 percent of global trade. The extraordinary profits available to those willing to assume the risks enrich criminals, terrorists, violent political insurgents, and corrupt politicians and governments. Many cities, states, and even countries in Latin America, the Caribbean, and Asia are reminiscent of Chicago under Al Capone—times 50. By bringing the market for drugs out into the open, legalization would radically change all that for the better.

More importantly, legalization would strip addiction down to what it really is: a health issue. Most people who use drugs are like the responsible alcohol consumer, causing no harm to themselves or anyone else. They would no longer be the state's business. But legalization would also benefit those who struggle with drugs by reducing the risks of overdose and disease associated with unregulated products, eliminating the need to obtain drugs from dangerous criminal markets, and allowing addiction problems to be treated as medical rather than criminal problems.

No one knows how much governments spend collectively on failing drug war policies, but it's probably at least $100 billion a year, with federal, state, and local governments in the United States accounting for almost half the total. Add to that the tens of billions of dollars to be gained annually in tax revenues from the sale of legalized drugs. Now imagine if just a third of that total were committed to reducing drug-related disease and addiction. Virtually everyone, except those who profit or gain politically from the current system, would benefit.

Some say legalization is immoral. That's nonsense, unless one believes there is some principled basis for discriminating against people based solely on what they put into their bodies, absent harm to others. Others say legalization would open the floodgates to huge increases in drug abuse. They forget that we already live in a world in which psychoactive drugs of all sorts are readily available—and in which people too poor to buy drugs resort to sniffing gasoline, glue, and other industrial products, which can be more harmful than any drug. No, the greatest downside to legalization may well be the fact that the legal markets would fall into the hands of the powerful alcohol, tobacco, and pharmaceutical companies. Still, legalization is a far more pragmatic option than living with the corruption, violence, and organized crime of the current system.

"Legalization Will Never Happen"

Never say never. Wholesale legalization may be a long way off—but partial legalization is not. If any drug stands a chance of being legalized, it's cannabis. Hundreds of millions of people have used it, the vast majority without suffering any harm or going on to use "harder" drugs. In

Switzerland, for example, cannabis legalization was twice approved by one chamber of its parliament, but narrowly rejected by the other.

Elsewhere in Europe, support for the criminalization of cannabis is waning. In the United States, where roughly 40 percent of the country's 1.8 million annual drug arrests are for cannabis possession, typically of tiny amounts, 40 percent of Americans say that the drug should be taxed, controlled, and regulated like alcohol. Encouraged by Bolivian President Evo Morales, support is also growing in Latin America and Europe for removing coca from international antidrug conventions, given the absence of any credible health reason for keeping it there. Traditional growers would benefit economically, and there's some possibility that such products might compete favorably with more problematic substances, including alcohol.

The global war on drugs persists in part because so many people fail to distinguish between the harms of drug abuse and the harms of prohibition. Legalization forces that distinction to the forefront. The opium problem in Afghanistan is primarily a prohibition problem, not a drug problem. The same is true of the narcoviolence and corruption that has afflicted Latin America and the Caribbean for almost three decades—and that now threatens Africa. Governments can arrest and kill drug lord after drug lord, but the ultimate solution is a structural one, not a prosecutorial one. Few people doubt any longer that the war on drugs is lost, but courage and vision are needed to transcend the ignorance, fear, and vested interests that sustain it.

POSTSCRIPT

Can the Global Community "Win" the Drug War?

The October 2003 Lisbon International Symposium on Global Drug Policy provided a forum for leading drug policymakers from national governments, senior representatives from various UN agencies, and other experts to address new ideas and innovative solutions. Speakers addressed such varied topics as an international framework for combating drugs, better public health policy, new approaches to the war on drugs, and the variety of new challenges facing the international community. Four key areas of division were spelled out by Martin Jelsma: (1) repression vs. protection; (2) zero tolerance vs. harm reduction; (3) the North-South or donors vs. recipients divide; and (4) demand vs. supply. The failure of nations of the world to reach agreement on these four major areas of contention has resulted, in the judgment of many, in the inability of the global community to address the drug problem successfully. Not enough funds are made available to international agencies like the United Nations, and money that is given is likely to have strings attached to it.

The conference was particularly timely because for the first time in the global war on drugs, policymakers did not debate the issue of whether the current policy was working. Instead, conference participants focused on how to organize a better drug control system. Honorary Secretary-General of Interpol, Raymond Kendall, echoed this view in his closing speech. While Kendall was pleased that debate had shifted to what he called "new levels," the conference did not develop a new plan of action. The issues outlined above were too great to overcome. Nonetheless, progress was made as national examples of successful alternative public policy programs were presented to the delegates.

The United Nations continued the theme of alternative approaches in its *"2004 World Drug Report."* Acknowledging that effective strategies are discovered through trial and error, the UN alluded to a number of recent developments that appear to have potential for helping the global war on drugs. Four major ideas were discussed under the rubric of a "holistic approach." The first is "Addressing the drug problem in a broader sustainable development context." On the one hand, the drug problem hinders development in poor countries and compromises peacemaking efforts in countries torn by civil strife. On the other hand, "poverty, strife and feeble governance are fertile ground for drug production, trafficking and abuse." These situations are interconnected and can only be addressed by a comprehensive approach that recognizes the causes as well as the symptoms of the drug problem.

The second idea is "Providing an integrated response to the drugs and crime nexus." The connections between drug trafficking, organized crime, and even the financing of terrorism has meant that those responsible for addressing each of these scourges must work within the same multilateral system rather than in isolation.

The third development is "Addressing the drugs and crime nexus under the new paradigm of human security." Growing out of the 2000 UN Millennium Summit, the Commission on Human Security is developing a new approach to security that combines human development and human rights. The UN Report suggests that this could provide a critical link between drugs/crime control and sustainable development.

The fourth development is termed "A more synergistic approach." This simply means that not only must there be an integrated and balanced approach to the war on drugs, but that much more needs to be learned. For example, the structure and dynamics of drug markets at the national, regional and global levels are a mystery beyond the simple belief that normal supply and demand principles are at work.

The 2004 UN report also called for deeper understanding of and a focus on controlling drug epidemics. The report summed it up this way. "The powerful dynamics created by the combination of the incentives and behavior of a ruthless market with the contagious characteristics of an epidemic explain why drug use can expand so rapidly and become so difficult to stem."

For Federico Mayor (in collaboration with Jérôme Bindé, *The World Ahead: Our Future in the Making*, UNESCO, 2001), the basic question of eliminating the supply or drying up the demand is raised. Mayor believes it critical that a major emphasis be placed on both sides of the equation. His motivation is based on the dual points that eliminating the supply is difficult but that the health issues associated with illegal drug use demand that we educate existing and potential users about the evils of such behavior. Addicts must be treated as patients, not criminals. At the same time, Mayor argues that the most effective way to fight the drug war is to destroy the financial power of organized crime. Both strategies are critically important.

Harry G. Levine argues that the emphasis on drug prohibition should be replaced by a focus on "harm reduction," creating mechanisms to address tolerance, regulation, and public health. He suggests that global drug prohibition and a focus on both punishing the supplier and the user have not worked very well. Instead, these approaches must be reexamined with a view toward addressing the plight of the drug user in a much different way.

A number of publications provide insight into the war on drugs. Twenty-eight speeches from the aforementioned 2003 Lisbon Conference are reproduced in *Global Drug Policy: Building a New Framework* (The Senlis Council, February 2004). A study prepared for the U.S. Congress by the Congressional Research Service describes U.S. international drug policy (Raphael Perl, "Drug Control: International Policy and Approaches," September 8, 2003). A balanced assessment of drug policies is found in

David R. Mares' *Drug Wars and Coffeehouses: The Political Economy of the International Drug Trade* (CQ Press, 2005). A description of international enforcement operations is found in Gregory D. Lee's *Global Drug Enforcement: Practical Investigative Techniques* (CRC, 2003). A book that examines the global war on drugs from a number of perspectives is Jurg Gerber's *Drug War American Style* (Routledge, 2000).

Criticism of the U.S.-dominated global approach can be found in a number of sources. The reading for this issue suggests a series of short rebuttals to some rather fundamental statements relating to the war on drugs. In response to the statement that "The Global War Can Be Won," Ethan Nadelmann responds: "No, it can't." Six other responses preceded by statements include: "We Can Reduce the Demand for Drugs" (Good luck.); "Reducing the Supply of Drugs Is the Answer" (Not if history is any guide.); "U.S. Drug Policy Is the World's Drug Policy" (Sad, but true.); "Afghan Opium Production Must Be Curbed" (Be careful what you wish for.); "Legalization Is the Best Approach" (It might Be.); and Legalization Will Never Happen" (Never say never.).

An important one focusing on Latin America is Ted Galen Carpenter's *Bad Neighbor Policy* (2003). *The Economist* suggested in its subtitle to an article on drugs that it was "Time to think again about the rules of engagement in the war on drugs" ("Breaking Convention," vol. 366, issue 8318, April 5, 2003). An article offering another perspective is Adam Isacson's "Washington's 'New War' in Colombia: The war on Drugs Meets the War on Terror" (*NACLA Report on the Americas,* vol. 36, issue 5, March/April 2003). Thomas C. Rowe's *Federal Narcotics Laws and the War on Drugs: Money Down a Rat Hole* (Haworth Press, 2006) focuses on the domestic situation in the United States.

A recent comprehensive official report is a U.S. Department of State publication, "International Narcotics Control Strategy Report" (March 2006). Its central message is that "international drug control efforts kept the drug trade on the defensive in 2005." Several long-sought drug kingpins were arrested during the year as well.

ISSUE 11

Is the International Community Adequately Prepared to Address Global Health Pandemics?

YES: Global Influenza Programme, from "Responding to the Avian Influenza Pandemic Threat," World Health Organization (2005)

NO: H. T. Goranson, from "A Primer for Pandemics," Global Envision www.globalenvision.org (2005)

ISSUE SUMMARY

YES: The document from the World Health Organization lays out a comprehensive program of action for individual countries, the international community, and WHO to address the next influenza pandemic.

NO: H. T. Goranson, a former top national scientist with the U.S. government, describes the grave dangers posed by global pandemics and highlights flaws in the international community's ability to respond.

Hear the words "global pandemics" and one thinks of the bubonic plague or Black Death of the Middle Ages where an estimated 30 percent of Europe's population died, or the influenza epidemic of 1918 that killed between 25 million and 50 million people worldwide. Both seem like stories from a bygone era, when modern medicine was unknown and people were simply at the mercy of the spreading tendencies of the virulent diseases. The world of medicine is different today, which leads many to assume that somewhere on the shelves of the local pharmacy or the Centers for Disease Control in Atlanta lies a counteragent to whatever killer lurks out there.

The world is far different from that of the fourteenth century or even 1918. Globalization is with us. The world has shrunk, literally and figuratively, as the human race's ability to move people, money, goods, information and also unwanted agents across national boundaries has increased exponentially. Viruses, germs, parasites, and other virulent disease agents can and do move much more easily than at any time in recorded history.

An article prepared for Risk Management LLC by Anup Shah of www.globalissues.org suggests that the problem is compounded by a number of other factors. One billion people have no access to health systems. Over 10 million people died in a recent year from infectious diseases and a similar number of children under the age of five suffer from malnutrition and other diseases. AIDS/HIV has spread rapidly with 40 million people living with HIV. These conditions help to facilitate the movement of major contagious diseases.

Throughout history, humankind has fallen victim to many such killers. As early as the Peloponnesian War in fifth-century B.C. Greece, typhoid fever was responsible for the deaths of upwards of 25 percent of combatants and civilians alike, necessitating major changes in military tactics. Imperial Rome felt the wrath of a plague thought to be smallpox, as did the eastern Mediterranean during its political height several centuries later. In the past 100 years, influenza (1918, 1957, and 1968), typhoid, and cholera were major killers. In recent years, other infectious diseases have made front page news: HIV, ebola virus, SARS, and most recently, avian or bird flu.

According to World Health Organization Europe, as many as 175 million to 360 million people could fall victim to bird flu if the outbreak was severe enough. The bird flu is front page news because more than 150 million birds have died worldwide from one of its strains, H5N1. This strain was first found in humans in 1997, and WHO estimates report that the human fatality rate has been 50 percent, with 69 deaths occurring as of December 2005. One might be prompted to ask: what is the "big deal, only 134 confirmed cases?" It is not quite so simple. Unlike previous pandemics that hit suddenly and without little or any warning, the avian flu is giving us a clear warning.

But there is good news as well. There does appear to be time to prepare for the worst-case scenario and diminish its likelihood. The flu has the attention of all relevant world health agencies and most national agencies, and steps have been undertaken and/or are currently underway to find a way to combat this contagious disease. While this global issue addresses pandemics in general, we have selected avian flu as a case study of world pandemics and global responses because of its current notoriety with the media and policymakers alike. In the first selection, the World Health Organization lays out a comprehensive program of action for individual countries, the international community, and WHO to address the next influenza pandemic. In the second selection, H. T. Goranson, a former top national scientist with the U.S. government, cautions us that the task is so enormously difficult. He describes the grave dangers posed by global pandemics and highlights flaws in the international community's ability to respond.

YES ↵ Global Influenza Programme

Responding to the Avian Influenza Pandemic Threat

Purpose

This document sets out activities that can be undertaken by individual countries, the international community, and WHO to prepare the world for the next influenza pandemic and mitigate its impact once international spread has begun. Recommended activities are specific to the threat posed by the continuing spread of the H5N1 virus. Addressed to policy-makers, the document also describes issues that can guide policy choices in a situation characterized by both urgency and uncertainty. Recommendations are phase-wise in their approach, with levels of alert, and corresponding activities, changing according to epidemiological indicators of increased threat.

In view of the immediacy of the threat, WHO recommends that all countries undertake urgent action to prepare for a pandemic. Advice on doing so is contained in the recently revised *WHO global influenza preparedness plan*[1] and a new *WHO checklist for influenza pandemic preparedness planning.*[2] To further assist in preparedness planning, WHO is developing a model country plan that will give many developing countries a head start in assessing their status of preparedness and identifying priority needs. Support for rehearsing these plans during simulation exercises will also be provided.

Opportunities to Intervene

As the present situation continues to evolve towards a pandemic, countries, the international community, and WHO have several phase-wise opportunities to intervene, moving from a pre-pandemic situation, through emergence of a pandemic virus, to declaration of a pandemic and its subsequent spread. During the present pre-pandemic phase, interventions aim to reduce the risk that a pandemic virus will emerge and gather better disease intelligence, particularly concerning changes in the behaviour of the virus that signal improved transmissibility. The second opportunity to intervene occurs coincident with the first signal that the virus has improved its transmissibility, and aims to change the early history of the pandemic. The final opportunity occurs after a pandemic has begun. Interventions at this point aim to reduce morbidity, mortality, and social disruption.

Objectives

The objectives of the strategic actions correspond to the principal opportunities to intervene and are likewise phase-wise.

Phase: pre-pandemic
1. Reduce opportunities for human infection
2. Strengthen the early warning system
Phase: emergence of a pandemic virus
3. Contain or delay spread at the source
Phase: pandemic declared and spreading internationally
4. Reduce morbidity, mortality, and social disruption
5. Conduct research to guide response measures

Strategic Actions

The document describes strategic actions that can be undertaken to capitalize on each opportunity to intervene. Given the many uncertainties about the evolution of the pandemic threat, including the amount of time left to prepare, a wise approach involves a mix of measures that immediately address critical problems with longer-term measures that sustainably improve the world's capacity to protect itself against the recurring pandemic threat.

Background

Influenza pandemics have historically taken the world by surprise, giving health services little time to prepare for the abrupt increases in cases and deaths that characterize these events and make them so disruptive. Vaccines—the most important intervention for reducing morbidity and mortality—were available for the 1957 and 1968 pandemic viruses, but arrived too late to have an impact. As a result, great social and economic disruption, as well as loss of life, accompanied the three pandemics of the previous century.

The present situation is markedly different for several reasons. First, the world has been warned in advance. For more than a year, conditions favouring another pandemic have been unfolding in parts of Asia. Warnings that a pandemic may be imminent have come from both changes in the epidemiology of human and animal disease and an expanding geographical presence of the virus, creating further opportunities for human exposure. While neither the timing nor the severity of the next pandemic can be predicted, evidence that the virus is now endemic in bird populations means that the present level of risk will not be easily diminished.

Second, this advance warning has brought an unprecedented opportunity to prepare for a pandemic and develop ways to mitigate its effects. To date, the main preparedness activities undertaken by countries have concentrated on preparing and rehearsing response plans, developing a pandemic vaccine, and securing supplies of antiviral drugs. Because these activities are costly, wealthy countries are presently the best prepared; countries where H5N1 is endemic—and where a pandemic virus is most likely to emerge—lag far behind. More countries now have pandemic preparedness plans: around one fifth of the world's countries have some form of a response plan, but these vary greatly in comprehensiveness and stage of completion. Access to antiviral drugs and, more importantly, to vaccines remains a major problem because of finite manufacturing capacity as well as costs. Some 23 countries have ordered antiviral drugs for national stockpiles, but the principal manufacturer will not be able to fill all orders for at least another year. Fewer than 10 countries have domestic vaccine companies engaged in work on a pandemic vaccine. A November 2004 WHO consultation reached the stark conclusion that, on present trends, the majority of developing countries would have no access to a vaccine during the first wave of a pandemic and possibly throughout its duration.

Apart from stimulating national preparedness activities, the present situation has opened an unprecedented opportunity for international intervention aimed at delaying the emergence of a pandemic virus or forestalling its international spread. Doing so is in the self-interest of all nations, as such a strategy could gain time to augment vaccine supplies. At present capacity, each day of manufacturing gained can mean an additional 5 million doses of vaccine. International support can also strengthen the early warning system in endemic countries, again benefiting preparedness planning and priority setting in all nations. Finally, international support is needed to ensure that large parts of the world do not experience a pandemic without the protection of a vaccine.

Pandemics are remarkable events in that they affect all parts of the world, regardless of socioeconomic status or standards of health care, hygiene and sanitation. Once international spread begins, each government will understandably make protection of its own population the first priority. The best opportunity for international collaboration—in the interest of all countries—is now, before a pandemic begins.

Situation Assessment

1. The risk of a pandemic is great.

Since late 2003, the world has moved closer to a pandemic than at any time since 1968, when the last of the previous century's three pandemics occurred. All prerequisites for the start of a pandemic have now been met save one: the establishment of efficient human-to-human transmission. During 2005, ominous changes have been observed in the epidemiology of the disease in animals. Human cases are continuing to occur, and the virus has expanded its geographical range to include new countries, thus increasing the size of the population at risk. Each new human case gives the virus an opportunity to evolve towards a fully transmissible pandemic strain.

2. The risk will persist.

Evidence shows that the H5N1 virus is now endemic in parts of Asia, having established an ecological niche in poultry. The risk of further human cases will persist, as will opportunities for a pandemic virus to emerge. Outbreaks have recurred despite aggressive control measures, including the culling of more than 140 million poultry. Wild migratory birds—historically the host reservoir of all influenza A viruses—are now dying in large numbers from highly pathogenic H5N1. Domestic ducks can excrete large quantities of highly pathogenic virus without showing signs of illness. Their silent role in maintaining transmission further complicates control in poultry and makes human avoidance of risky behaviours more difficult.

3. Evolution of the threat cannot be predicted.

Given the constantly changing nature of influenza viruses, the timing and severity of the next pandemic cannot be predicted. The final step— improved transmissibility among humans—can take place via two principal mechanisms: a reassortment event, in which genetic material is exchanged between human and avian viruses during co-infection of a human or pig, and a more gradual process of adaptive mutation, whereby the capability of these viruses to bind to human cells would increase during subsequent infections of humans. Reassortment could result in a fully transmissible pandemic virus, announced by a sudden surge of cases with explosive spread. Adaptive mutation, expressed initially as small clusters of human cases with evidence of limited transmission, will probably give the world some time to take defensive action. Again, whether such a "grace period" will be granted is unknown.

4. The early warning system is weak.

As the evolution of the threat cannot be predicted, a sensitive early warning system is needed to detect the first sign of changes in the behaviour of the virus. In risk-prone countries, disease information systems and health, veterinary, and laboratory capacities are weak. Most affected countries cannot adequately compensate farmers for culled poultry, thus discouraging the reporting of outbreaks in the rural areas where the vast majority of human cases have occurred. Veterinary extension services frequently fail to reach these areas. Rural poverty perpetuates high-risk behaviours, including the traditional home-slaughter and consumption of diseased birds. Detection of human cases is impeded by patchy surveillance in these areas. Diagnosis of human cases is impeded by weak laboratory support and the complexity and high costs of testing. Few affected countries have the staff and resources needed to thoroughly investigate human cases and, most importantly, to detect and investigate clusters of cases—an essential warning signal. In virtually all affected countries, antiviral drugs are in very short supply.

The dilemma of preparing for a potentially catastrophic but unpredictable event is great for all countries, but most especially so for countries affected by H5N1 outbreaks in animals and humans. These countries, in which rural subsistence farming is a backbone of economic life, have experienced direct and enormous agricultural losses, presently estimated at more than US$10 billion. They are being asked to sustain—if not intensify—resource-intensive activities needed to safeguard international public health while struggling to cope with many other competing health and infectious disease priorities.

5. Preventive intervention is possible, but untested.

Should a pandemic virus begin to emerge through the more gradual process of adaptive mutation, early intervention with antiviral drugs, supported by other public health measures, could theoretically prevent the virus from further improving its transmissibility, thus either preventing a pandemic or delaying its international spread. While this strategy has been proposed by many influenza experts, it remains untested; no effort has ever been made to alter the natural course of a pandemic at its source.

6. Reduction of morbidity and mortality during a pandemic will be impeded by inadequate medical supplies.

Vaccination and the use of antiviral drugs are two of the most important response measures for reducing morbidity and mortality during a pandemic. On present trends, neither of these interventions will be available in adequate quantities or equitably distributed at the start of a pandemic and for many months thereafter.

1. Reduce Opportunities for Human Infection

Strategic Actions

- **Support the FAO/OIE control strategy**

  The FAO/OIE technical recommendations describe specific control measures and explain how they should be implemented. The global strategy, developed in collaboration with WHO, takes its urgency from the risk to human health, including that arising from a pandemic, posed by the continuing circulation of the virus in animals. The strategy adopts a progressive approach, with different control options presented in line with different disease profiles, including such factors as poultry densities, farming systems, and whether infections have occurred in commercial farms or small rural holdings. The proposed initial focus is on Viet Nam, Thailand, Cambodia, and Indonesia, the four countries where human cases of infection with H5N1 avian influenza have been detected.

Clear and workable measures are proposed for different countries and situations within countries. Vaccination is being recommended as an appropriate control measure in some, but not all, epidemiological situations. Other measures set out in the strategy include strict biosecurity at commercial farms, use of compartmentalization and zoning concepts, control of animal and product movements, and a restructuring of the poultry industry in some countries. The strategy notes strong political will to tackle the problem. Nonetheless, time-frames for reaching control objectives are now being measured in years.

In July 2005, OIE member countries approved new standards, recognized by the World Trade Organization, specific to avian influenza and aimed at improving the safety of international trade of poultry and poultry products. The new standards cover methods of surveillance, compulsory international notification of low- and highly-pathogenic strains of avian influenza, the use of vaccination, and food safety of poultry products. Compliance with these standards should be given priority in efforts to strengthen early detection, reporting, and response in countries currently affected by outbreaks of H5N1 avian influenza.

- **Intensify collaboration between the animal and public health sectors**

WHO will appoint dedicated staff to increase the present exchange of information between agricultural and health sectors at the international level. Increased collaboration between the two sectors serves three main purposes: to pinpoint areas of disease activity in animals where vigilance for human cases should be intensified, to ensure that measures for controlling the disease in animals are compatible with reduced opportunities for human exposure, and to ensure that advice to rural communities on protective measures remains in line with the evolving nature of the disease in animals.

WHO will undertake joint action with FAO and OIE to understand the evolution of H5N1 viruses in Asia. Achieving this objective requires acquisition and sharing of a full inventory of H5N1 viruses, from humans, poultry, wild birds, and other animals, and sequences.

WHO will stress the importance of controlling the disease in rural areas. Measures to control the disease in animals of necessity consider how best to regain agricultural productivity and international trade, and this objective is reflected in the FAO/OIE strategy. While elimination of the virus from the commercial poultry sector alone will aid agricultural recovery, it may not significantly reduce opportunities for human exposure, as the vast majority of cases to date have been associated with exposure to small rural flocks. No case has yet been detected among workers in the commercial poultry sector. The FAO/OIE strategy fully recognizes that control of disease in rural "backyard" flocks will be the most difficult challenge; strong support from the health sector, as expressed by WHO, helps gather the political will to meet this challenge. In addition, it is imperative that measures for controlling disease in rural flocks are accompanied by risk communication to farmers and their families.

A joint FAO/OIE/WHO meeting, held in Malaysia in July 2005,[3] addressed the links between animal disease and risks of human exposures and infections, and defined preventive measures that should be jointly introduced by the animal and public health sectors. Priority was given to interventions in the backyard rural farming system and in so-called wet markets where live poultry are sold under crowded and often unsanitary conditions.

WHO, FAO, and OIE have jointly established a Global Early Warning and Response System (GLEWS) for transboundary animal diseases. The new mechanism combines the existing outbreak alert, verification, and response capacities of the three agencies and helps ensure that disease tracking at WHO benefits from the latest information on relevant animal diseases. The system formalizes the sharing of epidemiological information and provides the operational framework for joint field missions to affected areas.

- **Strengthen risk communication to rural residents**

WHO will, through its research networks and in collaboration with FAO and OIE, improve understanding of the links between animal disease, human behaviours, and the risk of acquiring H5N1 infection. This information will be used as the basis for risk communication to rural residents.

Well-known and avoidable behaviours with a high risk of infection continue to occur in rural areas. Ongoing risk communication is needed to alert rural residents to these risks and explain how to avoid them. Better knowledge about the relationship between animal and human disease, obtained by WHO in collaboration with FAO/OIE, can be used to make present risk communication more precise and thus better able to prevent risky behaviours.

- **Improve approaches to environmental detection of the virus**

WHO, FAO, and OIE will facilitate, through their research networks, the rapid development of new methods for detecting the virus in environmental samples. The purpose of these methods is to gain a better understanding of conditions that increase the risk of human infection and therefore favour emergence of a pandemic virus. Such knowledge underpins the success of primary prevention of a pandemic through disease control in animals. It also underpins advice to rural residents on behaviours to avoid. Reliance on routine veterinary surveillance, which is weak in most risk-prone countries, has not produced an adequate understanding of the relationship between animal and human disease. For example, in some cases, outbreaks in poultry are detected only after a human case has been confirmed. In other cases, investigation of human cases has failed to find a link with disease in animals.

2. Strengthen the Early Warning System

Strategic Actions

- **Improve the detection of human cases**

  WHO will provide the training, diagnostic reagents, and administrative support for external verification needed to improve the speed and reliability of case detection. To date, the vast majority of cases have been detected following hospitalization for respiratory illness. Hospitals in affected countries need support in case detection, laboratory confirmation, and reporting. Apart from its role in an early warning system, rapid laboratory confirmation signals the need to isolate patients and manage them according to strict procedures of infection control, and can thus help prevent further cases.

  Diagnostic support continues to be provided by laboratories in the WHO network. However, because the initial symptoms of H5N1 infection mimic those of many diseases common in these countries, accurate case detection requires the testing of large numbers of samples. Improved local capacity is therefore a more rational solution.

  Because of its high pathogenicity, H5N1 can be handled safely only by specially trained staff working in specially equipped laboratories operating at a high level of biosecurity. These facilities do not presently exist in the majority of affected countries. As an alternative, laboratory capacity can be enhanced by strengthening the existing system of national influenza centres or by providing mobile high-containment laboratories. Supportive activities include training in laboratory methods needed for H5N1 diagnosis, distribution of up-to-date diagnostic reagents, and coordination of work between national laboratories and epidemiological institutions.

  An infrastructure needs to be developed to complement national testing with rapid international verification in WHO certified laboratories, especially as each confirmed human case yields information essential to risk assessment. The capacity to do so already exists. WHO offers countries rapid administrative support to ship samples outside affected countries. Such forms of assistance become especially critical when clusters of cases occur and require investigation.

- **Combine detection of new outbreaks in animals with active searches for human cases**

  Using epidemiologists in its country offices and, when necessary, external partners, WHO will ensure that detection of new outbreaks of highly pathogenic H5N1 in poultry is accompanied by active searches for human cases. Surveillance in several countries where H5N1 is considered endemic in birds is inadequate and suspicions are strong that human cases have been missed. Cambodia's four human cases were detected only after patients sought treatment in neighbouring Viet Nam, where physicians are on high alert for cases and familiar with the clinical presentation.

- **Support epidemiological investigation**

Reliable risk assessment depends on thorough investigation of sporadic human cases and clusters of cases. Guidelines for outbreak investigation, specific to H5N1 and to the epidemiological situation in different countries, are being developed on an urgent basis for use in training national teams. These guidelines give particular emphasis to the investigation of clusters of cases and determination of whether human-to-human transmission has occurred. Teams assembled from institutions in the WHO Global Outbreak Alert and Response Network (GOARN) can be deployed for rapid on-site investigative support.

- **Coordinate clinical research in Asia**

Clinical data on human cases need to be compiled and compared in order to elucidate modes of transmission, identify groups at risk, and find better treatments. Work has begun to establish a network of hospitals, modelled on the WHO global influenza surveillance network, engaged in clinical research on human disease. The network will link together the principal hospitals in Asia that are treating H5N1 patients and conducting clinical research. Technical support will allow rapid exchange of information and sharing of specimens and research results, and encourage the use of standardized protocols for treatment and standardized sampling procedures for investigation.

Identification of risk groups guides preventive measures and early interventions. Provision of high-quality data on clinical course, outcome, and treatment efficacy meets an obvious and immediate need in countries with human cases. Answers to some key questions—the efficacy of antiviral drugs, optimum dose, and prescribing schedules—could benefit health services elsewhere once a pandemic is under way.

- **Strengthen risk assessment**

WHO's daily operations need to be strengthened to ensure constant collection and verification of epidemiological and virological information essential for risk assessment. Ministries of health and research institutions in affected countries need to be more fully engaged in the collection and verification of data. Ministries and institutions in non-affected countries should help assess the significance of these data, and the results should be issued rapidly. These activities, currently coordinated by WHO, need to escalate; influenza viruses can evolve rapidly and in unexpected ways that alter risk assessment, as evidenced by the recent detection of highly pathogenic H5N1 viruses in migratory birds. Functions of the WHO network of laboratories with expertise in the analysis of H5N1 viruses can be improved through tools, such as a genetic database, and a strong collaboration with veterinary laboratory networks to ensure that animal as well as human viruses are kept under constant surveillance.

- **Strengthen existing national influenza centres throughout the risk-prone region**

  Many existing national influenza centres, designated by WHO, already possess considerable infrastructure in the form of equipment and trained personnel. Additional support, particularly in the form of diagnostic reagents, could help strengthen the early warning system in risk-prone countries and their neighbours.

- **Give risk-prone countries an incentive to collaborate internationally**

  The promise of assistance is a strong motivation to report cases and share clinical specimens internationally. A high-level meeting should be convened so that heads of state in industrialized countries and in risk-prone countries can seek solutions and reach agreement on the kinds of support considered most desirable by individual countries.

3. Contain or Delay Spread at the Source

Strategic Actions

- **Establish an international stockpile of antiviral drugs**

  WHO will establish an international stockpile of antiviral drugs for rapid response at the start of a pandemic. The stockpile is a strategic option that serves the interests of the international community as well as those of the initially affected populations. Issues that need to be addressed include logistics associated with deployment and administration, and licensing for use in individual countries. Mechanisms for using an international stockpile need to be defined more precisely in terms of epidemiological triggers for deploying the stockpile and time-frames for emergency delivery and administration. WHO is working closely with groups engaged in mathematical modelling and others to guide the development of early containment strategies.

  While pursuit of this option thus has no guarantee of success, it nonetheless needs to be undertaken as it represents one of the few preventive options for an event with predictably severe consequences for every country in the world. It is also the best guarantee that populations initially affected will have access to drugs for treatment. Should early containment fail to completely halt spread of the virus, a delay in wide international spread would gain time to intensify preparedness. It can be expected that most governments will begin introducing emergency measures only when the threat of a pandemic is certain and immediate. A lead time for doing so of one month or more could allow many health services to build surge capacity and make the necessary conversion from routine to emergency services.

- **Develop mass delivery mechanisms for antiviral drugs**

  Several WHO programmes, such as those for the emergency response to outbreaks of poliomyelitis, measles, epidemic-prone meningitis, and yellow fever, have acquired considerable experience in the urgent mass delivery of vaccines in developing countries. Less experience exists for the mass delivery of antiviral drugs, where administration is complicated by the need for drugs to be taken over several days and the need for different dosing schedules according to therapeutic or prophylactic use. WHO will develop and pilot test delivery mechanisms for antiviral drugs in collaboration with national health authorities and industry. Studies will assess coverage rates that could be achieved, taking into account compliance rates, and ways to support this intervention with other measures, such as area quarantine.

- **Conduct surveillance of antiviral susceptibility**

  Using its existing network of influenza laboratories, WHO will establish a surveillance programme for antiviral susceptibility testing, modelled on a similar programme for anti-tuberculosis drugs. Use of an international stockpile to attempt to halt an outbreak will involve administration of drugs to large numbers of people for several weeks. A mechanism must be in place to monitor any resulting changes in virus susceptibility to these drugs. The development of drug resistance would threaten the effectiveness of national stockpiles of antiviral drugs established for domestic use. The work of WHO collaborating centres for influenza and reference laboratories for H5N1 analysis can be coordinated to include antiviral susceptibility testing.

4. Reduce Morbidity, Mortality, and Social Disruption

Strategic Actions

- **Monitor the evolving pandemic in real time**

  Many characteristics of a pandemic that will guide the selection of response measures will become apparent only after the new virus has emerged and begun to cause large numbers of cases. WHO, assisted by virtual networks of experts, will monitor the unfolding epidemiological and clinical behaviour of the new virus in real time. This monitoring will give health authorities answers to key questions about age groups at greatest risk, infectivity of the virus, severity of the disease, attack rates, risk to health care workers, and mortality rates. Such monitoring can also help determine whether severe illness and deaths are caused by primary viral pneumonia or secondary bacterial pneumonia, which responds to antibiotics, and thus guide the emergency provision of supplies. Experts in mathematical modelling will be included in the earliest field assessment teams to make the forecasting of trends as reliable as possible.

- **Introduce non-pharmaceutical interventions**

  Answers to these questions will help officials select measures—closing of schools, quarantine, a ban on mass gatherings, travel restrictions—that match the behaviour of the virus and thus have the greatest chance of reducing the number of cases and delaying geographical spread. WHO has produced guidance on the use of such measures at different stages at the start of a pandemic and after its international spread.

- **Use antiviral drugs to protect priority groups**

  WHO recommends that countries with sufficient resources invest in a stockpile of antiviral drugs for domestic use, particularly at the start of a pandemic when mass vaccination is not an option and priority groups, such as frontline workers, need to be protected.

- **Augment vaccine supplies**

  WHO, in collaboration with industry and regulatory authorities, has introduced fast-track procedures for the development and licensing of a pandemic vaccine. Strategies have also been developed that make the most of scarce vaccine antigen and thus allow more quantities of vaccine to be produced despite the limits of existing plant capacity. Once a pandemic is declared, all manufacturers will switch from production of seasonal vaccines to production of a pandemic vaccine. Countries need to address liability issues that could arise following mass administration of a pandemic vaccine and ensure adequate warehousing, logistics, and complementary supplies, such as syringes.

- **Ensure equitable access to vaccines**

  The present strong interdependence of commerce and trade means that the international community cannot afford to allow large parts of the world to experience a pandemic unprotected by a vaccine. The humanitarian and ethical arguments for providing such protection are readily apparent. As a matter of urgency, WHO must build a political process aimed at finding ways to further augment production capacity dramatically and make vaccines affordable and accessible in the developing world. WHO will also work with donor agencies on the latter issue.

- **Communicate risks to the public**

  As soon as a pandemic is declared, health authorities will need to start a continuous process of risk communication to the public. Many difficult issues—the inevitable spread to all countries, the short-age of vaccines and antiviral drugs, justification for the selection of priority groups for protection—will need to be addressed. Effective risk communication, supported by confidence in government au-thorities and the reliability of their information, may help mitigate some of the social and economic disruption attributed to an anxious public. Countries are advised to plan in advance. A communication strategy for a pandemic situation should include training in out-break communication and integration of communicators in senior management teams.

5. Conduct Research to Guide Response Measures

Strategic Actions

- **Assess the epidemiological characteristics of an emerging pandemic**

  At the start of a pandemic, policy-makers will face an immediate need for epidemiological data on the principal age groups affected, modes of transmission, and pathogenicity. Such data will support urgent decisions about target groups for vaccination and receipt of antiviral drugs. They can also be used to support forecasts on local and global patterns of spread as an early warning that helps national authorities intensify preparedness measures. WHO will identify epidemiological centres for collecting these data and establish standardized research protocols.

- **Monitor the effectiveness of health interventions**

  Several non-pharmaceutical interventions have been recommend-ed to reduce local and international spread of a pandemic and lower the rate of transmission. While many of these interventions have proved useful in the prevention and control of other infec-tious diseases, their effectiveness during a pandemic has never been comprehensively evaluated. More information is needed on their feasibility, effectiveness, and acceptability to populations. WHO will establish study sites and develop study protocols to evaluate these interventions at local, national, and international levels. Comparative data on the effectiveness of different interventions are also important, as several measures are associated with very high levels of social disruption.

- **Evaluate the medical and economic consequences**

  WHO will establish study sites and develop protocols for prospec-tive evaluation of the medical and economic consequences of the pandemic so that future health interventions can be adjusted accordingly. In the past, such evaluations have been conducted only after a pandemic had ended. Their value as a policy guide for the allocation of resources has been flawed because of inadequate data.

Notes

1. http://whqlibdoc.who.int/hq/2005/WHO_CDS_CSR_GIP_2005.5.pdf.
2. http://whqlibdoc.who.int/hq/2005/WHO_CDS_CSR_GIP_2005.4.pdf.
3. http://www.fao.org/ag/againfo/subjects/documents/ai/concmalaysia.pdf.

H. T. Goranson   ➔ **NO**

A Primer for Pandemics

A few times each year, the world is reminded that a pandemic threat is immanent. What can we do to prepare for the next one?

> According to Dr. Tim Evans, Assistant Director-General for Evidence and Information for Policy, World Health Organization: "There is a chronic global shortage of health workers, as a result of decades of underinvestment in their education, training, salaries, working environment and management. This has led to a severe lack of key skills, rising levels of career switching and early retirement, as well as national and international migration. In sub-Saharan Africa, where all the issues mentioned above are combined with the HIV/AIDS pandemic, there are an estimated 750,000 health workers in a region that is home to 682 million people. By comparison, the ratio is ten to 15 times higher in OECD countries, whose ageing population is putting a growing strain on an over-stretched workforce. Solutions to this crisis must be worked out at local, national and international levels, and must involve governments, the United Nations, health professionals, non-governmental organizations and community leaders."
>
> "There is no single solution to such a complex problem, but ways forward do exist and must now be implemented. For example, some developed countries have put policies in place to stop active recruitment of health workers from severely understaffed countries. Some developing countries have revised their pay scales and introduced non-monetary incentives to retain their workforce and deploy them in rural areas. Education and training procedures have been tailored to countries' specific needs. Community health workers are helping their communities to prevent and treat key diseases. Action must be taken now for results to show in the coming years."

This article takes a look at global pandemics, and how medical professionals worldwide trained as "detectors" would be the best way to halt the spread of a disease before it became a global threat.

·❀·

A few times each year, the world is reminded that a pandemic threat is immanent. In 2003, it was SARS. Today, it is a potential avian virus similar to the one that killed 30 million people after 1914.

"Bird flu" has already shown that it can jump from fowl to humans, and now even to cats, which indicates that it might be the next global killer. But there are many other potential pandemics, and many are not even viruses. Bacteria, prions, parasites, and even environmental factors could suddenly change in a way that slays us. It is widely predicted that when this happens, the economic and human losses will exceed that of any previous war.

Indeed, it is humbling to remember that some of history's most deadly invasions were carried out by single-cell organisms, such as cholera, bubonic plague, and tuberculosis. Countries with the resources to do so are making resistance plans against pandemics—limited strategies that would protect their own citizens. Most governments are hoping that early detection will make containment possible.

Containment depends heavily on vaccines, but vaccines are only part of the answer. While they are a good defense against many viruses, each vaccine is highly specific to the threat. Viruses are parasites to cells, and each virus attacks a particular type of cell. The virus is shaped so that it can drill into a particular feature of that cell and inject parts of itself inside, confusing the cell into making more viruses and destroying itself in the process. With their very specific forms, the most effective anti-viral vaccines must be designed for a narrow range of factors.

Sometimes the tailored nature of viruses works in our favor. For example, they usually find it difficult to jump between species, because they would have to change their structure. But if large numbers of a host—say, birds—encounter a great number of people, eventually the virus will find a way to prosper in a new type of cell.

Birds are the greatest concern today only because the spread is easy to see. But AIDS jumped from monkeys and several types of flu jumped from swine. Deadly mutations of any kind need to be identified urgently, so that an effective vaccine can be designed before the strain becomes comfortable in the human body. Unfortunately our present methods of detection are not sensitive enough.

This is even more worrying when you realize that scientists should also be monitoring bacteria, prions, and parasites. There are more bacteria than any other life form. Many live harmlessly in our bodies and perform useful functions. They evolve and adapt easily, which means that they learn to sidestep our drugs over time. Bacteria should be checked for two types of mutation: adaptation by a hostile form that enables it to become super-immune to drugs, or a deadly mutant strain that appears in one of the multitude of "safe" bacteria.

Prions are a relatively new discovery. They are made from proteins similar to those that the body uses during healthy operations, which means that they are able to fool the body's tools into making more prions. They have only recently been recognized as the cause of several infectious diseases, including mad cow disease and Creutzfeldt-Jakob Disease, which kill by crowding out healthy brain cells. Many nerve, respiratory and muscle diseases might also be caused by prions.

Finally, parasites, simple animals that infect us, are already classified as pandemics. Malaria afflicts 300 million people and is the world's biggest killer of children. Many parasites are worms: hookworm (800 million people infected), roundworm (1.5 billion), schistosomes (200 million), and the worm that causes Elephantiasis (150 million).

There are also antagonists that are currently ignored. Environmental chemicals and particulates might warrant their own categories. Or consider combinations of problems, such as these chemical infectors mixing with airborne pollens, and apparently pushing up incidences of asthma. New fungal infections are even scarier and might be harder to treat.

The bottom line is that we can't predict where the threat will emerge, so we need a distributed, intelligent detection system. In practical terms, how should it be built?

"Detectors" would have to be expert enough to know when an ordinary-looking symptom is actually an emergency. They would be located everywhere, with an emphasis on vulnerable regions. Initial warning signs of a pandemic are most likely to appear in the developing world, but detection nodes should be positioned in every country, with the least possible expense. This is not as difficult as it sounds. The key is to harness existing infrastructure.

Medical infrastructure exists everywhere, in some form. It also tends to be the least corrupt of institutions in regions where that is a problem. Medical centers and clinics would be expected to investigate the cause of ailments in a large number of their patients, even in cases where the symptoms seem common. A small amount of additional scientific expertise and lab equipment would need to be added to a public health system that serves ordinary needs.

Enhancing existing resources would be effective for two reasons. First, illness is more likely to be reported in a city hospital than at a specialist institute. Second, the investment would boost latent public health in that region. For poor regions, investment in equipment and training would have to come from wealthier counterparts. Rich countries could justify the expense in terms of the savings that would result from early detection of a major threat. Tropical climates and urban slums are humanity's front line against pandemics, and they should be equipped properly.

Public health is an important asset for any nation. With so much at stake, it makes sense to place sentinels near every swamp, city, public market, and farmyard on earth.

POSTSCRIPT

Is the International Community Adequately Prepared to Address Global Health Pandemics?

It is far too easy to adopt one of two extreme positions regarding the potential for a global pandemic such as influenza. The first assumes that since these outbreaks begin somewhere in the poorer regions of the globe far removed geographically from the United States, we in the developed world, particularly in the United States, are not at great risk. One should immediately pause, however, as each winter many Americans find themselves suffering from a much less virulent strain of the flu, which typically has its roots in the same poor regions of the globe. The second position with respect to the future potential for a global pandemic suggests that modern medical science will always find a way to counteract such diseases. As the world's experience with HIV/AIDS has taught us, however, modern viruses and other diseases are increasingly more complicated to address successfully, either in treating the symptoms of the problem or the actual problem itself.

Edwin D. Kilbourne addresses this issue in his analysis of twentieth-century pandemics and lessons learned there from ("Influenza Pandemics of the 20th Century," *Emerging Infectious Diseases*, vol. 12, no. 1, January 2006). Says Kilbourne, "Yes, we can prepare, but with the realization that no amount of hand washing, hand wringing, public education, or gauze masks will do the trick. The keystone of influenza prevention is vaccination." This raises a number of questions, Kilbourne continues. Primary among these are who shall be given the vaccine, the risks of mass administration, and the availability of sufficient quantities of a vaccine of "adequate antigenic potency."

Kilbourne suggests that an appropriate strategy was suggested by the World Health Organization as early as 1969 and endorsed repeatedly since then. The approach assumes that a new influenza outbreak will emerge from one of sixteen known subtypes HA in avian or mammalian species. This assumption has not yet resulted in a genetic vaccine that can address these subtypes. As the first reading reveals, however, WHO has developed a comprehensive set of strategic actions for the three phases of a pandemic: the pre-pandemic phase, the emergence of a pandemic virus, and the pandemic declared and spreading internationally. As the second reading suggests, however, national governments in the developing world, the likely place of origin of the next global pandemic, suffer from a shortage of skilled medical personnel that would serve as front-line defenders against such infectious diseases.

One piece of good news is that, unlike previous pandemics, the developed world has taken notice of a potential future threat. The U.S. government has pledged close to $4 billion for the current fiscal year, three times its expenditures of five years ago. Private philanthropists led by the Bill and Melinda Gates Foundation have also been active in global health programs.

Literature from both the medical and more general fields has also been more cognizant of the problem and has dramatically focused attention to the potential future problem. One place to begin is a major report from the World Health Organization called *Avian Influenza: Assessing the Pandemic Threat* (2005). It traces the evolution of the outbreaks of the H5N1 avian influenza, lessons from past pandemics, its origins in poultry, and future actions "in the face of an uncertain threat." A second WHO report spells out in greater detail that organization's plan of action, *WHO Global Influenza Preparedness Plan* (2005). One study cautions us about this report, however (Martin Enserink, "New Study Casts Doubt on Plans for Pandemic Containment," *Science*, vol. 311, no. 5764, February 24, 2006).

Several books are useful in understanding global health and pandemics. A most recent work is Barry Youngerman's *Pandemics and Global Issues* (Facts on File, 2008). Two books that focus on broader global health issues include *Understanding Global Health* by William Markle et al. (McGraw-Hill, 2007) and *Critical Issues in Global Health* (C. Everett Koop et al., eds., Jossey-Bass, 2002). Two books that address the link between globalization and health include *Globalization and Health: An Introduction* (Kelley Lee, Palgrave Macmillan, 2004) and *Health Impacts of Globalization: Towards Global Governance* (Kelley Lee, Palgrave Macmillan, 2003).

A historical overview of pandemics is R. S. Bray's *Armies of Pestilence: The Effects of Pandemics on History* (Lutterworth Press, 1998). Another general source is "Preparing for Pandemic: High Probability of a Flu Pandemic Prompts WHO to Offer Strategies" (*The Futurist*, vol. 40, no. 1, January/February 2006). A source that focuses on the value of global structures in the fight against pandemics is "Global Network Could Avert Pandemics" (J. P. Chretien, J. C. Gaydos, J. L. Malone and D. L. Blazes, *Nature*, vol. 440, 2006).

An excellent Internet Web site is bmj.com, a comprehensive source of resources by the medical field on global pandemics. One example is "An Iatrogenic Pandemic of Panic" by Luc Bonneux and Wim Van Damme (April 1, 2006).

Finally, a current report on the problem of HIV/AIDS is "The Global Challenge of HIV and AIDS" (Peter R. Lamptey, Jami L. Johnson and Marya Khan, *Population Reference Bureau*, vol. 61, no. 1, March 2006).

ISSUE 12

Do Adequate Strategies Exist to Combat Human Trafficking?

YES: Janie Chuang, from "Beyond a Snapshot: Preventing Human Trafficking in the Global Economy," *Indiana Journal of Global Legal Studies* (Winter 2006)

NO: Dina Francesca Haynes, from "Used, Abused, Arrested, and Deported: Extending Immigration Benefits to Protect the Victims of Trafficking and to Secure the Prosecution of Traffickers," *Human Rights Quarterly* (vol. 26, no. 2, 2004)

ISSUE SUMMARY

YES: Janie Chuang, practitioner-in-residence at the America University Washington College of Law, suggests that governments have been finally motivated to take action against human traffickers as a consequence of the concern over national security implications of forced human labor movement and the involvement of transnational criminal syndicates.

NO: Dina Francesca Haynes, associate professor of law at the New England School of Law, argues that none of the models underlying domestic legislation to deal with human traffickers is "terribly effective" in addressing the issue effectively.

Human trafficking is defined by the United Nations as "The recruitment, transportation, transfer, harbouring or receipt of persons, by means of the threat or use of force or other forms of coercion, of abduction, of fraud, of deception, of the abuse of power or of a position of vulnerability or of the giving or receiving of payments or benefits to achieve the consent of a person having control over another person, for the purpose of exploitation" ("Trafficking in Persons—Global Patterns," United Nations, Office on Drug and Crime, April 2006). Exploitation may take any one of several forms: prostitution, forced labor, slavery, or other forms of servitude. While slavery has been with us since ancient times, the existence of human trafficking across national borders, particularly involving major distances, is a relatively new escalation of a problem that in the past was addressed as a domestic issue, if addressed at all.

Its modern manifestation is eerily similar, as reported by the UN in the above source. People are abducted or "recruited" in the country of origin, transferred through a standard network to another region of the globe, and then exploited in the destination country. If at any point exploitation is interrupted or ceases, victims can be rescued and might receive support from the country of destination. Victims might be repatriated to their country of origin or, less likely, relocated to a third country. Too often, victims are treated as illegal migrants and treated accordingly. The UN estimates that 127 countries act as countries of origin while 137 countries serve as countries of destination. Profits are estimated by the UN to be $7 billion per year, with between 70,000 and four million new victims annually.

When one hears of human trafficking, one usually thinks of sexual exploitation rather than of forced labor. This is not surprising as not only are individual victim stories more compelling, the former type of exploitation represents the more frequent topic of dialogue among policymakers and is also the more frequent occurrence as reported to the UN by a three-to-one margin. With respect to victims, 77 per cent are woman, 33 per cent children, 48 per cent girls, 12 per cent boys, and 9 per cent males (the sum of percentages is over 100 because one source can indicate more than one victim profile). It is not surprising that most women and female children are exploited sexually, while most male adults and children are subjected to forced labor. Sexual exploitation is more typically found in Central and Southeastern Europe. Former Soviet republics serve as a huge source of origin. Africa ranks high as a region of victim origin as well, although most end up in forced labor rather than in sexual exploitation. Asia is a region of both origin and destination. Countries at the top of the list include Thailand, Japan, India, Taiwan, and Pakistan.

Two principal types of groups characterize the traffickers. The first group was highly structured and organized, following a disciplined hierarchical pattern of control. In addition to trafficking, they were involved in transnational movement of a variety of illegal goods, such as drugs and firearms. Violence was the norm in this group. The second type was a smaller group that was strictly profit-oriented and opportunistic.

In the first selection, Janie Chuang suggests that governments have adopted a three-pronged approach focusing on prosecuting traffickers, protecting trafficked persons, and preventing trafficking. She argues that there has been greater success with the first two foci, but that the current legal response appears to be having an effect or shows great promise in addressing all three areas. In the second selection, Dina Francesca Haynes suggests that while much rhetoric has occurred, the models underlying domestic legislation are not effective for a variety of reasons.

YES ↩

Janie Chuang

Beyond a Snapshot: Preventing Human Trafficking in the Global Economy

Introduction

Within the last decade, governments have hastened to develop inter-national, regional, and national laws to combat the problem of human trafficking, i.e., the recruitment or movement of persons for forced labor or slavery-like practices. Legal responses to the problem typically adopt a three-prong framework focused on prosecuting traffickers, protecting trafficked persons, and preventing trafficking. In practice, however, these responses emphasize the prosecution of traffickers and, to a lesser extent, the protection of their victims. Most legal frameworks address trafficking as an act (or a series of acts) of violence, with the perpetrators to be punished and the victims to be protected and reintegrated into society. While such responses might account for the consequences of trafficking, they tend to overlook its causes—that is, the broader socioeconomic conditions that feed the problem. Oft-repeated pledges to prevent trafficking by addressing its root causes seldom evolve from rhetoric into reality.

More often than not, trafficking is labor migration gone horribly wrong in our globalized economy. Notwithstanding its general economic benefits, globalization has bred an ever-widening wealth gap between countries, and between rich and poor communities within countries.[1] This dynamic has created a spate of "survival migrants"[2] who seek em-ployment opportunities abroad as a means of survival as jobs disappear in their countries of origin. The desperate need to migrate for work, com-bined with destination countries tightening their border controls (despite a growing demand for migrant workers), render these migrants highly vul-nerable to trafficking. For women in particular, this vulnerability is exacer-bated by well-entrenched discriminatory practices that relegate women to employment in informal economic sectors and further limit their avenues for legal migration.

Governments have been deeply reluctant, however, to view trafficking in this broader frame—that is, as a problem of migration, poverty,

From *Indiana Journal of Global Legal Studies,* vol. 13, no. 2, 2004, pp. 137–138, 147–157.
Copyright © 2004 by Indiana University Press. Reprinted by permission.

discrimination, and gender-based violence. They have tended to view trafficking as a "law and order" problem requiring an aggressive criminal justice response. Emerging studies reveal the drawbacks of this myopia. Notwithstanding the hundreds of millions of dollars already invested in the criminal justice response to the problem, we have yet to see an appreciable reduction in the absolute numbers of people trafficked worldwide.[3] And even in the rare cases where trafficked persons have received rights protective treatment and aftercare, they nonetheless are left facing the socioeconomic conditions that rendered them vulnerable to abuse in the first instance.

This article explores governments' reluctance to address trafficking in its broader socioeconomic context, and offers both a plea and a proposal for more comprehensive approaches to trafficking. Because close examination of these issues is beyond the scope of this short symposium piece, this article aims only to lay a foundation for further thought and discussion in this area. This article problematizes current approaches to trafficking by refraining the problem of trafficking as a global migratory response to current globalizing socioeconomic trends. It argues that, to be effective, counter-trafficking strategies must also target the underlying conditions that impel people to accept dangerous labor migration assignments in the first place. The article then examines how the international legal response to the problem is, as yet, inadequate to the task of fostering longterm solutions. Moreover, by failing to assess the long-term implications of existing counter-trafficking strategies, these responses risk being not only ineffective, but counterproductive. Observing the need for more focused inquiry into prevention strategies, the article advocates strategic use of the nondiscrimination principle to give more meaningful application to basic economic, social, and cultural rights, the violation of which sustains the trafficking phenomenon.[4]

Given the enduring nature of socioeconomic deprivation in many parts of the world, it is easy to dismiss calls for substantive prevention strategies as too lofty or impracticable. But the reality that millions of lives remain at risk for trafficking demands that we embrace this challenge.

I. Globalization, Migration, and Trafficking

While the problem of human trafficking has captured widespread public attention in recent years, it has mostly been in response to narrow portrayals of impoverished women and girls trafficked into the sex industry by shady figures connected to organized crime.[5] Considerably less attention has been devoted to the widespread practice of the trafficking of women, men, and children into exploitative agricultural work, construction work, domestic work, or other nonsexual labor.[6] Most portrayals—particularly of sex trafficking—depict trafficking as an act (or series of acts) of exploitation and violence, perpetrated by traffickers and suffered by desperate and poverty-stricken victims. While accurate in some respects, such depictions are incomplete. The problem of trafficking begins not with the traffickers themselves, but with the conditions that caused their victims to migrate under circumstances rendering them vulnerable to exploitation. Human trafficking is but "an opportunistic response" to the tension between the economic necessity to migrate, on the one hand, and the politically motivated restrictions on migration, on the other.[7] This section offers a broader view of trafficking as a product of the larger socioeconomic forces that feed the "emigration push" and "immigration pull" toward risky labor migration practices in our globalized economy.

A. Emigration "Push" Factors

Globalization and the opening of national borders have led not only to greater international exchange of capital and goods, but also to increasing labor migration.[8] The wealth disparities created by our globalized economy have fed increased intra- and transnational labor migration as livelihood options disappear in less wealthy countries and communities.[9] As Anne Gallagher explains, trafficking lies at one extreme end of the emigration continuum,[10] where the migration is for survival—that is, escape from economic, political, or social distress—as opposed to opportunity-seeking migration—that is, merely a search for better job opportunities. Contrary to the popular, sensationalized image of trafficked persons as either kidnapped or coerced into leaving their homes, more often than not the initial decision to migrate is a conscious one.[11] Yet, the decision to uproot oneself, leave one's home, and migrate elsewhere cannot be explained as a straightforward "rational choice by persons who assess the costs and benefits of relocating"; rather, an understanding of this decision must account for "macro factors that encourage, induce or often, compel migration."[12] "Push" factors are not created by the traffickers so much as this broader context, i.e., the economic impact of globalization.[13] Traffickers, being opportunity-seeking by nature, simply take advantage of the resulting vulnerabilities to make a profit.

Because women are over-represented among survival migrants, it is not surprising that women comprise the vast majority of trafficked persons. Recent estimates from the U.S. State Department place the figure at 80 per cent.[14] This gender disparity is often attributed to the "feminization of poverty" arising from the failure of existing social structures to provide equal and just educational and employment opportunities for women.[15] While women migrate in response to economic hardship, they also migrate to flee gender-based repression.[16] Women will accept dangerous migration arrangements in order to escape the consequences of entrenched discrimination against women, including unjust or unequal employment, gender-based violence, and the lack of access to basic resources for women.[17]

As the former U.N. Special Rapporteur on Violence against Women, Radhika Coomaraswamy, explains, gender discrimination underlying these migratory flows is maintained through the collusion of factors at the market, state, community, and family levels.[18] Women's role in the market tends to be derived from traditional sex roles and division of labor, e.g., housekeeping, childcare, and other unpaid/underpaid subsistence labor. At the community level, women face discrimination through "uneven division of wage labour and salaries, citizenship rights and inheritance rights,"[19] as well as certain religious and customary practices, which, reinforced by state policies, further entrench and validate the discrimination and perpetuate the cycle of oppression of women. At the family level, gender discrimination manifests, for example, in "the preference for male children and [a] culture of male privilege [that] deprives girls and women of access to basic and higher education."[20]

Women's lack of rights and freedoms is further exacerbated by certain (macro-level) globalizing trends that have produced an environment conducive to trafficking. Professor Jean Pyle has identified these trends to include: (1) the shift to "export-oriented" approaches, where the production of essential goods is targeted for external trade rather than countries' own internal markets; (2) the entry of multinational corporations (MNCs) into developing countries and the MNCs' extensive networks of subcontractors; (3) structural adjustment policies (SAPs) mandated by the International Monetary Fund (IMF) or the World Bank (WB) as a condition for loans, requiring governments to open their markets to further financial and trade flows and to undertake austerity measures which fall heavily on the poor, particularly women; and (4) the shift in the structure of power at the international level—that is, the rise in the power of international institutions focused on markets (such as MNCs, the IMF, the WB, and the World Trade Organization [WTO] relative to those that are more people-centered and concerned with sustainable human development (such as the ILO, many U.N. agencies, and nongovernmental organizations [NGOs].[21]

These global restructuring trends can have harsh effects on women in developing countries—either fostering exploitative conditions for women working in the formal sector, or pushing women directly into work in the informal sector. To the (limited) extent that women are even permitted to work in the formal economy—such as in small businesses or in agriculture—they are often forced out of business by the cheaper imports that trade liberalization brings.[22] As the manufacturing and service industries have entered developing economies, workers in these countries have joined the "global assembly line"; indeed, many MNCs prefer female workers due to their lower cost and lesser likelihood of resisting adverse working conditions.[23] While MNCs provide a source of jobs, they also create "a pool of low-skilled wage labour exposed to standards of western consumption and representing a potential source of emigration."[24]

Structural adjustment policies add to the pressure on women to migrate in search of work. These policies, which require governments to cut programs and reduce expenditures on social services, cause women to take on additional income-earning activities in order to maintain their families' standards of living, as governments decrease benefits in housing, health care, education, food, and fuel subsidies.[25] This often pushes women to work in the unregulated, informal sectors, thus contributing to the rise of gendered-labor networks—prostitution or sex work, domestic work, and low-wage production work.[26] Women often migrate in search of jobs in these largely unregulated sectors, rendering them all the more vulnerable to traffickers.

Compelled to leave their homes in search of viable economic options, previously invisible, low-wage-earning, migrant women are now playing a critical role in the global economy. Through this dynamic—which Professor Saskia Sassen terms the "feminization of survival"—entire households, communities, and even some governments are increasingly dependent on these women for their economic survival.[27] The changes to the international political economy have caused a number of states in the global south, especially in Asia, which is grappling with foreign debt and rising unemployment, to play a "courtesan's role" to global capital in ways that either directly or indirectly foster these gendered-labor networks.[28] Favored growth strategies include attracting direct foreign investment from MNCs and their subcontracting networks—often sacrificing labor standards to do so—or investing in tourism industries widely associated with recruitment of trafficked females for the entertainment of foreign tourists.[29] Moreover, in an effort to ease their unemployment problems and accumulate foreign currency earnings, deeply indebted countries make use of their comparative advantage in the form of women's surplus labor and encourage their labor force to seek employment in wealthier countries.[30] Through their work and remittances, women enhance the government revenue of deeply indebted countries,[31] helping to "narrow the trade gap, increase foreign currency reserves, facilitate debt servicing, reduce poverty and inequalities in wealth and support sustainable development."[32]

B. Immigration "Pull" Factors

The growth in trafficking reflects not just an increase of "push" factors in the globalized economy, but also the strong "pull" of unmet labor demands in the wealthier destination countries. Most have an aging population, with "[t]he proportion of adults over 60 in high income countries . . . expected to increase from eight per cent to 19 per cent by 2050, while the number of children will drop by one third" due to low fertility rates.[33] The resulting "labour shortages, skills shortages, and increased tax burdens on the working population . . . to support and provide social benefits to the wider population,"[34] means these economies will become increasingly dependent on migrant populations to fill the labor gaps.[35] A number of other factors strengthen the immigration "pull," including, for example, fewer constraints on travel (for example, less restrictions on freedom of movement and cheaper and faster travel opportunities); established migration routes and communities in destination countries plus the active presence of recruiters willing to facilitate jobs or travel; and the promise of higher salaries and standards of living abroad.[36] Advances in information technology, global media, and internet access provide the means to broadcast to even the most isolated communities the promise of better opportunities abroad.[37] This fosters high hopes and expectations of women from poor, unskilled backgrounds who are desperate for employment.[38] The prospect of any job is a strong "pull" factor for survival migrants.

Labor shortages in the informal sector are often filled by migrant workers, who are willing to take the "3-D jobs"—i.e., jobs that are dirty, dangerous, and difficult—rejected by the domestic labor force.[39] The employers' profit potential, particularly in the case of trafficked persons, is much higher than would be the case if local labor were employed. If trafficked persons are paid at all, it is invariably at a lower rate than local workers would require, and the trafficked persons do not receive the costly benefits required in many Western states.[40]

In addition to the cost differential, migrants' "foreignness" appears to be a factor in the demand for migrant workers in the domestic work and commercial sex sectors. As Professors Anderson and O'Connell Davidson report in a recent study of the "demand side" of trafficking, employers favor migrant domestic workers over local domestic workers because of the vulnerability and lack of choice that results from their foreign status.[41] Employers perceive them as more "flexible" and "cooperative" with respect to longer working hours, more vulnerable to "molding" to the requirements of individual households, and less likely to leave their jobs. Moreover, their racial "otherness" makes the hierarchy between employer and employee less socially awkward—it is easier to dress up an exploitative relationship as one of paternalism/maternalism toward the impoverished "other."[42]

Rather than publicly recognize their dependence on migrant labor (skilled and unskilled), destination countries have sought instead to promote increasingly restrictive immigration policies, particularly in the wake of the September 11, 2001, terrorist attacks in the United States. There remains considerable public and political resistance to liberalizing the migration policies of these countries,[43] despite strong demographic and economic evidence that migrants produce more benefit than burden for their host countries.[44] This resistance is linked to popular—yet mistaken—concerns about the negative impact of immigration flows on employment, national security, welfare systems, and national identity.[45] Rather than confront xenophobic reactions to issues of migration, many governments instead have sought electoral or political advantage by promoting increasingly restrictive immigration policies.[46] The tension between economic reality and political expedience thus fosters conditions that enable and promote human trafficking. In reducing the opportunities for regular migration, these policies provide greater opportunities for traffickers, who are "fishing in the stream of migration," to take advantage of the confluence of survival migrants' need for jobs, on the one hand, and the unrelenting market demand for cheap labor, on the other.[47] Indeed, as borders close and migration routes become more dangerous, smuggling costs increase to the point that smugglers turn to trafficking to make a profit.[48]

Situating the trafficking phenomenon in this broader context spotlights how deeply rooted trafficking is in the underlying socioeconomic forces that impel workers to migrate. It also demonstrates how the focus on the back end of the trafficking process—that is, entry of the trafficker and the abuses committed in the course of the trafficking—is but a narrow snapshot of the broader problem of trafficking. Solutions that fail to account for the broader picture can only hope to ameliorate the symptoms, rather than address the cause of the problem.

II. The International Legal Response

Throughout the 1980s and 1990s, human rights advocates worked diligently to draw attention to the problem of trafficking in its broader socioeconomic context.[49] But it was concern over the national security implications of increased labor migration and the involvement of transnational criminal syndicates in the clandestine movement of people that ultimately motivated governments to take action. Viewing trafficking as a border and crime control issue, governments seized the opportunity to develop a new international counter-trafficking law in the form of a trafficking-specific protocol to a new international cooperation treaty to combat transnational crime—the U.N. Convention Against Transnational Organized Crime (Crime Convention).[50] States' eagerness to combat the problem resulted in the conclusion of the U.N. Protocol to Prevent, Suppress and Punish Trafficking in Persons, Especially Women and Children (Palermo Protocol or Protocol) within two years and its entry into force three years later, on December 25, 2003.[51]

The development of the Protocol set the stage for a rapid proliferation of counter-trafficking laws in the past five years. The issue of human trafficking is now high on the agenda, the international community has devoted hundreds of millions of dollars in trafficking interventions.[52] Efforts to combat trafficking have proceeded from a narrow view of trafficking as a criminal justice problem, with a clear focus on targeting the traffickers and, to a lesser extent, protecting their victims. Addressing the socioeconomic factors at the root of the problem, by contrast, has largely fallen outside the purview of government action.

A. The Palermo Protocol

The Palermo Protocol is, at base, an international crime control cooperation treaty designed to promote and facilitate States Parties' cooperation in combating trafficking in persons. Together with the Crime Convention, the Protocol establishes concrete measures to improve communication and cooperation between national law enforcement authorities, engage in mutual legal assistance, facilitate extradition proceedings, and establish bilateral and multilateral joint investigative bodies and techniques.[53] While the criminal justice aspects of this framework are a clear priority, the Palermo Protocol also contains measures to protect trafficked persons and to prevent trafficking. Unlike the criminal justice measures, which are couched as hard obligations, these provisions are mostly framed in programmatic, aspirational terms. Thus, "in appropriate cases and to the extent possible under its domestic law," the Protocol requires states to consider implementing measures providing for trafficked persons' physical and psychological recovery and endeavor to provide for their physical safety, among other goals.[54] With respect to "prevention" efforts, states are to endeavor to undertake measures such as information campaigns and social and economic initiatives to prevent trafficking,[55] as well as "to alleviate the factors that make persons . . . vulnerable to trafficking, such as poverty, underdevelopment and lack of equal opportunity," and to discourage demand for trafficking.[56]

Just as the text of the Protocol reflects states' clear prioritization of the criminal justice response, so does that which was excluded from the Protocol. Human rights advocates lobbied to include a provision in the Protocol granting trafficked persons protections against prosecution for status-related offenses, such as illegal migration, undocumented work, and prostitution,[57] citing the well-documented reality that trafficked persons were frequently deported or jailed rather than afforded protection.[58] But states refused to include such a provision for fear that it would lead to the "unwarranted use of the 'trafficking defense' and a resulting weakening of states' ability to control both prostitution and migration flows through the application of criminal sanctions."[59]

States' concern over maintaining strong border controls was also reflected in their efforts to draw a legal distinction between trafficking and migrant smuggling,[60] despite the difficulty in distinguishing between the two in practice. Defined as the illegal movement of persons across borders for profit, "migrant smuggling" technically applies to any trafficked person who begins his/her journey as a smuggled migrant but is ultimately forced into an exploitative labor situation.[61] Consequently, a victim of incomplete trafficking—for example, a victim who is stopped at the border before the end purpose of the movement is realized—could be treated as a smuggled migrant and thus denied the victim status and protections afforded to trafficked persons.[62] As Anne Gallagher concludes, the Protocol drafters' failure to address this issue was "clear evidence of [states'] unwillingness . . . to relinquish any measure of control over the migrant identification process."[63]

States' refusal to adjust their migration control policies is perhaps symptomatic of states' deep reluctance to expand the rights afforded to migrant workers. Tellingly, it took thirteen years for the International Convention on the Protection of the Rights of All Migrant Workers and Members of their Families (the Migrant Workers Convention) to receive enough ratifications to enter into force on July 1, 2003.[64] By contrast, the Palermo Protocol entered into force three years after its adoption.[65] Despite well-documented abuses of migrant workers' rights in countries of destination, these countries discouraged ratification of the instrument on grounds that its provisions—which address the treatment, welfare, and human rights of migrant workers (documented and undocumented) and their families—are too ambitious and detailed to be practicable and realizable.[66] That states would maintain such a restrictive stance even when the violations are egregious enough to constitute trafficking reveals the strong priority placed on the crime and border control aspects of trafficking over concern for the welfare of trafficked persons.

B. Counter-Trafficking Efforts in Practice

In practice, the priorities set forth in the Palermo Protocol are mirrored in counter-trafficking law and policy initiatives undertaken across the globe. As the U.S. State Department's yearly Trafficking in Persons Report (TIP Report) reveals, most countries' counter-trafficking efforts focus on effectuating a strong criminal justice response to the problem.[67] Although there is a growing awareness of a need for stronger protection of trafficked persons' human rights,[68] current models of protection continue "to prioritise the needs of law enforcement over the rights of trafficked persons."[69] Most governments adopt restrictive immigration policies, which, at times, fail to distinguish between smuggling and trafficking and can lead to summary deportation or incarceration of trafficked persons.[70] This not only exposes trafficked persons to further harm, including possible retrafficking, but it deprives them of access to justice and undermines government efforts to prosecute the traffickers.[71] To the extent trafficked persons are afforded an opportunity to remain in the destination countries, their residency status is often conditioned on their willingness to assist in the prosecution of their traffickers, potentially exposing them to further trauma and reprisals from the traffickers.

Even well-intentioned efforts to adopt a more "victim-centered approach"[72] to the problem can promote a narrow conception of trafficking that diverts attention from its broader labor and migration causes and implications. A review of country practices reveals two trends, in particular, that foster this dynamic: (1) the deliberate de-emphasizing of the movement or recruitment element of the trafficking definition; and (2) an over-emphasis on sex trafficking, to the neglect or exclusion of labor trafficking.

Regarding the first trend, the United States, for example, has adopted an interpretation of the trafficking definition that shifts focus away from the movement or recruitment element to the "end purpose" of the trafficking:

> The means by which people are subjected to servitude—their recruitment and the deception and coercion that may cause movement—are impor-tant factors but factors that are secondary to their compelled service. It is the state of servitude that is key to defining trafficking. . . . The movement of [a] person to [a] new location is not what constitutes traf-ficking; the force, fraud or coercion exercised on that person by another to perform or remain in service to the master is the defining element of trafficking in modern usage.[73]

Granted, de-emphasizing the recruitment or movement aspect of the definition perhaps helps draw much-needed attention to the broader prob-lem of forced labor. But it also has the detrimental effect of diverting atten-tion from the fact that trafficking is a crime committed during migration and against migrants. It also departs from the international legal definition of trafficking, of which movement or recruitment of the person is a defining element:

> [Trafficking is defined as] (a) . . . the recruitment, transportation, transfer, harbouring or receipt of persons, by means of the threat or use of force or other forms of coercion, of abduction, of fraud, of deception, of the abuse of power or of a position of vulnerability or of the giving or receiving of payments or benefits to achieve the consent of a person having control over another person, for the purpose of exploitation. Exploitation shall include, at a minimum, the exploitation of the prostitution of others or other forms of sexual exploitation, forced labour or services, slavery or practices similar to slavery, servitude or the removal of organs; (b) the consent of a victim of trafficking to the intended exploitation set forth in subparagraph (a) shall be irrelevant where any of the means set forth in subparagraph (a) have been used.[74]

The migration element of the definition speaks to the particular vulnerability that migrants face as a result of living and working in an unfamiliar milieu, where language and cultural barriers can prevent the migrant from accessing assistance.[75] De-emphasizing the migration aspect of trafficking thus overlooks a substantial source of vulnerability. It also narrows the focus of state responsibility to the confines of that which has taken place within its borders—that is, the explorative end purpose of the facilitated movement. Moreover, it conveniently sets to the side thorny questions regarding how to address a victim's (often undocumented) immigration status—an issue of immediate and pressing concern to trafficked persons, who often fear return to their home communities. In sum, this formulation glosses over any responsibility on the part of the state for fostering emigration push or immigration pull factors discussed in Part I, above.

As for the second trend, despite the fact that the international legal definition of trafficking encompasses trafficking for nonsexual as well as sexual purposes, many states—including, until recently, the United States[76]—have focused their efforts on trafficking for sexual purposes.[77] Significantly less attention has been devoted to "labor trafficking" or trafficking for nonsexual purposes, despite recent estimates that this practice accounts for at least one-third of all trafficking cases.[78] The moral outrage that images of women trapped in "sexual slavery" so easily provoke has been a galvanizing force behind global efforts to combat trafficking. Sex trafficking and its associated sex crimes also fall neatly within the purview of a criminal justice response. By contrast, labor trafficking, though hardly benign, is perhaps less likely to engender a criminal justice response given our arguably greater moral tolerance for explorative labor conditions. An over-emphasis on sex trafficking thus not only risks overlooking a significant portion of the trafficked population, but it diverts attention away from states' responsibility to promote safe labor conditions.

If protection of the victims is of secondary concern to states, then prevention of trafficking (at least, in the long term) is practically an afterthought.

Despite the Protocol's requirement that states should take measures to alleviate the root causes of trafficking, such as "poverty, underdevelopment and lack of equal opportunity,"[79] in practice, "prevention" efforts focus on short-term strategies such as public awareness campaigns regarding the risks of migration. For instance, in her ground-breaking study assessing prevention efforts in southeastern Europe (SEE),[80] Barbara Limanowska found a tendency to adopt "repressive" prevention strategies that "focus on suppressing the negative (or perceived as negative) phenomena related to trafficking, such as [undocumented migration] . . . illegal and forced labor, prostitution, child labor or organized crime."[81] Common strategies include bar raids, computerized border checks, and databases that register the names of undocumented migrants, and public awareness campaigns that broadcast to the general public the risks of trafficking.[82] While efforts to prevent re-trafficking of victims are more victim-focused—providing housing, social services, and legal and medical assistance to victims to assist in reintegration into their home communities—these are only provided on a short-term basis.[83] As Limanowska has concluded with respect to SEE, "[t]here is no comprehensive long-term prevention strategy for the region, nor any clear understanding of what such a strategy should include."[84] Although prevention strategies from other regions of the world have yet to be assessed in as comprehensive a fashion,[85] a review of the country practices in other regions of the world reveals a similar focus on repressive approaches to prevention.[86]

Preliminary evaluation of these strategies indicates that they are ineffective, if not counterproductive. Rather than deterring risky migration, large-scale public awareness campaigns have been dismissed by their target audiences as anti-migration measures resulting from "the manipulation of the anti-trafficking agenda by rich countries that want to keep the poor away from their territory."[87] Efforts to "reintegrate" trafficked persons into their home communities cannot overcome the grim reality that the underlying social conditions that led to their trafficking—such as poverty and unemployment—still exist. Indeed, the myopic failure to recognize, much less address, the root causes of trafficking can actually increase vulnerability to trafficking. For example, as Limanowska reports with respect to SEE, the failure to link domestic violence to trafficking at the policy level has led to the creation of separate shelters for trafficked persons and victims of domestic violence, with the former underutilized and the latter underfunded and overcrowded.[88] Rather than recognizing domestic violence as a possible early warning sign of trafficking, the closing of domestic violence shelters has gone unaddressed, thus increasing the vulnerability to trafficking of an already at-risk population.

States' resistance to addressing the broader social problems that feed human trafficking is, in some respects, unsurprising. Treating trafficking as a criminal justice issue is far less resource-intensive and politically risky than developing long-term strategies to address the labor migration aspects of the problem. Moreover, addressing the socioeconomic root causes of trafficking means confronting vexing questions concerning the measure and content of states' obligations to achieve "progressive realization" of the social, economic, and cultural rights half of the human rights corpus.[89] A long-term strategy would thus require attention to deeper, systemic problems that states have proven highly reluctant to confront—for example, the economic need to migrate and the politically motivated restrictions against doing so, not to mention the cycle of poverty, discrimination, and violence that causes these migratory flows. As discussed below, however, such a strategy is critical to the success of global efforts to eliminate trafficking.

III. Prevention as Necessary Core of Counter-Trafficking Strategy

There is no doubt that a strong criminal justice response is a critical component of any effective global counter-trafficking strategy. Absent meaningful victim protection and long-term prevention measures, however, it is, at best, a temporary solution to a chronic and potentially growing problem.[90] Stopping the vicious cycle of trafficking demands a strategy that frames the problem within its broader socioeconomic context and takes seriously the project of targeting the root causes of this complex problem. As with any call to confront the world's ubiquitous social problems, it is an ambitious task, but one for which a few modest steps could help transform the rhetorical commitment to prevention into a substantive one. Two such measures are proposed and briefly described here.

The first proposed step is to undertake rigorous and independent assessment of the potential long-term effects of existing counter-trafficking strategies. This speaks to the need to ensure that existing counter-trafficking measures do not operate at cross-purposes with the goal of long-term prevention. In their haste to adopt counter-trafficking policies and legislation, governments have largely taken on faith that these strategies are effective with little or no basis in objective evaluations of their outcomes.[91] The sobering results of the few assessments that have been conducted—such as Limanowska's SEE study and even the United States' self-assessment[92]— illustrate the critical need for further evaluation. With data from at least five years of state practice since the adoption of the Protocol by the U.N. General Assembly, there is now a basis for some preliminary evaluations.

The second is to use international human rights law to provide a conceptual framework for addressing the root causes of trafficking. Framing the project of alleviating the root causes of trafficking as a human rights issue would encourage more proactive efforts to address these problems rather than the traditional assumption that such issues are solely within the province of broader development policy. The Palermo Protocol obliges states to "take or strengthen measures . . . to alleviate the factors that make persons . . . vulnerable to trafficking, such as poverty, underdevelopment and lack of equal opportunity."[93] While development policy can provide detailed prescriptions for action on the ground, international human rights law offers an important normative framework within which these strategies can be constructed. Most significantly, a human rights framework offers legal and political space for the disenfranchised to begin to claim these needs as rights, and thereby bring the scope of state responsibility into sharper focus.

A. Assessment of Existing Counter-Trafficking Strategies

A 2003 expert report to the U.N. Commission on the Status of Women concluded that, despite ten years of counter-trafficking laws and policies in the Balkans region, there was no evidence of a significant decrease in trafficking or increase in the number of assisted victims or number of traffickers punished.[94] Considering the hundreds of millions of dollars spent on counter-trafficking programs around the world—the United States contributed $96 million in 2004 alone[95]—and the vast numbers of lives affected by trafficking, this conclusion should give us pause. Regrettably, however, as the International Organization for Migration (IOM) recently reported, "there has been relatively little independent evaluation of counter-trafficking policies and programmes to assess the real impact and effectiveness of different interventions."[96]

The few assessments that have been conducted thus far demonstrate why further evaluation of state practices is vital. Studies such as those conducted by Limanowska not only provide critical, pragmatic insight into best (and worst) practices, but they also expose weaknesses and inaccuracies in the ways in which the problem is conceptualized. For instance, Limanowska's findings concerning the ineffectiveness of large-scale public awareness campaigns in the SEE region underscore how these efforts fail to appreciate fully the migrant perspective. That the target audiences of some of these campaigns so readily dismiss them as rich countries' anti-migration propaganda[97]—despite recognizing the accuracy of the risks portrayed—illustrates the depths of the migrants' need to migrate and the great risks they are willing to assume to do so. This is similarly demonstrated in the fact that the vast majority of calls to helplines created to reach victims of trafficking were "preventive and informative"—that is, to seek information regarding migration for work abroad.[98] Limanowska's evaluation of these and other counter-trafficking initiatives thus underscores governments' chronic failure to appreciate fully the power of the socioeconomic forces underlying migratory flows.

Another area where preliminary studies of programs have called into question the wisdom of existing counter-trafficking strategies relates to efforts to target the demand side of trafficking. Most of these programs are punitive in nature—that is, designed to clamp down on consumer demand, particularly with respect to the commercial sex industry. But as Anderson and O'Connell Davidson demonstrated in their pioneering study of the demand side of trafficking,[99] there are no easy solutions to reducing demand for trafficked labor—sexual or nonsexual. On the one hand, clamping down on demand for street prostitution may actually strengthen demand on other segments of the sex industry where trafficked labor can be an issue, such as pornography, escort agency prostitution, lap- and table-dance clubs, etc.[100] On the other hand, regulating the sex or domestic work sectors "does nothing, in itself, to counteract racism, xenophobia and prejudice against migrants and ethnic minority groups" who tend to comprise the trafficked end of these labor markets and could actually reinforce existing racial, ethnic, and national hierarchies in these sectors.[101] Accordingly, Anderson and O'Connell Davidson suggest that policy makers "pay much closer attention to the unintended and negative consequences of legislating prostitution . . . or of regulating . . . domestic work."[102] Policy makers instead ought to consider concentrating efforts on educational and preventive work targeting the social construction of demand—that is, the social norms that permit exploitation of vulnerable labor.

In addition to evaluating specific counter-trafficking programs and policies, governments should endeavor to assess their overall priorities vis-a-vis the types of programs they pursue—that is, whether oriented toward short-term or long-term results. The SEE experience reveals that funding for programs tends to be channeled toward anti-migration projects reflecting the interests of countries of destination, or in the alternative, "charity work" focused on direct assistance to victims.[103] This has had the unfortunate effect of diverting money away from programs focused on development, equality, and human rights, which hold greater promise of long-lasting change.[104] Trafficking research suffers from the same shortsightedness. Most of the research in the trafficking field is "action-oriented" or designed to prepare for specific counter-trafficking interventions on the ground, typically conducted within a six- to nine-month time frame. "There has been less funding for long-term research [into] the causes of trafficking and the best ways to prevent and combat it, or [into] the impacts of different interventions and policy responses."[105]

The importance of rigorous and independent assessment of existing counter-trafficking programs and research cannot be underestimated. Obtaining meaningful results requires a deeper understanding of the problem and the operational value of the proposed solutions than currently exists today.

B. Addressing Root Causes through a Human Rights Lens

Although there is a general understanding that trafficking has its root causes in poverty, unemployment, discrimination, and violence against women, no large-scale counter-trafficking program has been implemented to address these underlying problems.[106] Even at the level of legal analysis, there is a persistent failure to analyze how international human rights law could be used to address the root causes of the problem. While resource limitations might necessarily slow the implementation of programs targeting root causes on the ground, no such barrier exists to articulating a legal framework to address root causes. Emerging norms and analysis in the field of women's human rights, specifically, and economic, social, and cultural rights, generally, provide a basis upon which such a framework might be developed. Utilizing the principle of nondiscrimination is one potential avenue, as described briefly below.

When one considers trafficking in its broader socioeconomic context, it is not difficult to connect the root causes of trafficking to violations of economic, social, and cultural rights. These include violations of such rights as the right of opportunity to gain a living by work one freely chooses or accepts, the right to just and favorable conditions of work, the right to an adequate standard of living, and the right to education.[107] Race- and gender-based discrimination in the recognition and application of these rights are also critical factors rendering women particularly vulnerable to trafficking.[108] Many of the rights implicated in the root causes of trafficking are the subject of states' obligations under the International Covenant on Economic, Social, and Cultural Rights (ICESCR). With women arguably encountering the most severe deprivations in the area of economic, social, and cultural life,[109] the Convention on the Elimination of All Forms of Discrimination against Women (CEDAW) also plays a critical role in safeguarding these rights vis-a-vis women.

As readily identifiable as these rights violations are, however, legal analyses of trafficking have persistently neglected the economic, social, and cultural rights implications of trafficking. This likely has to do with the fact that, despite being touted as indivisible, interdependent, interrelated, and of equal importance for human dignity,[110] the norm development, monitoring, and implementation of economic, social, and cultural rights—half of the human rights corpus—has fallen far behind that of civil and political rights. The traditional view of economic, social, and cultural rights as merely "programmatic" or "aspirational" in nature—in contrast to the apparently immediately realizable civil and political rights—has fed their marginalization in human rights discourse. Vexing questions and enduring debates over the justiciability of economic, social, and cultural rights—or their capacity to be subject to formal third-party adjudication with remedies for noncompliance[111]—are another likely cause of this relative neglect.

Evolving jurisprudence regarding economic, social, and cultural rights, generally, and their application to women, specifically, nonetheless provides a basis for at least conceptualizing a legal framework to address the root causes of trafficking. The traditional assumption that economic, social, and cultural rights are inherently aspirational, necessarily resource-intensive, and therefore not immediately realizable, has now been cast into doubt.[112] By distinguishing between the types or levels of obligations human rights impose on States Parties—to respect, to protect, and to fulfill—commentators have demonstrated how certain aspects of economic, social, and cultural rights can be of immediate effect.[113] Many of these rights can be safeguarded by virtue of states' noninterference with the freedom and use of resources possessed by individuals. Accordingly, the Committee on Economic, Social and Cultural Rights (the treaty body charged with monitoring state compliance with the ICESCR) has made clear that states have an immediate obligation to ensure that ICESCR rights be exercised without discrimination.[114] Thus, states are obliged to abolish any laws, policies, or practices that affect enjoyment of these rights and, moreover, to take action to prevent discrimination by private persons and bodies in any field of public life.

Interpreted to have broad application under international human rights law, the nondiscrimination principle is particularly well-suited to a human rights analysis of the broad range of root causes of trafficking—poverty, unequal educational and employment opportunities, and violence against women, among others. Under the International Covenant for Civil and Political Rights, states are obliged not only to refrain from discriminatory practices, but also to adopt punitive measures to make equality and nondiscrimination a concrete reality.[115] As General Comment 18, issued by the Human Rights Committee, makes clear, the prohibition on discrimination in law or in fact applies "in any field regulated and protected by public authorities," and thus encompasses economic, social, and cultural rights.[116] In practice, the nondiscrimination principle has been applied to prohibit gender-based differential treatment in the allocation of social benefits, such as unemployment benefits.[117] It has also provided a framework for addressing gender-based violence, "or violence that is directed against a woman because she is a woman or that affects women disproportionately."[118] Poverty is another root cause of trafficking to which the nondiscrimination principle can be applied, as "poverty not only arises from a lack of resources—it may also arise from a lack of access to resources, information, opportunities, power, and mobility. . . . [D]iscrimination may cause poverty, just as poverty may cause discrimination."[119]

As discussed above in Part I, discrimination against women with respect to educational and employment opportunities, the disproportionate burden economic restructuring places on women, the feminization of migration due to violence against women, and the feminization of poverty, among other factors, render women particularly vulnerable to trafficking. "Gender-based discrimination [often] intersects with discriminations based on other forms of 'otherness,' such as race, ethnicity, [and] religion," among others.[120] The nondiscrimination principle, particularly as articulated, interpreted, and applied by treaty bodies such as the Committee on the Elimination of Discrimination against Women (Women's Committee) and the Committee on the Elimination of Racial Discrimination, thus offers a useful framework for addressing the root causes of trafficking.

Moreover, the recent entry into force of the CEDAW Optional Protocol contributes to the practical appeal of a nondiscrimination approach to root causes. The Optional Protocol provides individuals alleging violations of their CEDAW rights the opportunity to pursue complaints against States Parties to the Optional Protocol, and for the Women's Committee to conduct inquiries into allegations of systematic and gross violations of those rights.[121] Using the discrimination framework thus affords rare access to an enforcement mechanism otherwise unavailable for violations of economic, social, and cultural rights.

Conclusion

Situated within its broader frame, the problem of human trafficking demands that efforts to combat this international crime and human rights violation take seriously the need to address its root causes. Over a decade of global counter-trafficking initiatives adopting a "law and order" approach to the problem has yielded questionable, if not disappointing, results. The international community is coming to the growing realization that treating trafficking predominantly, if not solely, as a border and crime control issue is but to respond only to a snapshot view of a much larger problem. There is no question that confronting the poverty, unemployment, discrimination, and gender-based violence, among other factors, that increase an individual's vulnerability to trafficking is a tremendous task that demands creative and long-term strategic thinking. This article has provided a cursory view of two possible approaches by which we might begin to undertake this project. Far more analysis and deeper understanding of the trafficking problem are necessary prerequisites of the project, as is dispossessing ourselves of the traditional view that realization of economic, social, and cultural rights can wait. As daunting of a task as this may be, it is a necessary one if global efforts to eliminate trafficking are to succeed.

Notes

1. See United Nations High Commissioner for Human Rights, Report of the United Nations High Commissioner, [paragraph] 6, delivered to the Economic and Social Council, U.N. Doc. E/1999/96 (July 29, 1999) (noting that while globalization has had its benefits, there is a "clear trend towards a smaller percentage of the population receiving a greater share of wealth, while the poorest simultaneously lose ground"); see generally Executive Summary to U.N. Econ. & Soc. Council [ECOSOC], Comm'n on Human Rights, Integration of the Human Rights of Women and the Gender Perspective: Violence Against Women, at 4 U.N. Doc. E/CN.4/2000/68 (Feb. 29, 2000) (prepared by Radhika Coomaraswamy) [hereinafter Coomaraswamy Report].

2. BIMAL GHOSH, HUDDLED MASSES AND UNCERTAIN SHORES: INSIGHTS INTO IRREGULAR MIGRATION 35 (1998).

3. The number of people trafficked remains staggering. The International Labour Organization (ILO) estimates that 2.5 million people are trafficked at any point in time, generating $32 billion in profits for organized crime. INTERNATIONAL LABOUR OFFICE, A GLOBAL ALLIANCE AGAINST FORCED LABOUR: GLOBAL REPORT UNDER THE FOLLOW-UP TO THE ILO DECLARATION ON FUNDAMENTAL PRINCIPLES AND RIGHTS AT WORK 46, 55 (2005) [hereinafter ILO GLOBAL REPORT].

4. Michael J. Dennis & David P. Stewart, Justiciability of Economic, Social, and Cultural Rights: Should There Be an International Complaints Mechanism to Adjudicate the Rights to Food, Water, Housing, and Health?, 98 AM. J. INT'L L. 462, 464 (2004).

5. See, e.g., Peter Landesman, The Girls Next Door, N.Y. TIMES MAG., Jan. 25, 2004, at 30; Nicholas D. Kristof, Girls for Sale, N.Y. TIMES, Jan. 17, 2004, at A15; Nicholas D. Kristof, Bargaining for Freedom, N.Y. TIMES, Jan. 21, 2004, at A27; Nicholas D. Kristof, Loss of Innocence, N.Y. TIMES, Jan. 28, 2004, at A25; Nicholas D. Kristof, Stopping the Traffickers, N.Y. TIMES, Jan. 31, 2004, at Al7.

6. David A. Feingold, Think Again: Human Trafficking, FOREIGN POL'Y, Sept.–Oct. 2005, at 26.

7. ILO GLOBAL REPORT, supra note 3, at 46.

8. COMM. ON FEMINISM AND INT'L LAW, INT'L LAW ASS'N, WOMEN AND MIGRATION: INTERIM REPORT ON TRAFFICKING IN WOMEN 2 (2004), available at http://www.ila-hq.org/pdf/Feminism%20&%20International% 20Law/Report% 202004.pdf.

9. See generally GHOSH, SUpm note 2 (distinguishing between survival migration and opportunity seeking migration); MIKE KAYE, ANTI-SLAVERY INT'L, THE MIGRATION-TRAFFICKING NEXUS: COMBATING TRAFFICKING THROUGH THE PROTECTION OF MIGRANTS' HUMAN RIGHTS 13 (2003), available at http://www.antislavery.org/homepage/resources/the%20migration%20 trafficking%20nexus%202003.pdf.

10. ANNE GALLAGHER ET AL., CONSIDERATION OF THE ISSUE OF TRAFFICKING: BACKGROUND PAPER 16-17 (2002) (citing GHOSH, supra note 2, at 35), available at http://www.nhri.net/pdf/ACJ%20Trafficking%20Background%20 Paper.pdf.

11. Feingold, supra note 6, at 28.

12. Patrick A. Taran, Human Rights of Migrants: Challenges of the New Decade, INT'L MIGRATION, Vol. 38, No. 6 (Special Issue 2), Feb. 2001, at 12.

13. See Saskia Sassen, Women's Burden: Counter-Geographies of Globalization and the Feminization of Survival, 71 NORDIC J. INT'L L. 255, 257 (2002).

14. U.S. DEP'T OF STATE, TRAFFICKING IN PERSONS REPORT 6 (2005) [hereinafter 2005 TIP REPORT], available at http://www.state.gov/documents/organization/ 47255.pdf.

15. Coomaraswamy Report, supra note 1, [paragraph] 58.

16. Id. [paragraph][paragraph] 54–60.

17. See id. [paragraph] 60.

18. Id. [paragraph] 57.

19. Id.

20. Id.

21. See Jean L. Pyle, How Globalization Fosters Gendered Labor Networks and Trafficking 23 (Nov 13–15, 2002) (unpublished manuscript), available at http://www.hawaii.edu/global/projects_activities/Trafficking/Pyle.doc.

22. Id. at 5.

23. Id.

24. CHRISTINA BOSWELL & JEFF CRISP, POVERTY, INTERNATIONAL MIGRATION AND ASYLUM 6 (United Nations Univ., World Inst. for Dev. Econ. Research, Policy Brief No. 8, 2003).

25. See Sassen, supra note 13, at 263.

26. See U.N. Dip. for the Advancement of Women, The New Borderlanders: Enabling Mobile Women and Girls for Safe Migration and Citizenship Rights, at 5–6, U.N. Doc. CM/MMW/2003/ CRE3 (Jan. 14, 2004) (prepared by Jyoti Sanghera).

27. Sassen, supra note 13, at 258.

YES / Janie Chuang   **229**

28. Vidyamali Samarasinghe, Confronting Globalization in Anti-Trafficking Strategies in Asia, BROWN J. WORLD AFF., Summer–Fall 2003, at 91, 94 (citing JIM MITTLEMAN, THE GLOBALIZATION SYNDROME: TRANSFORMATION AND RESISTANCE 15 (2000)).

29. Id. at 92, 94.

30. Id. at 95.

31. Sassen, supra note 13, at 258. Thus, according to Professor Sassen, "[t]he growing immiseration of governments and whole economies in the global south has promoted and enabled the proliferation of survival and profit-making activities that involve migration and trafficking of women." Id. at 255 (from the Abstract). According to the International Organization for Migration, remittances through official channels totaled $93 billion in 2003, INTERNATIONAL ORGANIZATION FOR MIGRATION, WORLD MIGRATION 2005: COSTS AND BENEFITS OF INTERNATIONAL MIGRATION 491 (2005), approached $100 billion in 2004, id. at 124, and now seriously rival development aid in many countries; unofficial remittances are likely to be two to three times that figure. For example, in El Salvador, "remittances accounted for more than 80 per cent of the total financial inflows in 2000, with overseas development assistance and foreign direct investment accounting for less than 20 per cent." Kaye, supra note 9, at 14.

32. KAYE, supra note 9, at 14 (spending remittances on locally produced goods and services can have a multiplier effect by simulating demand).

33. Id. at 13.

34. Id.

35. "In order to stabilise the size of the working population in the 15 EU member states, there needs to be a net inflow of some 68 million foreign workers and professionals between 2003 and 2050." Id. (citing INT'L ORG. FOR MIGRATION) WORLD MIGRATION 2003, at 245 (2003)).

36. Id. at 11; accord BOSWELL & CRISP, supra note 24, at 10.

37. Samarasinghe, supra note 28, at 96–97.

38. See BOSWELL & CRISP, supra note 24, at 6.

39. See ILO GLOBAL REPORT, supra note 3, at 46.

40. See Taran, supra note 12, at 15–16.

41. BRIDGET ANDERSON & JULIA O'CONNELL DAVIDSON, IS TRAFFICKING IN HUMAN BEINGS DEMAND DRIVEN?: A MULTI-COUNTRY PILOT STUDY 29–32 (Int'l Org. for Migration, IOM Migration Research Series No. 15, 2003).

42. Id. at 32.

43. BOSWELL & CRISP, supra note 24, at 1.

44. INT'L ORG. FOR MIGRATION, supra note 31, at 170, 188–89 (noting that a recent U.K. study calculated that in 1999–2000, migrants contributed $4 billion more in taxes than they received in benefits, and a U.S. study estimated that national income had expanded $8 billion in 1997 because of immigration).

45. BOSWELL & CRISP, supra note 24, at 21–22.

46. KAYE, SUPRA note 9, at 13.

47. Helen Thomas, Fishing in the Stream of Migration, ADB REV. (ASIAN DEV. BANK, MANILA, PHIL.), February 2004, at 16, 16–17, available at http://www.adb.org/Documents/Periodicals/ADB_Review/2004/vo136_1/fishing.asp.

48. Migrant smuggling entails payment by a third party to facilitate the movement of the migrant. See Protocol Against the Smuggling of Migrants by Land, Sea and Air, Supplementing the United Nations Convention Against Transnational Organized Crime, G.A. Res. 55/25, annex III, pmbl. & art. 3, U.N. Doc. A/RES/55/25 (Nov. 2, 2000) [hereinafter Migrant Smuggling Protocol]. In addition to whatever profit is to be made from the facilitated migration, traffickers can also profit from the revenue generated from the exploitative end purpose of the movement—e.g., the forced labor or slavery-like practice.

49. See generally HUMAN RIGHTS WATCH, A MODERN FORM of SLAVERY: TRAFFICKING OF BURMESE WOMEN AND GIRLS INTO BROTHELS IN THAILAND (1993), available at http://www.hrw.org/reports/1993/thailand/; HUMAN RIGHTS WATCH, RAPE FOR PROFIT: TRAFFICKING OF NEPALI GIRLS AND WOMEN TO INDIAN BROTHELS (1995), available at http://www.hrw.org/reports/pdfs/c/crd/india957.pdf (report by Human Rights Watch demonstrating that unequal access to education and employment opportunities, among other factors, fed the feminization of poverty and migration and increased women's vulnerability to traffickers).

50. United Nations Convention Against Transnational Organized Crime, G.A. Res. 55/25, annex I, U.N. Doc. A/RES/55/25 (Nov. 2, 2000) [hereinafter Crime Convention].

51. Protocol to Prevent, Suppress and Punish Trafficking in Persons, Especially Women and Children, G.A. Res. 55/25, annex II, U.N. Doc. A/RES/55/25 (Nov. 2, 2000) [hereinafter Palermo Protocol].

52. See 2005 TIP REPORT, supra note 14, at 245 (reporting that the United States alone has invested $295 million in counter-trafficking efforts over the last four fiscal years).

53. Crime Convention, supra note 50, arts. 16, 18, 19, 27, 28.

54. Palermo Protocol, supra note 51, arts. 6–8.

55. Id. art. 9, [paragraph] 2.

56. Id. art. 9, [paragraph][paragraph] 4–5.

57. See Position Paper on the Draft Protocol to Prevent, Suppress and Punish Trafficking in Women and Children, submitted by the Special Rapporteur on Violence Against Women, Report of the Ad Hoc Committee on the Elaboration of a Convention Against Transnational Organized Crime on its Fourth Session, Held in Vienna June 28 to July 9, 1999, U.N. Doc. A/AC.254/CRP.13 (May 20, 1999) [hereinafter "Coomaraswamy Position Paper"].

58. See, e.g., Coomaraswamy Report, supra note 1, [paragraph] 44.

59. See Anne Gallagher, Human Rights and the New UN Protocols on Trafficking and Migrant Smuggling: A Preliminary Analysis, 23 HuM. RTs. Q. 975, 991 (2001).

60. See Migrant Smuggling Protocol, supra note 48 (migrant smuggling is the subject of one of the other two protocols to the Crime Convention).

61. Smuggling is defined as "the procurement, in order to obtain, directly or indirectly, a financial or other material benefit, of the illegal entry of a

person into a State Party of which the person is not a national or a permanent resident." Id. art. 3.

62. "Smuggled migrants are assumed to be acting voluntarily," and are thus afforded less protection under international law. Anne Gallagher, Trafficking, Smuggling and Human Rights: Tricks and Treaties, 12 FORCED MIGRATION REV. 25, 26 (2002).

63. Gallagher, supra note 59, at 1001.

64. For a current list of ratifications, see http://0-untreaty.un.org.unistar.uni.edu:80/ENGLISH/bible/englishinternetbible/partI/chapterIV/treaty25.asp.

65. For a current list of ratifications, see http://www.unodc.org/unodc/en/crime_cicp_signatures trafficking.html.

66. Taran, supra note 12, at 18–22.

67. 2005 TIP REPORT, SUPRA note 14, at 34.

68. The United States, for example, is increasingly recognizing how the failure to protect trafficked persons' human rights compromises efforts to prosecute traffickers. For example, noting the significant disparity between the numbers of people trafficked to the United States (14,500–17,500 each year) and the numbers of those who have reported the abuse to law enforcement (757 as of November 2003), the U.S. Department of Justice has made concerted efforts to collaborate more effectively with NGOs and consider more victim-centered approaches to prosecution. DEP'T OF JUSTICE, ASSESSMENT OF U.S. ACTIVITIES TO COMBAT TRAFFICKING IN PERSONS 5, 22, 26–27 (2004).

69. ELAINE PEARSON, ANTI-SLAVERY INT'L, HUMAN TRAFFIC, HUMAN RIGHTS: REDEFINING VICTIM PROTECTION 4 (2002).

70. See, e.g., U.S. DEP'T OF STATE, TRAFFICKING IN PERSONS REPORT 148, 165, 185 (2004) (citing the Italian, Portuguese, and British governments' failure to distinguish between trafficking and smuggling). The 2004 Trafficking in Persons Report also described how trafficked persons in the Czech Republic "were treated as illegal immigrants and expressed fear of testifying due to safety concerns," id. at 134, and in Morocco, were "jailed and/or detained for violating immigration or other laws [and were] not provided adequate legal representation." Id. at 199. In the 2005 Trafficking in Persons Report, Italy, the United Kingdom, and Portugal persisted in their failure to distinguish between trafficking and smuggling or illegal immigration. 2005 TIP REPORT, supra note 14, at 130, 181, 221. France has apparently adopted a practice of "arresting, jailing, and fining trafficking victims as a means of discouraging the operation of trafficking networks and to gain information to pursue cases against traffickers," which, as the U.S. State Department notes, "harms trafficking victims and allows for [their] deportation . . . regardless of possible threats [in their country of origin]." Id. at 106.

71. PEARSON, supra note 69, at 2.

72. See 2005 TIP RETORT, supra note 14, at 5 (referring to the "three P's" of prosecution, protection, and prevention, noting that "a victim-centered approach to trafficking requires us equally to address the 'three R's'—rescue, rehabilitation and reintegration').

73. Id. at 9–10.

74. Palermo Protocol, supra note 51, art. 3.

75. See Coomaraswamy Position Paper, supra note 57, at 3.

76. In the 2005 TIP REPORT, the United States expanded its coverage of trafficking for nonsexual purposes. 2005 TIP REPORT, supra note 14, at 1. This expansion was undoubtedly in response to years of NGO protests over the United States' focus on sex trafficking.

77. Frank Laczko, Introduction, INT'L MIGRATION, Jan. 2005, at 5, 9 (introduction to a special issue entitled "Data and Research on Human Trafficking: A Global Survey," noting that research on trafficking has focused on the sex trafficking of women and children, neglecting other forms of trafficking). Liz Kelly, "You Can Find Anything You Want": A Critical Reflection on Research on Trafficking in Persons Within and into Europe, INT'L MIGRATION, Jan. 2005, at 235, 239 (article in a special issue entitled "Data and Research on Human Trafficking: A Global Survey," noting how most of the content and data in the TIP Reports issued by the U.S. State Department for years 2002–2004 was "confined to sexual exploitation").

78. ILO GLOBAL REVORT, Supra note 3, at 46.

79. Palermo Protocol, supra note 51, art. 9, [paragraph] 4.

80. BARBARA LIMANOWSKA, TRAFFICKING IN HUMAN BEINGS IN SOUTH EASTERN EUROPE xiii (2005) [hereinafter SEE REPORT] (assessing prevention strategies in Albania, Bosnia and Herzegovina, Bulgaria, Croatia, the former Yugoslav Republic of Macedonia, Moldova, Romania, Servia and Montenegro, and Kosovo).

81. Id. at 2.

82. See generally SEE REPORT, Supra note 80.

83. Id. at 36–37.

84. Id. at xiii.

85. The SEE REPORT is one of the few to undertake an assessment of prevention programs. As the IOM found in its survey of data and research on trafficking, there is a lack of information regarding trafficking programs in many regions of the world, including the Middle East, the Americas, and Africa. See Laczko, supra note 77, at 7.

86. See generally 2005 TIP REPORT, Supra note 14.

87. SEE REPORT, supra note 80, at 22.

88. Id. at 20–21.

89. International Covenant on Economic, Social and Cultural Rights, G.A. Res. 2200, U.N. GAOR, 21st Sess., Supp. No. 16, at 49, U.N. Doc. A/6316 (Dec. 16, 1966) [hereinafter ICESCR].

90. The current reality is that the number of traffickers arrested is low compared to the efforts expended to capture them, and of those who are tried, few are convicted and even fewer serve sentences. Am. Soc'y of Int'l Law, Trafficking in Humans: Proceedings of the 99th Annual Meeting (forthcoming 2006) [hereinafter 2005 ASIL Human Trafficking Panel] (noting that "virtually no kingpins are brought to justice, and criminal networks remain largely undisturbed," and that sentences are relatively minor and often not served) (draft on file with author). It appears to be a socioeconomic reality that there will be others to take advantage of the substantial profit-making potential to be had wherever there is both economic

necessity to migrate, yet shrinking avenues for legal migration. See Sassen, supra note 13, at 266–70.

91. See Laczko, supra note 77, at 9.

92. See generally SEE REPORT, supra note 80; DEP'T OF JUSTICE, ASSESSMENT of U.S. ACTIVITIES TO COMBAT TRAFFICKING IN PERSONS (2004).

93. Palermo Protocol, supra note 51, art. 9, [paragraph] 4.

94. U.N. Comm'n on the Status of Women, Women's Human Rights and Elimination of All Forms of Violence Against Women and Girls as Defined in the Beijing Platform of Action and the Outcome Documents of the Twenty-third Special Session of the General Assembly, at 47, U.N. Doc. E/CN.6/ 2003/12 (Mar. 13, 2003) (prepared by Barbara Limanowska). This report was based on information from the Balkans region. Id. at 1 n.2. See also 2005 ASIL Human Trafficking Panel, supra note 90, at 2–3 (noting the disparity between the proliferation of new counter-trafficking legal and institutional mechanisms, on the one hand, and the achievement of meaningful results, on the other).

95. 2005 TIP REPORT, supra note 14, at 1.

96. Laczko, supra note 77, at 9.

97. See supra text accompanying note 87.

98. SEE REPORT, Supra note 80, at 32–33. On a positive note, however, this experience also suggests the potential preventive role that helplines can play.

99. See generally ANDERSON & O'CONNELL DAVIDSON, supra note 41.

100. Id. at 43. Reports of the Swedish experience illustrate this point. "[W]hen Sweden introduced laws in 1999 to criminalize men who purchase sex, while decriminalizing [the prostitutes/sex workers], the incidence of female sex trafficking dropped. . . . [W]hile the demand for prostitution decreased in Sweden, it increased in neighboring countries. The male clients simply went [elsewhere to satisfy their desires]." Samarasinghe, supra note 28, at 102.

101. ANDERSON & O'CONNELL DAVIDSON, supra note 41, at 44.

102. Id. at 46, 47.

103. SEE REPORT, supra note 80, at 54.

104. Id.

105. Laczko, supra note 77, at 9.

106. See 2005 ASIL Human Trafficking Panel, supra note 90, at 3.

107. ICESCR, supra note 89, arts. 6, 7, 11, 13.

108. See generally Convention on the Elimination of All Forms of Discrimination Against Women, G.A. Res. 34/180, U.N. Doc. A/RES/34/180 (Dec. 18, 1979), reprinted in 19 I.L.M. 33 (1980).

109. Katarina Frostell & Martin Scheinin, Women, in ECONOMIC, SOCIAL AND CULTURAL RIGHTS 331,331 (Asbjorn Eide et al. eds., 2d. rev. ed. 2001).

110. World Conference on Human Rights, June 14–25, 1993, Vienna Declaration and Programme of Action, art. 1, [paragraph] 5, U.N. Doc. A/CONE.157/23 (July 12, 1993), reprinted in 32 I.L.M. 1663 (1993).

111. See Martin Scheinin, Economic and Social Rights as Legal Rights, in ECONOMIC, SOCIAL AND CULTURAL RIGHTS, Supra note 109, at 29, Dennis & Stewart, supra note 4, at 463.

112. See, e.g., Asbjorn Eide, Economic, Social and Cultural Rights as Human Rights, in ECONOMIC, SOCIAL AND CULTURAL RIGHTS, supra note 109, at 9, 23–25.

113. See U.N. Comm'n on Econ., Soc. and Cultural Rights, General Comment 3, annex III, [paragraph] 10, U.N. Doc. E/1991/23 (Dec. 14, 1990) [hereinafter General Comment 3]. "Progressive realization" cannot be used as a "pretext for non-compliance." The Maostricht Guidelines on Violations of Economic, Social and Cultural Rights, reprinted in 20 HUM. RTS. Q. 691, 694 (1998).

114. General Comment 3, supra note 113, [paragraph] 1.

115. See International Covenant on Civil and Political Rights, G.A. Res. 2200, art. 26, U.N. GAOR, 21st Sess., Supp. No. 16, at 52, U.N. Doc. A/6316 (Dec. 16, 1966).

116. See Frostell & Scheinin, supra note 109, at 334 (citing General Comment 18).

117. Id. at 334 & n. 15.

118. U.N. Comm. on the Elimination of All Foms of Discrimination Against Women, General Recommendation 19, U.N. Doc. HRI/GEN/Rev. 3 (noting that "[p]overty and unemployment increase opportunities for trafficking in women").

119. UNITED NATIONS, OFFICE OF THE HIGH COMM'R FOR HUMAN RIGHTS, HUMAN RIGHTS AND POVERTY REDUCTION: A CONCEPTUAL FRAMEWORK 17 (2004).

120. Coomaraswamy Report, supra note 1, [paragraph] 55.

121. See Optional Protocol to the Convention on the Elimination of All Forms of Discrimination Against Women, G.A. Res. 54/4, annex, U.N. Doc. A/54/49 (Oct. 6, 1999).

Dina Francesca Haynes

NO

Used, Abused, Arrested, and Deported: Extending Immigration Benefits to Protect the Victims of Trafficking and to Secure the Prosecution of Traffickers

Prologue

Madeleina was a slight, delicate-looking sixteen-year-old girl from Moldova. She left Moldova in 1998, when her sister's husband convinced her and another girl to go with his friend who promised to find them hostess jobs in Italy. She was given a fake passport, and after about a week of traveling, found herself locked in a brothel in what she later discovered was the Republika Srpska, Bosnia and Herzegovina (Bosnia).[1] A woman interpreting for the brothel owner told her that she had been sold to him to be his "wife." The brothel owner forced Madeleina to have sex with him and his friends and told her that she could begin working off her debt to him immediately. He told her that she already owed him more than $2000 for her purchase price and working papers.

Madeleina had no money and no friends. She could not speak the local language and the owner threatened her regularly, beating her and telling her that police would arrest her if she tried to leave. There were at least eleven other girls and women at this brothel, all foreigners. Most of them were from Moldova or Romania, and the brothel owner tried to keep them separated as much as possible to prevent their collusion and escape. The owner sometimes forced them to take drugs to keep them more compliant, the cost of which was added to their debt. The brothel owner kept Madeleina for about five months, forcing her to have sex with as many as twenty men a day. She thought that some of the customers at the brothel were local police. She also knew that Russian and either American, Canadian, or British men, and she thinks Italian, had visited her and had sex with her, in addition to local men.

When police raided that brothel, she was taken by car to Arizona Market, near Brcko, where cars, goods, and women are sold. Two foreign

From *Human Rights Quarterly,* 26:2 (2004), 222–237. Copyright © The John Hopkins University Press. Reprinted with permission of the John Hopkins University Press.

men purchased her; she thinks they were Swiss and American peacekeepers. These two men put her in a car and took her to an apartment in Tuzla where they kept her locked up and came to visit her every day or two, often with friends, and forced her to have sex with them. Over the course of these months, Madeleina had begun to teach herself some of the Serbian language.

One day, after no one had visited her for several days and she was running out of food, the landlord of the apartment opened the door and told her to get out. It was winter, and with no warm clothes Madeleina went out to find the local police, not because she believed the police would help her, but because she knew she would freeze to death with no place to go.

The local police promptly jailed her for prostitution. A Human Rights Officer with the Organization for Security and Co-operation in Europe (OSCE) intervened, and Madeleina was transported to a makeshift shelter in Sarajevo.[2] International and local nongovernmental organizations were then just establishing the shelter.

I. Introduction

Trafficking in human beings is an extremely lucrative business, with profits estimated at $7 billion per year[3] and a seemingly endless supply of persons to traffic, estimated at between 700,000 and four million new victims per year.[4] Trafficked persons, typically women and children, can be sold and resold, and even forced to pay back their purchasers for the costs incurred in their transport and purchase.[5] In fact, the United States Central Intelligence Agency estimates that traffickers earn $250,000 for each trafficked woman.[6] Economic instability, social dislocation, and gender inequality in transitioning countries foster conditions ripe for trafficking.

Trafficking in human beings involves moving persons for any type of forced or coerced labor, for the profit of the trafficker.[7] Several countries are finally adopting domestic legislation to criminalize trafficking in human beings, although many continue to punish the victims of trafficking, charging them with prostitution, possession of fraudulent documents, or working without authorization.[8] Many international organizations and consortiums of grassroots anti-trafficking organizations have also put forward models for combating trafficking.

None of these models is yet terribly effective, for a variety of reasons. At the forefront of these reasons is the fact that several countries have yet to adopt anti-trafficking laws.[9] Second, of those that have, many completely fail to implement those laws even after undertaking domestic and international obligations.[10] A third major reason is that some governments have failed to incorporate the advice of grassroots and international anti-trafficking organizations that have worked for years drafting recommended legislation based upon their observations in the field.[11]

A particular contemporary problem is trafficking for the sexual exploitation of women[12] in and from Central and Southeastern Europe.[13]

Currently, Central and Southeastern Europe are the primary sources from which women are drawn into global sex traffic through Europe,[14] and some countries in this region are actively engaged in developing anti-trafficking initiatives pursuant to their obligations as signatories to the 2000 Protocols to the UN Convention on Transnational Organized Crime.[15] In addition, some countries in the Balkans have the added presence of international peacekeepers and humanitarian workers, which in many respects exacerbates the problem.[16]

This paper will, in Part II, discuss the recent increase in trafficking. Part II will explore how and why governments have failed to effectively address the problem, despite being aware of its existence for decades. Part IV illustrates that two dominant anti-trafficking models have emerged in recent years, one of which is oriented toward prosecution of traffickers while the other emphasizes victim protection. Part V proposes a specific combination of the best of the two models, recommending several additional elements to create a new model that will more effectively combat trafficking, highlighting immigration benefits, and responds to anticipated arguments against such an expansion.

The principal recommendation of this article is that the best of the "jail the offender" and "protect the victim" models should be combined. The new model should incorporate advice from grassroots organizations that work directly with trafficked persons, in order to craft anti-trafficking programs that promote protection of victims. This new model should include immigration protection, should hit traffickers where it hurts, and should prioritize full implementation.

II. The Recent Rise of Trafficking in Human Beings

The horrific practice of trafficking in human beings has long been a serious problem throughout the world, but in the last fifteen years trafficking from European countries has been on the rise. Trafficking in Europe has been fueled by the social dislocations, increasing pockets of poverty, gender imbalance, bureaucratic chaos, and legislative vacuums resulting from the collapse of communism.[17]

Women already disenfranchised within their communities are most often those who fall prey to traffickers: ostracized minorities, women without employment or future economic prospects, and girls without family members to look out for them or who have fallen outside of the educational system.[18] These girls and women are lured by traffickers into leaving their countries, believing that they will work in the West as dancers, hostesses, or nannies, and instead find themselves forced to have sex for the profit of the men and women who purchased them.[19]

In order to secure their silence and compliance, traffickers threaten, beat, rape, drug, and deprive their victims of legitimate immigration or work documents. Women are forced to sell themselves in brothels, often receiving several clients per day.[20] They rarely see any wages for their work;

in fact, most victims are kept in indentured servitude and told that they owe their traffickers or the brothel owners for their own purchase price and for the price of procuring working papers and travel documents.[21]

The rings of traffickers are often vast, extremely well connected to police and government officials, well hidden, and reach across borders and continents.[22] Traffickers in human beings are also known to traffic in weapons and drugs, and to use trafficking in human beings to bring in initial cash flow to support the riskier traffic in drugs and arms.[23] Human beings, being reusable commodities that can be sold and resold, are both more lucrative[24] and less risky to traffic than drugs and arms, in that traffickers of human beings are rarely prosecuted for this particular offense.[25]

While between 700,000 and four million women are trafficked each year,[26] only a fraction of those are known to have received assistance in order to escape trafficking.[27] Many are re-victimized by being deported from the countries in which they are found,[28] sanctioned by law when attempting to return to their countries of origin,[29] and ostracized within their communities and families.[30]

Governments appear to have recognized the importance of the issue, many having ratified international instruments established to eradicate trafficking in human beings. Nevertheless, trafficking is neither slowing, nor is the prosecution of traffickers or the protection of their victims becoming any more certain.

III. Governmental Failures to Confront the Issue

As early as 1904, concern over "white slavery," in which European women were exported to the colonies, prompted the adoption of the International Agreement for the Suppression of White Slave Traffic, addressing the fraudulent or abusive recruitment of women for prostitution in another country.[31] The issue was addressed again in 1933 with the International Convention on the Suppression of the Traffic in Women of Full Age, by which parties agreed to punish those who procured prostitutes or ran brothels.[32] In 1949, the United Nations adopted the Convention for the Suppression of the Traffic in Persons and of the Exploitation of the Prostitution of Others.[33] Until 2000, the only other international treaty to address trafficking was the 1979 UN Convention on the Elimination of All Forms of Discrimination Against Women (CEDAW), which required states to take all measures to suppress both trafficking and "exploitation of prostitution," meaning forced prostitution.[34]

Beginning in the late 1980s, the European Union and the United Nations began addressing the issue repeatedly, yet little progress was made and the collapse of communism flooded trafficked persons throughout Europe. With trafficking recognized as a distinct problem since 1903, with the ratification of four treaties by many nations, and with trafficking recently and dramatically on the rise, why has so little progress been made?

A. Some Politicians Use Trafficking to Direct Attention to Unrelated Political Agendas

Trafficking is a low priority for many governments who pay lip service to solving the problem only to harness more support for other political objectives. Because of the visceral reaction trafficking elicits with the public, it has recently been used by politicians and governments to bolster other political agendas, such as curtailing illegal migration, fighting prostitution, and even combating terrorism.

Some governments pretend to care about trafficking when the real objective is controlling unwanted migration.[35] Trafficking in human beings is a very serious topic in its own right, but the gravity and emotional impact of the topic unfortunately render it vulnerable to political manipulation. With illegal migration, smuggling, terrorism, and prostitution now on many political agendas, the pledge to combat trafficking is misused as justification for "clamping down" on these other threats that also have immigration implications.[36] Authorities have remained cynical and hardened to the plight of victims who are easier to treat as prostitutes or illegal immigrants.[37]

In fact, some countries seem to view the existence of trafficked women within their sovereign borders as evidence of a breach of security or the failure of their domestic immigration mechanisms, and accordingly attempt to address trafficking through simple reconfiguration of their border control mechanisms.[38] Traffickers are often extremely savvy transnational organized criminals, while their victims are most often women and children already victimized by economic, political, or social conditions in their home countries. Viewing trafficking as an immigration issue overly simplifies the complexity of preparing effective anti-trafficking measures.

As this section will demonstrate, politicians and governments have blurred the distinctions between illegal migration, trafficking, and smuggling, taking advantage of the current world fear of terrorism committed by legal and illegal immigrants, to restrict immigration and freedom of movement further. They have purposely co-mingled anti-trafficking initiatives with anti-prostitution initiatives. They have tried to further curtail migration by blurring the distinction between trafficking and smuggling. Finally, it is my opinion that some governments are motivated not by a keen belief in the necessity of curtailing trafficking, but by a desire to secure international financial assistance or enter the European Union.

1. Prostitution

Prostitution and trafficking are not one and the same, yet some would treat them as such.[39] Prostitution involves persons willingly engaging in sex work. Although there may be a gray area involving different degrees of consent, choice, and free will, trafficking goes well outside of this gray area. While a valid argument could be made that gender imbalances in economic or social factors drive a woman to consent to such labor as her chosen profession, thus effectively removing her "will,"[40] trafficking involves clear deprivation of choice at some stage, either through fraud, deception, force, coercion, or threats.

Whether a trafficked woman was initially willing or unwilling when she entered into sex work should make no legal difference when the outcome is enslavement or forced servitude; a person cannot consent to enslavement or forced labor of any kind.[41] While some trafficked persons may be willing to work in the sex industry, they do not anticipate being forced to pay off large forcibly imposed debts, being kept against their will, having their travel documents taken from them, or being raped, beaten, and sold like chattel.[42]

Nevertheless, within the community of NGOs, international organizations, governments, and working groups laboring to define and combat trafficking, the issue of prostitution regularly enters the deliberation. As recently as 2001, for example, some persons working for the United Nations Mission in Bosnia and Herzegovina (UNMIBH) and partner organizations tasked with assisting the Bosnian government to eradicate trafficking refused to provide trafficking protection assistance to women who at any point willingly engaged in prostitution.[43]

The Organized Crime Convention has encouraged countries to focus on coercion and use of force in identifying whether a woman is a victim of trafficking, rather than on whether she has ever engaged in prostitution. Nevertheless, the US government agency tasked with distributing funding to international trafficking initiatives recently determined that it would refuse to fight trafficking where doing so might appear to treat prostitution as a legitimate activity.[44] Thus, trafficking is politicized, a volatile topic easily used to affix other political agendas. Even while most experts working in anti-trafficking initiatives agree that trafficking and prostitution are separate issues, to be handled separately as a matter of law, the United States took a step backwards in attempting to tackle prostitution under the guise of combating trafficking.

2. Smuggling

Politicians have also attempted to link smuggling and trafficking in order to achieve tightened border controls. While most governments acknowledge that smuggling and trafficking are two distinct crimes, they nonetheless use trafficking statistics and horrific trafficking stories to justify tightened border controls when the primary goal is not the elimination of trafficking, but the reduction of illegal migration, some of which occurs via smugglers, and perhaps preventing terrorism.

The United States Department of State, for instance, opened the Migrant Smuggling and Trafficking in Persons Coordination Center in December 2000, even while acknowledging, "at their core . . . these related problems are distinct."[45] The US government nevertheless justified combining the two issues by pointing out that "these related problems result in massive human tragedy and affect our national security, primarily with respect to crime, health and welfare, and border control."[46] By way of another example, the Canadian government supported a study jointly reviewing both smuggling and trafficking, even while pointing out the legal distinctions between the two.[47] The study was justified under the premise that "as human smuggling and trafficking are increasing, the tightening of border controls has taken on a new urgency from the fear of terrorism in the West, as well as restrictive measures placed on irregular migratory movements."[48]

Smuggling involves delivering persons to the country they wish to enter, initiated by the potential migrant. Smuggling often takes place under horrible and possibly life threatening conditions, but smuggled persons are left to their own devices upon delivery. Smuggling is not as lucrative for the perpetrators, as smugglers usually make only a short-term profit on the act of moving a person, while traffickers regard people as highly profitable, reusable, re-sellable, and expendable commodities.[49]

In order for anti-trafficking initiatives to be effective, politicians must make the eradication of trafficking and the protection of trafficked persons into a prioritized goal, distinct from the elimination of smuggling or the tightening of border controls.

3. Some Governments are Motivated by a Desire to Meet EU Entrance Requirements or to Obtain Financial Assistance

Not surprisingly, the European Union and the United States, among other institutions and governments, are conditioning financial assistance[50] and entry into the European Union on the country's willingness to develop legislation curtailing trafficking within and across its borders[51]. Countries set to enter the European Union in 2004[52] are eager to pass legislation recommended by the European Union and the Council of Europe (CoE), and join working groups that address stemming the flow of trafficking and smuggling.[53]

Passing recommended legislation and making real efforts to stem the flow of trafficking, however, are often two different things. When countries simply adopt legislation in order to secure entry into the European Union or to meet financial assistance requirements, there is no real ownership or commitment to eradicating trafficking. The legislation, no matter how meticulously in conformity with international standards, will not be fully or adequately implemented at the local level without serious political will.

B. Governments Ignore Obvious Problems with Anti-Trafficking Initiatives

Many countries have now finally adopted some domestic legislation addressing trafficking, and most have eradicated earlier laws that punished trafficked persons for immigration or prostitution offenses.[54] This section points out reasons no current laws are very effective in the fight to eradicate trafficking.

By no means, however, have all countries adopted laws to specifically target trafficking.[55]

1. Governments Fail to Prioritize the Implementation of Anti-Trafficking Laws

A piece of legislation is useful to trafficked persons and threatening to violators only if it is implemented and known by the traffickers to be fully in force. No matter how great the economic or political pressure applied by the European Union or the United States to encourage countries to introduce legislation to prosecute traffickers, no incentive can create the political will to *implement* legislation if such will or ability does not exist or is not prioritized.[56]

In Bosnia, for example, UNMIBH reported that of sixty-three cases brought against traffickers in 2000, only three were successfully prosecuted.[57] Of those three, the defendants were *all* tried on charges related to prostitution, not trafficking. According to the HRW Report, all of the thirty-six cases brought involved charges related to prostitution and not trafficking—not just the three successful ones.[58] In one of the three cases, three trafficked women and two brothel owners were arrested in a raid. Although the defendants admitted that they had purchased the women for prices ranging between $592 and $1162, the court convicted the three women for prostitution and dropped the charges against the male defendants.[59]

Coordination among responsible agencies to implement the law is often flawed in the best of circumstances, further obstructing implementation.[60] Meetings are held at the highest levels and those in attendance come away full of self-congratulations that plans are being made and laws adopted. Yet out in the community, brothels are raided and no screening is done for victims of trafficking; victims identify themselves to police and face prosecution;[61] traffickers supply false passports to border police,[62] and the girls and traffickers are waived through.

For example, during the author's tenure in Belgrade, Serbia, and Montenegro, a brothel was raided and trafficked women were placed in jail, rather than the new shelter for trafficked persons, on the very same day that a high-level regional meeting took place in Belgrade between ministries and Stability Pact, UN, and OSCE officials to discuss follow up victim protection mechanisms for the new shelter. There seemed to be no communication between those making the decisions to adopt new laws and practices and those carrying them out in the field, and there was an inability or unwillingness to train these low-level government employees.

2. Governments Fail to Penalize or Even Acknowledge the Complicity of Peacekeepers and International Workers in Trafficking

Despite a growing awareness that peacekeeping forces and humanitarian workers regularly and knowingly obtain the services of trafficked women and sometimes even engage in or aid and abet trafficking, governments have failed to publicly address this issue. Trafficked women in Bosnia, for instance, report that approximately 30 per cent of their clients are internationals.[63] Countries that had never before been countries of destination began receiving trafficked women when peacekeepers and international aid workers moved into Bosnia, Croatia, and Kosovo.[64] Neighboring countries quickly became countries of transit and origin. While the use of trafficked women by international workers might constitute only a fraction of the total number of trafficked women and the fraction of those trafficked by international workers is even less, the participation of international humanitarian workers and peacekeeping forces in trafficking conveys a powerful symbolic message to local authorities and traffickers. The message is this: governments working to "democratize" developing countries do not really care about eradicating trafficking.

For years international organizations operating in the Balkans have been unwilling to determine how they can best prevent their employees from frequenting brothels known to harbor trafficked women. In recent years, when it has become clear that most brothels in the Balkans, for instance, do contain trafficked women,[65] these international organizations have still failed to enforce internal rules or laws against frequenting brothels.[66]

Ninety per cent of foreign sex workers in the Balkans are estimated to be trafficked, although less than 35 per cent are identified and deemed eligible to receive protection assistance, and less than 7 per cent actually do receive long-term support.[67] It is therefore well known among those charged with teaching Bosnians how to better enforce their laws, e.g. peacekeepers, the International Police Task Force [IPTF][68], and international humanitarian workers, that by visiting a prostitute, one stands a good chance of visiting a trafficked woman.[69] One would think, therefore, that workers paid by the foreign ministries whose goals are combating trafficking and promoting safety and democracy would be strictly forbidden to visit brothels, but they are not. In fact, sometimes they receive no punishment whatsoever even when caught engaging in such activity.[70] How can a victim of trafficking be expected to escape her captor and seek safety with the very men paying her captors for her services?

Some international organizations such as the OSCE and some branches of the United Nations have recently developed "Codes of Conduct" which implicitly forbid their personnel from seeing prostitutes by exhorting that they not "engage in any activity unbecoming of a mission member," subsequent to widely-publicized scandals involving international troops engaged in trafficking.[71] Nevertheless, several recent articles indicate that local police, international peacekeepers, and humanitarian aid workers continue to be major users of brothels in the Balkans in particular.[72] Developing and enforcing prohibitions against this practice are crucial, because the international police, peacekeepers, and humanitarian workers are the very persons whose duty it is to work with local authorities to eradicate trafficking in this part of the world, and the victims are supposed to be looking to international police and peacekeepers for protection.[73]

Notes

1. Bosnia is currently divided into two entities and a district: the Republika Srpska, the Federation, and Brcko District.
2. As related to the author during her work with the OSCE in Bosnia. For

similar stories, see Human Rights Watch, Hopes Betrayed: Trafficking of Women and Girls to Post-Conflict Bosnia and Herzegovina for Forced Prostitution (2002) [hereinafter HRW Report]; John McGhie, *Bosnia— Arizona Market: Women for Sale* (UK Channel 4 News television broadcast, 8 June 2000), *available at* fpmail.friends-partners.org/pipermail/stop-traffic/2000-August/000113; William J. Kole & Aida Cerkez-Robinson, *U.N. Police Accused of Involvement in Prostitution in Bosnia,* Assoc. Press, 28 June 2001; Colum Lynch, *U.N. Halted Probe of Officers' Alleged Role in Sex Trafficking,* Wash. Post, 27 Dec. 2001, at A17, *available at* www.washingtonpost.com/wp-dyn/articles/A28267-2001Dec26.

3. United Nations Children's Fund (UNICEF) et al., Trafficking in Human Beings in Southeastern Europe xiii (2002) [hereinafter Joint Report on Trafficking] (stating that trafficking in human beings is the third most lucrative organized crime activity after, and often conjoined with, trafficking in arms and drugs). *See also* Gillian Caldwell et al., Crime and Servitude: An Exposé of the Traffic in Women for Prostitution from the Newly Independent States 14 (1997), *available at* www.qweb.kvinnoforum.se/misc/crimeru.rtf (citing 1988 German police estimates that "traffickers earned US $35–50 million annually in interest on loans to foreign women and girls entering Germany to work as prostitutes").

4. U.S. Dep't of State Office to Monitor and Combat Trafficking in Persons, Trafficking in Persons Report 1 (2002).

5. *The Sex Trade: Trafficking of Women and Children in Europe and the United States: Hearing before the Commission on Security and Cooperation in Europe,* 106th Cong., 1st Sess. 22 (1999) (testimony of Laura Lederer) [hereinafter, The Lederer Report] (stating that women trafficked into North America are sold for as much as $16,000 to each new brothel owner, and have to pay or work off a debt of $20,000 to $40,000); *see also,* Jennifer Lord, *EU Expansion Could Fuel Human Trafficking,* United Press Int'l, 9 Nov. 2002, *available at* cayman netnews.com/Archive/Archive%20Articles/November%202002/Issue%20286%20Wed/EU%20Expansion.html.

6. Caldwell, *supra* note 3, at 10.

7. While there are a multitude of definitions of trafficking, the most widely used definition derives from the current legal standard bearer, the Protocol to Prevent, Suppress and Punish Trafficking in Persons, Especially Women and Children, Supplementing the United Nations Convention Against Transnational Organized Crime, *adopted* 15 Nov. 2000, G.A. Res. A/55/25, Annex II, 55 U.N. GAOR Supp. (No. 49), at 60, U.N. Doc. A/45/49 (Vol. I) (2001) (*entered into force* 25 Dec. 2003) [hereinafter Trafficking Protocol]. Article 3 of The Protocol defines trafficking as:

> the recruitment, transportation, transfer, harbouring or receipt of persons, by means of the threat or use of force or other forms of coercion, of abduction, of fraud, of deception, of the abuse of power or of a position of vulnerability or of the giving or receiving of payments or benefits to achieve the consent of a person having control over another person, for the purpose of exploitation.

See United Nations, Office of Drugs and Crime *available at* www.unodc.org/unodc/en/trafficking_human_beings. Solely for the purposes of narrowing discussion, this article will emphasize trafficking for sex work. This narrow focus should not be viewed as support for a definition of trafficking that bifurcates trafficking that results in sex work from other forms of trafficking (such as indentured domestic service, forced labor, forced marriage, subjugation in making pornography, etc.). All trafficking in human beings is a violation of human rights in that it involves affronts to human dignity and arguably constitutes a form of slavery.

8. *See infra* text and accompanying notes pt. IV(A).

9. In South Eastern Europe, for instance, Croatia, Serbia, and Montenegro, have no distinct criminal offense for trafficking, despite being known countries of origin, transit, or destination, although a law is under consideration in Serbia. For review of laws related to trafficking in these countries, *see* Kristi Severance, ABA: Central European an Eurasian Law Initiative Survey of Legislative Frameworks for Combating Trafficking in Persons (2003) [hereinafter ABA CEELI Report] *available at* www.abanet.org/ceeli/publications/conceptpapers/humantrafficking/home. *See infra* note 109. In March 2003, the Office of the High Representative imposed a law criminalizing trafficking as a distinct offense, as the Bosnian authorities had failed to do. As yet, however, no traffickers have been charged under this new law.

10. *See infra* text pt. III(B)(1).

11. *See infra* text pt. IV(B)(1)(b).

12. For the purposes of simplicity, the paper will refer to women in particular, and use the feminine pronouns when referring to victims of trafficking, as the majority of victims of trafficking for sexual exploitation are women and girls.

13. Since the early 1990s countries in political and economic transition in Central, Eastern, and South Eastern Europe and the Former Soviet Union have not only become main countries of origin for trafficked persons, but also of transit and destination. See Office for Democratic Institutions and Human Rights, Organization for Security and Co-operation in Europe, Reference Guide for Anti-Trafficking Legislative Review 20 (2001) [hereinafter OSCE Reference Guide]. South Eastern European countries offer the unique combination of being countries deeply mired in trafficking, and simultaneously interested in entering the European Union (EU). As such, they are in the process of bringing their legislation and administrative bodies into compliance with European standards, and are particularly useful for viewing the process of developing anti-trafficking initiatives. Cyprus, the Czech Republic, Estonia, Hungary, Latvia, Lithuania, Malta, Poland, the Slovak Republic, and Slovenia, and are set to join the EU in 2004, while Romania, Bulgaria, and Turkey all have active applications for EU membership. See European Union Website, Candidate, Countries, *available at* europa.eu.int/comm/enlargement/candidate.

14. Central and Eastern Europe have surpassed Asia and Latin America as countries of origin since the breakdown of the Soviet Union in 1989. See OSCE Reference Guide, *supra* note 13, at 7.

15. U.N. Convention Against Transnational Organized Crime, G.A. Res. 55/25, Annex I, U.N. GAOR 55th Sess., Supp. No. 49, at 44, U.N. Doc. A/45/49 (Vol. 1) (2000), *entered into force 29 Sept.* 2003 [hereinafter Organized Crime

Convention]. Serbia, Montenegro, and Bosnia have ratified the Organized Crime Convention, and its Protocols. All other South Eastern European countries are parties and it remains unclear as to how they will implement their commitments.

16. *See infra* text pt. III(B)(2). International Administration is still in effect in Kosovo (through the U.N. Mission in Kosovo, pursuant to U.N. Resolution 1244 (S.C. Res 1244, U.N. SCOR, 4011th mtg., S/RES/1244 (1999)), and partially in Bosnia and Herzegovina.

17. *See* Jenna Shearer Demir, the Trafficking of Women for Sexual Exploitation: A Gender-Based and Well-founded Fear of Persecution? 4–5 (2003), *available at* www.unhcr.ch/cgi-bin/texis/vtx/home/opendoc.pdf?tbl=RESEARCH&id=3e71f 84c4&page=publ (arguing that women disproportionately suffer the effects of an economic upheaval); Sergei Blagov, *Equal Opportunities Remain a Pipedream*, Asia Times Online, 10 Mar. 2000, *available at* www.atimes.com/c-asia/ BC10Ag01.html (stating that "[s]ome 70 per cent of Russian unemployed with college degrees are women. In some regions, women make up almost 90 per cent of the unemployed.")

18. Based on the author's discussion with anti-trafficking NGOs and UN officials in Bosnia and Serbia, and on direct discussion with trafficking victims.

19. *Id.*

20. HRW Report, *supra* note 2, at 18.

21. *Id.* at 4, 11.

22. *Report of the Special Rapporteur on Violence Against Women, its Causes and Consequences, Ms. Radhika Coomaraswamy*, U.N. ESCOR, Comm'n on Hum. Rts., 53rd Sess., U.N. Doc. E/CN.4/1997/47 (1997) § IV (expressing concern about government complicity in trafficking).

23. *See* Amy O'Neill Richard, U.S. Dep't of State Center for the Study of Intelligence: International Trafficking in Women to the United States: A Contemporary Manifestation of Slavery and Organized Crime 1 (1999), *available at* www.odci.gov/csi/monograph/women/trafficking.pdf [hereinafter CSI Report]. *See also* IOM, Applied Research and Data Collection on a Study of Trafficking in Women and Children for Sexual Exploitation to through and from the Balkan Region 7 (2001) [hereinafter IOM Report].

24. *See* CSI Report, *supra* note 23, at 19–20.

25. *See infra* text pt. IV (C)(2)(a).

26. U.S. Dep't of State, Office to Monitor and Combat Trafficking in Persons, Trafficking in Persons Report 1, *supra* note 4, at 1. The numbers for South Eastern Europe in particular are difficult to specify. For example, one Swedish NGO estimates that "500,000 women . . . are trafficked each year into Western Europe alone. A large proportion of these come from the former Soviet Union countries." Joint Report on Trafficking, *supra* note 3, at 4. IOM estimates that in 1997, "175,000 women and girls were trafficked from Central and Eastern Europe and the Newly Independent States." *Id.* As of 2002, IOM estimates that 120,000 women and children are trafficked into the EU each year, mostly through the Balkans, and that 10,000 are working in Bosnia alone, mostly from Moldova, Romania and the Ukraine. *Id.*

27. Joint Report on Trafficking, *supra* note 3, at xv (only 7 per cent of the foreign migrant sex workers known to be victims of trafficking receive any long term assistance and support).

28. HRW Report, *supra* note 2, at 38.

29. Global Alliance Against Traffic in Women et al., Human Rights Standards for the Treatment of Trafficked Persons 13, 15 (1999), *available at* www. hrlawgroup.org/resources/content/IHRLGTraffickin_tsStandards.pdf. Countries from which trafficked persons originate are referred to as countries of origin. Countries through which victims are trafficked are called countries of transit, and destination countries are those in which victims ultimately find themselves engaged in sex work.

30. *Id.* at 13.

31. International Agreement for the Suppression of White Slave Traffic, 1 U.N.T.S. 83 (*signed* 18 May 1904) (*entered into force* 18 July 1905) (amended by the Protocol signed at Lake Success, New York, 4 May 1949). The Agreement was ratified by Belgium, Denmark, France, Germany, Italy, the Netherlands, Portugal Russia, Spain, Sweden, and Norway, Switzerland, and the United Kingdom and consented to by their respective colonies, and dealt with European women being exported to the colonies for prostitution, sometimes forcibly.

32. International Convention for the Suppression of the Traffic in Women of Full Age, Concluded at Geneva 11 Oct. 1933, as amended by the Protocol signed at Lake Success, New York, on 12 Nov. 1947, *registered* 24 Apr. 1950, No. 772.

33. Convention for the Suppression of the Traffic in Persons and of the Exploitation of the Prostitution of Others, *opened for signature* 21 Mar. 1950, 96 U.N.T.S. 271 (*entered into force* 25 July 1951). Parties agreed to "punish any person who, to gratify the passions of another: (1) Procures, entices or leads away, for purposes of prostitution, another person, even with the consent of that person; (2) Exploits the prostitution of another person, even with the consent of that person." *Id.* art. 1.

34. Convention on the Elimination of All Forms of Discrimination Against Women, *adopted* 18 Dec. 1979, G.A. Res. 34/180, U.N. GAOR, 34th Sess., Supp. No. 46, U.N. Doc. A/34/46 (1980) (*entered into force* 3 Sept. 1981), 1249 U.N.T.S. 13, *reprinted in* 19 I.L.M. 33 (1980).

35. *See* CSI Report, *supra* note 23, at 31 (stating that "[d]efinitional difficulties still persist regarding trafficking in women. . . . Distinctions regarding trafficking in women, alien smuggling, and irregular migration are sometimes blurred with INS [former US immigration department] predisposed to jump to the conclusion that most cases involving illegal workers are alien smuggling instead of trafficking cases").

36. *See, e.g.,* Richard Monk, Organization for Security and Co-operation in Europe Mission to the Fry: Study on Policing in the Federal Republic of Yugoslavia 21 (2001), *available at* www.osce.org/yugoslavia/documents/reports/files/report-policing-e.pdf [hereinafter Monk Report] (Commenting: "Additionally, these statistics [on successful anti-trafficking ventures] are used for various political purposes—for example, prevention of trafficking is used as an argument for refusing young women entry to a country or for refusing to issue them a visa, and then, in the police statistics, these cases are relabeled as successful cases of rescuing 'victims of trafficking.'").

37. *See,* e.g., CSI Report, *supra* note 23, at 35 (US government officials cited as holding the opinion that trafficking victims are part of the conspiracy and therefore view them as accomplices).

38. "More often than not, anti-trafficking laws, be it domestic or international, tend to be conceived and are employed as border-control and immigration mechanisms," Agnes Khoo, *Trafficking and Human Rights: Some Observations and Questions,* 12 Asia Pacific-Forum on Law, Women and Development 3 (Dec. 1999), *available at* www.apwld.org/vol123-02.htm.

39. In explaining its priorities for 2003, the Stability Pact of South-Eastern Europe stated: "Attention will be drawn to maintain the differentiation between victims of human trafficking and prostitutes, which is currently becoming blurred, to the detriment of effective and targeted victim protection." Special Co-ordinator of the Stability Pact for South Eastern Europe Task Force on Trafficking in Human Beings, Anti-Trafficking Policy-Outline for 2003 [hereinafter SP Trafficking Task Force Priorities], *available at* www.stabilitypact.org/trafficking/info.html#four. For more discussion on the Stability Pact, see discussion *infra* pt. IV(D)(3).

40. NGO Consultation with the UN/IGO's on Trafficking in Persons, Prostitution and the Global Sex Industry, Trafficking and the Global Sex Industry: The Need for a Human Rights Framework, 21–22 (1999), Room XII Palais des Nations, Geneva, Switzerland [Panel A and Panel B] (some IGO's arguing that all prostitution is forced prostitution and calling for its abolition, with others arguing for a distinction between voluntary and forced prostitution in order to focus on preventing the worst forms of exploitation of prostitutes).

41. *See,* e.g., CSI Report, *supra* note 23, at vi ("The Thirteenth Amendment outlawing slavery prohibits an individual from selling himself or herself into bondage, and Western legal tradition prohibits contracts consenting in advance to assaults and other criminal wrongs."). This argument is further developed in pt. V(A)(1).

42. *See* HRW Report, *supra* note 2, at 15–20 (detailing common treatment and expectations of trafficked women).

43. *Id.* at 13. This practice of excluding prostitutes from victim protection results from criteria set by donor agencies rather than international law; *see e.g., infra* note 44 and accompanying text.

44. In its report entitled "Trafficking in Persons, The USAID Strategy for Response," designed to implement several provisions within the Trafficking Victim's Protection Act (TVPA), the US Agency for International Development (USAID) states that it will only work with [e.g. fund] local NGOs "committed . . . to combat trafficking *and prostitution,*" [emphasis added], explaining that: "organizations advocating prostitution as an employment choice or which advocate or support the legalization of prostitution are not appropriate partners," US Agency for International Development, Trafficking in Persons: The USAID Strategy for Response (Feb. 2003), *available at* www.usaid.gov/wid/pubs/pd-abx-358-final.pdf.

45. U.S. Dep't of State International Information Programs, Fact Sheet: Migrant Smuggling and Trafficking in Persons (2000), *available at* www.usembassy.it/file2000_12/alia/a0121523. htm.

46. *Id.*

47. *See* Jacqueline Oxman-Martinez, Human Smuggling and Traficking: Achieving the Goals of the UN Protocols? 1 (2003), *available at* www.maxwell.syr.edu/campbell/XBorder/OxmanMartinez%20oped.pdf.

48. *Id.* at 1.

49. In the last decade, Southeast Asia alone has produced nearly three times as many victims of trafficking than produced during the entire history of slavery from Africa. Melanie Nezer, *Trafficking in Women and Children: "A Contemporary Manifestation of Slavery,"* 21 Refugee Reports 1, 3 (2000) (400 years of slavery from Africa produced 11.5 million victims; victims of trafficking in the 1990s within and from Southeast Asia are estimated to be more than 30 million).

50. The United States Trafficking Victims Protection Act of 2000, Pub. L. No. 106-386, 114 Stat. 1464 (2000) [hereinafter TVPA], for instance, requires an annual submission to Congress by the Department of State on the status of trafficking in each country. Financial assistance is tied directly to the level of each country's compliance with US directives. U.S. Dep't of State Office to Monitor and Combat Trafficking in Persons, Trafficking in Persons Report 10 (2002). (Beginning in 2003, those countries ranked lowest in this report "will be subject to certain sanctions, principally termination of non-humanitarian, non-trade-related assistance. Consistent with the Act, such countries also would face U.S. opposition to assistance . . . from international financial institutions.")

51. In the case of the European Union, entry into the Union is conditioned upon compliance with general respect for human rights and compliance with human rights standards.

52. For list of applicant countries to the European, *see supra* note 13.

53. In the author's experience working with ministries of justice, interior, and human rights in Bosnia, Croatia, and Serbia and Montenegro, high level government authorities were typically keen to attend high level working groups addressing the drafting of trafficking legislation, but were much harder to pin down when it came to establishing work plans to train field level government authorities.

54. *See infra* text pt. IV(A). For example, in Israel as recently as 1998, a victim's best hope was to have the brothel or massage parlor she worked in raided by police. She would then be taken to prison, not a shelter or detention center, and offered two options: be deported and have criminal prostitution charges dropped, or file a complaint against her trafficker or those holding her in involuntary servitude. If she chose to file charges, however, she would remain in prison until a trial was held. Not surprisingly, no women between 1994 and 1998 chose to testify against their traffickers in Israel. Most traffickers were well aware that the laws favored them, if only because the women they trafficked were illegally in the country and were engaging in criminal activity. Michael Specter, *Traffickers' New Cargo: Naïve Slavic Women,* N.Y. Times, 11 Jan. 1998, at A1.

55. Serbia, Montenegro, and Croatia, for example, have no distinct criminal offense for trafficking. *See* generally ABA CEELI Report, *supra* note 9, for updates on domestic trafficking legislation. Although Bosnia's law criminalizing trafficking was imposed in March 2003, it has yet to yield a prosecution. *See infra* note 109.

56. One way to encourage implementation of anti-trafficking laws is for the European Union and United States to condition their assistance on implementation, rather than on simple passage of anti-trafficking laws, a recommendation made in this paper, and finally acknowledged in the 2003 Trafficking in Persons Report, U.S. Dep't of State Office to Monitor and Combat Trafficking in Persons, Trafficking in Persons Report 2 (2003) [hereinafter 2003 Trafficking in Persons Report], *available at* www.state.gov/documents/ organization/21555.pdf.

57. HRW Report, *supra* note 2, at 36.

58. *Id.*

59. *Id.*

60. CSI Report, *supra* note 23, at 31. Questions about whether the United States can be considered an example of the "best of circumstances" aside, the CSI Report states that at least in 1999, prior to passage of the TVPA, "information sharing among the various entities remain[ed] imperfect. Several Department of Justice [DOJ] offices look at the trafficking issue through the prism of their particular offices' interest, be it eliminating civil rights violations, tackling organized crime, or protecting minors. Even within the [DOJ], information is not always shared." *See also* Monk Report, *supra* note 36, at 76. Although Serbia and Montenegro are actively participating in high level working groups to combat trafficking, including suggesting progressive programs for victim protection, the police force is incapable of coping with the scale of the phenomenon:

> Apart from within the border police departments, there is poor awareness and interest generally on the part of police and the public about the subject [of trafficking], and the prevailing disregard for gender equality contributes to indifference about the plight of victims. . . . Because of the lack of reciprocal agreements with neighboring States, the incompatibility of laws, the absence of [domestic] laws which enable successful prosecutions to be brought against the traffickers and pimps and the lack of [domestic] legal authority to produce evidence obtained by the internal use of technical and surveillance aids, victim's cases are generally viewed as time and energy consuming and inevitably unproductive. The very fact that victim's statements, both verbal and written, will be in a foreign language further reduces responsiveness.

61. HRW Report, *supra* note 2, at 61.

62. *See id.* at 16.

63. *Id.* at 11. *See also,* 2003 Trafficking in Persons Report, *supra* note 56, at 35 (acknowledging that the international civilian and military personnel have contributed to trafficking in Bosnia).

64. *See, e.g.,* HRW Report, *supra* note 2, at 4, 11. ("According to [IGOs and NGOs] trafficking first began to appear [in Bosnia] in 1995," and "[l]ocal NGOs believe that the presence of thousands of expatriate civilians and soldiers has been a significant motivating factor for traffickers to Bosnia and Herzegovina.")

65. *See id.* at 4 (227 of the nightclubs in Bosnia are suspected of harboring trafficked women).

66. *Id.* at 46–60.

67. *See* Joint Report on Trafficking, *supra* note 3, at xv.

68. In January 2003, the duties of the IPTF were assumed by the European Union, and are now referred to as "European Union Police Mission."

69. In Serbia for example, of 600 women questioned by police during brothel raids between January 2000 and July 2001, 300 were determined to be victims of trafficking. *See id.,* at 78.

70. HRW Report, *supra* note 2, at 62–67.

71. The author, a member of the OSCE Mission to Bosnia, signed such a Code of Conduct.

72. *See, e.g.,* McGhie, *supra* note 2; Kole, *supra* note 2; Lynch, *supra* note 2; Daniel McGrory, *Woman Sacked for Revealing UN Links with Sex Trade,* The Times Online (London), 7 Aug. 2002; Robert Capps, *Crime Without Punishment,* SALON.COM, 27 Jun. 2002, *available at* www.salon.com/news/feature/2002/06/27/military; Robert Capps, Outside the Law, SALON.COM, 26 June. 2002, *available at* www.salon.com/news/feature/2002/06/26/bosnia/index_np; *US Scandal, Prostitution, Pimping and Trafficking,* Bosnia Daily, Daily e-newspaper, 25 Jul. 2001, No. 42, at 1 (on file with author).

73. UNHCHR recently addressed this issue openly in its guideline covering "Obligations of peacekeepers, civilian police and humanitarian and diplomatic personnel," asking states to consider "[e]nsuring that staff employed in the context of peacekeeping, peace-building, civilian policing, humanitarian and diplomatic missions do not engage in trafficking and related exploitation or use the services of persons in relation to which there are reasonable grounds to suspect that they may have been trafficked." *Recommended Principles and Guidelines on Human Rights and Human Trafficking, U.N. High Commissioner for Human Rights,* E/2002/68/Add.1, Guideline 10, ¶ 3 [hereinafter *Recommended Principles and Guidelines*]. *See infra* text pt. IV(C)(2).

POSTSCRIPT

Do Adequate Strategies Exist to Combat Human Trafficking?

Human trafficking has been part of the global landscape for centuries. What is different today are the magnitude and scope of the trafficking and the extent to which organized crime is involved in facilitating such nefarious activity. And yet the global community is still only in the position of trying to identify the nature and extent of the problem, let alone ascertaining how to deal with it. In April 2006, the UN Office on Drugs and Crime released its most recent report on the human trafficking problem. Titled *Trafficking in Persons: Global Patterns* (United Nations Office on Drugs and Crime, April 2006), its message was clear. The starting point for addressing the problem is the implementation of the Protocol to Prevent, Suppress and Punish Trafficking in Persons, especially Women and Children. National governments are called upon to take a leading role in: (1) the prevention of trafficking, (2) prosecution of violators, and (3) protection of victims.

Consider the task of prevention. Nations are expected to establish comprehensive policies and programs to prevent and combat trafficking, including research, information and media campaigns. Nations must attempt to alleviate the vulnerability of people, especially women and children. They must create steps to discourage demand for victims. Nations must also prevent transportation opportunities for traffickers. Finally, they must exchange information and increase cooperation among border control agencies.

The UN report also suggests several steps with respect to prosecution. The first step is to "ensure the integrity and security of travel and identity documents" and thus prevent their misuse. Domestic laws must be enacted making human trafficking a criminal offense, and these laws must apply to victims of both genders and all ages. Penalties must be adequate to the crime. Finally, victims must be protected and possibly compensated.

The third role outlined in the UN report focuses on protection of victims. Specifically, victims must be able to achieve "physical, psychological and social recovery." The physical safety of victims is also paramount. The final step relates to the future home of victims, whether they want to remain in the location where found or whether they wish to return home.

The essence of the report suggests the changing character of global issues in this age of globalization. No longer can nation-states solve problems alone. Moreover, no longer can they simply create a new international organization to address the problem. The issue is simply too complex. An array of interlocking structures, agreements, international law, and national initiatives (what was termed an international regime earlier) is needed and is well on the way to being created. As with other issues in this volume, modern technology combined with the process of globalization demands such a strategy if the international community is going to successfully address the evils of human trafficking.

On February 1, 2008, European nations signed an historic treaty termed the Council of Europe Convention on Action against Trafficking in Human Beings. For the first time, these countries will have a comprehensive treaty that addresses both efforts to prevent trafficking and steps to prosecute traffickers.

The UN report cited above represents an excellent starting point for additional readings about human trafficking. A second comprehensive source is "Victims of Trafficking for Forced Prostitution: Protection Mechanisms and the Right to Remain in the Destination Countries" (*Global Migration Perspectives*, Global Commission on International Migration, no. 2, July 2004).

A 2005 book edited by Kamala Kempadoo, *Trafficking and Prostitution Reconsidered: New Perspectives on Migration, Sex Work, and Human Rights* (Paradigm Publishers) examines the contemporary situation in Asia. Other useful books include: *Data and Research on Human Trafficking: A Global Survey* (Frank Laczko, United Nations, 2005); *Global Trafficking in Women and Children* (Obi N.I. Ebbe and Dilip K. Das, eds., CRC, 2007); *Human Trafficking, Human Security, and the Balkans* (H. Richard Friman and Simon Reich, eds., University of Pittsburgh Press, 2007); *Not for Sale: The Return of the Global Slave Trade—and How We Can Fight It* (David Batstone, HarperOne, 2007); and *Unspeakable: The Hidden Truth Behind the World's Fastest Growing Crime* (Raymond Bechard, 2006).

A number of articles provide useful insights into aspects of the problem. Ilana Kramer's "Modern-Day Sex Slavery" (*Lilith*, vol. 31, no. 1, Spring 2006) describes the problem as it relates to Israel. John R. Miller's "Modern-Day Slavery" (*Sheriff*, vol. 58, no. 2, March/April 2006) describes trafficking problems within the United States. Gail Kligman and Stephanie Limoncelli address the trafficking of women in post-Communist Eastern Europe in "Trafficking Women after Socialism: To, Through, and From Eastern Europe" (*Social Politics: International Studies in Gender, State and Society*, Spring 2005). Amy Fraley provides information about national anti-trafficking legislation in "Child Sex Tourism Legislation Under the Protect Act: Does It Really Protect?" (St. John's Law Review Association, 2005). An assessment of UN progress as of 2003 can be found in "Global Trafficking in Human Beings: Assessing the Success of the United Nations Protocol to Prevent Trafficking in Persons" (LeRoy G. Potts, Jr., *The George Washington International Law Review*, 2003). See also the work of Professor Cynthia Messer, University of Minnesota, at http://www.tourism.umn.edu/about/staff/messer.html. Two official reports provide comprehensive information about the problem of human trafficking: *2007 Trafficking in Persons Report* (U.S. Department of State) and *Combating Child Trafficking* (UNICEF, 2005). A comprehensive look at the new agreements can be found in Anne Gallagher, "Human Rights and the New UN Protocols on Trafficking and Migrant Smuggling: A Preliminary Analysis" (*Human Rights Quarterly*, vol. 23, 2001). The UN Web site for its Office on Drugs and Crime is http://www. unodc.org/unodc/multimedia.html. For information about the Council of Europe's efforts, see http//:www.coe.int?T/E/human_rights/trafficking. "Federal Government Efforts to Combat Human Trafficking" provides links to multiple U.S. Government sites on human trafficking.

A number of other Web sites are also useful. Among these are http:// www.wnhcr.ch (the UN High Commissioner for Refugees); http://www.unicef. org (International Child Development Center); http://www.unifem.org (United Nations Development Fund for Women); http://www.ecre.org/research/smuggle.shtml (European Council on Refugees and Exiles); http://www.bayswan. org?FoundTraf.html (Foundation against Trafficking in Women); http://www. trafficked-women.org (Coalition to Abolish Slavery and Trafficking); http://www. uri.edu/artsci/wms/hughes/pubvio.htm (Coalition Against Trafficking in Women); www.gaatw.org (Global Alliance against Traffic in Women); www.ecpatw.org (End Child Prostitution and Trafficking); and http://www.antislavery.org (Antislavery International). Additional sites include http://www.endhumantrafickingnow. com (End Human Trafficking Now); http://www.sharedhope.org (Shared Hope International); http://www.freetheslaves.net (Free the Slaves); and http:// humantrafficking.org.

ISSUE 13

Is Globalization a Positive Development for the World Community?

YES: Robyn Meredith and **Suzanne Hoppough,** from "Why Globalization Is Good," *Forbes* (April 16, 2007)

NO: Steven Weber, Naazneen Barma, Matthew Kroenig, and **Ely Ratner,** from "How Globalization Went Bad," *Foreign Policy* (January/February 2007)

ISSUE SUMMARY

YES: Meredith and Hoppough argue that the data supports the conclusion that globalization works for both rich and poor. They particularly point to the growing middle class in many countries throughout Asia, Africa and Latin America to support this conclusion.

NO: Weber et al. argue that globalization and the American predominance that drives it amplify a myriad of evils including terrorism, global warming, and interethnic conflict creating a less stable and less just world community.

Globalization is a phenomenon and a revolution. It is sweeping the world with increasing speed and changing the global landscape into something new and different. Yet, like all such trends, its meaning, development, and impact puzzle many. We talk about globalization and experience its effects, but few of us really understand the forces that are at work in the global political economy.

When people use their cell phones, log onto the Internet, view events from around the world on live television, and experience varying cultures in their own backyards, they begin to believe that this process of globalization is a good thing that will bring a variety of new and sophisticated changes to people's lives. Many aspects of this technological revolution bring fun, ease, and sophistication to people's daily lives. Yet the anti–World Trade Organization (WTO) protests in Seattle, Washington, in 1999 and

Washington, D.C., in 2000 are graphic illustrations of the fact that not everyone believes that globalization is a good thing. Many Americans who have felt left out of the global economic boom, as well as Latin Americans, Africans, and Asians who feel that their job skills and abilities are being exploited by multinational corporations (MNCs) in a global division of labor, believe that this system does not meet their needs. Local cultures who believe that Wal-Mart and McDonald's bring cultural change and harm rather than inexpensive products and convenience criticize the process. In this way, globalization, like all revolutionary forces, polarizes people, alters the fabric of their lives, and creates rifts within and between people.

Many in the West, along with the prominent and elite—among MNCs, educators, and policymakers—seem to have embraced globalization. They argue that it helps to streamline economic systems, disciplines, labor and management, brings forth new technologies and ideas, and fuels economic growth. They point to the relative prosperity of many Western countries and argue that this is proof of globalization's positive effects. They see little of the problems that critics identify. In fact, those who recognize some structural problems in the system argue that despite these issues, globalization is like an inevitable tide of history, unfortunate for some but unyielding and impossible to change. Any problems that are created by this trend, they say, can be solved.

Many poor and middle-class workers, as well as hundreds of millions of people across the developing world, view globalization as an economic and cultural wave that tears at the fabric of centuries-old societies. They see jobs emerging and disappearing in a matter of months, people moving across the landscape in record numbers, elites amassing huge fortunes while local cultures and traditions are swept away, and local youth being seduced by promises of American material wealth and distanced from their own cultural roots. These critics look past the allure of globalization and focus on the disquieting impact of rapid and system-wide change.

The irony of such a far-ranging and rapid historical process such as globalization is that both proponents and critics may be right. The realities of globalization are both intriguing and alarming. As technology and the global infrastructure expand, ideas, methods, and services are developed and disseminated to greater and greater numbers of people. As a result, societies and values are altered, some for the better and others for the worse.

In the selections that follow, the authors explore the positive and negative impacts of globalization and reach different conclusions. Meredith and Hoppough argue that the facts of globalization show that it works for rich and poor alike. They point to the elevation into middle class of literally hundreds of millions of people across Asia, Latin America, and Africa as a proof, along with the realization that by lifting bans and restrictions, people around the globe can elevate their own economic condition and have done so. Weber et al. contend that globalization combined with America's predominance has created a kind of warping of globalization that accentuates the bad aspects (terrorism, global warming, cultural conflict) while mitigating its more positive effects.

256

YES ⤶

Robyn Meredith and
Suzanne Hoppough

Why Globalization Is Good

A ragtag army of save-the-world crusaders has spent years decrying multinational corporations as villains in the wave of globalization overwhelming the Third World. This ominous trend would fatten the rich, further impoverish and oppress the poor and crush local economies.

The business-bashing group Public Citizen argued as much in a proclamation signed by almost 1,500 organizations in 89 countries in 1999. Whereupon hundreds of protesters rioted outside a conference of the World Trade Organization in Seattle, shattering windows, blocking traffic and confronting cops armed with tear gas and pepper spray. Six hundred people were arrested.

Cut to 2007, and the numbers are in: The protesters and do-gooders are just plain wrong. It turns out globalization is good—and not just for the rich, but *especially* for the poor. The booming economies of India and China—the Elephant and the Dragon—have lifted 200 million people out of abject poverty in the 1990s as globalization took off, the International Monetary Fund says. Tens of millions more have catapulted themselves far ahead into the middle class.

It's remarkable what a few container ships can do to make poor people better off. Certainly more than $2 trillion of foreign aid, which is roughly the amount (with an inflation adjustment) that the U.S. and Europe have poured into Africa and Asia over the past half-century.

In the next eight years almost 1 billion people across Asia will take a Great Leap Forward into a new middle class. In China middle-class incomes are set to rise threefold, to $5,000, predicts Dominic Barton, a Shanghai managing partner for McKinsey & Co.

As the Chindia revolution spreads, the ranks of the poor get smaller, not larger. In the 1990s, as Vietnam's economy grew 6% a year, the number of people living in poverty (42 million) fell 7% annually; in Uganda, when GDP growth passed 3%, the number fell 6% per year, says the World Bank.

China unleashed its economy in 1978, seeding capitalism first among farmers newly freed to sell the fruits of their fields instead of handing the produce over to Communist Party collectives. Other reforms let the Chinese create 22 million new businesses that now employ 135 million

As seen in *Forbes Magazine*, April 16, 2007. Adapted from *The Elephant and the Dragon: The Rise of India and China, and What It Means for All of Us*, by Robyn Meredith (W.W. Norton & Co., 2007). Copyright © 2007 by Robin Meredith. Reprinted by permission of W.W. Norton & Co. and Forbes Inc.

people who otherwise would have remained peasants like the generations before them.

Foreign direct investment, the very force so virulently opposed by the do-gooders, has helped drive China's gross domestic product to a more than tenfold increase since 1978. Since the reforms started, $600 billion has flooded into the country, $70 billion of it in the past year. Foreigners built hundreds of thousands of new factories as the Chinese government built the coal mines, power grid, airports and highways to supply them.

As China built infrastructure, it created Special Economic Zones where foreign companies willing to build modern factories could hire cheap labor, go years without paying any taxes and leave it to government to build the roads and other infrastructure they needed. All of that, in turn, drove China's exports from $970 million to $974 billion in three decades. Those container loads make Americans better off, too. You can get a Chinese DVD player at Wal-Mart for $28, and after you do you will buy some $15 movies made in the U.S.A.

Per-person income in China has climbed from $16 a year in 1978 to $2,000 now. Wages in factory boomtowns in southern China can run $4 a day—scandalously low in the eyes of the protesters, yet up from pennies a day a generation ago and far ahead of increases in living costs.

Middle-class Chinese families now own TVs, live in new apartments and send their children to private schools. Millions of Chinese have traded in their bicycles for motorcycles or cars. McDonald's has signed a deal with Sinopec, the huge Chinese gasoline retailer, to build drive-through restaurants attached to gas stations on China's new roads.

Today 254 Starbucks stores serve coffee in the land of tea, including one at the Great Wall and another at the Forbidden Palace. (The latter is the target of protesters.) In Beijing 54 Starbucks shops thrive, peddling luxury lattes that cost up to $2.85 a cup and paying servers $6 for an 8-hour day. That looks exploitative until you peek inside a nearby Chinese-owned teahouse where the staff works a 12-hour day for $3.75.

Says one woman, 23, who works for an international cargo shipper in Beijing: "My parents were both teachers when they were my age, and they earned 30 yuan [$3.70] a month. I earn 4,000 yuan ($500) a month, live comfortably and feel I have better opportunities than my parents did."

Tony Ma, age 51, was an unwilling foot soldier in Mao's Cultural Revolution. During that dark period from 1966 to 1976 universities were closed, and he was sent at age 16 to work in a steel mill for $2 a month. He cut metal all day long for seven years and feared he might never escape.

When colleges reopened, he landed a spot to study chemistry, transferred to the U.S., got a Ph.D. in biochemistry and signed on with Johnson & Johnson at $45,000 a year. Later he returned to the land he fled and now works for B.F. Goodrich in Hong Kong.

The young college grads in China today wouldn't bother immigrating to the U.S. for a job that pays $45,000, he says—because now they have better opportunities at home.

Capitalism alone, however, isn't enough to remake Third World economies—globalism is the key. A big reason India trails behind its bigger neighbor to the northeast in lifting the lower classes is that, even after embracing capitalism, it kept barriers to the flow of capital from abroad.

Thus 77% of Indians live on $2 a day or less, the Asian Development Bank says, down only nine percentage points from 1990. A third of the population is illiterate. In 1980 India had more of its population in urban centers than China did (23% versus 20% for China). But by 2005 China had 41% in cities, where wages are higher; India's urbanites had grown to only 29%.

Freed of British colonial rule in 1947 and scarred by its paternalistic effects, India initially combined capitalism with economic isolationism. It thwarted foreign companies intent on investing there and hampered Indian firms trying to sell abroad. This hurt Indian consumers and local biz: A $100 Microsoft operating system got slapped with duties that brought the price to $250 in India, putting imported software and computers further from reach for most people and businesses. Meanwhile, the government granted workers lavish job protections and imposed heavy taxes and regulations on employers. Government jobs usually were by rote and paid poorly, but they guaranteed lifetime employment. They also ensured economic stagnation.

Financial crisis struck in 1991. Desperate for cash, India flew a planeload of gold reserves to London and began, grudgingly, to open its economy. Import duties were lowered or eliminated, so India's consumers and companies could buy modern, foreign-made goods and gear. Overseas firms in many industries were allowed to own their subsidiaries in India for the first time since 1977. India all but banned foreign investment until 1991. Since then foreign companies have come back, but not yet on the scale seen in China. Foreign companies have invested $48 billion in India since 1991—$7.5 billion of that just in the last fiscal year—the same amount dumped into China every six weeks. By the mid-1990s the economy boomed and created millions of jobs.

By the late 1990s U.S. tech companies began turning to India for software design, particularly in the Y2K crunch. The Indians proved capable and cheap, and the much-maligned offshoring boom began. Suddenly Indian software engineers were programming corporate America's computers. New college graduates were answering America's customer service phone calls. Builders hired construction workers to erect new high-rise buildings suddenly in demand as American and European firms rushed to hire Indian workers.

The new college hires, whose older siblings had graduated without finding a job, tell of surpassing their parents' salaries within five years and of buying cell phones, then motorcycles, then cars and even houses by the time they were 30. All of that would have been impossible had India failed to add globalization to capitalism.

Today, despite its still dilapidated airports and pothole-riddled highways, the lumbering Elephant now is in a trot, growing more than 7% annually for the last decade. In 2005, borrowing from the Chinese, India began a five-year, $150 billion plan to update its roads, airports, ports and electric plants. India is creating free trade zones, like those in China, to encourage exports of software, apparel, auto parts and more.

S.B. Kutwal manages the assembly line where Tata Motors builds Safari SUVs. He remembers how, in the 1980s, people waited five years to buy a scooter and cars were only for the rich. "Since we've liberated the economy, lots of companies have started coming into India," says Kutwal. "People couldn't afford cars then. Now the buying power is coming."

In Mumbai (formerly Bombay), Delhi, Bangalore and other big cities, shopping malls have sprung up, selling everything from Levi's jeans to Versace. India still has raggedy street touts, but when they tap on car windows at stoplights, instead of peddling cheap plastic toys, they sell to the new India: copies of *Vogue* and *House & Garden* magazines. Western restaurants are moving in, too: Domino's Pizza and Ruby Tuesday's have come to India, and 107 McDonald's have sprung up, serving veggie burgers in the land where cattle are sacred.

None of this gives pause to an entity called International Forum on Globalization. The group declares that globalism's aim is to "benefit transnational corporations over workers; foreign investors over local businesses; and wealthy countries over developing nations. While promoters . . . proclaim that this model is the rising tide that will lift all boats, citizen movements find that it is instead lifting only yachts."

"The majority of people in rich and poor countries aren't better off" since the World Trade Organization formed in 1995 to promote global trade, asserts Christopher Slevin, deputy director of Global Trade Watch, an arm of Ralph Nader's Public Citizen. "The breadth of the opposition has grown. It's not just industrial and steel workers and people who care about animal rights. It includes high-tech workers and the offshoring of jobs, also the faith-based community."

While well-off American techies may be worried, it seems doubtful that an engineer in Bangalore who now earns $40,000 a year, and who has just bought his parents' house, wants to ban foreign investment.

Slevin's further complaint is that globalism is a creature of WTO, the World Bank and other unelected bodies.

But no, the people do have a voice in the process, and it is one that is equivocal on the matter of free market capitalism. The Western World's huge agriculture subsidies—$85 billion or more annually, between the U.S., Japan and the European Union—are decreed by democratically elected legislatures. The EU pays ranchers $2 per cow in daily subsidies, more than most Indians earn. If these farmers weren't getting handouts, and if trade in farm products were free, then poor farmers in the Third World could sell more of their output, and could begin to lift themselves out of poverty.

Steven Weber et al.

→ **NO**

How Globalization Went Bad

From terrorism to global warming, the evils of globalization are more dangerous than ever before. What went wrong? The world became dependent on a single superpower. Only by correcting this imbalance can the world become a safer place.

The world today is more dangerous and less orderly than it was supposed to be. Ten or 15 years ago, the naive expectations were that the "end of history" was near. The reality has been the opposite. The world has more international terrorism and more nuclear proliferation today than it did in 1990. International institutions are weaker. The threats of pandemic disease and climate change are stronger. Cleavages of religious and cultural ideology are more intense. The global financial system is more unbalanced and precarious.

It wasn't supposed to be like this. The end of the Cold War was supposed to make global politics and economics easier to manage, not harder. What went wrong? The bad news of the 21st century is that globalization has a significant dark side. The container ships that carry manufactured Chinese goods to and from the United States also carry drugs. The airplanes that fly passengers nonstop from New York to Singapore also transport infectious diseases. And the Internet has proved just as adept at spreading deadly, extremist ideologies as it has e-commerce.

The conventional belief is that the single greatest challenge of geopolitics today is managing this dark side of globalization, chipping away at the illegitimate co-travelers that exploit openness, mobility, and freedom, without putting too much sand in the gears. The current U.S. strategy is to push for more trade, more connectivity, more markets, and more openness. America does so for a good reason—it benefits from globalization more than any other country in the world. The United States acknowledges globalization's dark side but attributes it merely to exploitative behavior by criminals, religious extremists, and other anachronistic elements that can be eliminated. The dark side of globalization, America says, with very little subtlety, can be mitigated by the expansion of American power, sometimes unilaterally and sometimes through multilateral institutions, depending

From *Foreign Policy,* January/February 2007, pp. 48+. Copyright © 2007 by the Carnegie Endowment for International Peace. Reprinted with permission. www.foreignpolicy.com

on how the United States likes it. In other words, America is aiming for a "flat," globalized world coordinated by a single superpower.

That's nice work if you can get it. But the United States almost certainly cannot. Not only because other countries won't let it, but, more profoundly, because that line of thinking is faulty. The predominance of American power has many benefits, but the management of globalization is not one of them. The mobility of ideas, capital, technology, and people is hardly new. But the rapid advance of globalization's evils is. Most of that advance has taken place since 1990. Why? Because what changed profoundly in the 1990s was the polarity of the international system. For the first time in modern history, globalization was superimposed onto a world with a single superpower. What we have discovered in the past 15 years is that it is a dangerous mixture. The negative effects of globalization since 1990 are not the result of globalization itself. They are the dark side of American predominance.

The Dangers of Unipolarity

A straightforward piece of logic from market economics helps explain why unipolarity and globalization don't mix. Monopolies, regardless of who holds them, are almost always bad for both the market and the monopolist. We propose three simple axioms of "globalization under unipolarity" that reveal these dangers.

Axiom 1: Above a certain threshold of power, the rate at which new global problems are generated will exceed the rate at which old problems are fixed.

Power does two things in international politics: It enhances the capability of a state to do things, but it also increases the number of things that a state must worry about. At a certain point, the latter starts to overtake the former. It's the familiar law of diminishing returns. Because powerful states have large spheres of influence and their security and economic interests touch every region of the world, they are threatened by the risk of things going wrong—anywhere. That is particularly true for the United States, which leverages its ability to go anywhere and do anything through massive debt. No one knows exactly when the law of diminishing returns will kick in. But, historically, it starts to happen long before a single great power dominates the entire globe, which is why large empires from Byzantium to Rome have always reached a point of unsustainability.

That may already be happening to the United States today, on issues ranging from oil dependency and nuclear proliferation to pandemics and global warming. What Axiom 1 tells you is that more U.S. power is not the answer; it's actually part of the problem. A multipolar world would almost certainly manage the globe's pressing problems more effectively. The larger the number of great powers in the global system, the greater the chance that at least one of them would exercise some control over a given combination of space, other actors, and problems. Such reasoning doesn't rest on hopeful notions that the great powers will work together. They might do so. But even if they don't, the result is distributed governance, where some great power is interested in most every part of the world through productive competition.

Axiom 2: In an increasingly networked world, places that fall between the networks are very dangerous places—and there will be more ungoverned zones when there is only one network to join.

The second axiom acknowledges that highly connected networks can be efficient, robust, and resilient to shocks. But in a highly connected world, the pieces that fall between the networks are increasingly shut off from the benefits of connectivity. These problems fester in the form of failed states, mutate like pathogenic bacteria, and, in some cases, reconnect in subterranean networks such as al Qaeda. The truly dangerous places are the points where the subterranean networks touch the mainstream of global politics and economics. What made Afghanistan so dangerous under the Taliban was not that it was a failed state. It wasn't. It was a partially failed and partially connected state that worked the interstices of globalization through the drug trade, counterfeiting, and terrorism.

Can any single superpower monitor all the seams and back alleys of globalization? Hardly. In fact, a lone hegemon is unlikely to look closely at these problems, because more pressing issues are happening elsewhere, in places where trade and technology are growing. By contrast, a world of several great powers is a more interest-rich environment in which nations must look in less obvious places to find new sources of advantage. In such a system, it's harder for troublemakers to spring up, because the cracks and seams of globalization are held together by stronger ties.

Axiom 3: Without a real chance to find useful allies to counter a superpower, opponents will try to neutralize power, by going underground, going nuclear, or going "bad."

Axiom 3 is a story about the preferred strategies of the weak. It's a basic insight of international relations that states try to balance power. They protect themselves by joining groups that can hold a hegemonic threat at bay. But what if there is no viable group to join? In today's unipolar world, every nation from Venezuela to North Korea is looking for a way to constrain American power. But in the unipolar world, it's harder for states to join together to do that. So they turn to other means. They play a different game. Hamas, Iran, Somalia, North Korea, and Venezuela are not going to become allies anytime soon. Each is better off finding other ways to make life more difficult for Washington. Going nuclear is one way. Counterfeiting U.S. currency is another. Raising uncertainty about oil supplies is perhaps the most obvious method of all.

Here's the important downside of unipolar globalization. In a world with multiple great powers, many of these threats would be less troublesome. The relatively weak states would have a choice among potential partners with which to ally, enhancing their influence. Without that more attractive choice, facilitating the dark side of globalization becomes the most effective means of constraining American power.

Sharing Globalization's Burden

The world is paying a heavy price for the instability created by the combination of globalization and unipolarity, and the United States is bearing most of the burden. Consider the case of nuclear proliferation. There's effectively a market out there for proliferation, with its own supply (states willing to share nuclear technology) and demand (states that badly want a nuclear weapon). The overlap of unipolarity with globalization ratchets up both the supply and demand, to the detriment of U.S. national security.

It has become fashionable, in the wake of the Iraq war, to comment on the limits of conventional military force. But much of this analysis is overblown. The United States may not be able to stabilize and rebuild Iraq. But that doesn't matter much from the perspective of a government that thinks the Pentagon has it in its sights. In Tehran, Pyongyang, and many other capitals, including Beijing, the bottom line is simple: The U.S. military could, with conventional force, end those regimes tomorrow if it chose to do so. No country in the world can dream of challenging U.S. conventional military power. But they can certainly hope to deter America from using it. And the best deterrent yet invented is the threat of nuclear retaliation. Before 1989, states that felt threatened by the United States could turn to the Soviet Union's nuclear umbrella for protection. Now, they turn to people like A.Q. Khan. Having your own nuclear weapon used to be a luxury. Today, it is fast becoming a necessity.

North Korea is the clearest example. Few countries had it worse during the Cold War. North Korea was surrounded by feuding, nuclear-armed communist neighbors, it was officially at war with its southern neighbor, and it stared continuously at tens of thousands of U.S. troops on its border. But, for 40 years, North Korea didn't seek nuclear weapons. It didn't need to, because it had the Soviet nuclear umbrella. Within five years of the Soviet collapse, however, Pyongyang was pushing ahead full steam on plutonium reprocessing facilities. North Korea's founder, Kim Il Sung, barely flinched when former U.S. President Bill Clinton's administration readied war plans to strike his nuclear installations preemptively. That brinkmanship paid off. Today North Korea is likely a nuclear power, and Kim's son rules the country with an iron fist. America's conventional military strength means a lot less to a nuclear North Korea. Saddam Hussein's great strategic blunder was that he took too long to get to the same place.

How would things be different in a multipolar world? For starters, great powers could split the job of policing proliferation, and even collaborate on some particularly hard cases. It's often forgotten now that, during the Cold War, the only state with a tougher nonproliferation policy than the United States was the Soviet Union. Not a single country that had a formal alliance with Moscow ever became a nuclear power. The Eastern bloc was full of countries with advanced technological capabilities in every area except one—nuclear weapons. Moscow simply wouldn't permit it. But today we see the uneven and inadequate level of effort that non-superpowers devote to stopping proliferation. The Europeans dangle carrots at Iran, but they are unwilling to consider serious sticks. The Chinese refuse to admit that there is a problem. And the Russians are aiding Iran's nuclear ambitions. When push comes to shove, nonproliferation today is almost entirely America's burden.

The same is true for global public health. Globalization is turning the world into an enormous petri dish for the incubation of infectious disease. Humans cannot outsmart disease, because it just evolves too quickly. Bacteria can reproduce a new generation in less than 30 minutes, while it takes us decades to come up with a new generation of antibiotics. Solutions are only possible when and where we get the upper hand. Poor countries where humans live in close proximity to farm animals are the best place to breed extremely dangerous zoonotic disease. These are often the same countries, perhaps not entirely coincidentally, that feel threatened by American power. Establishing an early warning system for these diseases—exactly what we lacked in the case of SARS a few years ago and exactly what we lack for avian flu today—will require a significant level of intervention into the very places that don't want it. That will be true as long as international intervention means American interference.

The most likely sources of the next ebola or HIV-like pandemic are the countries that simply won't let U.S. or other Western agencies in, including the World Health Organization. Yet the threat is too arcane and not immediate enough for the West to force the issue. What's needed is another great power to take over a piece of the work, a power that has more immediate interests in the countries where diseases incubate and one that is seen as less of a threat. As long as the United States remains the world's lone superpower, we're not likely to get any help. Even after HIV, SARS, and several years of mounting hysteria about avian flu, the world is still not ready for a viral pandemic in Southeast Asia or sub-Saharan Africa. America can't change that alone.

If there were rival great powers with different cultural and ideological leanings, globalization's darkest problem of all—terrorism—would also likely look quite different. The pundits are partly right: Today's international terrorism owes something to globalization. Al Qaeda uses the Internet to transmit messages, it uses credit cards and modern banking to move money, and it uses cell phones and laptops to plot attacks. But it's not globalization that turned Osama bin Laden from a small-time Saudi dissident into the symbolic head of a radical global movement. What created Osama bin Laden was the predominance of American power.

A terrorist organization needs a story to attract resources and recruits. Oftentimes, mere frustration over political, economic, or religious conditions is not enough. Al Qaeda understands that, and, for that reason, it weaves a narrative of global jihad against a "modernization," "Westernization," and a "Judeo-Christian" threat. There is really just one country that both spearheads and represents that threat: the United States. And so the most efficient way for a terrorist to gain a reputation is to attack the United States. The logic is the same for all monopolies. A few years ago, every computer hacker in the world wanted to bring down Microsoft, just as every aspiring terrorist wants to create a spectacle of destruction akin to the September 11 attacks inside the United States.

Al Qaeda cells have gone after alternate targets such as Britain, Egypt, and Spain. But these are not the acts that increase recruitment and fund-raising, or mobilize the energy of otherwise disparate groups around the world. Nothing enhances the profile of a terrorist like killing an American, something Abu Musab al-Zarqawi understood well in Iraq. Even if al Qaeda's deepest aspirations lie with the demise of the Saudi regime, the predominance of U.S. power and its role supporting the house of Saud makes America the only enemy really worth fighting. A multipolar world would surely confuse this kind of clear framing that pits Islamism against the West. What would be al Qaeda's message if the Chinese were equally involved in propping up authoritarian regimes in the Islamic, oil-rich Gulf states? Does the al Qaeda story work if half its enemy is neither Western nor Christian?

Restoring the Balance

The consensus today in the U.S. foreign-policy community is that more American power is always better. Across the board. For both the United States and the rest of the globe. The National Security Strategy documents of 2002 and 2006 enshrine this consensus in phrases such as "a balance of power that favors freedom." The strategy explicitly defines the "balance" as a continued imbalance, as the United States continues "dissuading potential competitors . . . from challenging the United States, its allies, and its partners."

In no way is U.S. power inherently a bad thing. Nor is it true that no good comes from unipolarity. But there are significant downsides to the imbalance of power. That view is hardly revolutionary. It has a long pedigree in U.S. foreignpolicy thought. It was the perspective, for instance, that George Kennan brought to the table in the late 1940s when he talked about the desirability of a European superpower to restrain the United States. Although the issues today are different than they were in Kennan's time, it's still the case that too much power may, as Kennan believed, lead to overreach. It may lead to arrogance. It may lead to insensitivity to the concerns of others. Though Kennan may have been prescient to voice these concerns, he couldn't have predicted the degree to which American unipolarity would lead to such an unstable overlap with modern-day globalization.

America has experienced this dangerous burden for 15 years, but it still refuses to see it for what it really is. Antiglobalization sentiment is coming today from both the right and the left. But by blaming globalization for what ails the world, the U.S. foreign-policy community is missing a very big part of what is undermining one of the most hopeful trends in modern history—the reconnection of societies, economies, and minds that political borders have kept apart for far too long.

America cannot indefinitely stave off the rise of another superpower. But, in today's networked and interdependent world, such an event is not entirely a cause for mourning. A shift in the global balance of power would, in fact, help the United States manage some of the most costly and dangerous consequences of globalization. As the international playing field levels, the scope of these problems and the threat they pose to America will only decrease. When that happens, the United States will find globalization is a far easier burden to bear.

POSTSCRIPT

Is Globalization a Positive Development for the World Community?

It is hard to argue that this kind of revolution is all positive or all negative. Many will find the allure of technological growth and expansion too much to resist. They will adopt values and ethics that seem compatible with a materialistic Western culture. And they will embrace speed over substance, technical expertise over knowledge, and wealth over fulfillment.

Others will reject this revolution. They will find its promotion of materialism and Western cultural values abhorrent and against their own sense of humanity and being. They will seek enrichment in tradition and values rooted in their cultural pasts. This resistance will take many forms. It will be political and social, and it will involve actions ranging from protests and voting to division and violence.

Trying to determine whether a force as dominant and all-encompassing as globalization is positive or negative is like determining whether the environment is harsh or beautiful. It is both. One can say that in the short term, globalization will be destabilizing for many millions of people because the changes that it brings will cause some fundamental shifts in beliefs, values, and ideas. Once that period is past, it is conceivable that a more stable environment will result as people come to grips with globalization and either learn to embrace it, cope with it, or keep it at bay.

The literature on globalization is growing rapidly, much of it centering on defining its parameters and evaluating its impact. Any analysis of globalization should begin with Thomas Friedman's work, which helps shape the boundaries of globalization while arguing strongly for its promotion and inherent strengths. Friedman's work *The Lexus and the Olive Tree* (Farrar, Straus & Giroux, 1999) and *The World Is Flat* (Farrar, Straus & Giroux, 2005) map the terrain and discuss globalization's revolutionary impact. Some counter-perspectives have emerged, and they cover a range of thought and depth of analysis. Two interesting and accessible efforts include William Grieder's *One World Ready or Not: The Manic Logic of Global Capitalism* (Simon & Schuster, 1997) and David Korten's *When Corporations Rule the World* (Kumarian Press, 1996). Also, see Anthony Gidden's work *Runaway World* and John Micklethwait and Adrian Wooldridge's *A Future Perfect: The Challenge and Hidden Promise of Globalization.*

The literature that will help us to understand the full scope of globalization has not yet been written. Also, the determination of globalization's positive or negative impact on the international system has yet to be decided. For certain, globalization will bring profound changes that will cause people from America to Zimbabwe to rethink assumptions and beliefs about how the world works. And equally certain is the realization that globalization will empower some people but that it will also leave others out, helping to maintain and perhaps exacerbate the divisions that already exist in global society.

ISSUE 14

Is the World a Victim of American Cultural Imperialism?

YES: Julia Galeota, from "Cultural Imperialism: An American Tradition," *The Humanist* (2004)

NO: Philippe Legrain, from "In Defense of Globalization," *The International Economy* (Summer 2003)

ISSUE SUMMARY

YES: Julia Galeota contends that the world today is flooded with American culture, and while some would argue that this is simply a matter of tastes and choices, she argues that it is a strategy to impose American principles and ideals on the world community and as a result destroy other cultures.

NO: Philippe Legrain is a British economist who presents two views of cultural imperialism and argues that the notion of American cultural imperialism "is a myth" and that the spreading of cultures through globalization is a positive, not negative, development.

In 1989 the Berlin Wall collapsed. Two years later the Soviet Union ceased to exist. With this relatively peaceful and monumental series of events, the cold war ended, and with it one of the most contentious and conflict-ridden periods in global history. It is easy to argue that in the wake of those events the United States is in ascendancy. The United States and its Western allies won the cold war, defeating communism politically and philosophically. Since 1990 democracies have emerged and largely flourished as never before across the world stage. According to a recent study, over 120 of the world's 190 nations now have a functioning form of democracy. Western companies, values, and ideas now sweep across the globe via airwaves, computer networks, and fiber-optic cables that bring symbols of U.S. culture and values (such as Michael Jordan and McDonald's) into villages and schools and cities around the world.

If American culture is embodied in the products sold by many multinational corporations (MNCs), such as McDonald's, Ford, IBM, The Gap, and others, then the American cultural values and ideas that are embedded in these products are being bought and sold in record numbers around the world. Globalization largely driven by MNCs and their control of technology brings with it values and ideas that are largely American in origin and expression. Values such as speed and ease of use, a strong emphasis on leisure time over work time, and a desire for increasing material wealth and comfort dominate the advertising practices of these companies. For citizens of the United States, this seems a natural part of the landscape. They do not question it; in fact, many Americans enjoy seeing signs of "home" on street corners abroad: a McDonald's in Tokyo, a Sylvester Stallone movie in Djakarta, or a Gap shirt on a student in Nairobi, for example.

While comforting to Westerners, this trend is disquieting to the hundreds of millions of people around the world who wish to partake of the globalizing system without abandoning their own cultural values. Many people around the globe wish to engage in economic exchange and develop politically but do not want to abandon their own cultures amidst the wave of values embedded in Western products. This tension is most pronounced in its effect on the youth around the world. Millions of impressionable young people in the cities and villages of the developing world wish to emulate the American icons that they see on soft drink cans or in movie theaters. They attempt to adopt U.S. manners, language, and modes of dress, often in opposition to their parents and local culture. These young people are becoming Americanized and, in the process, creating huge generational rifts within their own societies. Some of the seeds of these rifts and cultural schisms can be seen in the actions of the young Arab men who joined Al Qaeda and participated in the terrorist attacks of September 11, 2001.

In this section, the authors examine the realities of globalization and America's preeminence within it and reach different conclusions. Julia Galeota, a young writer and student, articulates the fear and opposition to American cultural imperialism in her essay. Here she contends that the dissemination of American values and mores through consumerism is destroying other cultures, and as a result millions are losing their identity. Legrain counters that it is fashionable to argue that globalization leads to imperialism, but it is simply a myth. He postulates that identity and culture cannot be taken away by the products that you buy or the clothes that you wear. He contends that our culture stays with us and defines us based on our own choices and not from insidious external forces.

YES

Julia Galeota

Cultural Imperialism: An American Tradition

Travel almost anywhere in the world today and, whether you suffer from habitual Big Mac cravings or cringe at the thought of missing the newest episode of MTV's *The Real World,* your American tastes can be satisfied practically everywhere. This proliferation of American products across the globe is more than mere accident. As a byproduct of globalization, it is part of a larger trend in the conscious dissemination of American attitudes and values that is often referred to as *cultural imperialism.* In his 1976 work *Communication and Cultural Domination,* Herbert Schiller defines cultural imperialism as:

> The sum of the processes by which a society is brought into the modern world system, and how its dominating stratum is attracted, pressured, forced, and sometimes bribed into shaping social institutions to correspond to, or even to promote, the values and structures of the dominant center of the system.

Thus, cultural imperialism involves much more than simple consumer goods; it involves the dissemination of ostensibly American principles, such as freedom and democracy. Though this process might sound appealing on the surface, it masks a frightening truth: many cultures around the world are gradually disappearing due to the overwhelming influence of corporate and cultural America.

The motivations behind American cultural imperialism parallel the justifications for U.S. imperialism throughout history: the desire for access to foreign markets and the belief in the superiority of American culture. Though the United States does boast the world's largest, most powerful economy, no business is completely satisfied with controlling only the American market; American corporations want to control the other 95 percent of the world's consumers as well. Many industries are incredibly successful in that venture. According to the *Guardian,* American films accounted for approximately 80 percent of global box office revenue in January 2003. And who can forget good old Micky D's? With over 30,000 restaurants in over one hundred

From *The Humanist,* by Julia Galeota, vol. 64, no. 3, May/June 2004, pp. 22–24, 46. Copyright © 2004 by American Humanist Association. Reprinted by permission.

countries, the ubiquitous golden arches of McDonald's are now, according to Eric Schlosser's *Fast Food Nation*, "more widely recognized than the Christian cross." Such American domination inevitably hurts local markets, as the majority of foreign industries are unable to compete with the economic strength of U.S. industry. Because it serves American economic interests, corporations conveniently ignore the detrimental impact of American control of foreign markets.

Corporations don't harbor qualms about the detrimental effects of "Americanization" of foreign cultures, as most corporations have ostensibly convinced themselves that American culture is superior and therefore its influence is beneficial to other, "lesser" cultures. Unfortunately, this American belief in the superiority of U.S. culture is anything but new; it is as old as the culture itself. This attitude was manifest in the actions of settlers when they first arrived on this continent and massacred or assimilated essentially the entire "savage" Native American population. This attitude also reflects that of the late nineteenth-century age of imperialism, during which the jingoists attempted to fulfill what they believed to be the divinely ordained "manifest destiny" of American expansion. Jingoists strongly believe in the concept of social Darwinism: the stronger, "superior" cultures will overtake the weaker, "inferior" cultures in a "survival of the fittest." It is this arrogant belief in the incomparability of American culture that characterizes many of our economic and political strategies today.

It is easy enough to convince Americans of the superiority of their culture, but how does one convince the rest of the world of the superiority of American culture? The answer is simple: marketing. Whether attempting to sell an item, a brand, or an entire culture, marketers have always been able to successfully associate American products with modernity in the minds of consumers worldwide. While corporations seem to simply sell Nike shoes or Gap jeans (both, ironically, manufactured *outside* of the United States), they are also selling the image of America as the land of "cool." This indissoluble association causes consumers all over the globe to clamor ceaselessly for the same American products.

Twenty years ago, in his essay "The Globalization of Markets," Harvard business professor Theodore Levitt declared, "The world's needs and desires have been irrevocably homogenized." Levitt held that corporations that were willing to bend to local tastes and habits were inevitably doomed to failure. He drew a distinction between weak multinational corporations that operate differently in each country and strong global corporations that handle an entire world of business with the same agenda.

In recent years, American corporations have developed an even more successful global strategy: instead of advertising American conformity with blonde-haired, blue-eyed, stereotypical Americans, they pitch diversity. These campaigns—such as McDonald's new international "I'm lovin' it" campaign—work by drawing on the United State's history as an ethnically integrated nation composed of essentially every culture in the world. An early example of this global marketing tactic was found in a Coca-Cola commercial from 1971 featuring children from many different countries innocently singing, "I'd like to teach the world to sing in perfect harmony/ I'd like to buy the world a Coke to keep it company." This commercial illustrates an attempt to portray a U.S. goods as a product capable of transcending political, ethnic, religious, social, and economic differences to unite the world (according to the Coca-Cola Company, we can achieve world peace through consumerism).

More recently, Viacon's MTV has successfully adapted this strategy by integrating many different Americanized cultures into one unbelievably influential American network (with over 280 million subscribers worldwide). According to a 1996 "New World Teen Study" conducted by DMB&B's BrainWaves division, of the 26,700 middle-class teens in forty-five countries surveyed, 85 percent watch MTV every day. These teens absorb what MTV intends to show as a diverse mix of cultural influences but is really nothing more than manufactured stars singing in English to appeal to American popular taste.

If the strength of these diverse "American" images is not powerful enough to move products, American corporations also appropriate local cultures into their advertising abroad. Unlike Levitt's weak multinationals, these corporations don't bend to local tastes; they merely insert indigenous celebrities or trends to present the facade of a customized advertisement. MTV has spawned over twenty networks specific to certain geographical areas such as Brazil and Japan. These specialized networks further spread the association between American and modernity under the pretense of catering to local taste. Similarly, commercials in India in 2000 featured Bollywood stars Hrithik Roshan promoting Coke and Shahrukh Khan promoting Pepsi (Sanjeev Srivastava, "Cola Row in India." BBC News Online). By using popular local icons in their advertisements, U.S. corporations successfully associate what is fashionable in local cultures with what is fashionable in America. America essentially samples the world's cultures, repackages them with the American trademark of materialism, and resells them to the world.

Critics of the theory of American cultural imperialism argue that foreign consumers don't passively absorb the images America bombards upon them. In fact, foreign consumers do play an active role in the reciprocal relationship between buyer and seller. For example, according to Naomi Klein's *No Logo*, American cultural imperialism has inspired a "slow food movement" in Italy and a demonstration involving the burning of chickens outside of the first Kentucky Fried Chicken outlet in India. Though there have been countless other conspicuous and inconspicuous acts of resistance, the intense, unrelenting barrage of American cultural influence continues ceaselessly.

Compounding the influence of commercial images are the media and information industries, which present both explicit and implicit messages about the very real military and economic hegemony of the United States. Ironically, the industry that claims to be the source for "fair and balanced" information plays a large role in the propagation of American influence around the world. The concentration of media ownership during the 1990s enabled both American and British media organizations to gain control of the majority of the world's news services. Satellites allow over 150 million households in approximately 212 countries and territories worldwide to subscribe to CNN, a member of Time Warner, the world's largest media conglomerate. In the words of British sociologist Jeremy Tunstall, "When a government allows news importation, it is in effect importing a piece of another country's politics—which is true of no other import." In addition to politics and commercials, networks like CNN also present foreign countries with unabashed accounts of the military and economic superiority of the United States.

The Internet acts as another vehicle for the worldwide propagation of American influence. Interestingly, some commentators cite the new "information economy" as proof that American cultural imperialism is in decline. They argue that the global accessibility of this decentralized medium has decreased the relevance of the "core and periphery" theory of global influence. This theory describes an inherent imbalance in the primarily outward flow of information and influence from the stronger, more powerful "core" nations such as the United States. Additionally, such critics argue, unlike consumers of other types of media, Internet users must actively seek out information; users can consciously choose to avoid all messages of American culture. While these arguments are valid, they ignore their converse: if one so desires, anyone can access a wealth of information about American culture possibly unavailable through previous channels. Thus, the Internet can dramatically increase exposure to American culture for those who desire it.

Fear of the cultural upheaval that could result from this exposure to new information has driven governments in communist China and Cuba to strictly monitor and regulate their citizens' access to websites (these protectionist policies aren't totally effective, however, because they are difficult to implement and maintain). Paradoxically, limiting access to the Internet nearly ensures that countries will remain largely the recipients, rather than the contributors, of information on the Internet.

Not all social critics see the Americanization of the world as a negative phenomenon. Proponents of cultural imperialism, such as David Rothkopf, a former senior official in Clinton's Department of Commerce, argue that American cultural imperialism is in the interest not only of the United States but also of the world at large. Rothkopf cites Samuel Huntington's theory from *The Clash of Civilizations and the Beginning of the World Order* that, the greater the cultural disparities in the world, the more likely it is that conflict will occur. Rothkopf argues that the removal of cultural barriers through U.S. cultural imperialism will promote a more stable world, one in which American culture reigns supreme as "the most just, the most tolerant, the most willing to constantly reassess and improve itself, and the best model for the future." Rothkopf is correct in one sense: Americans are on the way to establishing a global society with minimal cultural barriers. However, one must question whether this projected society is truly beneficial for all involved. Is it worth sacrificing countless indigenous cultures for the unlikely promise of a world without conflict?

Around the world, the answer is an overwhelming "No!" Disregarding the fact that a world of homogenized culture would not necessarily guarantee a world without conflict, the complex fabric of diverse cultures around the world is a fundamental and indispensable basis of humanity. Throughout the course of human existence, millions have died to preserve their indigenous culture. It is a fundamental right of humanity to be allowed to preserve the mental, physical, intellectual, and creative aspects of one's society. A single "global culture" would be nothing more than a shallow, artificial "culture" of materialism reliant on technology. Thankfully, it would be nearly impossible to create one bland culture in a world of over six billion people. And nor should we want to. Contrary to Rothkopf's (and George W. Bush's) belief that, "Good and evil, better and worse coexist in this world," there are no such absolutes in this world. The United States should not be able to relentlessly force other nations to accept its definition of what is "good" and "just" or even "modern."

Fortunately, many victims of American cultural imperialism aren't blind to the subversion of their cultures. Unfortunately, these nations are often too weak to fight the strength of the United States and subsequently to preserve their native cultures. Some countries—such as France, China, Cuba, Canada, and Iran—have attempted to quell America's cultural influence by limiting or prohibiting access to American cultural programming through satellites and the Internet. However, according to the UN Universal Declaration of Human Rights, it is a basic right of all people to "seek, receive, and impart information and ideas through any media and regardless of frontiers." Governments shouldn't have to restrict their citizens' access to information in order to preserve their native cultures. We as a world must find ways to defend local cultures in a manner that does not compromise the rights of indigenous people.

The prevalent proposed solutions to the problem of American cultural imperialism are a mix of defense and compromise measures on behalf of the endangered cultures. In *The Lexus and the Olive Tree,* Thomas Friedman advocates the use of protective legislation such as zoning laws and protected area laws, as well as the appointment of politicians with cultural integrity, such as those in agricultural, culturally pure Southern France. However, many other nations have no voice in the nomination of their leadership, so those countries need a middle-class and elite committed to social activism. If it is utterly impossible to maintain the cultural purity of a country through legislation, Friedman suggests the country attempt to "glocalize," that is:

> to absorb influences that naturally fit into and can enrich [a] culture, to resist those things that are truly alien and to compartmentalize those things that, while different, can nevertheless be enjoyed and celebrated as different.

These types of protective filters should help to maintain the integrity of a culture in the face of cultural imperialism. In *Jihad vs. McWorld,*

Benjamin Barber calls for the resuscitation of nongovernmental, noncapitalist spaces—to the "civic spaces"—such as village greens, places of religious worship, or community schools. It is also equally important to focus on the education of youth in their native values and traditions. Teens especially need a counterbalance to images of American consumerism they absorb from the media. Even if individuals or countries consciously choose to become "Americanized" or "modernized," their choice should be made freely and independently of the coercion and influence of American cultural imperialism.

The responsibility for preserving cultures shouldn't fall entirely on those at risk. The United States must also recognize that what is good for its economy isn't necessarily good for the world at large. We must learn to put people before profits. The corporate and political leaders of the United States would be well advised to heed these words of Gandhi:

> I do not want my house to be walled in on all sides and my windows to be stuffed. I want the culture of all lands to be blown about my house as freely as possible. But I refuse to be blown off my feet by any.

The United States must acknowledge that no one culture can or should reign supreme, for the death of diverse cultures can only further harm future generations.

Philippe Legrain

➡ **NO**

In Defense of Globalization

Fears that globalization is imposing a deadening cultural uniformity are as ubiquitous as Coca-Cola, McDonald's, and Mickey Mouse. Many people dread that local cultures and national identities are dissolving into a crass all-American consumerism. That cultural imperialism is said to impose American values as well as products, promote the commercial at the expense of the authentic, and substitute shallow gratification for deeper satisfaction.

Thomas Friedman, columnist for the *New York Times* and author of *The Lexus and the Olive Tree,* believes that globalization is "globalizing American culture and American cultural icons." Naomi Klein, a Canadian journalist and author of *No Logo,* argues that "Despite the embrace of poly-ethnic imagery, market-driven globalization doesn't want diversity; quite the opposite. Its enemies are national habits, local brands, and distinctive regional tastes."

But it is a myth that globalization involves the imposition of Americanized uniformity, rather than an explosion of cultural exchange. And although— as with any change—it can have downsides, this cross-fertilization is overwhelmingly a force for good.

The beauty of globalization is that it can free people from the tyranny of geography. Just because someone was born in France does not mean they can only aspire to speak French, eat French food, read French books, and so on. That we are increasingly free to choose our cultural experiences enriches our lives immeasurably. We could not always enjoy the best the world has to offer.

Globalization not only increases individual freedom, but also revitalizes cultures and cultural artifacts through foreign influences, technologies, and markets. Many of the best things come from cultures mixing: Paul Gauguin painting in Polynesia, the African rhythms in rock 'n' roll, the great British curry. Admire the many-colored faces of France's World Cup-winning soccer team, the ferment of ideas that came from Eastern Europe's Jewish diaspora, and the cosmopolitan cities of London and New York.

Fears about an Americanized uniformity are overblown. For a start, many "American" products are not as all-American as they seem; MTV in Asia promotes Thai pop stars and plays rock music sung in Mandarin. Nor

From *The International Economy,* by Phillippe Legrain, vol. 17, no. 3, Summer 2003, pp. 62–65. Copyright © 2003 by The International Economy. Reprinted by permission.

are American products all-conquering. Coke accounts for less than two of the 64 fluid ounces that the typical person drinks a day. France imported a mere $620 million in food from the United States in 2000, while exporting to America three times that. Worldwide, pizzas are more popular than burgers and Chinese restaurants sprout up everywhere.

In fashion, the ne plus ultra is Italian or French. Nike shoes are given a run for their money by Germany's Adidas, Britain's Reebok, and Italy's Fila. American pop stars do not have the stage to themselves. According to the IFPI, the record-industry bible, local acts accounted for 68 percent of music sales in 2000, up from 58 percent in 1991. And although nearly three-quarters of television drama exported worldwide comes from the United States, most countries' favorite shows are homegrown.

Nor are Americans the only players in the global media industry. Of the seven market leaders, one is German, one French, and one Japanese. What they distribute comes from all quarters: Germany's Bertelsmann publishes books by American writers; America's News Corporation broadcasts Asian news; Japan's Sony sells Brazilian music.

In some ways, America is an outlier, not a global leader. Baseball and American football have not traveled well; most prefer soccer. Most of the world has adopted the (French) metric system; America persists with antiquated British Imperial measurements. Most developed countries have become intensely secular, but many Americans burn with fundamentalist fervor—like Muslims in the Middle East.

Admittedly, Hollywood dominates the global movie market and swamps local products in most countries. American fare accounts for more than half the market in Japan and nearly two-thirds in Europe. Yet Hollywood is less American than it seems. Top actors and directors are often from outside America. Some studios are foreign-owned. To some extent, Hollywood is a global industry that just happens to be in America. Rather than exporting Americana, it serves up pap to appeal to a global audience.

Hollywood's dominance is in part due to economics: Movies cost a lot to make and so need a big audience to be profitable; Hollywood has used America's huge and relatively uniform domestic market as a platform to expand overseas. So there could be a case for stuffing subsidies into a rival European film industry, just as Airbus was created to challenge Boeing's near-monopoly. But France's subsidies have created a vicious circle whereby European film producers fail in global markets because they serve domestic demand and the wishes of politicians and cinematic bureaucrats.

Another American export is also conquering the globe: English. By 2050, it is reckoned, half the world will be more or less proficient in it. A common global language would certainly be a big plus—for businessmen, scientists, and tourists—but a single one seems far less desirable. Language is often at the heart of national culture, yet English may usurp other languages not because it is what people prefer to speak, but because, like Microsoft software, there are compelling advantages to using it if everyone else does.

But although many languages are becoming extinct, English is rarely to blame. People are learning English as well as—not instead of—their native tongue, and often many more languages besides. Where local languages are dying, it is typically national rivals that are stamping them out. So although, within the United States, English is displacing American Indian tongues, it is not doing away with Swahili or Norwegian.

Even though American consumer culture is widespread, its significance is often exaggerated. You can choose to drink Coke and eat at McDonald's without becoming American in any meaningful sense. One newspaper photo of Taliban fighters in Afghanistan showed them toting Kalashnikovs—as well as a sports bag with Nike's trademark swoosh. People's culture—in the sense of their shared ideas, beliefs, knowledge, inherited traditions, and art—may scarcely be eroded by mere commercial artifacts that, despite all the furious branding, embody at best flimsy values.

The really profound cultural changes have little to do with Coca-Cola. Western ideas about liberalism and science are taking root almost everywhere, while Europe and North America are becoming multicultural societies through immigration, mainly from developing countries. Technology is reshaping culture: Just think of the Internet. Individual choice is fragmenting the imposed uniformity of national cultures. New hybrid cultures are emerging, and regional ones re-emerging. National identity is not disappearing, but the bonds of nationality are loosening.

Cross-border cultural exchange increases diversity within societies— but at the expense of making them more alike. People everywhere have more choice, but they often choose similar things. That worries cultural pessimists, even though the right to choose to be the same is an essential part of freedom.

Cross-cultural exchange can spread greater diversity as well as greater similarity: more gourmet restaurants as well as more McDonald's outlets. And just as a big city can support a wider spread of restaurants than a small town, so a global market for cultural products allows a wider range of artists to thrive. If all the new customers are ignorant, a wider market may drive down the quality of cultural products: Think of tourist souvenirs. But as long as some customers are well informed (or have "good taste"), a general "dumbing down" is unlikely. Hobbyists, fans, artistic pride, and professional critics also help maintain (and raise) standards.

A bigger worry is that greater individual freedom may undermine national identity. The French fret that by individually choosing to watch Hollywood films they might unwittingly lose their collective Frenchness. Yet such fears are overdone. Natural cultures are much stronger than people seem to think. They can embrace some foreign influences and resist others. Foreign influences can rapidly become domesticated, changing national culture, but not destroying it. Clearly, though, there is a limit to how many foreign influences a culture can absorb before being swamped. Traditional cultures in the developing world that have until now evolved (or failed to evolve) in isolation may be particularly vulnerable.

In *The Silent Takeover,* Noreena Hertz describes the supposed spiritual Eden that was the isolated kingdom of Bhutan in the Himalayas as being defiled by such awful imports as basketball and Spice Girls T-shirts. But is that such a bad thing? It is odd, to put it mildly, that many on the left support multiculturalism in the West but advocate cultural purity in the developing world—an attitude they would tar as fascist if proposed for the United States. Hertz appears to want people outside the industrialized West preserved in unchanging but supposedly pure poverty. Yet the Westerners who want this supposed paradise preserved in aspic rarely feel like settling there. Nor do most people in developing countries want to lead an "authentic" unspoiled life of isolated poverty.

In truth, cultural pessimists are typically not attached to diversity per se but to designated manifestations of diversity, determined by their preferences. Cultural pessimists want to freeze things as they were. But if diversity at any point in time is desirable, why isn't diversity across time? Certainly, it is often a shame if ancient cultural traditions are lost. We should do our best to preserve them and keep them alive where possible. Foreigners can often help, by providing the new customers and technologies that have enabled reggae music, Haitian art, and Persian carpet making, for instance, to thrive and reach new markets. But people cannot be made to live in a museum. We in the West are forever casting off old customs when we feel they are no longer relevant. Nobody argues that Americans should ban nightclubs to force people back to line dancing. People in poor countries have a right to change, too.

Moreover, some losses of diversity are a good thing. Who laments that the world is now almost universally rid of slavery? More generally, Western ideas are reshaping the way people everywhere view themselves and the world. Like nationalism and socialism before it, liberalism is a European philosophy that has swept the world. Even people who resist liberal ideas, in the name of religion (Islamic and Christian fundamentalists), group identity (communitarians), authoritarianism (advocates of "Asian values") or tradition (cultural conservatives), now define themselves partly by their opposition to them.

Faith in science and technology is even more widespread. Even those who hate the West make use of its technologies. Osama bin Laden plots terrorism on a cellphone and crashes planes into skyscrapers. Antiglobalization protesters organize by e-mail and over the Internet. China no longer turns its nose up at Western technology: It tries to beat the West at its own game.

Yet globalization is not a one-way street. Although Europe's former colonial powers have left their stamp on much of the world, the recent flow of migration has been in the opposite direction. There are Algerian suburbs in Paris, but not French ones in Algiers. Whereas Muslims are a growing minority in Europe, Christians are a disappearing one in the Middle East.

Foreigners are changing America even as they adopt its ways. A million or so immigrants arrive each year, most of them Latino or Asian. Since 1990, the number of foreign-born American residents has risen by 6 million to just over 25 million, the biggest immigration wave since the turn of the 20th century. English may be all-conquering outside America, but in some parts of the United States, it is now second to Spanish.

The upshot is that national cultures are fragmenting into a kaleidoscope of different ones. New hybrid cultures are emerging. In "Amexica" people speak Spanglish. Regional cultures are reviving. The Scots and Welsh break with British monoculture. Estonia is reborn from the Soviet Union. Voices that were silent dare to speak again.

Individuals are forming new communities, linked by shared interests and passions, that cut across national borders. Friendships with foreigners met on holiday. Scientists sharing ideas over the Internet. Environmentalists campaigning together using e-mail. Greater individualism does not spell the end of community. The new communities are simply chosen rather than coerced, unlike the older ones that communitarians hark back to.

So is national identity dead? Hardly. People who speak the same language, were born and live near each other, face similar problems, have a common experience, and vote in the same elections still have plenty in common. For all our awareness of the world as a single place, we are not citizens of the world but citizens of a state. But if people now wear the bonds of nationality more loosely, is that such a bad thing? People may lament the passing of old ways. Indeed, many of the worries about globalization echo age-old fears about decline, a lost golden age, and so on. But by and large, people choose the new ways because they are more relevant to their current needs and offer new opportunities.

The truth is that we increasingly define ourselves rather than let others define us. Being British or American does not define who you are: It is part of who you are. You can like foreign things and still have strong bonds to your fellow citizens. As Mario Vargas Llosa, the Peruvian author, has written: "Seeking to impose a cultural identity on a people is equivalent to locking them in a prison and denying them the most precious of liberties—that of choosing what, how, and who they want to be."

POSTSCRIPT

Is the World a Victim of American Cultural Imperialism?

Globalization is a process of technological change and economic expansion under largely capitalist principles. The key actors driving the globalization process are multinational corporations like McDonald's, Coca-Cola, Nike, and Exxon Mobil. These companies are rooted in the American-Western cultural experience, and their premise is based on a materialistic world culture that is striving for greater and greater wealth. That value system is Western and American in origin and evolution. It is therefore logical to assume that as globalization goes, so goes American culture.

Evidence of "American" culture can be seen across the planet: kids in Djakarta or Lagos wearing Michael Jordan jerseys and Nike shoes, for example, and millions of young men and women from Cairo to Lima listening to Michael Jackson records. Symbols of American culture abound in almost every corner of the world, and most of that is associated with economics and the presence of multinational corporations.

As the youth of the world are seduced into an American cultural form and way of life, other cultures are often eclipsed. They lose traction and fade with generational change. Many would argue that this loss is unfortunate, but others would counter that it is part of the historical sweep of life. Social historians suggest that the cultures of Rome, Carthage, Phoenicia, and the Aztecs, while still influential, were eclipsed by a variety of forces that were dominant and historically rooted. While tragic, it was inevitable in the eyes of some social historians.

Regardless of whether this eclipse is positive or negative, the issue of cultural imperialism remains. Larger and more intrusive networks of communication, trade, and economic exchange bring values. In this world of value collision comes choices and change. Unfortunately, millions will find themselves drawn toward a lifestyle of materialism that carries with it a host of value choices. The losers in this clash are local cultures and traditions that, as so often is the case among the young, are easily jettisoned and discarded. It remains to be seen whether or not they will survive the onslaught.

Works on this subject include Benjamin Barber, "Democracy at Risk: American Culture in a Global Culture," *World Policy Journal* (Summer 1998); "Globalism's Discontents," *The American Prospect* (January 1, 2002); Seymour Martin Lipset, *American Exceptionalism: A Double-Edged Sword* (W. W. Norton, 1996); and Richard Barnet and John Cavanagh, *Global Dreams: Imperial Corporations and the New World Order* (Simon & Schuster, 1995).

ISSUE 15

Do MySpace and YouTube Make Private Globalization Democratized?

YES: David Brain, from "The Democratisation of Everything," *The Sixty-Second View* (October 18, 2006)

NO: Andrew Keen, from *The Cult of the Amateur: How Today's Internet Is Killing Our Culture* (Doubleday, 2007)

ISSUE SUMMARY

YES: Brain argues that the Internet and elements like MySpace, YouTube, and others allow for instant dissemination of information, response, and change empowering millions in the marketplace of things and ideas. He contends that top-down control is melting away amidst this onslaught and everyone is becoming their own creator, critic, and controller, thus democratizing everything from corporate products to tastes and politics.

NO: Keen contends that the Internet is destroying culture and rubbing outlines between knowledge and whimsy, experts and neophytes. He argues that MySpace and YouTube do not empower, but rather water down, values and ideals such that a lowest common denominator prevails, leading to less democracy and not more.

There is perhaps no greater revolution of the last 20 years than the Internet. An entire dimension of existence has exploded onto the global scene in a way that few understand, but everyone embraces. Social networking, politics, education, commerce, and cultural awareness all have been revolutionized by the reach and force of the Internet. It has empowered hundreds of millions in ways few could have imagined just a few short years ago. At the same time, governments and other institutions have been slow to understand the impact of this revolution or adapt to it.

Let's just take the examples of entertainment and politics. With video technology readily available to average people, millions have become their own filmmakers, posting everything from social commentary to comedy, from drama to pornography. In every case, millions are able to communicate, share ideas and values, explore and stretch social norms, and also break down territorial boundaries and cultural divides in both good and challenging ways. The concept of viral media and marketing is born, along with new ways of thinking about the dissemination of ideas, facts, and also, rumors and lies.

Political candidates in democracies are able to reach broad audiences, respond quickly to critics, raise vast sums of money from individual small donors, and project their image without relying on the cumbersome dimensions of broadcast media with its own time schedules and, largely financial motivations. In states without democratic expression, the Internet has become the underground where people and groups share ideas, grievances and perspectives usually through open exchange or through their own encoded language. As a result, governments are not able to control information flow to any degree that they could do in the middle of the twentieth century, and thus, power becomes more elusive.

MySpace and YouTube represent the most pronounced examples of this phenomenon. Born out of simple ideas, they have grown like viruses such that their worth is measured in hundreds of millions of dollars and they are essentially electronic blackboards for people to post lives, loves, views, and products. The young with their technological savvy have been the first to seize and take advantage of these mediums, but others, including political candidates, have now embraced their power.

In this section the authors explore the potential impact of these new phenomena as forces for democratization and empowerment or as forces for social decay and destruction. Brain contends that these tools empower people and lead to a much wider dissemination of ideas and perspectives that are naturally good for any society, and indeed, global society as a whole. Keen argues that MySpace, YouTube and others water down culture and values and so trivialize many of the important ideals and values that societies hold dear. Essentially, he sees these devices are ultimately corrosive on the social fabric of society and the world.

YES

David Brain

The Democratisation
of Everything

When I was asked to write this piece on trends in PR and communications I was reminded of a David Ogilvy quotation: "It's easier to write a great a speech about advertising than it is to write a great ad." He was right on that as on so many things.

I was also aware that I've heard many people speak or write as if the world we have all happily lived in for years is about to change completely at that very moment and everything we have always done is wrong and whatever brand of communications snake-oil the writer or the speaker is offering is our only hope of salvation. And it can be really annoying and patronising. So with these two little grains of self awareness out of the way, let me clear my throat and claim with gleaming eye and foaming mouth that: "this is the most exciting and challenging time I have witnessed in our business for the 22 years I have been in it and the changes that have just begun will fundamentally alter what we do and the role that PR plays."

If this was a speech and not an article there would now be an embarrassed silence and the sound of polite coughing.

Bear with me. Take a look at www.ihatedell.net when you get a chance. A little over a year ago a blogger named *Jeff Jarvis* complained on his blog about a Dell pc he had bought and the service he had received. Within minutes hundreds responded and within days there were thousands agreeing and weighing in with their own stories. In Jeff's words he had set off a "raging mob with pitchforks" and they were determined to storm 'Castle Dell'. They came together on the www.ihatedell.net site and a strange thing happened. After they got over complaining a number of them began helping each other, technically in terms of fixing faults mainly, but also on how to get the best out of their machines. Dell did nothing. Well officially, Dell did nothing. Unofficially Dell employees started responding and as you can see from the site they chipped in with advice and comments, totally separately to the official help-lines (many of which were outsourced, which added some spice). And another odd thing happened. When people 'Googled' Dell they discovered pretty high up the results table the www.ihatedell.net site and if you look at it now you can see conversations between employees and people that are about to be interviewed for a job at Dell. And journalists went there, and business partners and families of employees and, of course, customers. It became a landing site for anybody disaffected with Dell and very soon after that, a site for anyone interested in anything to do with Dell—only Dell had nothing to do with it themselves. The whole incident became totemic for the company's corporate and product brand and was related and re-told in many news stories.

So what does it mean? It means I think that the days of trying to control corporate message from the top down are gone. Spokespeople in this new age are increasingly customers, employees, interviewees and, occasionally also senior management. Dell's corporate reputation was turned inside out by some angry customers and their own employees. It was democratised.

Another example. [There were] picture[s] from the London Tube on July 7th last year after the bombs went off. [Shots] of passengers walking along the track to safety [were taken] on a mobile phone camera. [These images and others like it were] run on news outlets around the world and it highlighted that people armed with digital devices can now bring us personal views of big news events that the traditional news organisations can't get to or don't have the resources to deliver. Check these sites out for an on-the-ground perspective of what is happening in Lebanon and Iraq at the moment: http://www.aliveinbaghdad.org/, http://colddesert.blogspot.com/, http://lebanesebloggers.blogspot.com/ and if you can't be bothered then let me tell you that they include very personal views of what it is like on the ground in those conflicts; views you will not and cannot really get on TV or mainstream media. The point of all this? People can tell the news and with no more than a mobile phone and pc connected to the web, they can broadcast the news. To each other via social network media and to traditional news organisations who are now very happy to take their footage and comments. News is being democratized too.

And it's not just the sources of news; it's the editorial decision-making as well. The BBC is tracked by 13 different blogs (last time I looked) each of which analyse the TV news bulletins within minutes for perceived bias and wrong facts. Any journalist will tell you that they take pride in getting facts and tone right, and these sites which track many major news outlets in Europe and around the world now, do have an affect on editorial decision-making. BBC editors now blog daily on their own news policy and editorial decision-making. News is also much more democratic than it used to be. Richard Sambrook of the BBC said "the crowd are now well and truly on the pitch" (see my interview with Kevin Bakhurst of BBC news 24 on www.sixtysecondview.com) for his view on this.

Entertainment is becoming democratized too. Look at Rocketboom and YouTube (www.rocketboom.com and www.YouTube.com) which have become global phenomena and have massive viewing figures eclipsing those of many national broadcasters. People making shows and broadcasting themselves with equipment that can be bought for a couple of hundred euros. And if you do get onto YouTube, take a look at the footage by combatants in

Iran, Afghanistan and Lebanon . . . soldiers (on all sides) filming themselves fighting and making that film available to everyone with a pc and a broadband connection and an interest in the issue. The coverage of war has also become democratized.

Your friends these days do not have to be restricted to the people that live near you or you met at school or work. MySpace (www.myspace.com) has getting on for 70 million subscribers, most of whom have not physically met, but who would tell you that they have (in some cases) long and rich relationships with each other.

Ebay democratized commerce . . . we don't need shops or middlemen any more; we can just trade with each other. Ask any author and he or she will tell you that the reviews they crave most are positive ones on Amazon, not from a newspaper art critic writing for a tiny and highly informed audience. The same goes for the reviews of music on iTunes. The democratization of opinion?

Personal blogs are increasing at a rate of 70,000 a day (doubling every five months). They are mad, bad, brilliant and indifferent but they are being written and they are being read. . . . some by thousands of people. They are of course 'just' conversations and we have always talked to each other, but we have never had the potential for so many to listen to us if we really are engaged in a particular issue or have a perspective that is interesting to others. Who knew that conversation needed democratizing too?

Ask any doctor about the main difference between their patients today and just a few years ago and the answer is: "information." Patients enter surgeries all over the world now clutching printouts from the net and have often tried not only to diagnose themselves, but have views on the their treatment or prescription. Does this mean they are qualified to diagnose and prescribe? No, but it does mean that doctors and health professionals have now to engage patients in the process and make them understand their decisions. The democratization of healthcare is arguably one of the most important of these changes for every country in the world.

And I know I have focused on the on-line world but it's not just there. Many countries in Europe have their version of the TV show *Big Brother* where we are fascinated to witness normal people being elevated to celebrity status; and sometimes in Celebrity *Big Brother*, celebrities being reduced to citizen level. More people voted for the winner of the last *American Idol* than did for George Bush. Celebrity too has been democratised.

And all this at a time when participation in the traditional field of democracy (i.e. politics and voting) is at record lows pretty much everywhere. Established authority in the form of governments, politicians and business leaders score badly in terms of trust. According to the *Edelman annual Trust Barometer,* a CEO is trusted to "do the right thing" by only 29 percent of people in Europe. However, a 'regular' employee of a company is trusted by 33 percent. But a 'person like myself' is trusted by a huge 61 percent of people in Europe.

So what? So in communications and in the way brands and companies deport themselves to their customers and to their stakeholders the game is changing fast. The new model citizen who is increasingly participating and demanding a say and respect and, even a relationship, is not the person we used to know. They don't believe us in the way the way they used to (just like they don't believe a doctor enough not to check the net before visiting the surgery) and the change required is not just about a new media buying strategy it is fundamental for most companies, brands, PR people and communicators.

We used to drive brand preference through awareness vehicles like advertising. But advertising can't reach people like it used to and it is one-way and it is not trusted or believed as it used to be anywhere in Europe. And we used to drive corporate preference through the idea of a few messages, strictly controlled and repeated as often as possible through top down opinion forming media most often by the CEO themselves.

For the new model citizens increasingly used to making more and more decisions for themselves (or at least having a say) being shouted at in traditional forms of static bought media is often a jarring experience. They don't want to hear from the CEO about his product or his latest CSR initiative because "he would say that wouldn't he" (for most CEOs for most of the time, in today's world, formal communication should be restricted to financial results, company strategy announcement and crisis—though informally they can say much more as I'll discuss later).

Much more effective in driving corporate or brand preference are the techniques of dialogue, loyalty and involvement. And that brings me to the re-emergence of an old friend. Word of mouth marketing.

Malcolm Gladwell's book, *The Tipping Point,* some years ago illustrated the power of word of mouth in moving markets and changing behaviour on a mass scale. It was a book before it's time, because in a world populated by these new model citizens, who trust each other's opinions and are very happy to say what they think, word of mouth is more powerful than ever.

Jeff Bezos the founder of *Amazon* said; "Word of mouth has been incredibly important to us, and ultimately that's what a brand is; the things people say about you when you are not there." The net (but not the net alone) gives a powerful boost to word of mouth (through viral techniques and the blogosphere), but more importantly, people seem more willing to make up their own view on brands and companies and [are] much more willing to tell other people (and again the increasing availability of the net and broadband access boost this affect).

Word of mouth now influences around 80 percent of purchase decisions according to NOP and has an impact on 67 percent of the US economy according to McKinsey.

And of course, PR has always been about this. In the corporate, business-to-business, tech, health and brand areas, the power of what we do is related to how successful we are at getting third parties to speak on our behalf. But there is a mass dimension to this now which is different. And many of the new web-based social media mean for the first time that we can directly communicate and have relationships with customers, end users or the people we want to influence. That is new and brings fresh challenges and some issues to deal with—PR is out of the back-room and onto the front line.

The proof of the pudding is in the eating according to my mum (who I trust in all things by the way). Does all this change anything in how we do what we do for our companies and clients? Demonstrably yes I believe. Take a look at some of the Edelman case studies on Edelman movies on www.edelmanfilms.com and especially the Microsoft Xbox and Halo 2 cases where anticipation, massive awareness and then sales were created through word-of-mouth. In the most successful of these for brands, there are some common elements:

- Make use of people's most trusted source of information—other people
- Identify the most influential and active and get them to act as catalysts (the Halo 2 case is a good example of that)
- Give them reasons to talk on your behalf

This last point is often the most difficult. Increasingly this is about having content that is either interesting and useful or just plain entertaining. People pass things on verbally or virally on-line if they are invested enough in it; if it makes them look "in the know"; if they think they can do a service to other people; if they think they have something funny or amazing that will get that second or two of amazement from the person they are addressing it to. Or if they believe it and are passionate about it.

The band the Arctic Monkeys became huge in the US (they are British) because they were adopted by a few people on MySpace who then passed them on to others and they quickly became a phenomena, without the formal and traditional backing of a big record label. There is some debate about how accidental or not this viral affect was for them, but the principle remains the same whether planned or accidental.

In the more traditional media realm, Dove's Real Beauty campaign worked because the PR and advertising created a real 'talk factor' and gave the brand a hero role in that . . . again, great case on Edelman movies on www.edelmanfilms.com.

Much of what we do on PR is about this obviously, but the impact we can now have in all areas of our business is far greater. In the corporate realm blogs are having a huge affect in many sectors. Dell shows how this can be a challenge but look at how some companies through blogging of staff and CEO can be a huge asset for corporate reputation. Robert Scoble (http://scobleizer.wordpress.com) who until recently blogged about his then employer Microsoft is credited with a lot of that firm's improved corporate image. CEO bloggers like Federico at Ducati in Italy and Bob Lutz at General Motors have succeeded in putting a very human face on some of the heavy corporate challenges that face them and their firms (CEOs seem to be better believed on bloggs, possibly because of their frequent and informal conversational style and so have a better chance of being "trusted").

And around any major corporate event now like an IPO or merger or acquisition, check out the blogs that are putting investors together with management (on both sides) with employees with political groups and media.

These are some of the reasons why I think that we are living through the era of greatest change our industry has seen. It's not just as the old monolithic broadcasting and publishing blocs are crumbling and that the channels that have principally served them (advertising) are struggling to find new ways of targeting people . . . it is more a fundamental shift in who people are believing and how they want to be treated. The agencies and companies that figure this out and begin to listen and enter conversations with customers and stakeholders will be the winners.

Andrew Keen  **NO**

The Cult of the Amateur: How Today's Internet Is Killing Our Culture

Introduction

If I didn't know better, I'd think it was 1999 all over again. The boom has returned to Silicon Valley, and the mad utopians are once again running wild. I bumped into one such evangelist at a recent San Francisco mixer.

Over glasses of fruity local Chardonnay, we swapped notes about our newest new things. He told me his current gig involved a new software for publishing music, text, and video on the Internet.

"It's MySpace meets YouTube meets Wikipedia meets Google," he said. "On steroids."

In reply, I explained I was working on a polemic about the destructive impact of the digital revolution on our culture, economy, and values.

"It's ignorance meets egoism meets bad taste meets mob rule," I said, unable to resist a smile. "On steroids."

He smiled uneasily in return. "So it's Huxley meets the digital age," he said. "You're rewriting Huxley for the twenty-first century." He raised his wine glass in my honor. "To *Brave New World 2.0!*"

We clinked wine glasses. But I knew we were toasting the wrong Huxley. Rather than Aldous, the inspiration behind this book comes from his grandfather, T. H. Huxley, the nineteenth-century evolutionary biologist and author of the "infinite monkey theorem." Huxley's theory says that if you provide infinite monkeys with infinite typewriters, some monkey somewhere will eventually create a masterpiece—a play by Shakespeare, a Platonic dialogue, or an economic treatise by Adam Smith.

In the pre-Internet age, T. H. Huxley's scenario of infinite monkeys empowered with infinite technology seemed more like a mathematical jest than a dystopian vision. But what had once appeared as a joke now seems to foretell the consequences of a flattening of culture that is blurring the lines between traditional audience and author, creator and consumer, expert and amateur. This is no laughing matter.

Today's technology hooks all those monkeys up with all those type-writers. Except in our Web 2.0 world, the typewriters aren't quite type-writers, but rather networked personal computers, and the monkeys aren't quite monkeys, but rather Internet users. And instead of creating master-pieces, these millions and millions of exuberant monkeys—many with no more talent in the creative arts than our primate cousins—are creating an endless digital forest of mediocrity. For today's amateur monkeys can use their networked computers to publish everything from uninformed politi-cal commentary, to unseemly home videos, to embarrassingly amateurish music, to unreadable poems, reviews, essays, and novels.

At the heart of this infinite monkey experiment in self-publishing is the Internet diary, the ubiquitous blog. Blogging has become such a mania that a new blog is being created every second of every minute of every hour of every day. We are blogging with monkeylike shamelessness about our private lives, our sex lives, our dream lives, our lack of lives, our Second Lives. At the time of writing there are fifty-three million blogs on the Internet, and this number is doubling every six months. In the time it took you to read this paragraph, ten new blogs were launched.

If we keep up this pace, there will be over five hundred million blogs by 2010, collectively corrupting and confusing popular opinion about everything from politics, to commerce, to arts and culture. Blogs have become so dizzyingly infinite that they've undermined our sense of what is true and what is false, what is real and what is imaginary. These days, kids can't tell the difference between credible news by objective profes-sional journalists and what they read on joeshome.blogspot.com. For these Generation Y utopians, every posting is just another person's version of the truth; every fiction is just another person's version of the facts.

Then there is Wikipedia, an online encyclopedia where anyone with opposable thumbs and a fifth-grade education can publish anything on any topic from AC/DC to Zoroastrianism. Since Wikipedia's birth, more than fifteen thousand contributors have created nearly three million entries in over a hundred different languages—none of them edited or vetted for accuracy. With hundreds of thousands of visitors a day, Wikipedia has be-come the third most visited site for information and current events; a more trusted source for news than the CNN or BBC Web sites, even though Wiki-pedia has no reporters, no editorial staff, and no experience in newsgather-ing. It's the blind leading the blind—infinite monkeys providing infinite information for infinite readers, perpetuating the cycle of misinformation and ignorance.

On Wikipedia, everyone with an agenda can rewrite an entry to their liking—and contributors frequently do. *Forbes* recently reported, for example, a story of anonymous McDonald and Wal-Mart employees furtively using Wikipedia entries as a medium for deceptively spreading corporate propaganda. On the McDonald's entry, a link to Eric Schlosser's *Fast Food Nation* conveniently disappeared; on Wal-Mart's somebody elim-inated a line about underpaid employees making less than 20 percent of the competition.

But the Internet's infinite monkey experiment is not limited to the written word. T. H. Huxley's nineteenth-century typewriter has evolved into not only the computer, but also the camcorder, turning the Internet into a vast library for user-generated video content. One site, YouTube, is a portal of amateur videos that, at the time of writing, was the world's fastest-growing site, attracting sixty-five thousand new videos daily and boasting sixty million clips being watched each day; that adds up to over twenty-five million new videos a year, and some twenty-five billion hits. In the fall of 2006, this overnight sensation was bought by Google for over a billion and a half dollars.

YouTube eclipses even the blogs in the inanity and absurdity of its content. Nothing seems too prosaic or narcissistic for these videographer monkeys. The site is an infinite gallery of amateur movies showing poor fools dancing, singing, eating, washing, shopping, driving, cleaning, sleeping, or just staring into their computers. In August 2006, one hugely popular video called "The Easter Bunny Hates You" showed a man in a bunny suit harassing and attacking people on the streets; according to *Forbes* magazine, this video was viewed more than three million times in two weeks. A few other favorite subjects include a young woman watching another YouTube user who is watching yet another user—a virtual hall of mirrors that eventually leads to a woman making a peanut butter and jelly sandwich in front of the television; a Malaysian dancer in absurdly short skirts grooving to Ricky Martin and Britney Spears; a dog chasing its tail; an Englishwoman instructing her viewers how to eat a chocolate and marmalade cookie; and, in a highly appropriate addition to the YouTube library, a video of dancing stuffed monkeys.

What's more disturbing than the fact that millions of us willingly tune in to such nonsense each day is that some Web sites are making monkeys out of us without our even knowing it. By entering words into Google's search engine, we are actually creating something called "collective intelligence," the sum wisdom of all Google users. The logic of Google's search engine, what technologists call its algorithm, reflects the "wisdom" of the crowd. In other words, the more people click on a link that results from a search, the more likely that link will come up in subsequent searches. The search engine is an aggregation of the ninety million questions we collectively ask Google each day; in other words, it just tells us what we already know.

This same "wisdom" of the crowd is manifested on editor-free news-aggregation sites such as Digg and Reddit. The ordering of the headlines on these sites reflects what other users have been reading rather than the expert judgment of news editors. As I write, there is a brutal war going on in Lebanon between Israel and Hezbollah. But the Reddit user wouldn't know this because there is nothing about Israel, Lebanon, or Hezbollah on the site's top twenty "hot" stories. Instead, subscribers can read about a flat-chested English actress, the walking habits of elephants, a spoof of the latest Mac commercial, and underground tunnels in Japan. Reddit is a mirror of our most banal interest . It makes a mockery of traditional news media and turns current events into a childish game of Trivial Pursuit.

The *New York Times* reports that 50 percent of all bloggers blog for the sole purpose of reporting and sharing experiences about their personal lives. The tagline for YouTube is "Broadcast Yourself" And broadcast ourselves we do, with all the shameless self-admiration of the mythical Narcissus. As traditional mainstream media is replaced by a personalized one, the Internet has become a mirror to ourselves. Rather than using it to seek news, information, or culture, we use it to actually BE the news, the information, the culture.

This infinite desire for personal attention is driving the hottest part of the new Internet economy—social-networking sites like MySpace, Facebook, and Bebo. As shrines for the cult of self-broadcasting, these sites have become tabula rasas of our individual desires and identities. They claim to be all about "social networking" with others, but in reality they exist so that we can advertise ourselves: everything from our favorite books and movies, to photos from our summer vacations, to "testimonials" praising our more winsome qualities or recapping our latest drunken exploits. It's hardly surprising that the increasingly tasteless nature of such self-advertisements has led to an infestation of anonymous sexual predators and pedophiles.

But our cultural standards and moral values are not all that are at stake. Gravest of all, the very traditional institutions that have helped to foster and create our news, our music, our literature, our television shows, and our movies are under assault as well. Newspapers and news-magazines, one of the most reliable sources of information about the world we live in, are flailing, thanks to the proliferation of free blogs and sites like Craigslist that offer free classifieds, undermining paid ad placements. In the first quarter of 2006, profits plummeted dramatically at all the major newspaper companies—down 69 percent at the New York Times Company, 28 percent at the Tribune Company, and 11 percent at Gannett, the nation's largest newspaper company. Circulation is down, too. At the *San Francisco Chronicle,* ironically one of the newspapers of record for Silicon Valley, readership was down a dizzying 16 percent in the middle two quarters of 2005 alone. And in 2007, Time, Inc., laid off almost 300 people, primarily from editorial, from such magazines as *Time, People,* and *Sports Illustrated.*

Those of us who still read the newspaper and magazines know that people are buying less music, too. Thanks to the rampant digital piracy spawned by file-sharing technology, sales of recorded music dropped over 20 percent between 2000 and 2006.

In parallel with the rise of YouTube, Hollywood is experiencing its own financial troubles. Domestic box office sales now represent less than 20 percent of Hollywood's revenue and, with the levelling off of DVD sales and the rampant global piracy, the industry is desperately searching for a new business model that will enable it to profitably distribute movies on the Internet. According to *The New Yorker* film critic David Denby, many studio executives in Hollywood are now in a "panic" over declining revenue. One bleak consequence is cuts. Disney, for example, announced 650 job cuts in 2006, and an almost 50 percent drop in the number of animated movies produced annually.

Old media is facing extinction. But if so, what will take its place? Apparently, it will be Silicon Valley's hot new search engines, social media sites, and video portals. Every new page on MySpace, every new blog post, every new YouTube video adds up to another potential source of advertising revenue lost to mainstream media. Thus, Rupert Murdoch's canny—or desperate—decision in July 2005 to buy MySpace for five hundred and eighty million dollars. Thus, the $1.65 billion sale of YouTube and the explosion of venture capital funding YouTube copycat sites. And, thus, the seemingly unstoppable growth at Google where, in the second quarter of 2006, revenue surged to almost two and a half billion dollars.

What happens, you might ask, when ignorance meets egoism meets bad taste meets mob rule?

The monkeys take over. Say good-bye to today's experts and cultural gatekeepers—our reporters, new anchors, editors, music companies, and Hollywood movie studios. In today's cult of the amateur, the monkeys are running the show. With their infinite typewriters, they are authoring the future. And we may not like how it reads.

POSTSCRIPT

Do MySpace and YouTube
Make Private Globalization
Democratized?

There is perhaps no more difficult question in this volume to answer. The sheer force and speed of the Internet revolution makes speculation regarding its profound impact murky at best. It is undeniable that hundreds of millions of people are now wired into a world that they could never reach just a few short years ago. People are "connecting" in myriad ways that shape politics, economics, and civil society. People are able to express themselves to wide audiences, display talents, embark on new projects, and shape attitudes all from their bedrooms. This is empowering, intoxicating, and a bit scary.

What makes the Internet and social networking sites like YouTube and MySpace so alluring also raises some real concerns. How will people be able to distinguish between friendly banter, postings, and opinions from truly informed analysis, facts, and knowledge? Many argue that the watering down of culture, values, and expectations is occurring and will continue to occur, and there is some strong evidence to support this. Since young people seem to be leading the way here and arguably they are the least experienced in society in terms of judgment, it stands to reason that ways of organizing knowledge and information will be haphazard and ultimately detrimental. Real ability or art as distinguished from mere expression, gossip as distinguished from information, and opinion as distinguished from wisdom—all of these have yet to be sorted out in the Wild West of the Internet.

Our authors clearly see the impact of these phenomena differently and articulate two very different Internet worlds. In the final analysis, perhaps, they are both right and wrong. Since we have yet to understand the full impact and scope of the Internet nor have we seen its complete global dissemination, we will have to wait for a more thorough analysis of its long-term impact. Needless to say, the literature on this subject is being developed as we speak. Some interesting works include Hubert Dreyfus' *On the Internet* (Routledge, 2001), Manuel Hinds' *The Triumph of the Flexible Society: The Connectivity Revolution and Resistance to Change* (Greenwood Publishing Group, 2003), and Ian Graham's *Internet Revolution* (Heinemann, 2002).

Internet References . . .

Nuclear Terrorism: How to Prevent It

This site of the Nuclear Control Institute discusses nuclear terrorism and how best to prevent it. Topics include terrorists' ability to build nuclear weapons, the threat of "dirty bombs," and whether or not nuclear reactors are adequately protected against attack. This site features numerous links to key nuclear terrorism documents and Web sites as well as to recent developments and related news items.

http://www.nci.org/nuketerror.htm

CDI Terrorism Project

The Center for Defense Information's (CDI) Terrorism Project is designed to provide insights, in-depth analysis, and facts on the military, security, and foreign policy challenges of terrorism. The project looks at all aspects of fighting terrorism, from near-term issues of response and defense to long-term questions about how the United States should shape its future international security strategy.

http://www.cdi.org/terrorism/

Exploring Global Conflict: An Internet Guide to the Study of Conflict

Exploring Global Conflict: An Internet Guide to the Study of Conflict is an Internet resource designed to provide understanding of global conflict. Information related to specific conflicts in areas such as Northern Ireland, the Middle East, the Great Lakes region in Africa, and the former Yugoslavia is included on this site. Current news and educational resource sites are listed as well.

http://www.uwm.edu/Dept/CIS/conflict/congeneral.html

Central Intelligence Agency

The U.S. government agency with major responsibility for the war on terrorism provides substantial information on its Web site.

http://www.cia.gov/terrorism/

The Cato Institute

This U.S. public organization conducts research on a wide range of public policy issues. It subscribes to what it terms "basic American principles." One important research issue is civil liberties concerns relating to the war on terrorism.

http://cato.org/current/civil-liberties/

Center for Strategic and International Studies (CSIS)

CSIS now provides substantial information on terrorism in the aftermath of 9/11. The URL noted here leads directly to its thinking on the issue of homeland defense.

http://www.csis.org/homeland

The New Global Security Dilemma

*W*ith the end of the Cold War, the concept of security was freed from its bipolar constraints of great power calculations. And as a consequence of 9/11, the definition of security and how to achieve it were once again redefined to encompass new kinds of threats from a new group of perpetrators. In short, our concept of security in a post-modern age has broadened considerably.

These include concerns over religious extremism and ethnic conflicts, the impact of immigration on a nation's security, the prospects of a nuclear terrorism, the rise of potential nuclear powers like Iran, and the growing emergence of China as a global superpower.

This section examines some of the key issues shaping the security dilemma of the twenty-first century.

- Does Immigration Policy Affect Terrorism?

- Are We Headed Toward a Nuclear 9/11?

- Is Religious and Cultural Extremism a Global Security Threat?

- Is a Nuclear Iran a Global Security Threat?

- Will China Be the Next Superpower?

ISSUE 16

Does Immigration Policy Affect Terrorism?

YES: Mark Krikorian, from "Keeping Terror Out," *The National Interest* (Spring 2004)

NO: Daniel T. Griswold, from "Don't Blame Immigrants for Terrorism," *The Age Peace Foundation* (October 6, 2003)

ISSUE SUMMARY

YES: Mark Krikorian argues that immigration and security are directly and inexorably linked. He contends that the nature of terrorism is such that individual and small group infiltration of our U.S. borders is a prime strategy for terrorists, and thus undermine individual calls for relaxed or open immigration.

NO: Daniel T. Griswold argues that by coupling security and immigration, we simplify a complex issue and, in fact, do little to enhance security while we demonize a huge segment of the population who are by and large law abiding and not a threat.

Immigration has always been a social, economic, and cultural issue. Countries around the world struggle with their attitudes regarding the migration of people both into and out of their countries. Also, attitudes and acceptance of immigration change over time. Certainly this is true in the United States where attitudes regarding immigration have changed dramatically over the decades in response to a number of factors.

Today, with the expansion of terrorism as a form of conflict and with the extension of that into the United States with 9/11, security and immigration have become irrevocably linked. Attitudes regarding immigration policy, whether in favor of relaxed restrictions or greater exclusion, are now intertwined with debates regarding security. Also, who are the immigrants and where do they come from is now central to the debate regarding immigration policy and any person's potential threat to a states' security.

For countries like the United States where immigration has become a central feature of the history and culture of society, this debate is both emotional and complex. Attitudes about immigrants, their status in society, and their rights and responsibilities are intertwined with views regarding certain ethnic groups and their perceived propensity to engage in acts that may be a threat to the nation's security. In the United States this debate has already become heated with extreme views expressed on all sides.

As security has become paramount in the American mindset, concerns over illegal immigration and the large and porous borders that the United States possesses have accelerated. Those who see security as central to our policy see these borders and the illegal immigration as a shield to future terrorists and more 9/11s. They see no choice but to restrict our borders, shut down illegal immigration and begin mass deportations if necessary. Those who see immigration as a cultural socio-economic issue want a more complex approach that meets security needs but does not change the fundamental character of an America committed to sheltering those in search of greater opportunity.

Mark Krikorian places this debate within a security policy mindset and argues that 9/11 changed our notions of security, free movement of people, what the "Home Front" means, and what our obligations are to immigrants. Essentially he contends that a policy designed to thwart 9/11s must take into account that the hijackers were from outside the United States and that this fact illustrates the reality that immigrants can be a threat to U.S. security. Krikorian argues that only through stricter enforcement and a greater acceptance of the potential immigrant threat will we be able to prevent another 9/11.

Daniel Griswold sees immigration and terrorism as separate issues and policy concerns. He sees immigration as a vital part of who America is and what it represents and by demonizing immigrants through a policy of "cracking down" we run the risk of destroying what is a noble legacy of American acceptance of immigrants. He sees security as a matter of making sure we keep out the wrong people without changing our fundamental approach to the vast majority of immigrants who simply want a better life.

YES

Mark Krikorian

Keeping Terror Out

Supporters of open immigration have tried to de-link 9/11 from security concerns. "There's no relationship between immigration and terrorism," said a spokeswoman for the National Council of the advocacy group La Raza. "I don't think [9/11] can be attributed to the failure of our immigration laws," claimed the head of the immigration lawyers' guild a week after the attacks.

President Bush has not gone that far, but in his January 7 speech proposing an illegal alien amnesty and guest worker program, he claimed the federal government is now fulfilling its responsibility to control immigration, thus justifying a vast increase in the flow of newcomers to America. Exploring the role of immigration control in promoting American security can help provide the context to judge the president's claim that his proposal is consistent with our security imperatives, and can help to sketch the outlines of a secure immigration system.

Home Front

The phrase "Home Front" is a metaphor that gained currency during World War I, with the intention of motivating a civilian population involved in total war. The image served to increase economic output and the purchase of war bonds, promote conservation and the recycling of resources and reconcile the citizenry to privation and rationing.

But in the wake of 9/11, "Home Front" is no longer a metaphor. As Deputy Secretary of Defense Paul Wolfowitz said in October 2002,

> *"Fifty years ago, when we said, 'home front,' we were referring to citizens back home doing their part to support the war front. Since last September, however, the home front has become a battlefront every bit as real as any we've known before."*

Nor is this an aberration unique to Al-Qaeda or to Islamists generally. No enemy has any hope of defeating our armies in the field and must therefore resort to asymmetric means.[1] And though there are many facets to asymmetric or "Fourth-Generation" warfare—as we saw in Al-Qaeda's pre-9/11

From *The National Interest,* Spring 2004. Copyright © 2004 by National Interest. Reprinted by permission.

assaults on our interests in the Middle East and East Africa and as we are seeing today in Iraq. The Holy Grail of such a strategy is mass-casualty attacks on America.

The military has responded to this new threat with the Northern Command, just as Israel instituted its own "Home Front Command" in 1992, after the Gulf War. But our objective on the Home Front is different, for this front is different from other fronts; the goal is defensive, blocking and disrupting the enemy's ability to carry out attacks on our territory. This will then allow offensive forces to find, pin, and kill the enemy overseas.

Because of the asymmetric nature of the threat, the burden of homeland defense is not borne mainly by our armed forces but by agencies formerly seen as civilian entities—mainly the Department of Homeland Security (DHS). And of DHS's expansive portfolio, immigration control is central. The reason is elementary: no matter the weapon or delivery system—hijacked airliners, shipping containers, suitcase nukes, anthrax spores—operatives are required to carry out the attacks. Those operatives have to enter and work in the United States. In a very real sense, the primary weapons of our enemies are not inanimate objects at all, but rather the terrorists themselves—especially in the case of suicide attackers. Thus keeping the terrorists out or apprehending them after they get in is indispensable to victory. As President Bush said recently, "Our country is a battlefield in the first war of the 21st century."

In the words of the July 2002 National Strategy for Homeland Security:

> *Our great power leaves these enemies with few conventional options for doing us harm. One such option is to take advantage of our freedom and openness by secretly inserting terrorists into our country to attack our homeland. Homeland security seeks to deny this avenue of attack to our enemies and thus to provide a secure foundation for America's ongoing global engagement.*

Our enemies have repeatedly exercised this option of inserting terrorists by exploiting weaknesses in our immigration system. A Center for Immigration Studies analysis of the immigration histories of the 48 foreign-born Al-Qaeda operatives who committed crimes in the United States from 1993 to 2001 (including the 9/11 hijackers) found that nearly every element of the immigration system has been penetrated by the enemy.[2] Of the 48, one-third were here on various temporary visas, another third were legal residents or naturalized citizens, one-fourth were illegal aliens, and the remainder had pending asylum applications. Nearly half of the total had, at some point or another, violated existing immigration laws.

Supporters of loose borders deny that inadequate immigration control is a problem, usually pointing to flawed intelligence as the most important shortcoming that needs to be addressed. Mary Ryan, for example, former head of the State Department's Bureau of Consular Affairs (which issues visas), testified in January 2004 before the 9/11 Commission that

> *"Even under the best immigration controls, most of the September 11 terrorists would still be admitted to the United States today . . . because they had no*

*criminal records, or known terrorist connections, and had not been identified
by intelligence methods for special scrutiny."*

But this turns out to be untrue, both for the hijackers and for earlier
Al-Qaeda operatives in the United States. A normal level of visa scrutiny,
for instance, would have excluded almost all the hijackers. Investigative reporter Joel Mowbray acquired copies of 15 of the 19 hijackers' visa
applications (the other four were destroyed—yes, destroyed—by the State
Department), and every one of the half-dozen current and former consular
officers he consulted said every application should have been rejected on its
face.[3] Every application was incomplete or contained patently inadequate
or absurd answers.

Even if the applications had been properly prepared, many of the
hijackers, including Mohammed Atta and several others, were young,
single, and had little income—precisely the kind of person likely to overstay his visa and become an illegal alien, and thus the kind of applicant
who should be rejected. And, conveniently, those *least* likely to overstay
their visas—older people with close family, property and other commitments in their home countries—are also the very people least likely to
commit suicide attacks.

9/11 was not the only terrorist plot to benefit from lax enforcement
of ordinary immigration controls—every major Al-Qaeda attack or conspiracy in the United States has involved at least one terrorist who violated
immigration law. Gazi Ibrahim Abu Mezer, for example, who was part of
the plot to bomb the Brooklyn subway, was actually caught three times
by the Border Patrol trying to sneak in from Canada. The third time the
Canadians would not take him back. What did we do? Because of a lack of
detention space, he was simply released into the country and told to show
up for his deportation hearing. After all, with so many millions of illegal
aliens here already, how much harm could one more do? . . .

Prior to the growth of militant Islam, the only foreign threat to our
population and territory in recent history has been the specter of nuclear
attack by the Soviet Union. To continue that analogy, since the terrorists
are themselves the weapons, immigration control is to asymmetric warfare
what missile defense is to strategic warfare. There are other weapons we must
use against an enemy employing asymmetric means—more effective international coordination, improved intelligence gathering and distribution,
special military operations—but in the end, the lack of effective immigration control leaves us naked in the face of the enemy. This lack of defensive
capability may have made sense with regard to the strategic nuclear threat
under the doctrine of Mutual Assured Destruction, but it makes no sense
with regard to the asymmetric threats we face today and in the future.

Unfortunately, our immigration response to the wake-up call
delivered by the 9/11 attacks has been piecemeal and poorly coordinated.
Specific initiatives that should have been set in motion years ago have
finally begun to be enacted, but there is an *ad hoc* feel to our response, a
sense that bureaucrats in the Justice and Homeland Security departments

are searching for ways to tighten up immigration controls that will not alienate one or another of a bevy of special interest groups.

Rather than having federal employees cast about for whatever enforcement measures they feel they can get away with politically, we need a strategic assessment of what an effective immigration-control system would look like.

Homeland Security Begins Abroad

To extend the missile defense analogy, there are three layers of immigration control, comparable to the three phases of a ballistic missile's flight: boost, midcourse, and terminal. In immigration the layers are overseas, at the borders, and inside the country. But unlike existing missile defense systems, the redundancy built into our immigration control system permits us repeated opportunities to exclude or apprehend enemy operatives.

Entry to America by foreigners is not a right but a privilege, granted exclusively at the discretion of the American people. The first agency that exercises that discretion is the State Department's Bureau of Consular Affairs, whose officers make the all-important decisions about who gets a visa. Consular Affairs is, in effect, America's other Border Patrol.[4] In September 2003, DHS Under Secretary Asa Hutchinson described the visa process as "forward-based defense" against terrorists and criminals.

The visa filter is especially important because the closer an alien comes to the United States the more difficult it is to exclude him. There is relatively little problem, practically or politically, in rejecting a foreign visa applicant living abroad. Once a person presents himself at a port of entry, it becomes more difficult to turn him back, although the immigration inspector theoretically has a free hand to do so. Most difficult of all is finding and removing people who have actually been admitted; not only is there no specific chokepoint in which aliens can be controlled, but even the most superficial connections with American citizens or institutions can lead to vocal protests against enforcement of the law. . . .

Despite improvements, the most important flaw in the visa filter still exists: the State Department remains in charge of issuing visas. State has a corporate culture of diplomacy, geared toward currying favor with foreign governments. In the context of visa issuance, this has fostered a "customer-service" approach, which sees the foreign visa applicant as the customer who needs to be satisfied. The attitude in management is summed up by the catchphrase of the former U.S. consul general in Saudi Arabia: "People gotta have their visas!"[5] Such an approach views high visa-refusal rates as a political problem, rather than an indicator of proper vigilance.

Nor will oversight of visa officers by DHS officials be an adequate antidote. As long as the decisions about raises, promotions, and future assignments for visa officers are made by the State Department, the culture of diplomacy will win out over the culture of law enforcement. In the end, the only remedy may be to remove the visa function from the State Department altogether.

Order at the Border

The next layer of immigration security is the border, which has two elements: "ports of entry," which are the points where people traveling by land, sea, or air enter the United States; and the stretches between those entry points. The first are staffed by inspectors working for DHS's Bureau of Customs and Border Protection, the second monitored by the Border Patrol and the Coast Guard, both now also part of DHS.

This is another important chokepoint, as almost all of the 48 Al-Qaeda operatives who committed terrorist acts through 2001 had had contact with immigration inspectors. But here, too, the system failed to do its job. For instance, Mohammed Atta was permitted to reenter the country in January 2001 even though he had overstayed his visa the last time. Also, before 9/11 hijacker Khalid Al-Midhar's second trip to the United States, the CIA learned that he had been involved in the bombing of the U.S.S. *Cole*—but it took months for his name to be placed on the watch list used by airport inspectors, and by then he had already entered the country. And in any case, there still are 12 separate watch lists, maintained by nine different government agencies. . . .

There were also failures *between* the ports of entry. Abdelghani Meskini and Abdel Hakim Tizegha, both part of the Millennium Plot that included Ahmed Ressam, first entered the country as stowaways on ships that docked at U.S. ports. Tizegha later moved to Canada and then returned to the United States by sneaking across the land border. And of course, Abu Mezer, though successfully apprehended by the U.S. Border Patrol, was later released.

And finally, perhaps the biggest defect in this layer of security is the lack of effective tracking of departures. Without exit controls, there is no way to know who has overstayed his visa. This is especially important because most illegal alien terrorists have been overstayers. The opportunities for failure are numerous and the system is so dysfunctional that the INS's own statistics division declared that it was no longer possible to estimate the number of people who have overstayed their visas.

Certainly, there have been real improvements since 9/11. The US-VISIT system has begun to be implemented, with arriving visa-holders being digitally photographed and having their index fingerprints scanned; this will eventually grow into a "check in/check out" system to track them and other foreign visitors. Also, the 45-minute maximum for clearing foreign travelers has been repealed. Lastly, all foreign carriers are now required to forward their passenger manifests to immigration before the plane arrives.

But despite these and other improvements in the mechanics of border management, the same underlying problem exists here as in the visa process: lack of political seriousness about the security importance of immigration control. The Coast Guard, for instance, still considers the interdiction of illegal aliens a "nonsecurity" mission. More importantly, pressure to expedite entry at the expense of security persists; a DHS memo leaked in January outlined how the US-VISIT system would be suspended if lines at airports grew too long. And, to avoid complaints from businesses in Detroit, Buffalo, and elsewhere, most Canadian visitors have been exempted from the requirements of the US-VISIT system. . . .

Safety Through Redundancy

The third layer of immigration security—the terminal phase, in missile defense jargon—is interior enforcement. Here, again, ordinary immigration control can be a powerful security tool. Of the 48 Al-Qaeda operatives, nearly half were either illegal aliens at the time of their crimes or had violated immigration laws at some point prior to their terrorist acts.

Many of these terrorists lived, worked, opened bank accounts, and received driver's licenses with little or no difficulty. Because such a large percentage of terrorists violated immigration laws, enforcing the law would be extremely helpful in disrupting and preventing terrorist attacks.

But interior enforcement is also the most politically difficult part of immigration control. While there is at least nominal agreement on the need for improvements to the mechanics of visas and border monitoring, there is no elite consensus regarding interior enforcement. This is especially dangerous given that interior enforcement is the last fallback for immigration control, the final link in a chain of redundancy that starts with the visa application overseas.

There are two elements to interior enforcement: first, conventional measures such as arrest, detention, and deportation; and second, verification of legal status when conducting important activities. The latter element is important because its goal is to disrupt the lives of illegal aliens so that many will return home on their own (and, in a security context, to disrupt the planning and execution of terrorist attacks).

Inadequacies in the first element of interior enforcement have clearly helped terrorists in the past. Because there is no way of determining which visitors have overstayed their visas, much less a mechanism for apprehending them, this has been a common means of remaining in the United States—of the 12 (out of 48) Al-Qaeda operatives who were illegal aliens when they took part in terrorism, seven were visa overstayers.

Among terrorists who were actually detained for one reason or another, several were released to go about their business inside America because of inadequate detention space. This lack of space means that most aliens in deportation proceedings are not detained, so that when ordered deported, they receive what is commonly known as a "run letter" instructing them to appear for deportation—and 94 percent of aliens from terrorist-sponsoring states disappear instead. . . .

Perhaps the most outrageous phenomenon in this area of conventional immigration enforcement is the adoption of "sanctuary" policies by cities across the country. Such policies prohibit city employees—including police—from reporting immigration violations to federal authorities or even inquiring as to a suspect's immigration status. It is unknown whether any terrorists have yet eluded detention with the help of such policies, but there is no doubt that many ordinary murderers, drug dealers, gang members, and other undesirables have and will continue to do so.

The second element of interior enforcement has been, if anything, even more neglected. The creation of "virtual chokepoints," where an alien's legal status would be verified, is an important tool of immigration control, making it difficult for illegals to engage in the activities necessary for modern life.

The most important chokepoint is employment. Unfortunately, enforcement of the prohibition against hiring illegal aliens, passed in 1986, has all but stopped. This might seem to be of little importance to security, but in fact holding a job can be important to terrorists for a number of reasons. By giving them a means of support, it helps them blend into society. Neighbors might well become suspicious of young men who do not work, but seem able to pay their bills. Moreover, supporting themselves by working would enable terrorists to avoid the scrutiny that might attend the transfer of money from abroad. Of course, terrorists who do not work can still arrive with large sums of cash, but this too creates risks of detection.

That said, the ban on employment by illegal aliens is one of the most widely violated immigration laws by terrorists. Among those who worked illegally at some point were CIA shooter Mir Aimal Kansi; Millennium plot conspirator Abdelghani Meskini; 1993 World Trade Center bombers Eyad Ismoil, Mohammed Salameh and Mahmud and Mohammed Abouhalima.

Other chokepoints include obtaining a driver's license and opening a bank account, two things that most of the 9/11 hijackers had done. It is distressing to note that, while Virginia, Florida, and New Jersey tightened their driver's license rules after learning that the hijackers had used licenses from those states, other states have not. Indeed, California's then-Governor Gray Davis signed a bill last year intended specifically to provide licenses to illegal aliens (which was repealed after his recall).

As for bank accounts, the trend is toward making it easier for illegal aliens to open them. The governments of Mexico and several other countries have joined with several major banks to promote the use of consular identification cards (for illegals who can't get other ID) as a valid form of identification, something the U.S. Department of the Treasury explicitly sanctioned in an October 2002 report.

Finally, the provision of immigration services is an important chokepoint, one that provides the federal government additional opportunities to screen the same alien. There is a hierarchy of statuses a foreign-born person might possess, from illegal alien to short-term visitor, long-term visitor, permanent resident (green card holder) and finally, naturalized citizen. It is very beneficial for terrorists to move up in this hierarchy because it affords them additional opportunities to harm us. To take only one example: Mahmud Abouhalima—one of the leaders of the first World Trade Center bombing—was an illegal-alien visa overstayer; but he became a legal resident as part of the 1986 illegal-alien amnesty by falsely claiming to be a farmworker, and he was only then able to travel to Afghanistan for terrorist training and return to the United States. . . .

Former INS Commissioner James Ziglar expressed the general resist-ance to linking immigration law with homeland security when he said a month after the 9/11 attacks that "We're not talking about immigration, we're talking about evil." It is as if the terrorists were summoned from a magic lamp, rather than moving through our extensive but neglected immigration control system, by applying for visas, being admitted by inspectors, and violating laws with impunity inside America.

Upholding the Law

Such ambivalence about immigration enforcement, at whatever stage in the process, compromises our security. It is important to understand that the security function of immigration control is not merely opportunistic, like prosecuting Al Capone for tax violations for want of evidence on his other numerous crimes. The FBI's use of immigration charges to detain hundreds of Middle Easterners in the immediate aftermath of 9/11 was undoubtedly necessary, but it cannot be a model for the role of immigration law in homeland security. If our immigration system is so lax that it can be penetrated by a Mexican busboy, it can surely be penetrated by an Al-Qaeda terrorist.

Since there is no way to let in "good" illegal aliens but keep out "bad" ones, countering the asymmetric threats to our people and terri-tory requires sustained, across-the-board immigration law enforcement. Anything less exposes us to grave dangers. Whatever the arguments for the president's amnesty and guest worker plan, no such proposal can plausibly be entertained until we have a robust, functioning immigration-control system. And we are nowhere close to that day.

Endnotes

1. See the National Defense University's Institute for National Strategic Studies 1998 Strategic Assessment: "Put simply, asymmetric threats or tech-niques are a version of not 'fighting fair,' which can include the use of sur-prise in all its operational and strategic dimensions and the use of weapons in ways unplanned by the United States. Not fighting fair also includes the prospect of an opponent designing a strategy that fundamentally alters the terrain on which a conflict is fought."

2. Steven A. Camarota, "The Open Door: How terrorists entered and remained in the United States, 1993–2001" (Washington, DC: Center for Immigration Studies, 2002).

3. "Visas for Terrorists: They were ill-prepared. They were laughable. They were approved," *National Review*, October 28, 2002.

4. "America's Other Border Patrol: The State Department's Consular Corps and Its Role in U.S. Immigration," by Nikolai Wenzel, Center for Immigra-tion Studies Backgrounder, August 2000, http://www.cis.org/articles/2000/back800.html

5. Joel Mowbray, "Perverse Incentives; The State Department rewards officials responsible for terror visas." *National Review Online*, October 22, 2002.

Daniel T. Griswold   ➡ **NO**

Don't Blame Immigrants for Terrorism

In the wake of the September 11 terrorist attacks on the Pentagon and the World Trade Center, the U.S. government must strengthen its efforts to stop terrorists or potential terrorists from entering the country. But those efforts should not result in a wider effort to close our borders to immigrants.

Obviously, any government has a right and a duty to "control its borders" to keep out dangerous goods and dangerous people. The U.S. federal government should implement whatever procedures are necessary to deny entry to anyone with terrorist connections, a criminal record, or any other ties that would indicate a potential to commit terrorist acts.

This will require expanding and upgrading facilities at U.S. entry points so that customs agents and immigration officials can be notified in a timely manner of persons who should not be allowed into the country. Communications must be improved between law enforcement, intelligence agencies and border patrol personnel. Computer systems must be upgraded to allow effective screening without causing intolerable delays at the border. A more effective border patrol will also require closer cooperation from Mexico and Canada to prevent potential terrorists from entering those countries first in an attempt to then slip across our long land borders into the United States.

Long-time skeptics of immigration, including Pat Buchanan and the Federation for American Immigration Reform, have tried in recent days to turn those legitimate concerns about security into a general argument against openness to immigration. But immigration and border control are two distinct issues. Border control is about who we allow to enter the country, whether on a temporary or permanent basis; immigration is about whom we allow to stay and settle permanently.

Immigrants are only a small subset of the total number of foreigners who enter the United States every year. According to the U.S. Immigration and Naturalization Service, 351 million aliens were admitted through INS ports of entry in fiscal year 2000—nearly a million entries a day. That total includes individuals who make multiple entries, for example, tourists and business travelers with temporary visas, and aliens who hold border-crossing cards that allow them to commute back and forth each week from Canada and Mexico.

The majority of aliens who enter the United States return to their homeland after a few days, weeks, or months. Reducing the number of people we allow to reside permanently in the United States would do nothing to protect us from terrorists who do not come here to settle but to plot and commit violent acts. And closing our borders to those who come here temporarily would cause a huge economic disruption by denying entry to millions of people who come to the United States each year for lawful, peaceful (and temporary) purposes.

It would be a national shame if, in the name of security, we were to close the door to immigrants who come here to work and build a better life for themselves and their families. Like the Statue of Liberty, the World Trade Center towers stood as monuments to America's openness to immigration. Workers from more than 80 different nations lost their lives in the terrorist attacks. According to the *Washington Post,* "The hardest hit among foreign countries appears to be Britain, which is estimating about 300 deaths . . . Chile has reported about 250 people missing, Colombia nearly 200, Turkey about 130, the Philippines about 115, Israel about 113, and Canada between 45 and 70. Germany has reported 170 people unaccounted for, but expects casualties to be around 100." Those people were not the cause of terrorism but its victims.

The problem is not that we are letting too many people into the United States but that the government is not keeping out the wrong people. An analogy to trade might be helpful: We can pursue a policy of open trade, with all its economic benefits, yet still exclude goods harmful to public health and safety, such as diseased meat and fruits, explosives, child pornography, and other contraband materials. In the same way, we should keep our borders open to the free flow of people, but at the same time strengthen our ability to keep out those few who would menace the public.

Immigrants come here to realize the American dream; terrorists come to destroy it. We should not allow America's tradition of welcoming immigrants to become yet another casualty of September 11.

POSTSCRIPT

Does Immigration Policy Affect Terrorism?

Immigration policy is a complex issue. It reflects attitudes regarding the socio-cultural fabric and history of a society. It also reaches deep into the core attitudes regarding each person's relationship to the society in which they live. Terrorism, too, is a complex issue. It is a form of warfare that demands dexterous responses, excellent intelligence, and awareness that civilian areas are targets and must be protected in ways heretofore not considered in modern warfare.

As these issues have been linked together in the United States and elsewhere, the debates regarding immigrants and security have become heated, contentious, and filled with polemic on both sides. Those who wish to build walls and those who wish for open door policies have become entrenched in mindsets that lend little to the complexities of the issues at hand.

If one is to ask whether an open door policy on immigration might allow more terrorists into a country like the United States than a closed door policy, statistical analysis tells us that the former would lead to more terrorists "getting in." However, if one embraces the notion that only a fraction (less than 1/10 of 1%) of people trying to enter the United States are of suspicious motives, then it seems that proper and effective intelligence services could prevent such entry without demonizing thousands of immigrants.

What position you take will often come down to what value you see as more important. Is it the value of a country willing to open its doors to those who are seeking a better life or security and the desire to protect one's own citizens? Clearly, U.S. society has not reached a consensus on which value has greater importance in terms of policy and it may never reach that consensus given our long and storied history as a country welcoming immigration.

Some important literature on this subject includes "Playing Games With Security: Taking Two Steps Back for Every Step Forward on Immigration" Mark Krikorian, *The National Review Online* (August 18, 2004), "Keeping Extremists Out: The History of Ideological Exclusion and the Need for Its Revival," James R. Edwards, Jr. *Center for Immigration Studies* (September 2005), *Globalization and the Future of Terrorism: Patterns and Predications,* Brynjar Lia, (Routledge 2005), and *Terrorism as a Challenge for National and International Law: Security Versus Liberty?* Christian Walter, Silva Vwneky, and Volker Rwben (Springer 2004).

Are We Headed Toward a Nuclear 9/11?

YES: David Krieger, from "Is a Nuclear 9/11 in Our Future?" *Nuclear Age Peace Foundation* (October 6, 2003)

NO: Graham Allison, from "Preventing Nuclear Terrorism," *Los Angeles World Affairs Council* (September 22, 2005)

ISSUE SUMMARY

YES: David Kreiger, president of the Nuclear Age Peace Foundation, argues that a nuclear 9/11 is very likely in a U.S. city due to the prevalence of nuclear weapons and the failure of nuclear member states to adequately enforce a true non-proliferation regime.

NO: Graham Allison, noted international scholar, argues that a nuclear 9/11 is preventable, provided that the United States and other states halt proliferation to states predisposed toward assisting terrorists, particularly North Korea.

Since the terrorist attacks of September 11, 2001, much has been written about the specter of nuclear terrorism and the releasing of a dirty bomb (one loaded with radioactive material) in an urban/civilian setting. The events of September 11 have all but ensured the world's preoccupation with such an event for the foreseeable future. Indeed, the arrest of a U.S. man with dirty bomb materials indicates that such plans may indeed be in the works between Al Qaeda and other terrorist cells. When this horror is combined with the availability of elements of nuclear-related material in places like the states of the former Soviet Union, Pakistan, India, Iraq, Iran, North Korea, and many other states, one can envision a variety of sobering scenarios.

Hollywood feeds these views with such films as *The Sum of All Fears* and *The Peacemaker,* in which nuclear terrorism is portrayed as all too easy to carry out and likely to occur. It is difficult in such environments to separate fact from fiction and to ascertain objectively the probabilities of such events. So many factors go into a successful initiative in this area. One needs to find a committed cadre of terrorists, sufficient financial backing, technological know-how, intense security and secrecy, the means of delivery, and many other variables, including luck. In truth, such acts may have already been advanced and thwarted by governments, security services, or terrorist mistakes and incompetence. We do not know, and we may never know.

Regional and ethnic conflicts of a particularly savage nature in places like Chechnya, Kashmir, Colombia, and Afghanistan help to fuel fears that adequately financed zealots will see in nuclear weapons a swift and catastrophic answer to their demands and angers. Osama bin Laden's contribution to worldwide terrorism has been the success of money over security and the realization that particularly destructive acts with high levels of coordination can be "successful." This will undoubtedly encourage others with similar ambitions against real or perceived enemies.

Conversely, many argue that fear of the terrorist threat has left us imagining that which is not likely. They point to a myriad of roadblocks to terrorist groups' obtaining all of the elements necessary for a nuclear or dirty bomb. They cite technological impediments, monetary issues, lack of sophistication, and inability to deliver. They also cite governments' universal desire to prevent such actions. Even critics of [former] Iraqi leader Saddam Hussein have argued that were he to develop such weapons, he would not deliver them to terrorist groups nor would he use them except in the most dire of circumstances, such as his own regime's survival. They argue that the threat is overblown and, in some cases, merely used to justify increased security and the restriction of civil liberties.

The following selections reflect this dichotomy of views. While both authors see proliferation as key, Krieger feels that a new approach to proliferation must be undertaken to ensure that such an attack won't take place. He takes the U.S. and other nuclear weapons states to task for not setting an example by removing nuclear weapons and as such, this ensures a nuclear terrorist attack eventually.

Allison also believe proliferation is the key to terrorism but argues that more pro-action and stricter proliferation enforcement will ensure that rogue states don't get the bomb and thus transfer it to terrorist groups for use.

YES ↰

David Krieger

Is a Nuclear 9/11 in Our Future?

Sooner or later there will be a nuclear 9/11 in an American city or that of a US ally unless serious program is undertaken to prevent such an occurrence. A terrorist nuclear attack against an American city could take many forms. A worst case scenario would be the detonation of a nuclear device within a city. Depending upon the size and sophistication of the weapon, it could kill hundreds of thousands or even millions of people.

Terrorists could obtain a nuclear device by stealing or purchasing an already created nuclear weapon or by stealing or purchasing weapons-grade nuclear materials and fashioning a crude bomb. While neither of these options would be easy, they cannot be dismissed as beyond the capabilities of a determined terrorist organization.

If terrorists succeeded in obtaining a nuclear weapon, they would also have to bring it into the US, assuming they did not already obtain or create the weapon in this country. While this would not necessarily be easy, many analysts have suggested that it would be within the realm of possibility. An oft-cited example is the possibility of bringing a nuclear device into an American port hidden on a cargo ship.

Another form of terrorist nuclear attack requiring far less sophistication would be the detonation of a radiation weapon or "dirty bomb." This type of device would not be capable of a nuclear explosion but would use conventional explosives to disperse radioactive materials within a populated area. The detonation of such a device could cause massive panic due to the public's appropriate fears of radiation sickness and of developing cancers and leukemias in the future.

A bi-partisan task force of the Secretary of Energy's Advisory Board, headed by former Senate Majority Leader Howard Baker and former White House Counsel Lloyd Cutler, called upon the US in 2001 to spend $30 billion over an eight to ten year period to prevent nuclear weapons and materials in the former Soviet Union from getting into the hands of terrorists or so called "rogue" states. The task force called the nuclear dangers in the former USSR "the most urgent unmet national security threat facing the United States today." At present, the US government is spending only about one-third of the recommended amount, while it pours resources into paying for the invasion, occupation and rebuilding of Iraq as well

From *Waging Peace,* October 6, 2003, pp. 1. Copyright © 2003 by David Krieger. Reprinted by permission. www.wagingpeace.org

as programs unlikely to provide effective security to US citizens such as missile defense.

The great difficulty in preventing a nuclear 9/11 is that it will require ending the well-entrenched nuclear double standards that the US and other nuclear weapons states have lived by throughout the Nuclear Age. Preventing nuclear terrorism in the end will not be possible without a serious global program to eliminate nuclear weapons and control nuclear materials that could be converted to weapons. Such a program would require universal agreement in the form of an enforceable treaty providing for the following:

- full accounting and international safeguarding of all nuclear weapons, weapons-grade nuclear materials and nuclear reactors in all countries, including the nuclear weapons states;
- international tracking and control of the movement of all nuclear weapons and weapons-grade materials;
- dismantling and prohibiting all uranium enrichment facilities and all plutonium separation facilities, and the implementation of a plan to expedite the phasing out all nuclear power plants;
- full recognition and endorsement by the nuclear weapons states of their existing obligation pursuant to the Nuclear Non-Proliferation Treaty for an "unequivocal undertaking" to eliminate their nuclear arsenals;
- rapidly dismantling existing nuclear weapons in an orderly and transparent manner and the transfer of nuclear materials to international control sites; and criminalizing the possession, threat or use of nuclear weapons.

While these steps may appear extreme, they are in actuality the minimum necessary to prevent a nuclear 9/11. If that is among our top priorities as a country, as surely it should be, the US government should begin immediately to lead the world in this direction. Now is the time to act, before one or more US cities are devastated by nuclear terrorism.

Graham Allison   **NO**

Preventing Nuclear Terrorism

$\mathbf{E}$ven when talking about a subject that on the one hand is so gloomy if realistic, the main message here is actually quite a hopeful message. The most important part of this story is the subtitle of my book: *The Ultimate Preventable Catastrophe.* So, while some part of what I'm going to say at the beginning may seem a little frightening, don't give up before the end of the presentation. For those of you who get the book, make sure to read part two, not just part one, because after part one you might be tempted to do something else rather than your normal day-to-day business.

All of us can remember 9/11, three years ago just this month, when Al Qaeda hijacked airplanes and crashed them into the World Trade Center and the Pentagon. Probably for most of us we can remember where we were, what we were doing, what we thought. My wife was supposed to have been on American Flight 77 coming to Los Angeles that day for a board meeting here in town, but [the meeting] was postponed for a day so she was on the plane for the 12th, not for the 11th. Obviously, the plane never went.

One month to the day after those events—one month to the day—George Tenet, who was the Director of the CIA, walked into the Oval Office for the president's morning intelligence briefing and informed the president that a CIA agent code-named Dragonfire—a wonderful name—had reported that Al Qaeda had acquired a ten-kiloton nuclear weapon. That's a very small nuclear weapon, but one that would make a ten-kiloton blast, and it had this weapon in New York City. There was a stunned silence followed by a series of interrogating questions in which the president was essentially trying to see if this was a real possibility or just another story. Were there ten-kiloton weapons in the former Soviet arsenal? and they say "yes." Are all these weapons accounted for? The answer, "uncertain." Could Al Qaeda have acquired one of these weapons? The answer, "of course." Could Al Qaeda have bought a weapon like this to New York City and have it there without us otherwise knowing about it? The answer "certainly." So on this, Vice President Cheney evacuated, he left Washington. He stayed for some considerable period of time in a secret alternative site for our government called "Site R," which is a site in the hole of a mountain. At that point they set up very rapidly an alternative government consisting of

From *Los Angeles World Affairs Council,* September 22, 2005, pp. 1–3, 5–6. Copyright © 2005 by Los Angeles World Affairs Council. Reprinted by permission.

several hundred people who worked in the government most of the time but who were there in this alternative site in the case that a weapon was in Washington as well. If it were to explode in Washington, all the current government would likely be killed, but the country would still survive and we would need a government to try to see what we could do to put the pieces together thereafter.

The point of this story, which is told in the introduction of the book, is that as the U.S. government confronted this report there was no basis in science, there was no basis in technology, no basis in logic, no basis in politics for dismissing this as a real possibility. Our government took it as a possible fact. Nuclear Emergency Support Teams were dispatched to New York City to search to see if they could find any signals of radioactivity, and other pieces of information in the report by Dragonfire were traced down. After less than a week it was concluded that this was a false alarm. Mayor Giuliani was never informed of this at the time—something that he expressed some considerable dissatisfaction about after he learned about it. But I believe the president made the right decision. If he had told Giuliani, he would undoubtedly have told his Commissioner of Police, and the more people that knew the more likely it would become a fact, and if you turned on your television and heard that the president thought that there might be a nuclear bomb in Los Angeles you wouldn't be here listening to a lecture tonight. I wouldn't be here giving it, so it can have a lot of consequences.

For tonight there are four things to remember. The first one was Dragonfire. The second story I tell in the introduction is four million. What is four million? Four million is the answer to the question, "How many Americans does Bin Laden say Al Qaeda needs to kill?" Four million. Several months after the 9/11 attack, Bin Laden's press spokesman, a fellow named Abu Gheith, put up on the Al Qaeda website Al Qaeda's objective for America in which he said, "our goal is to kill four million Americans, including two million children and to maim an equivalent number." He then goes on to explain in a fascinating, if grotesque, calculus that this number is not picked up out of thin air. This number is actually what is required, he says, to balance the scales of justice for the deaths and destruction that have been caused to Muslims by what they call "Jewish-Christian crusaders," by whom they mean Israel and the United States. He then goes through a whole series of incidents and gives us his body count, and I describe this in the introductory chapter—Chatilla, how many? sanctions against Iraq, how many? And even when I wrote the book, which was just published a month ago, I never quite got the thing about the children. It seemed kind of strange. Four million. I couldn't see how he gets this calculus. I think it's crazy but at least I can see some logic in it. The children point came home to me more vividly recently with this horrible action in Russia with the kids at the school in Beslan where killing children was also part of a conception of what's imagined, in some crazed way, to balance the scales of justice.

So, the second thing to remember is four million, and there's a debate about this among people that try to study Bin Laden and Al Qaeda in the international security community who say, "Oh, no. They're not really serious about this, it's too hard to believe." Actually, when people say they want to kill large numbers of people, most people find it unbelievable, and any of us who study history know that this is not the first time claims about proposals to kill millions of people were discounted. So I myself take this quite seriously. I think it's a serious effort. If you ask yourself how many 9/11 attacks would it take to kill four million Americans, we can do the math. It would be about 1,400. So, you're not going to get this goal by hijacking airplanes and crashing them into buildings. Someone is going to have to go upscale in terms of consequences.

Now, imagine, God forbid, a terrorist nuclear bomb like the bomb that Dragonfire said, and we thought, was in New York City, was in Los Angeles. How big is a ten-kiloton bomb out of the former Soviet arsenal? Less than half the size of one of these tables. You could put it in a big wheelie—these huge suitcase-types that you wheel around. And there are a large number of nuclear weapons much smaller than that. People have an idea that nuclear weapons are these huge things that you couldn't possibly haul about. There are some nuclear weapons that are quite small. So, in any case what would a ten-kiloton explosion look like? Think of Hiroshima—that was twelve and a half kilotons, so it's about the same size. In Los Angeles, if you imagine the bomb was at the intersection of Hollywood and Highland, a ten-kiloton explosion would vaporize everything a third of a mile from ground zero. So, that would be the Chinese Theatre, the Walk of Fame, the home of the Academy Awards would look like the Federal Office Building in Oklahoma City. Then you'd have raging fires out to past the Hollywood hill sign. So, in New York City, at Time Square on a work day, you could imagine killing half a million people instantaneously and about that many as well would die over the following several days.

Because nuclear weapons, even for those of you old enough to remember the Cold War, have kind of got out of people's heads, we put up a website called nuclearterrorism.org, which you can go to and you can put in the zip code you're interested in and see the consequences of a ten-kiloton weapon in that neighborhood. Just think of ground zero, a third of a mile gone completely, and out to beyond a mile looking like the federal office building in Oklahoma City. So, for a small nuclear weapon this is a huge consequence.

I go through this much detail in an introductory fashion, not to try to be just doom and gloom, but to say this is a real possibility that we face. I not only believe this is a great threat for us now, today, but President Bush has said that this is our ultimate nightmare. As he says, "the world's most destructive technologies in the hands of the world's most dangerous actors"—that's his bumper sticker for it, and it's a very good bumper sticker, I believe. What's the world's most destructive technology? Nuclear. Who are the world's most dangerous actors? Terrorists, because, as Bin Laden says, there are people who love death more than we love life. They also don't have a return address. A good part of the reason why the Soviet Union never attacked the U.S. was that those of us who are old Cold War warriors, and that would include me, built up a vast arsenal of nuclear weapons so that they would know—any Soviet leader would know—that the moment an attack occurred on the U.S. they had signed a suicide note for their country. Well, that clarifies the mind, but in the case of a nuclear bomb, if it went off tonight in San Francisco or in Boston or in Los Angeles, who did it? Let's imagine even that Bin Laden says, "Good for us. Five hundred thousand down, three and one-half million to go." So, we would be unhappy, we would be angry, we would be eager to attack somebody but, excuse me, if we knew where Bin Laden was we would be capturing him tonight. So, a person who has no return address is very difficult to deter.

Okay, point two, four million. Dragonfire and four million.

Two more points. The book consists of part one and part two. Part one says "inevitable," part two says "preventable." Let me say a word about each. Part one is for an ordinary citizen who reads the newspapers, not for national security experts. This is kind of speaking to people as citizens and is written for somebody who is running for Congress, but not a national security expert, who wants to play a role and cares about the country. I go through who, what, where, when, and how. So, who could want to do this? Al Qaeda? I go through the history of their search for nuclear weapons. Bin Laden says it's their religious duty, but I point out they're not the only game in town. There's a group called Hezbollah. This is a very, very sophisticated terrorist group that operates in conjunction with Iran. They are, as the Deputy Secretary of State Rich Armitage says, the A-Team of terrorists. They're much more sophisticated than Bin Laden and Al Qaeda. They actually blew up the barracks of the U.S. soldiers at Khobar Towers, and they've mounted a number of terrorist attacks upon Israel. This is a sophisticated group, but there are a whole number of others. The Chechens, actually. I pointed out that their most likely target for their first weapon would be Moscow, not the U.S. And when I talk to the Russians about this I tell them, "Wake up. These guys would toast Moscow first." I'm worried about their second nuclear weapon more, that they might actually sell it to Al Qaeda, that it would come to the U.S., but I'm also interested in Moscow. So that's the who.

What might they do with a weapon? There are two versions: A ready-made bomb—like the ten-kiloton bomb that Dragonfire warned about—or a homemade bomb. The ready-made bombs come in many varieties. I discuss in the book the suitcase bombs that the former Soviet arsenal included, some of which you can carry around literally in a suitcase or a backpack and some number of which it is unclear what happened to them.

But the other side of this is homemade nuclear bombs. The book has an appendix of frequently asked questions in which I discuss dirty bombs and attacks on nuclear power plants, but in the book I'm talking about nuclear bombs, which are bombs that create a mushroom cloud, and their vast destructive effect. It's conceivable for a terrorist to make a nuclear bomb if they start with one hundred pounds of highly enriched uranium. The hard thing to do is make highly enriched uranium or plutonium—that is actually beyond the capacity of the terrorist groups. That's a multi-billion dollar investment over many years in a big facility. Iran is now in its 18th year of this project and is just now coming to the finish line. It's possible to do. Pakistan did it over a decade with a very successful effort, but terrorists are not going to do this by themselves. But if terrorists got 100 pounds of highly enriched uranium that had been made by somebody else and stolen or given to them—from that to a nuclear bomb like Hiroshima is a very straight path. As President Bush said in the run-up to the war with Iraq, if Saddam got a soft-ball-size lump of highly enriched uranium he could make a bomb in a year. That's true, but so could Al Qaeda or any other group. If you start with the highly enriched uranium the rest of the design is unfortunately quite straightforward and simple. The rest of the material that's required is stuff that's industrially available. So, either a pre-made bomb or a ready-made bomb or a homemade bomb. . . .

Preventable. We have Dragonfire, four million, inevitable and this is the last point—preventable. Unlike other catastrophic terrorism of which there's a number of varieties, and unlike the fact that there will be additional catastrophic terrorist attacks on America of 9/11 proportions—that is, kills hundreds *or* thousands of people—I would say the chances of that are 100 percent, unlike bio-terrorism, where I'm sure there will be additional attacks like the anthrax attacks, the ultimate terrorist weapon, a nuclear bomb, is preventable. How can this be? Because there's fortunately in this issue a strategic narrow [window] to check this issue, this challenge.

There are only two elements in the world from which you can make a fissionable explosion: They are highly enriched uranium and plutonium. Neither of these elements exists in nature. You can't go dig them up. Neither of these can be made in somebody's basement. As I say, it's a multi-billion dollar, multi-year undertaking. So all we have to do, though "all" is big, is prevent terrorists acquiring highly enriched uranium and plutonium and we can prevent nuclear terrorism. Now, what's required to do that? Well, locking down all the stuff that now exists, preventing any more being produced and cleaning it out of the places where you can't lock it down successfully. That is the big picture.

I tried to organize a campaign for doing this under a doctrine of three "nos." Let me say just a word about each of them, because each of them is a lot of stuff, but I'm just going to do it briefly. The nos are: no loose nukes, no new nascent nukes and no new nuclear weapon states. Let's go through them very quickly. No loose nukes means developing with Russia a new gold standard and locking down all weapons and all materials, first in the U.S. and Russia and then everywhere else on the fastest feasible timetable to this new gold standard.

The U.S. loses how much gold from Fort Knox? Zero. Not an ounce. Russia loses how many treasures from the Kremlin armory? None. So do human beings know how to lock things down that they really care about people not stealing? Yes. There's no lock that's 100 percent, but relative to the people who want to steal gold, the chances of them getting it out of Ft. Knox is very, very slim—almost nonexistent. I had a debate with a senator whose name I won't mention but who kept saying, "You can't be serious about this! You mean locking down nuclear weapons as good as gold?" I said, "Yeah, I'm absolutely serious about that. Why not? What is gold?" Gold will become a relatively uninteresting substance after a nuclear terrorist attack, I believe. So, no loose nukes.

Second. No new nascent nukes. We haven't appreciated the extent to which if people get highly enriched uranium or plutonium they are about 90 percent of the way to having a nuclear bomb. So, no new national production of highly enriched uranium or plutonium. The specific test case for this today is Iran. Iran is just about to get across the finish line. So, I outline a strategy which I believe could be implemented today, but the window keeps narrowing all the time, for stopping Iran where they are right now and backing them down step-by-step in a verifiable process in which there would be no new production of highly enriched uranium or plutonium in Iran—which means stopping these factories from being completed.

The third one is no new nuclear weapons states. There are eight states that have nuclear weapons in the world today. Five acknowledged. India and Pakistan have tested and say that they're nuclear weapons states, but other people haven't "accepted" them in any official status, and Israel, which is an undeclared nuclear weapons state. So, that's eight. I say draw a bright line there and say simply, "We're not having any more." Yes, it is unfair that these eight should have them and other people shouldn't, to which the answer is we're going to work in the longer run on getting this problem solved—the eight—but in the short run it's not advanced by having more. In any case the current challenge to this is called North Korea. North Korea is *the* most dangerous property on earth. Why? Because with Americans hardly even noticing, since January of 2003—so just the last 18 months— while we've been consumed by Iraq, Kim Jong Il has noticed that we've been giving him a pass and he's been moving rapidly to build additional nuclear weapons or to produce material for additional nuclear weapons. Since January 2003 he withdrew from the non-proliferation treaty, he kicked out the IAE inspectors, turned off the video cams that were watching these fuel rods that had enough stuff for six more nuclear bombs, he put that stuff on trucks and took them off to factories that are reprocessing them to produce more plutonium and at some point he's going to announce "We're finished. We have a nuclear arsenal."

Indeed, when this mysterious explosion occurred in North Korea last week, one of the worries within the intelligence community is that it could be a nuclear bomb. This could be the wake-up call to that fact and the intelligence community tonight is still sitting on their seat thinking, "Is this going to happen and if it didn't happen, when could it happen?" So, if North Korea succeeds with this project they're going to be a nuclear weapon state and they're going to have a nuclear weapons production line for another dozen weapons a year.

What do we know about North Korea? We know that it sells what-ever it makes to anybody that will pay for it. So, they are in the business of Missiles-R-Us. They sell missiles to whom? People who pay, Iran, Iraq, Egypt, Libya, and others.

They have two other products: illegal drugs and counterfeit hundred dollar bills. That's it. The rest of the place has no income. Ten percent of the citizens have been starved to death in North Korea in the last half dozen years. So it's a genuine basket case as a country, ruled by a strange fellow, Mr. Kim Jong Il, who, if he has a nuclear arsenal and a nuclear weapons production line, will for sure sell nuclear weapons to other states and terrorist groups and we will not know that the weapon has been sold. So, I think this is the most dangerous site. In the book I outline the strategy for trying to deal with North Korea now. This window is closing, very, very fast, but if North Korea makes its way into this status as a nuclear weapon state with a nuclear weapon production line, then the likelihood of nuclear terrorist attacks on the U.S. goes right up the scale. So, this would be the worst failure in American security policy ever, I believe, if this is allowed to happen and it's just about to happen. But I have a strategy, which some people will regard as slightly crazy, but if I were in charge I would do it tonight. I would have done it two years ago.

So, three nos: no loose nukes, no new nascent nukes, no new nuclear weapons states.

My final point is just a question. There's a strategy group that met in the summer in Colorado, Republicans and Democrats from the national security community. There were two or three former secretaries of defense, a couple of former secretaries of state, three or four former directors of CIA, and several former national security advisors. A broad base of sensible people in my view, plus some people in the academic community. The subject this past summer was nuclear terrorism and my book was some part of the argument about it and at the end of the conversation Bill Perry, who's one of the genuine wise men, in my view, in the national security world, who was Secretary of Defense under Clinton and a very calm man, he hardly ever raises his blood pressure, said, "We are racing towards unprecedented catastrophe. I see no sense of urgency in the public about this threat. What in the world can we do to awaken the public and energize the administration?" I would say that's the question before the house. I don't have a very good answer to that. I saw Bill in San Francisco Monday night, and he's still worrying about that question.

Thank you.

POSTSCRIPT

Are We Headed Toward a Nuclear 9/11?

There are many arguments to support the contention that nuclear and dirty bombs are hard to obtain, difficult to move and assemble, and even harder to deliver. There is also ample evidence to suggest that most, if not all, of the U.S. government's work is in one way or another designed to thwart such actions because of the enormous consequences were such acts to be carried out. These facts should make Americans rest easier and allay fears if only for the reasons of probability.

However, Allison's contention that failure to assume the worst may prevent the thwarting of such terrorist designs is persuasive. Since September 11 it is clear that the world has entered a new phase of terrorist action and a new level of funding, sophistication, and motivation. The attitude that because something is difficult it is unlikely to take place may be too dangerous to possess. The collapse of the USSR has unleashed a variety of forces, some positive and some more sinister and secretive. The enormous prices that radioactive material and nuclear devices can command on the black market make the likelihood of temptation strong and possibly irresistible.

If states are to err, perhaps they should err on the side of caution and preventive action rather than on reliance on the statistical probability that nuclear terrorism is unlikely. We may never see a nuclear terrorist act in this century, but it is statistically likely that the reason for this will not be for lack of effort on the part of motivated terrorist groups.

Some important research and commentary on nuclear terrorism can be found in Elaine Landau, *Osama bin Laden: A War Against the West* (Twenty-First Century Books, 2002); Jan Lodal, *The Price of Dominance: The New Weapons of Mass Destruction and Their Challenge to American Leadership* (Council on Foreign Relations Press, 2001); Jessica Stern, *The Ultimate Terrorists* (Harvard University Press, 1999); Graham Allison, *Nuclear Terrorism: The Ultimate Preventable Catastrophe* (Times Books, 2004); and Zbigniew Brzezinski, *The Choice: Global Domination or Global Leadership* (Basic Books, 2005).

ISSUE 18

Is Religious and Cultural Extremism a Global Security Threat?

YES: Hussein Solomon, from "Global Security in the Age of Religious Extremism," *PRISM* (August 2006)

NO: Shibley Telhami, from "Testimony Before the House Armed Services Committee: Between Terrorism and Religious Extremism" (November 3, 2005)

ISSUE SUMMARY

YES: Solomon argues that when religious extremism, which is a security threat in and of itself, is merged with state power, the threat to global security is potentially catastrophic and must be met with clear and uncompromising policies. He contends that this is present across all religions, and he uses both a born-again George Bush and a fundamentalist Mahmoud Ahmadinejad as his examples.

NO: Telhami, on the other hand, does not argue that religious extremism is the threat, but rather that global security threats are from political groups with political agendas and not extremism as such.

Religious and cultural extremism has been a part of the global landscape for millennia. Since the dawn of civilization, groups of people have defined themselves by their language, religious beliefs, race, and other factors distinguishing their culture from "the other." Once this occurred, conflicts over resources, land, and allegiances began and have continued to varying degrees. Religion as a catalyst for this conflict has always been present particularly in Europe, the Middle East, and Asia throughout the Greek—Roman period and the Middle Ages.

While religious and cultural extremism is not a new force, the methods of idea dissemination and the speed with which groups can connect certainly are. Today in the age of globalization, religious extremism has a variety of mediums through which it can transmit its messages and as such, appears at least, to be a very potent force. This is certainly true in the Islamic world. Fundamentalist Islam has seized the mantle of religious extremism even though there are such extremists among all major religious groups. The increasing radicalism of the Palestinian movement combined with the high-profile acts of al-Qaeda has underscored this perception. The concept of martyrdom has now permeated the extremist culture such that suicide attacks, be they in a Jerusalem school or at the World Trade Center, are offered as pure manifestations of allegiance to one's faith. While it is often difficult to extract the political and economic motivations of these groups from their religious zealotry, one dimension is clear. Whatever the real politick motives of the leaders of these groups may be, the rank and file truly believe that they are martyrs in a cause ordained and blessed by their God.

The globalization of media in all of its forms has transformed more localized fundamentalist extremism into global movements with reach through every computer terminal and into the home of every disgruntled believer. As such, extremist cells have emerged throughout the world with a small, but highly motivated, minority of believers committed to violence as their only means of political and social expression. While the highest profile acts appear to be committed by Islamic fundamentalists, all faiths possess such zealotry and have examples of violence in the name of "pure belief."

With this reality comes the prevalence and proliferation of weaponry, be it biological, chemical, or nuclear that can transform an extremist act from local to global in seconds.

In the following section, two noted scholars argue whether it is religious extremism or simply political goals that are the security threat. Dr. Soloman contends that when religious extremism is combined with state power in any system, violence, conflict, and death will follow. He makes the controversial argument that a George Bush with his fundamentalist Christian beliefs and Mahmoud Ahmadinejad with his Islamic fundamentalism present global security threats. He contends that their fundamentalism when merged with instruments of state power leads to abuses, conflict, and death for their own citizens and innocents in arenas of conflict.

Shibley Telhami presents the case that states and interests compete and extremism, in and of itself, is not the culprit. He argues that the extremism of the Iranian regime or al-Qaeda is not what makes them a threat but rather the anti-western sentiment that they have tapped into. Their goals and interests combined with a willingness to engage in violent terrorism constitutes the security threat and not the fact that they have a religious base.

YES

Hussein Solomon

Global Security in the Age of Religious Extremism

A World Caught between Hope and Despair

We live in a world fecund with both hope and despair. Images of hope are aplenty. From Ireland, comes the story of the Irish Republican Army (IRA) formally giving up its armed struggle. From the Gaza strip, we see Israel's evacuation of Jewish settlers from occupied Palestinian land; and from Kashmir we witness rapprochement and reconciliation overcoming the enmity and quest for vengeance of the past. At the same time there is despair; which emanates from the fact that religion, which brings meaning to one's life and preaches peace, love and generosity has morphed into something ugly and violent. In Japan, we have seen Aum Shinrikyo (the Supreme Truth) cult release sarin gas in Tokyo's subways. From India's Gujarat State, we saw Hindu fundamentalists kill hundreds of their fellow Muslim citizens. In northern Uganda, Joseph Kony and his Christian fundamentalist Lord's Resistance Army aim to overthrow the secular government of Yoweri Museveni and to replace it with a government observant of the biblical Ten Commandments. In the process, the commandment "Thou Shall Not Kill" has been violated thousands of times. From the United States, we see people motivated by strong Christian principles bombing abortion clinics or federal buildings as in the case of Timothy McVeigh—the infamous Oklahoma bomber. The world has also witnessed Jewish fundamentalism in the form of Yigal Amir's assassination of former Israeli Prime Minister Yitzhak Rabin after he signed the Oslo Peace Accords. The rise of a violent Islamic fundamentalism was vividly illustrated by the tragic events of 9/11 in New York and Washington and by the atrocities committed more recently in Amman, Jordan.

While the violent religious fundamentalism of these non-state actors constitute a grave threat to national, regional and international security—this article will focus rather on the threat posed by state-sanctioned religious fundamentalism. The underlying premise here is that when religious extremists capture state power, the threat posed to international security is infinitely worse than that posed by non-state actors given the control that

From *PRISM* (www.e-prism.org), August 2006. Copyright © 2006 by Hussein Solomon. Reprinted by permission of the author.

they can now exercise over the resources of the state. Two cases illustrate the point well: the United States under George W. Bush and Iran under Mahmoud Ahmadinejad.

George W. Bush Finds God

In 1985 George W. Bush found God by way of a Bible study group and studied the scriptures intensely for the next two years. In the process he developed an ideology, which dovetailed neatly with the mentality of the conservative evangelicals in the US. Later when he decided to run for public office, his political strategist Karl Rove drew the link between Bush's Christian beliefs and the evangelical sector. This proved to be an immensely successful strategy given the evangelical voting bloc—one in three American Christians call themselves evangelical. To put it another way, there are 80 million born-again Christians of voting age in the United States—George W. Bush is one of them. As he prepared for elections first as Governor and later for the presidency, whilst others candidates spoke about their political platform, Bush spoke about his faith. Thus when a reporter asked him who his favourite philosopher was, Bush replied: "*Christ, because he changed my heart.*" Using religion to get elected, however, was one thing; acting on those strong Christian beliefs as president is quite another. Yet this is exactly what the Christian right sought to achieve—after all, their man occupied the White House. Their efforts ranged across the social spectrum from the issue of euthanasia to same sex marriage to the teaching of intelligent design (another term for creationism) as opposed to evolution in school textbooks.

However, it is perhaps in the realm of foreign policy that the religious views of George Bush hold the greatest menace. For one thing, he subscribes to Manichaeism that divides reality into Absolute Good and Absolute Evil. Juan Stam notes that the Christian Church rejected this as heretical many centuries ago. Yet, time and time again George W. Bush uses this rather simple dichotomy of good versus evil. The U.S. and its allies are good and have been 'called' by God to serve as his instrument against the evildoers. On the other hand—the other side is described as the "Axis of Evil". Such a simplistic dichotomy is extremely problematic. First, does Iran and North Korea really have so much in common with one another that one lumps them together? Second, using phrases like "Axis of Evil" suggest that a regime, a country or a set of countries are merely evil but does not point to the level of factionalism occurring inside a country or how one might capitalise on it to serve one's own national interest. To sum up then "Axis of Evil" is a primitive and simple term for a complex world that is characterised less by black and white and more by shades of grey.

Beyond the terminology however there are even more serious problems with George W. Bush occupying the Oval Office and this relates to the idea that God speaks to him. Arnon Regular writing in Israel's *Haaretz* newspaper reported that when George Bush met with then Palestinian Prime Minister Abbas in Aqaba he said: "*God told me to strike at Al-Qaeda and I struck them and then He instructed me to strike at Saddam, which I did, and now I am determined to solve the problem in the Middle East"*. Such statements do irreparable harm to US policy in the Middle East. How does one promote secular democracies in the Middle East when the President of the United States is himself undermining the First Amendment as it relates to the separation of Church and State?

Meanwhile Ira Chernus raised other objections against such a statement: *"If he truly believes that he hears the voice of God, there is no telling what God might say tomorrow. This is a man who can launch the world's biggest arsenal of weapons of mass destruction—biological, chemical, and nuclear at any moment. . . . When the President let's God tell him what to do, it violates the spirit of democracy. In a democracy, it is the people, not God who make the decisions. The president is supposed to represent the will of the people. Yes, he must seek the best advice he can get and use his own best judgement. That means relying on facts, intelligent analysis, and rational thought—not divine inspiration. Once the President lets God's voice replace the human mind, we are back in the Middle Ages, back in the very situation our revolution was supposed to get us out of."*

Professor Ira Chernus' perspective was echoed almost fifty years previously by that formidable First Lady, Eleanor Roosevelt: *"Anyone who knows history, particularly the history of Europe, will, I think, recognize that the domination of education or of government by any one particular religious faith is never a good arrangement for the people."*

Throughout the Afghan and Iraqi wars, President Bush did not shy away from identifying God with his own project. Thus when he appeared in his flight suit on the aircraft carrier Abraham Lincoln, he said to US troops: *"And wherever you go, you carry a message of hope—a message that is ancient and ever new. In the words of the prophet Isaiah, 'To the captives, come out! To those who are in darkness, be free'!"* It should be noted that Bush's use of God and the Bible is unprecedented in US political history and stands in sharp contrast to, for instance, President Abraham Lincoln. During the American Civil War, Lincoln did not claim that God was on his side. Indeed in his famous second inaugural address, he said that the war was a curse on both armies.

Mahmoud Ahmadinejad and the Mahdi

June 2005 witnessed the election of Mahmoud Ahmadinejad as President of the Islamic Republic of Iran. Amongst the people voting for him some cited his anti-corruption stance, others his desire to better the lot of the common Iranian man and woman, and still others his piety. Few could have guessed where this piety was to lead him and Iran as soon as he assumed the presidency. For one thing, the delicate balance between conservatives and reformists that the regime sought to preserve has been destroyed with Ahmadinejad's election. Before the June elections, Iran's supreme leader Ayatollah Ali Khamenei, stated that: *". . . the existence of two factions [conservative and reformist] serves the regime, like the two wings of a bird."* But Ahmadinejad has been removing reformists as well as those conservatives allied to his political rivals from positions of power and has been replacing them with incompetent cronies who share his ideological vision. The political establishment in Tehran is bound to experience further shocks following the announcement by Ahmadinejad's spiritual advisor, the extremist Ayatollah Mohammed Taqi Mesbah-Yazdi, that ". . . *with a true Islamic government at hand, Iran has no need for future elections.*" The delicate balance that Ayatollah Khamenei has sought to preserve has been utterly destroyed.

At this point it might be useful to ask what this pious ideological vision that Ahmadinejad subscribes to is. Much of his vision relates to his devotion to the 12th Imam, also known as the Mahdi who vanished in 941. According to Shiite Muslims this Imam will return at the end of time to lead an era of Islamic justice. The fact that Ahmadinejad fervently believes in this should not be viewed as a problem. The fact that President Ahmadinejad is prepared to act out on this belief as Iranian President should be cause for alarm. As mayor of Tehran, Ahmadinejad refurbished a major boulevard on the grounds that the Mahdi was to travel along it upon his return. Similarly, soon after winning the presidency, Ahmadinejad allocated the equivalent of 12 million British pounds of government funds to enlarge the shrine and mosque of the Mahdi. Diverting public funds in this manner, from pressing social needs towards the "imminent" return of an Imam who has not made his appearance in eleven centuries, borders on either the criminal or the insane.

However, it is not only at the level of social expenditure that the Mahdi intrudes on Ahmadinejad's thoughts. Indeed, Ahmadinejad believes in reorienting the country's economic, cultural and political policies based on the Mahdi's return and judgement day. Moreover, the urgency to reorient the country's policies emanates from Ahmadinejad's belief that the Hidden Imam will appear in two years. How he knows that the Mahdi will appear in two years time is anyone's guess though some supporters of the Iranian President suggest that he must have heard it from the Mahdi himself. Ahmadinejad was also quite prepared to share his penetrating insights with the world when he addressed the United Nations in September calling for the reappearance of the Imam.

Nevertheless, Ahmadinejad's address to the UN General Assembly was memorable for other reasons as well. When recounting his address to Ayatollah Javadi Amoli, one of Iran's leading clerics, Ahmadinejad stated that he felt that there was a light around him during his entire address at the podium "*during which time the world leaders did not blink. They were astonished as if a hand held them there and made them sit. It had opened their eyes and ears for the message of the Islamic Republic.*" Some commentators have taken this mysticism of the Iranian President seriously and wonder if him saying these things serve a political purpose—transforming Ahmadinejad into the instrument of the Mahdi thereby placing him above political reproach. In that case, the comment by Ayatollah Mesbah-Yazdi on there not being a need for future elections does fit into this broader political strategy.

Ahmadinejad's strong belief in the imminent return of the Mahdi does hold grave foreign policy implications. The fact that the Mahdi will only return at the End Times—a period characterised by intense international turmoil, is in itself instructive and may help to explain Ahmadinejad's foreign policy. Some analysts commented on how unfazed he was following the tremendous international outcry after he stated that Israel should be wiped off the map. However, from his ideological position both his statement and the reaction to it only contributed to the intense international turmoil that is a necessary precondition for the reappearance of the Mahdi. In that sense any punitive measures embarked upon by the international community would, rather than prompting a moderation of Tehran's current bellicose foreign policy, prompt the hawks around Ahmadinejad to congratulate themselves on a job well done. Moreover, such punitive measures may also serve to push moderates in Iran into the camp of Ahmadinejad, not because they share his ideology, but in order to provide a united front in defence of the national interest.

The Response

So how does one defeat the religious fundamentalists occupying high office? The first thing to realise is that, whilst both Bush and Ahmadinejad need to be neutralised in that as presidents of their respective countries they have tremendous power in order to engage in their religious fantasies, we should not personalise the issue either. Both Bush and Ahmadinejad head up powerful constituencies who share the beliefs of their president. The Reverend Pat Robertson calling for the removal of Venezuelan President Hugo Chavez illustrates the point well. Thus the ideology of the movement that has brought them into high office needs to be delegitimised by their co-religionists. This is already happening in both the US and Iran.

In the US, clerics like Fritz Ritsch, Presbyterian minister in Bethesda, Maryland are deeply offended by Bush's simple dichotomy of good and evil and the characterisation that the US is on the side of angels. As he stated: *"It is by no means certain that we are as pure as the driven snow or that our international policy is so pure."* Indeed nearly all the mainstream Churches, including Bush's own United Methodists are opposed to the war in Iraq. Meanwhile, academics, journalists, and various civil society groupings in the US have started opposing various aspects of the agenda of the Christian right. Amongst the most prominent of these has been former US President Jimmy Carter. In his latest book entitled *Our Endangered Values: America's Moral Crisis* Carter, a devout Southern Baptist, raised serious concerns about the religious right's openly political agenda. He also argues that their open hostility to a range of sinners from homosexuals to the federal judiciary run counter to America's democratic freedom. Finally he calls for a clear separation of Church and State.

In Iran, too, the religious, academic and political establishment have taken on Ahmadinejad in a dramatic way. Akbar Alami, an Iranian legislator, has questioned the President's claims of being surrounded by an aura of light, noting that not even Islam's holiest figures have made such claims. Ayatollah Mohammed Ali Abtahi, a former vice president, expressed his concern with the use of religious slogans and Ayatollah Yusuf Saanei urged: *"We should rule the country according to Islamic law, but we should not use religious ideas in politics. Even Ayatollah Khomeini did not believe we should do this."* Professor Hamid Reza Jalaipour at Tehran University also casts doubt on the broader politico-religious project of the President: *"The question is, can his reliance on Imam Mahdi be turned into a political ideology? I don't think so. Even the leading theologians in Qum do not take these allusions seriously."*

The second aspect of a response relates to neutralising the incumbent politically. In the US, this process is well advanced and George W. Bush has been transformed into a lame-duck president. What is interesting is that Republicans have also turned against their president as they vote with the Democrats. From Plamegate and Scooter Libby to the spiralling deficit, to the war in Iraq, and to the issue of illegal wiretaps, the Bush Administration is under extreme pressure. In recent weeks, the Administration suffered two humiliating setbacks. The first relates to it accepting the anti-torture amendment proposed by Republican Senator John McCain after initially making clear its objection to it. This underscores the weakness of the Bush Administration at this moment. Second, Bush and his fellow hawks had to fight tooth and nail to get the Patriot Act renewed. In the process major concessions were made on the part of the Administration.

In Iran, too, the process of vigorously neutralising President Ahmadinejad has begun. Inside the country, Ahmadinejad has been criticised for his seeming lack of tact and his confrontational style. For instance, shortly after Ahmadinejad's statement that Israel should be wiped off the map, Ali Akbar Rafsanjani, a former Iranian President and currently a major ally of Ayatollah Khamenei, stated at Friday prayers in Tehran: *"We have no problems with the Jews and highly respect Judaism as a holy religion."* Those opposed to Ahmadinejad's bellicose foreign policy have also established discreet back-channel contacts with the Americans over Iran's nuclear programme.

The Iranian Parliament has also moved to politically neutralise Ahmadinejad in two ways, firstly, by undermining his populist political programme. In this regard it has already dismantled the centrepiece of Ahmadinejad's populist programme—the Imam Reza Care Fund that sought to provide interest-free loans for young people to marry as well as various employment programmes. Second, parliament has sought to weaken the President and strengthen the hand of Ayatollah Khamenei. For instance, the Speaker of Parliament, Gholamali Haddad-Adel urged support for the concept of *Velayat-e-Faqih* (leadership of the supreme jurisprudent), introduced by Ayatollah Khomeini. However Ayatollah Khamenei is also taking active measures to weaken Ahmadinejad. Recently he gave the Expediency Council, a 32-member non-elected political arbitration body sweeping new powers to supervise parliament, the judiciary and the executive. This body is headed up by Rafsanjani. More ominously for Ahmadinejad, the Expediency Council's secretary, Mohsen Razaie, announced: *"The adjudication of the Expediency Council is the final word. And even if other state actors do not agree with it, it is still the final word and they have to accept that.*" Here it is interesting to note that Razaie used to be the commander of the Islamic Revolutionary Guard Corps (IRGC). This has led some commentators to believe that the senior echelons of the Revolutionary Guards may still be loyal to Ayatollah Khamenei as opposed to Ahmadinejad.

The third response has been to capitalise on the failure of the incumbent, thereby neutralising him further. Iraq has been such a failure for the Bush Administration. According to US statistics, 2,071 US soldiers have lost their lives and 16,000 others were wounded. Moreover, 39 percent of soldiers returning from Iraq are suffering from psychological trauma. In addition to the human costs, the Iraq and Afghanistan wars have already cost the American taxpayer $300 billion. Seen in the light of the US budget deficit, these economic costs are staggering. Opponents of the Bush Administration— Republican and Democrat—have been quick to attack and they have pressed Bush for a timetable for the withdrawal of US troops from Iraq. The senior military echelons have also voiced their concern on the sustainability of current troop levels in Iraq vis-à-vis securing other US interests. Failure in Iraq has certainly tempered the messianic zeal of Bush's foreign policy hawks. Thus their approach to the nuclear programme of Tehran and the already nuclear-armed Pyongyang regime has been radically different to that of Baghdad under Saddam Hussein when they refused to give Hans Blix and his nuclear weapons inspectors more time.

Whilst it is still early days for the Ahmadinejad administration, it is equally clear that a strategy of setting the incumbent up for failure that would then be used against him is being pursued. Consider the way the Iranian parliament has been dismantling aspects of Ahmadinejad's populist programme as described above. Whilst Ayatollah Khamenei's supporters may hope that this might undermine Ahmadinejad in the eyes of his supporters in that he will be unable to make good on his promises, it is equally clear that such a strategy is a high risk one. Ahmadinejad might well fail in his social programme and this might well anger his support base. However Ahmadinejad could also direct this popular anger towards parliament, towards Ayatollah Khamenei and Rafsanjani. In the process, he could become stronger.

We also need to realise that Ahmadinejad is not simply passively allowing these machinations against him to take place. He has also gone on the offensive against his political rivals. For instance, he has recently purged the upper echelons of Iran's diplomatic corps. According to some reports, these may number as many as 40 of Iran's senior diplomats. These were inevitably allies of Rafsanjani or others who were appointed by the reformist Ayatollah Mohammed Khatami, Ahmadinejad's predecessor. Even more disconcerting is the fact that, amongst those purged were Iran's ambassadors to London, Paris, Geneva, Berlin and Kuala Lumpur. This has resulted in Ed Blanche speculating on whether the purge of these particular diplomats was also an attempt on the part of Ahmadinejad to close the back-channel contacts existing between Tehran and Washington.

Conclusion

As this titanic power struggle continues in Tehran, there are deeper questions that need to be posed in the short-to-medium term. In the medium term, we do believe that the political power of the religious right-wing in the US will weaken as developments deteriorate in Iraq, Afghanistan and elsewhere, such as Latin America where we have seen the roll-back of American influence most dramatically in Evo Morales' Bolivia and Hugo Chavez' Venezuela. Indeed some pollsters are comparing George Bush's low popularity ratings with those of President Nixon at the time of the Watergate scandal. More importantly, the United States was established as a secular state and increasingly we see prominent individuals like President Carter as well as a plethora of civil society groups fighting back for the secular state promised in the US Constitution and the Bill of Rights. They seem to be winning the battle.

It is a very different situation in Iran. The 1979 Iranian revolution established a theocratic state that, in its current composition, cannot be secular. Nor, indeed can it be democratic. To understand this, we need to understand the fundamental split between Shiites and Sunnis in Islam. The democratic tradition is strong in Islam. Concepts such as freedom (*hurriyyah*), equality (*musawat*) and justice (*'adl*) are all intrinsic to the Qur'an. The fact that the first caliph after Prophet Muhammad's death in 632 C.E. was elected by majority consensus by a council of various Muslim tribes is ample proof of the democratic credentials of Islam. But this very election of the first Caliph saw the split between Sunnis and Shiites. Shiites broke away from mainstream Muslims after the election of the first Caliph since they wanted Imam Ali who was the cousin and son-in-law of Prophet Muhammad to succeed as Caliph. The majority (Sunnis) did not vote for Ali on the basis of his youth and inexperience. Thus the very origins of Shi'ism as a political doctrine lay in its anti-democratic foundations.

These anti-democratic foundations have been built upon by Ayatollah Khomeini, the founder of the Islamic Republic in 1979 when he established such concepts as the *Velayat-e-Faqih* or Leadership of the Supreme Jurisprudent. This concept has more in common with Plato's Philosopher-King and the Divine Right of Kings in the Middle Ages than with Islamic political thought and serves no other purpose than to consolidate the power of the ruling mullahs over a hapless population. It is important to understand this structure of the Iranian state in order to understand the limitation of reform of the state itself. This limitation was patently obvious during the presidency of Ahmadinejad's predecessor, Ayatollah Khatami. Despite him stressing moderation and a dialogue of civilizations as opposed to clash of civilizations, the reform movement foundered on the bedrock of a totalitarian theocratic state. One should also bear in mind that even without Ahmadinejad, the Iranian state will continue to be a source of insecurity to its own people as well as to the region—notice here Tehran's support for Hamas and Hezbollah.

In the short-term the most troubling aspect relates to Iran's nuclear programme. Whilst the Iranian regime stresses that their nuclear programme is for civilian purposes, as Mohammed El-Khawas notes the problem is that much of the technology used for civilian power generation could also be used for weapons as well. However the problem goes beyond merely dual use technology in that the Iranian government did conceal its nuclear programme for eighteen years. It should be noted here that failure to notify the International Atomic Energy Agency (IAEA) is a clear breach of Iran's nuclear obligations under the Nuclear Non-Proliferation Treaty (NPT). Iran also failed to disclose to the IAEA all its uranium enrichment facilities. Other worrying indicators that Tehran may not be interested in nuclear energy for purely civilian purposes are the fact that *". . . IAEA inspectors discovered traces of highly enriched uranium far above the levels needed for civilian use".* Moreover, El-Khawas also notes that Iran is building the infrastructure for nuclear weapons production like the heavy-water reactor at Arak that can produce plutonium.

   Still another reason to hold a somewhat sceptical stance towards the Iranian regime lies in the cat-and-mouse game it has been playing with the IAEA. In November 2004, for instance, Tehran agreed in Paris to freeze its entire uranium enrichment programme until a long-term agreement was reached. Some weeks later, however, when UN inspectors tried to confirm Iran's compliance with the suspension, they were not permitted to put UN seals on some enrichment equipment at Natanz. These developments clearly do not inspire confidence in the regime. In the final instance, the international community cannot allow President Ahmadinejad's bellicose regime to possess nuclear weapons. More so, the international community cannot allow a man who believes in the return of the Mahdi and with him the End Times in two years time. The international community cannot allow a man who believes that a halo of light surrounds him to have his finger on a nuclear button.

Testimony Before the House Armed Services Committee Between Terrorism and Religious Extremism

Let me say at the outset that the gravest threat to the United States today is neither Islamic groups nor Islamic fundamentalism as such. The central threat facing the United States of America is the threat of catastrophic terror by al-Qaeda and its allies. The nature of this threat justifies the allocation of significant resources to counter the threat and defeat al-Qaeda and its allies. But we must be very careful in identifying who the core enemy is and not waste resources and energies on strategies that do not confront the primary threat, and worse yet, could backfire.

First, while we must oppose all terrorism, and we have many local enemies in various parts of the world, most such enemies do not pose the kind of catastrophic threat that al-Qaeda does, and thus do not warrant the kind of resources that could take away from our effort to directly confront the primary threat.

Second, although religious extremism is something most of us would oppose, we have to be very careful not to jump to the conclusion that the threat to the United States stems from religious extremism as such. We have extremists all over the world, as we do in our own country, but most of them do not seek to cause catastrophic harm to us and most do not have the capacity or the support to do so even if they wanted to.

Third, al-Qaeda presents such a high threat to the United States primarily for three reasons: Unlike most local extremist groups around the world, it has a demonstrated capacity to organize on a global scale and a demonstrated global reach. As a non-state actor, it is not sensitive to deterrence and thus is capable of being maximally reckless in its operations and thus poses the potential for catastrophic attacks that are limited only by its capabilities. And while it may care about local issues in the Muslim world, in the end its agenda is broader and more dangerous and could thus not be realistically satisfied by political means. In the end, it is reasonable to conclude that al-Qaeda does aim to overthrow the existing political order in the Muslim world and replace it with a Taliban-like fanatical order, and it sees the United States as the anchor of the existing order.

From "Testimony Before the House Armed Services Committee Between Terrorism and Religious Extremism," November 3, 2005.

But it is wrong and even dangerous to assume that this aim of al-Qaeda is their primary strength, or that it is the primary reason some in the Muslim countries have expressed sympathy with it. It is also wrong to assume that most Muslim groups, including local extremist groups, share its objectives. We must differentiate above all what we see as pervasive unfavorable views in the Muslim world from the views of al-Qaeda and like-minded groups. We must also differentiate between the causes of anti-Americanism and the causes of al-Qaeda terrorism. If we don't, we risk helping push vastly diverse groups together in a way that undermines our effort to defeat al-Qaeda.

It is no secret that the United States has faced significant resentment in the past few years in Muslim countries. Is this a consequence of a rising clash of values that plays into the strengths of al-Qaeda? Most public opinion surveys in Arab and Muslim countries indicate otherwise. In my most recent survey completed October 24th, 2005, (with Zogby International) among 3900 Arabs in Saudi Arabia, Egypt, the United Arab Emirates, Jordan, Lebanon, and Morocco, 78 percent say that they base their views on American policies and only 12 percent say they base them on values. When given a number of Western, Muslim, and other non-Western countries to choose from as possible places to live or send family members to study, most of them name Western European countries or the US and those who name the other countries, including Muslim Pakistan, are in the single digit.

More importantly the cause of the sympathy that some have for al-Qaeda is vastly different from al-Qaeda's own aims: When asked what aspects of al-Qaeda, if any, they sympathize with most, only six percent said they sympathize with the aim of establishing a Taliban-like state, and only seven percent sympathized with al-Qaeda's methods. On the other hand, 35 percent said they sympathize with its standing up to the US and another 19 percent said they sympathize with its stand on behalf of Muslim causes such as the issue of Palestine. Twenty-six percent said "none."

These results are bolstered by other findings. Contrary to the Taliban world view, the vast majority of Arabs (88 percent), including in Saudi Arabia, want women to have the right to work outside the home either always or when economically necessary. That is precisely why al-Qaeda primarily highlights issues that resonate with the public in its recruitment tapes and strategies, such as Iraq, Palestine, and authoritarianism. Even those who oppose the US presence in Iraq and want to see the US defeated do not wish to have Abu Musaab al-Zarqawi as their ruler. That is not what they wish for their own children.

It is dangerous to have a high level of resentment of the United States, whatever its sources, not only because it may increase the ability of al-Qaeda and its allies to recruit, but also because people's incentives to help the United States to effectively combat the threat of al-Qaeda diminishes. If they resent us more than they fear al-Qaeda, our challenge increases dramatically. If they start believing, as most have, that one of our real aims is to weaken the Muslim world, not just to defeat al-Qaeda, al-Qaeda gains by default.

What are the issues for most Muslims in their attitudes toward the U.S.? What makes a difference in bridging the gap? Before I make some ending remarks on this issue, allow me to note that the Muslim world is not the only place where resentment of the United States runs high today, so some of the answers are not particular to the Muslim world and may have to do with the role of the United States in the current international system. But in the Arab and Muslim world there are some specific issues that we can identify.

From the public opinion surveys that I have conducted in the Middle East, the single most important demographic variable in the Arab world explaining unfavorable views of the United States was income. It speaks volumes about the rampant poverty and unemployment, linked to poor education, which must be confronted.

Second, regional issues are paramount. Iraq is certainly central, but the Palestinian-Israeli conflict remains the "prism of pain" through which Arabs see the United States. This speaks to the need for active American diplomacy to resolve regional conflict.

Third, Zogby International polls have shown clearly that those who have visited the United States or studied here, and those who have had other encounters with Americans in the region, were far more disposed to having a favorable opinion of the United States than those who didn't. This speaks to the need for major public diplomacy programs to encourage interactions.

In the end, we must define the central enemy correctly. It is primarily al-Qaeda and its allies as organizations that must be defeated. It is not terrorism broadly and it is not Islamism broadly. Terrorism is not an ideology, and al-Qaeda's ideology of seeking a Taliban-like world order is its source of weakness in the Muslim world, not its source of strength. Our strategy must isolate it by addressing the issues that most Muslims care about—not blur the distinction between the vast majorities with whom we have no principled quarrel and those few whose aims can never be reconciled with America's.

Allow me to end on a cautionary note. In broadly defining the threat as "Islamic extremism" without specifying what we mean exactly, we risk much. In fighting serious threats like that posed by al-Qaeda there is certainly a need to rely in part on significant covert operations as well as overt ones. But, there have recently been reports of the possible broadening of such operations to include extremist groups, leaders, and clergy. My worry is that we do not have, and probably never will, the kind of expertise that allows us to determine who's a friend and who's an enemy simply on the basis of utterances. One could end up targeting as suspects millions of people in a world of 1.2 billion Muslims. Given the deficient expertise in our bureaucracies in the languages, religions, and cultures of the Muslim world, we risk the chance of mistakes that could backfire, relying on locals who have their own agendas, and wasting precious resources. The strategy in the first place must remain focused on the operational and the logistical, not on what people say.

POSTSCRIPT

Is Religious and Cultural Extremism a Global Security Threat?

The events of 9/11 did not happen in a vacuum. They are merely one of several thousand acts of terrorism and violence perpetrated by groups bent on destroying their perceived enemy for professed reasons of faith. Clearly, anyone who is a victim of such attacks identifies the attacker as a threat to their security and, of course, global security. The central issues or questions arising from this are as follow:

- Is it religious and cultural extremism that fuels these attacks on security or merely geopolitical interests couched as faith?
- Do the organizers of these actions like Osama bin Laden and others really believe their rhetoric?
- Is this violence any more or less pronounced than it has been in the past and thus is it truly an emerging global security threat, or is it merely a continuing historical threat from the global fringe?

Scholars have been researching cultural and religious extremism for decades. The work is usually cyclical and results from the ebbs and flows of violence perpetrated by such groups. Whether it is Christian, Hindu, Muslim, or Jewish extremism fueling attacks on "non-believers," the focus is always on whether this behavior is growing, is it in response to external threats, and is it state sanctioned. Solomon argues with some persuasiveness that when political leaders develop devout fundamentalist views, they tend to be willing to engage in "extreme," that is, violent behavior to promote their perceived righteousness. They do this with all of the instruments of state power and, of course, are able to couch their policies as consistent with the national interest. His argument that Bush and Ahmadinejad share these dimensions and thus lead their countries to extremist policies bears further objective analysis. Yet it is still difficult to disentangle belief systems from policy decisions. We may believe that a Bush or Ahmadinejad used his spiritual fundamentalism as the central gyroscope on which all decisions are based; but in the final analysis we may never know.

Telhami tends to take a more real politic perspective when he contends that we must objectively analyze Islamic extremism for what it is and who it represents or, more importantly, the vast majority that it does not represent. It is al-Qaeda as a political organization that is the enemy, not Islam or fundamentalism per se? The rhetoric that we use and the tools that we employ must realize this fact and be consistent with it, lest we fuel religious "holy wars" that are frankly neither.

Ultimately, the question of whether religious or cultural extremism is a global security threat rests not with how we define such extremism or who believes what. It may simply be a function of two objective dimensions of a globalizing society. One is the ability of extremist groups to have global projection through technology and thus activate like-minded souls and second the prevalence of weapons of mass destruction that, if allowed to fall into extremist hands, will most definitely pose a grave threat to global security.

The experience of the cold war tells us that rational, national interest usually wins out over mass destruction; the Cuban Missile Crisis is the quintessential example. But can anyone argue that rational self-interest will guide al-Qaeda zealots or anti-abortion activists or Jewish extremists when confronting their perceived enemies and possessing of nuclear or biological weapons? The likelihood of that catastrophe clarifies the question of extremism as a security threat and that is merely a function of weapons possession.

Some interesting work in this area includes Sam Harris' controversial argument regarding religion and terror, *The End of Faith: Religion, Terror and the Future of Reason* (W.W. Norton & Company, 2004) and Christopher Hutchins, *God is Not Great: How Religion Poisons Everything* (Warner Books, 2007). In addition, take a look at Mark Juergensmeyer's, *Terror in the Mind of God: The Global Rise of Religious Violence* (University of California Press, 2003) and J. P. Larsson's, *Understanding Religious Violence: Thinking Outside the Box on terrorism* (Ashgate Publishing, 2004).

ISSUE 19

Is a Nuclear Iran a Global Security Threat?

YES: U.S. House of Representatives Permanent Select Committee on Intelligence Subcommittee on Intelligence Policy, from "Recognizing Iran as a Strategic Threat: An Intelligence Challenge for the United States" (August 23, 2006)

NO: Office of Director of National Intelligence, from "Iran: Nuclear Intentions and Capabilities," *National Intelligence Estimate* (November 2007)

ISSUE SUMMARY

YES: The House Select Committee concludes that Iran's weapons program and missile development technology combined with the nature of fundamentalist regimes pose a grave security threat and thus must be addressed.

NO: The National Intelligence Estimate contends that Iran is not a global security threat because they have decided to suspend their nuclear weapons program and would not be able to develop the capacity for such weapons until at least 2015.

The issue of nuclear proliferation has been a global concern since the first atomic explosion at Alamogordo, New Mexico, in 1945. That event ushered in a new era in weaponry, war, strategy, and tactics that still resonates today. Each successive nuclear power and the proclaimed nuclear club of states (the United States, Russia, China, Great Britain, France, India, Pakistan) and unproclaimed countries (Israel, South Africa) have been deeply aware of the issue of proliferation. In fact, all of these states, to one degree or another, have largely agreed on the need to maintain the smallness of the nuclear club.

The fall of the Soviet Union did much to change the dynamics of nuclear proliferation policy. Essentially, many regional states with interests opposed to the United States now saw no countervailing superpower to protect their interests and thus faced a bandwagon or balancing dilemma.

Do we move toward the United States as the preeminent power to satisfy our interests or balance against it by developing our own regional weapon deterrent to U.S. hegemony? States across the globe chose either of these approaches and acted accordingly. Iran in rhetoric and actions has chosen the path of balancing against U.S. policy interests in a myriad of ways. They have supported groups opposed to U.S. policy interests, funded terrorism against Israel and the United States, and of course to some degree, pursued nuclear technology with the assistance of the French, Russians, and others.

In the following section, the U.S. government through two separate branches articulates the dichotomy of views regarding Iran as a global security threat. The House Select Committee report argues that Iran may indeed be the gravest threat to global security should they achieve nuclear status, which the report clearly argues they are committed to doing. They piece together Iranian rhetoric, policy positions, intelligence, and supposition to contend that Iran poses the gravest of threats to U.S. interests and thus to global security. The National Intelligence Estimate, which was released earlier this year, argues that Iran has suspended its nuclear program and as such does not pose a grave security threat and will not do so for the foreseeable future should they maintain their current course.

While both analyses agree that Iran pursues interests antithetical to the U.S. policy, they have different conclusions regarding Iran's current level of security threat and future scenarios.

YES ↵

Recognizing Iran as a Strategic Threat: An Intelligence Challenge for the United States

"The annihilation of the Zionist regime will come . . . Israel must be wiped off the map . . . And God willing, with the force of God behind it, we shall soon experience a world without the United States and Zionism."[1]

"They have invented a myth that Jews were massacred and place this above God, religions and the prophets."[2]

"I officially announce that Iran has joined countries with nuclear technology."[3]

—Iranian President Mahmoud Ahmadinejad

Summary

Threats against the United States and Israel by Iranian President Ahmadinejad—coupled with advances in the Iranian nuclear weapons program, support for terror, and resistance to international negotiations on its nuclear program—demonstrate that Iran is a security threat to our nation that requires high caliber intelligence support. The seriousness of the Iranian threat has been amplified by the recent rocket attacks against Israel by the Iranian-backed Lebanese terrorist group Hezbollah, which, according to press accounts, has received as many as 10,000 rockets from Iran.[4]

Director of National Intelligence John Negroponte provided his assessment in his 2006 Annual Threat Report that Iran is seeking nuclear weapons.[5] America's intelligence agencies have also assessed the following about the Iranian threat:

• Iran has conducted a clandestine uranium enrichment program for nearly two decades in violation of its International Atomic Energy Agency (IAEA) safeguards agreement, and despite its claims to the

From "Staff Report of the House Permanent Select Committee on Intelligence Subcommittee on Intelligence Policy," August 23, 2006, pp. 3–10; 11–13, 15–29. Published by the U.S. House of Representatives Permanent Select Committee on Intelligence Subcommittee on Intelligence Policy.

contrary, Iran is seeking nuclear weapons. The U.S. Intelligence Community believes that Tehran probably has not yet produced or acquired the fissile material (weapons-grade nuclear fuel) needed to produce a nuclear weapon; Director of National Intelligence John Negroponte has stated that Iran will not be "in a position to have a nuclear weapon" until "sometime between the beginning of the next decade and the middle of the next decade".[6]

- Iran likely has an offensive chemical weapons research and development capability.[7]
- Iran probably has an offensive biological weapons program.[8]
- Iran has the largest inventory of ballistic missiles in the Middle East. The U.S. Intelligence Community has raised the concern that Tehran may integrate nuclear weapons into its ballistic missiles.[9]
- Iran provides funding, training, weapons, rockets, and other material support to terrorist groups in Lebanon, the Palestinian Territories, and elsewhere.
- Elements of the Iranian national security apparatus are actively supporting the insurgency in Iraq.

Iran's August 22, 2006 letter expressing its willingness to enter into "serious negotiations" on its nuclear program presents significant challenges for U.S. policymakers who must assess Iranian intentions, the likelihood that it would abide by a new diplomatic agreement, and whether Iran would exploit a new agreement to advance its nuclear weapons program. The U.S. Intelligence Community will play an important role in helping policymakers evaluate these questions. U.S. intelligence agencies will have to devote resources to verify adherence to whatever result negotiations might produce—Iran's compliance with any agreement that may be reached, or the international community's compliance with any new trade sanctions the international community may place on Iran should efforts to use negotiations to resolve the crisis fail.

Intelligence Gaps and Why They Are Critical

Accurate and comprehensive intelligence is critical for the development of good policy. There is a great deal about Iran that we do not know. It would be irresponsible to list the specific intelligence gaps in an unclassified paper, as identifying our specific shortcomings would provide critical insights to the Iranian government. Suffice it to say, however, that the United States lacks critical information needed for analysts to make many of their judgments with confidence about Iran and there are many significant information gaps. A special concern is major gaps in our knowledge of Iranian nuclear, biological, and chemical programs. U.S. policymakers and intelligence officials believe, without exception, that the United States must collect more and better intelligence on a wide range of Iranian issues—its political dynamics, economic health, support for terrorism, the nature of its involvement in Iraq, the status of its nuclear, biological, and chemical weapons efforts, and many more topics of interest. The national security community must dedicate the personnel and resources necessary to better assess Iran's plans, capabilities, and intentions, and the Director of National Intelligence (DNI) must identify, establish, and report on intelligence goals and performance metrics to measure progress on critical fronts.

This report provides an unclassified assessment of the Iran question to help the American public understand the seriousness of the Iranian threat and to discuss ways U.S. intelligence collection and analysis against Iran must be improved.

The Nature of the Threat

Iran poses a threat to the United States and its allies due to its sponsorship of terror, probable pursuit of weapons of mass destruction, and support for the insurgency in Iraq. The profile of the Iranian threat has increased over the last year due to the election of President Mahmoud Ahmadinejad, who has made public threats against the United States and Israel, the continuation of Iranian nuclear weapons research, and the recent attacks by Hezbollah, an Iranian terrorist proxy, against Israel. Iran has provided Hezbollah with financial support and weapons, including the thousands of rockets Hezbollah fired against Israel in July and August 2006. Iran thus bears significant responsibility for the recent violence in Israel and Lebanon.

Iran's efforts since December 2005 to resume enrichment of uranium, in defiance of the international community, Tehran's willingness to endure international condemnation, isolation, and economic disruptions in order to carry out nuclear activities covertly indicate Iran is developing nuclear weapons. It is worth noting, however, that some outside experts hold another view and believe that senior Iranian leaders are divided on whether to proceed with a nuclear weapons program, and contend that some Iranian officials argue that Iran should pursue nuclear research within the guidelines of the Nuclear Non-Proliferation Treaty (NPT) so Iran can maintain international trade links.[10] These outside experts hold that until the leadership's intentions and decisions are known, it is difficult to assert with confidence that Iran is actually pursuing nuclear weapons.

A nuclear-armed Iran would pose a serious strategic threat to the United States and its allies because:

- A nuclear-armed Iran would likely embolden the leadership in Tehran to advance its aggressive ambitions in and outside of the region, both directly and through the terrorists it supports—ambitions that gravely threaten stability and the security of U.S. friends and allies.
- An Iranian leadership which believes a nuclear arsenal protects it from retaliation may be more likely to use force against U.S. forces and allies in the region, the greater Middle East, Europe, and Asia. Nuclear weapons could thus lower the threshold for Iran's use of conventional force.

The principal method Iran is pursuing at this time to produce fissile material for nuclear weapons is a process known as uranium enrichment. This method involves spinning gaseous uranium hexafluoride (UF6) in large numbers of centrifuge machines to increase the fraction of uranium-235 (U-235), the uranium isotope that can be used as weapons fuel. Naturally occurring uranium contains only a very small fraction of this isotope (0.71%), thus the need for enrichment process. Weapons-grade uranium contains about 90% U-235.

The IAEA has also uncovered evidence that Iran has pursued another route for nuclear weapons by producing plutonium. Plutonium can be separated from irradiated nuclear material such as "spent" fuel rods from a nuclear power reactor. North Korea is believed to have produced plutonium for nuclear weapons by separating plutonium from spent fuel rods.

- A nuclear-armed Iran would likely exacerbate regional tensions. Israel would find it hard to live with a nuclear armed Iran and could take military action against Iranian nuclear facilities. A deliberate or miscalculated attack by one state on the other could result in retaliation, regional unrest, and an increase in terrorist attacks.

Iran's Nuclear Weapons Program

Two decades ago, Iran embarked on a secret program to acquire the capability to produce weapons-grade nuclear material. Iran has developed an extensive infrastructure, from laboratories to industrial facilities, to support its research for nuclear weapons. Producing fissile material is a complicated process and Tehran faces several key obstacles to acquiring a nuclear capability: its inability to produce or purchase fissile material, the challenges of marrying a nuclear warhead to a missile, and the difficulty of adjusting its existing missiles to carry a nuclear payload.

Since 2002, the IAEA has issued a series of reports detailing how Iran has covertly engaged in dozens of nuclear-related activities that violate its treaty obligations to openly cooperate with the IAEA. These activities included false statements to IAEA inspectors, carrying out certain nuclear activities and experiments without notifying the IAEA, and numerous steps to deceive and mislead the IAEA.[11]

Recent Diplomatic Developments

From late 2003 until early 2006, the United Kingdom, France, and Germany (the "EU-3") attempted to find a diplomatic solution to the Iranian nuclear program that addressed unanswered questions about Tehran's nuclear activities and its lack of cooperation with the IAEA. Despite some signs of progress in 2004 and 2005, a major turning point occurred on September 24, 2005 when the IAEA Board of Governors passed a resolution concluding that Iran's "many failures and breaches" to comply with its obligations under the Nuclear Nonproliferation Treaty constituted noncompliance with the IAEA statute.[12] The resolution also expressed an "absence of confidence that Iran's nuclear program is exclusively for peaceful purposes" and called for Iran to reestablish a full and sustained suspension of uranium enrichment and reprocessing. The EU-3 effort collapsed in early 2006 when Iran defied the September 2005 IAEA resolution by announcing it would break IAEA seals placed on uranium enrichment facilities and end its moratorium on enriching uranium. As a result, on February 4, 2006, the IAEA Board of Governors reported Iran's failure to allay concerns about the nature of its nuclear program to the United Nations Security Council.[13] The Security Council met to discuss the Iranian nuclear program in March 2006 but was only able to pass a mild statement urging Iran to abide by its IAEA obligations due to opposition to tougher action by China and Russia.[14]

On June 6, 2006, Iran was presented with an incentives package backed by the United States, Russia, UK, France, and China to convince it to suspend its uranium enrichment program and begin negotiations with the EU-3 and the United States. After Iran refused to provide a clear answer as to whether or when it would respond to the offer, the UN Security Council passed Resolution 1696 on July 31, 2006 giving Iran until August 31, 2006 to fully implement a suspension of its uranium enrichment program as mandated by the IAEA Board of Governors resolution of February 4, 2006. If Iran does not comply by this date, Resolution 1696 states the Security Council's intention to take "additional measures" to compel Iran to comply. The United States is prepared to propose trade sanctions against Iran as the "additional measures."[15] Iranian President Ahmadinejad rejected Resolution 1696 on August 1, 2006, indicating that his country would not be pressured into stopping its nuclear program and stating "if some think they can still speak with threatening language to the Iranian nation, they must know that they are badly mistaken." Iran responded to the incentives package on August 22, 2006, claiming it had provided a "new formula" to resolve the dispute and was ready to enter into "serious negotiations." The details of this response were not available when this report went to press.

The recent attempt by the United States, the United Kingdom, France, and Germany to begin a new round of negotiations with Iran on ending its nuclear weapons program raises a number of difficult issues. U.S. policymakers must carefully evaluate Iran's August 22, 2006 response to the incentives package, Iranian intentions, and past behavior to make a judgment as to whether Tehran would abide by a new agreement curtailing its nuclear weapons program or would attempt to exploit a new agreement to advance its weapons program, such as by harvesting plutonium from new light water reactors an agreement might provide to Iran or continuing nuclear weapons research using the small uranium enrichment capability that EU-3 states are proposing to permit Iran to retain as part of an agreement. This evaluation will determine our participation in any negotiations and whether America could ultimately agree to be a party to a diplomatic agreement with Iran. A determination also needs to be made as to whether Iran's August 22, 2006 response addresses the requirements of UN Security Council Resolution 1696—which requires Iran to suspend its uranium enrichment program—and whether additional action by the Council, such as trade sanctions against Iran, are warranted. We expect the U.S. Intelligence Community would play an important role in assisting U.S. policymakers with these questions—including whether Iran can be trusted to abide by a diplomatic agreement—and to assess the effectiveness and implementation of trade sanctions against Iran that could be employed if diplomatic efforts fail.

Evidence for an Iranian Nuclear Weapons Program

The WMD Commission (officially known as the Commission on the Intelligence of the United States Regarding Weapons of Mass Destruction) concluded in its March 2005 unclassified report that "across the board, the Intelligence Community knows disturbingly little about the nuclear programs of many of the world's most dangerous actors."[16] American intelligence agencies do not know nearly enough about Iran's nuclear weapons program. However, based on what is known about Iranian behavior and Iranian deception efforts, the U.S. Intelligence Community assesses that Iran is intent on developing a nuclear weapons capability. Publicly available information also leads to the conclusion that Iran has a nuclear weapons program, especially taking into account the following facts:

- Iran has covertly pursued two parallel enrichment programs—a laser process based on Russian technology and a centrifuge process. The Russian government terminated cooperation with Iran on laser enrichment in 2001, following extensive consultations with the United States, and it appears to be no longer active.[17]
- In February 2004, Iran admitted to obtaining uranium centrifuge technology on the black market shortly after Dr. A.Q. Khan, the father of Pakistan's nuclear weapons program, confessed to secretly providing this technology to Iran, Libya, and North Korea.[18] Khan also sold nuclear bomb plans to Libya.[19] It is not known whether Khan sold nuclear weapon plans to Iran.
- The IAEA reported on February 27, 2006 that Iran has produced approximately 85 tons of uranium hexafluoride ($UF6$).[20] If enriched through centrifuges to weapons-grade material—a capability Iran is working hard to master—this would be enough for 12 nuclear bombs.[21]
- To produce plutonium, Iran has built a heavy water production plant and is constructing a large, heavy water-moderated reactor whose technical characteristics are well-suited for the production of weapons-grade plutonium. In support of this effort, Iran admitted in October 2003 to secretly producing small quantities of plutonium without notifying the IAEA, a violation of its treaty obligations.[22]

- The IAEA has discovered documentation in Iran for casting and machining enriched uranium hemispheres, which are directly relevant to production of nuclear weapons components.[23] The IAEA is also pursuing information on nuclear-related high-explosive tests[24] and the design of a delivery system,[25] both of which point to a military rather than peaceful purpose of the Iranian nuclear program.
- The IAEA discovered evidence in September 2003 that Iran had covertly produced the short-lived radioactive element polonium 210 (Po-210), a substance with two known uses: a neutron source for a nuclear weapon and satellite batteries. Iran told the IAEA that the polonium 210 was produced for satellite batteries but could not produce evidence for this explanation.[26] The IAEA found Iran's explanation about its polonium experiments difficult to believe, stating in a September 2004 report that "it remains, however, somewhat uncertain regarding the plausibility of the stated purpose of the experiments given the very limited applications of short lived Po-210 sources."[27] . . .

Dubious Claims and Explanations for Iran's Nuclear Activities

Iran has engaged in an extensive campaign to conceal from the IAEA and the world the true nature of its nuclear program.

- Iran claims that its nuclear program is peaceful and for civilian electricity. While there are differences among some experts as to whether Iran may have an interest in a civilian nuclear program in addition to a weapons program, recent findings by the Department of Energy make a convincing case that the Iranian nuclear program is inconsistent with the Iranian Government's stated purpose of developing civil nuclear power in order to achieve energy independence.[28] Iran's claims that its nuclear program is peaceful also is belied by its record of non-cooperation with the IAEA, its decision to pursue nuclear technology covertly, and the fact that Iran does not have enough indigenous uranium resources to fuel even one power-generating reactor over its lifetime,[29] although it does have enough uranium to make several nuclear bombs.
- Aside from Iran's lack of uranium deposits, Iran's claim that its nuclear program is for electricity production appears doubtful in light of its large oil and natural gas reserves. Iran's natural gas reserves are the second largest in the world and the energy industry estimates that Iran flares enough natural gas annually to generate electricity equivalent to the output of four Bushehr reactors. Iran's energy reserves are compared in Figure 1.

Figure 1

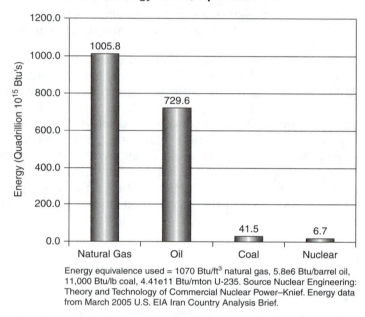

Iranian Energy Reserves by Type U.S. Department of Energy Chart, April 2006 [30]

Energy equivalence used = 1070 Btu/ft³ natural gas, 5.8e6 Btu/barrel oil, 11,000 Btu/lb coal, 4.41e11 Btu/mton U-235. Source Nuclear Engineering: Theory and Technology of Commercial Nuclear Power–Knief. Energy data from March 2005 U.S. EIA Iran Country Analysis Brief.

- Furthermore, there is no rational reason for Iran to pursue a peaceful nuclear program in secret and risk international sanctions when the International Atomic Energy Agency encourages and assists peaceful nuclear programs. If Iran sincerely wanted a peaceful nuclear program, the IAEA would have helped it develop one provided that Tehran agreed to IAEA supervision and monitoring.

In an October 1, 2003 agreement with the EU-3, Iran pledged "to engage in full cooperation with the IAEA to address and resolve through full transparency all requirements and outstanding issues of the Agency." In spite of this, Iran has admitted to conducting certain nuclear activities to IAEA inspectors only after the IAEA presented it with clear evidence or asked Tehran to correct prior explanations that were inaccurate, implausible, or fraught with contradictions. Iran's admissions have been grudging and piecemeal, and its cooperation with IAEA inspectors has been accompanied by protests, accusations, and threats. Iran's recalcitrant behavior toward IAEA inspections drove IAEA Director Mohammed ElBaradei to declare in a November 2003 report:

> "The recent disclosures by Iran about its nuclear program clearly show that, in the past, Iran had concealed many aspects of its nuclear activities, with resultant breaches of its obligation to comply with the provisions

of the Safeguards Agreement. Iran's policy of concealment continued until last month, with co-operation being limited and reactive, and information being slow in coming, changing and contradictory."[31]

Although it is likely that Iran is pursuing nuclear weapons, there is the possibility that Iran could be engaged in a denial and deception campaign to exaggerate progress on its nuclear program such as Saddam Hussein apparently did concerning his WMD programs. U.S. leaders need more definitive intelligence to judge the status of the Iranian nuclear program and whether there have been any related deception efforts.

While not an instance of Iranian perfidy, the spring 2006 decision by IAEA Director General ElBaradei to remove Mr. Christopher Charlier, the chief IAEA Iran inspector, for allegedly raising concerns about Iranian deception regarding its nuclear program and concluding that the purpose of Iran's nuclear program is to construct weapons, should give U.S. policymakers great pause. The United States has entrusted the IAEA with providing a truly objective assessment of Iran's nuclear program. IAEA officials should not hesitate to conclude that the purpose of Iranian nuclear program is to produce weapons if that is where the evidence leads. If Mr. Charlier was removed for not adhering to an unstated IAEA policy barring IAEA officials from telling the whole truth about the Iranian nuclear program, the United States and the international community have a serious problem on their hands.[32] . . .

The Threat from the Iranian Ballistic Missile Program

One of the most disturbing aspects of the Iranian WMD program is its determined effort to construct ballistic missiles that will enable Tehran to deliver conventional or, potentially, chemical, biological, or nuclear warheads against its neighbors in the region and beyond. Iran claimed last fall that its Shahab-3 missile can currently strike targets at distances up to 2,000 km (1,200 miles), including Israel, Egypt, Turkey, Saudi Arabia, Afghanistan, India, Pakistan, and southeastern Europe.[33] It is believed that Iran's Shahab-4 will have a range of 4,000 km (2,400 miles), enabling Iran to strike Germany, Italy, and Moscow. The below map by the Congressional Research Service[34] illustrates the estimated ranges of the ballistic missiles Iran is developing.

The U.S. Intelligence Community concluded in its November 2004 *721 Report:*

"Iran's ballistic missile inventory is among the largest in the Middle East and includes some 1,300-km-range Shahab-3 medium-range ballistic missiles (MRBMs) and a few hundred short-range ballistic missiles (SRBMs)—including the Shahab-1 (Scud-B), Shahab-2 (Scud C), and

Figure 2

Ranges of Iran's Missiles

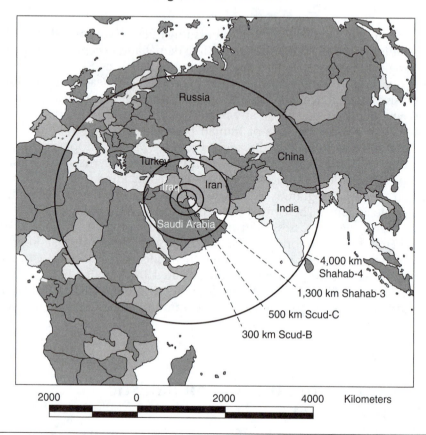

Tondar-69 (CSS-8)—as well as a variety of large unguided rockets. Already producing Scud SRBMs, Iran announced that it had begun production of the Shahab-3 MRBM and a new solid-propellant SRBM, the Fateh-110. In addition, Iran publicly acknowledged the development of follow-on versions of the Shahab-3. It originally said that another version, the Shahab-4, was a more capable ballistic missile than its predecessor but later characterized it as solely a space launch vehicle with no military applications. Iran is also pursuing longer-range ballistic missiles."[35]

DNI Negroponte stated a similar finding in February 2006, adding his concern that Iran may weaponize missiles to deliver nuclear warheads:

> ". . . the danger that it [Iran] will acquire a nuclear weapon and the ability to integrate it with the ballistic missiles Iran already possesses is a reason for immediate concern. Iran already has the largest inventory of ballistic missiles in the Middle East, and Tehran views its ballistic missiles as an integral part of its strategy to deter—and if necessary retaliate against—forces in the region, including US forces."[36]

IAEA Director General ElBaradei also raised the specter of Iran adapting its missiles to transport nuclear warheads when he wrote in a February 2006 report that the IAEA had asked Iran to meet to discuss "tests related to high explosives and the design of a missile re-entry vehicle, all of which could involve nuclear material." ElBaradei reported that Iran refused to discuss its alleged missile re-entry vehicle with the IAEA.[37] These and other recent reported developments about Iran's ballistic missile program are alarming and pose a serious threat to America's allies, especially in the Middle East.

Iran's WMD and Missile Programs: What Policymakers Need from U.S. Intelligence Agencies

Although Iran, being a denied area with active denial and deception efforts, is a difficult target for intelligence analysis and collection, it is imperative that the U.S. Intelligence Community devote significant resources against this vital threat. Detection and prevention are the two most important intelligence challenges concerning Iran's WMD and ballistic missile programs.

The U.S. Intelligence Community needs to improve its analysis and collection on the problem of detecting and characterizing Iran's WMD programs. This is particularly important regarding Iran's nuclear program, where U.S. efforts to reach a diplomatic agreement are at a critical and sensitive point. The IC's ability to provide accurate and timely intelligence on a number of facets of Iran's program will be equally critical whether there is a negotiated solution to the current nuclear impasse or if sanctions are imposed.

Improving intelligence collection and analysis to better understand and counter Iranian influence and intentions is vital to our national security. The Intelligence Community lacks the ability to acquire essential information necessary to make judgments on these essential topics, which have been recognized as essential to U.S. national security for many, many years.

An important dimension of the detection of Iran's WMD program is how intelligence analysts use intelligence to characterize these programs in their analysis. Intelligence Community managers and analysts must provide their best analytic judgments about Iranian WMD programs and not shy away from provocative conclusions or bury disagreements in consensus assessments.

It is vital that the Intelligence Community also provide intelligence the United States can use to prevent Iran from acquiring WMD technology and materials. This is a global challenge and the U.S. Intelligence Community must be prepared to play an important role as the Administration seeks the cooperation of like-minded government officials in efforts to prevent Iran from acquiring WMD or discouraging the Iranian regime and people from continuing to pursue such programs.

How Iran Is Destabilizing Iraq

Iranian involvement in Iraq is extensive, and poses a serious threat to U.S. national interests and U.S. troops. It is enabling Shia militant groups to attack Coalition forces and is actively interfering in Iraqi politics. General John Abizaid told the Senate Armed Service Committee on March 14, 2006:

> "Iran is pursuing a multi-track policy in Iraq, consisting of overtly supporting the formation of a stable, Shia Islamist-led central government while covertly working to diminish popular and military support for U.S. and Coalition operations there. Additionally, sophisticated bomb making material from Iran has been found in improvised explosive devices (IEDs) in Iraq."[38]

DNI Negroponte stated in February 2006 that Iran has demonstrated a degree of restraint in its support of violent attacks against Coalition forces in Iraq:

> "Tehran's intentions to inflict pain on the United States in Iraq has been constrained by its caution to avoid giving Washington an excuse to attack it, the clerical leadership's general satisfaction with trends in Iraq, and Iran's desire to avoid chaos on its borders."[39]

Some Iranian assistance to Iraqi insurgents already has been provided. However, through its terrorist proxies, intelligence service, Revolutionary Guard Corps (IRGC), and other tools of power projection and influence, Iran could at any time significantly ramp up its sponsorship of violent attacks against U.S. forces in Iraq and elsewhere in the Middle East if it believed doing so would keep the United States distracted or would otherwise be in Iran's national interest. Iran's support of the June 25, 1996 truck bombing of the Khobar Towers in Saudi Arabia, a terrorist act that killed 19 U.S. Servicemen and wounded 500, demonstrated that Tehran is willing to organize attacks on U.S. personnel.[40]

Iranian Involvement in Iraq's Political Process

In February 2005, then-Defense Intelligence Agency (DIA) Director Lowell E. ("Jake") Jacoby testified to the Senate Select Committee on Intelligence that Iran seeks a "weakened and Shia-dominated Iraq that is incapable of posing a threat to Iran."[41] Iran has long supported Iraqi Shia political parties, both in Iraq and in exile, and it continues to work through these groups to affect the political process. Non-government observers believe that Tehran consciously works to gain leverage with multiple political leaders, parties and organizations in the current Iraqi political system—even those who are no fans of Iran, such as Shia cleric and Mahdi Army leader Muqtada al-Sadr—to ensure it has options for influencing events no matter which group gains prominence in the Iraqi polity.[42]

On March 16, 2006, Ali Larijani, Secretary of Iran's Supreme National Security Council, indicated Iran was prepared to begin direct talks with the U.S. on Iraq, stating that, "the important thing for us is an established government in Iraq and that security is restored." Larijani was responding to Secretary of State Condoleezza Rice's authorization for U.S. Ambassador to Iraq Zalmay Khalilzad to hold bilateral talks limited to the situation in Iraq. Secretary Rice responded on March 24th that such talks would place "at the appropriate time." National Security Adviser Hadley expressed skepticism about the sincerity of Iran's offer to engage in talks with the U.S., noting that "Iran waited months to agree to a U.S. proposal to take up the issue, and did so only after its atomic program was referred to the UN Security Council for possible sanctions.[43]

Some have raised concerns about opening a dialogue with Iran while it is backing death squads in Iraq and insurgent attacks on U.S. forces. Ambassador Khalilzad said during a March 23, 2006 *Washington Post* interview that he believed Iran was publicly professing its support for Iraq's stalemated political process while its military and intelligence services back outlawed militias and insurgent groups. *The Washington Post* quoted Khalilzad stating that

> "Our judgment is that training and supplying, direct or indirect, takes place, and that there is also provision of financial resources to people, to militias, and that there is presence of people associated with Revolutionary Guard and with MOIS [Ministry of Intelligence and Security]"[44]

Iranian Support to Iraqi Militias

The U.S. Intelligence Community, the Department of State, and the Department of Defense have reported that Iran provides training, funds, and weapons to a variety of Shia militias in Iraq which have been linked to assassinations, human rights abuses, and the planting of improvised explosive devices (IEDs) designed to maim and kill U.S. troops.[45] The full extent of Iranian support to these militias is unknown, but three groups in particular have received Iranian support.

- Badr Brigade: The 20,000 strong Badr Brigade (recently renamed the Badr Organization to symbolize a transformation to a political organization) is widely believed by experts inside and outside of the U.S. Government to be controlled by the Iranian-supported Supreme Council for the Islamic Revolution in Iraq (SCIRI). It has been accused of running "death squads" that kidnap, torture, and kill Sunnis, including the 173 Sunnis found in a secret prison in a Ministry of Interior building in Jadriyah in November 2005.[46] General George Casey, the U.S. military commander in Iraq, said on December 12, 2005 that the Badr Brigade openly placed its personnel in security units in the Iraqi internal security forces, and that the loyalty of these forces remains primarily to the militia, not the national security forces.[47] Given the degree of Iranian influence over the group, the Badr Organization is widely seen as a means through which Iran has "taken over many of the Iraqi Interior Ministry's intelligence activities and infiltrated its elite commando units," to the point that "the Interior Ministry had become what amounted to an Iranian fifth column inside the U.S.- backed Iraqi government."[48] The organization is also believed to help Iran move agents, weapons, and materiel into Iraq.[49] If Iran indeed has such influence inside the Ministry of Interior, it will have great insights into the Iraqi police force's strategies, plans and possibly even operations, thus giving Iran opportunities to defeat Iraqi efforts to undermine Shia extremists in Iraq.

• Wolf Brigade: The 2,000-member "Wolf Brigade," a Badr offshoot, is led by SCIRI member Abu Walid and reported to be under the control of Iranian-influenced officials at the Interior Ministry.[50] It is reputed to have targeted Iraqi Sunnis for kidnapping, torture, and murder.[51]

Iranian Involvement in Attacks on U.S. and Coalition Forces

Evidence has mounted that Iran has facilitated IED attacks on U.S. forces. In a March 13 speech, President Bush stated that "coalition forces have seized IEDs and components that were clearly produced in Iran" and that "some of the most powerful IED's we're seeing in Iraq today include components that came from Iran."[52] DNI Negroponte echoed the president's remarks when he told Congress in February 2006 that:

> "Iran provides guidance and training to select Iraqi Shia political groups and weapons and training to Shia militant groups to enable anti-Coalition attacks. Tehran has been responsible for at least some of the increasing lethality of anti-Coalition attacks by providing Shia militants with the capability to build IEDs with explosively formed projectiles similar to those developed by Iran and Lebanese Hezbollah."[53]

While there appears to be clear evidence that Iraqi insurgent groups receive assistance from entities in Iran, however, Joint Chiefs Chairman General Peter Pace asserted that he has seen no evidence Iran's *government* is the driving force behind such activity.[54] Better intelligence collection and analysis is needed to determine the nature and extent of Iranian ties to Iraqi insurgent groups.

Iran's Role in Iraq: What Policymakers Need from U.S. Intelligence Agencies

The United States needs a range of information to adequately assess Iran's intentions and activities in Iraq. The U.S. needs to understand better Tehran's ongoing support to Shia militants conducting lethal attacks in

Iraq in order to save Coalition lives and ensure the future of a stable, democratic Iraqi government. Insights into Tehran's efforts to exert long-term influence over Iraqi institutions will be important as well.

Iranian Support for Terrorism Outside Iraq

The July 2006 Hezbollah attacks on Israel likely is the latest use of terrorism by Iran to advance its regional policy goals. Iran has used terrorism over the years as a means of projecting power, mostly against Israel but also against internal dissidents and other adversaries in Europe. The State Department's annual *Country Reports on Terrorism 2004* (issued April 2005) calls Iran "the most active state sponsor of terrorism," stating that the MOIS and the IRGC both "provided Lebanese Hezbollah and Palestinian terrorist groups—notably HAMAS, the Palestinian Islamic Jihad, the al-Aqsa Martyrs' Brigade, and the Popular Front for the Liberation of Palestine-General Command—with funding, safe haven, training and weapons."[55] Secretary of State Condoleezza Rice has referred to Iran as the "central banker for terrorism."[56]

Iran's links are strongest to Lebanese Hezbollah and Palestinian rejectionist groups, both of which have been designated by the United States as foreign terrorist organizations. Tehran is reported to have links to al-Qaeda, though U.S. intelligence information is insufficient to make a conclusive judgment on this relationship.

Hezbollah

Iran's influence over Hezbollah gives it a role in the Israeli-Palestinian peace process, making Tehran a player on an issue of global importance. Its ties to Hezbollah also provide Iran with a power projection tool—"an extension of their state," according to State Department Counterterrorism Coordinator Henry Crumpton—allowing it to authorize (or prevent) terror attacks as a way to exercise influence in the region or beyond.[57] Iran also employs the threat of stepped-up terror attacks as a deterrent against hostile powers; the possibility that Iran might unleash its terrorist proxies against the United States and its allies undoubtedly gives pause to those who might call for aggressive action against Iran.

The extent to which Iran directed the July/August 2006 Hezbollah attacks against Israel is unknown, as are possible Iranian objectives for provoking hostilities with Israel at this point in time. Certainly, Iran could benefit if the international community's attention was diverted away from Iran's nuclear program. It is urgent that the U.S. Intelligence Community redouble its efforts to uncover any Iranian agenda behind the attacks and learn how Iran may be directing them.

Iranian assistance to Hezbollah consists of funds, training, equipment, and intelligence.[58] Hezbollah leader Hassan Nasarallah stated in a May 2005 speech that Hezbollah had more than 12,000 rockets with ranges of 25–45 miles.[59] The IRGC reportedly has a strong presence in Lebanon to coordinate aid to Hezbollah, including Stinger surface-to-air missiles, Katyusha rockets, mortars, and other weaponry.[60] The State Department *Country Reports on Terrorism* stated that Iran provided Hezbollah an unmanned aerial vehicle that it flew in November 2004 into Israeli airspace, providing target reconnaissance regarding northern Israeli cities.[61] There were several unconfirmed news accounts in August 2006 of Hezbollah UAVs crashing or being shot down by Israeli forces. The press accounts claimed the UAVs may have been packed with explosives.[62]

Hezbollah has also served as a conduit for Iranian provision of weapons to Palestinian groups inside Israel. The ship *Karine-A*, seized by Israel in the Red Sea in January 2002, was filled with weapons destined for the Palestinian Authority; Hezbollah reportedly provided the funds for purchasing the weapons and hiring the ship, which was loaded in Iran.[63]

Palestinian Groups

The State Department *2004 Country Reports on Terrorism* stated that "Iran provided Palestinian terrorist groups—notably HAMAS, the Palestinian Islamic Jihad, the al-Aqsa Martyr's Brigades, and the Popular Front for the Liberation of Palestine-General Command—with funding, safe haven, training, and weapons."[64]

- HAMAS: While Iran has provided funding to HAMAS in the past, Tehran has increased its promise of support since the beginning of 2006. After HAMAS won Palestinian legislative elections in January, leading Western governments to cut off aid to the PA government, Iran has pledged to provide $250 million in financial support and urged other Muslim countries to do so as well.[65] It is not clear, however, whether Iran (or other countries) will actually provide such funding.
- Palestinian Islamic Jihad (PIJ): As early as 1993, PIJ founder Fathi Shiqaqi publicly acknowledged receiving funding from Iran, which it then provided to operatives in the West Bank and Gaza.[66] Israeli intelligence agencies assert that Iran continues to influence the group and that Tehran has urged PIJ to launch attacks ahead of the March 2006 Knesset elections.[67]
- Popular Front for the Liberation of Palestine-General Command (PFLP-GC): The PFLP-GC was the first Palestinian group to receive funding from Iran, in 1989. Its guerrillas launched numerous attacks against Israel in the 1980s and 1990s and has served in recent years as a leading conduit through which Iran provided weapons and materiel to HAMAS and PIJ.

Al-Qaeda

It is unclear whether and to what extent Iran may have ties to al-Qaeda. The primarily Sunni Arab terrorist group is an unlikely partner for the overwhelmingly Shia Persian nation; its leader, Osama bin Laden, recently referred to Shia in Iraq as "rejectionist," "traitors" and "agents of the

Americans."[68] Bin Laden's primary lieutenant in Iraq, the recently killed Abu Musab al-Zarqawi, declared a Sunni jihad against Iraqi Shia, targeting the community that hosts Iran's primary allies and proxies in Iraq.

That said, some observers believe that Iran is actively supporting al-Qaeda operatives; others suggest that Iran may passively tolerate the group's activities in the country. In November 2005, Under Secretary of State for Political Affairs R. Nicholas Burns said the U.S. believed "that some Al Qaeda members and those from like-minded extremist groups continue to use Iran as a safe haven and as a hub to facilitate their operations," without stating whether the Iranian government is actively complicit in these activities.[69] Similarly, without claiming that the Iranian regime actively provides assistance, Secretary of Defense Rumsfeld stated as early as April 2002 that "there is no question but that al-Qaeda have moved into and found sanctuary in Iran. And there is no question but that al-Qaeda has moved into Iran and out of Iran to the south and dispersed to some other countries."[70]

Iran has had a number of senior al-Qaeda operatives in custody since 2003, and the United States has repeatedly called for Iran to bring these individuals to justice. The Iranian government appears to have little willingness to do so, though it is not clear whether its reasons stem from sympathy for al-Qaeda's shared hostility toward the United States or simply a desire to use the terrorists as a future bargaining chip with Washington.[71] The nature of Iran's relationship with al-Qaeda, if any, is unclear, and U.S. intelligence must enhance its insights into this critical dynamic.[72]

WMD Terrorism

The Department of State provided a persuasive assessment of Iran and WMD terrorism in its *2005 Country Reports on Terrorism:*

> "State sponsors of terrorism pose a grave WMD threat. A WMD program in a state sponsor of terrorism could enable a terrorist organization to acquire a sophisticated WMD. State sponsors of terrorism and nations that fail to live up to their international obligations deserve special attention as potential facilitators of WMD terrorism. Iran presents a particular concern, given its active sponsorship of terrorism and continued development of a nuclear program. Iran is also capable of producing biological and chemical agents or weapons. Like other state sponsors of terrorism with WMD programs, Iran could support terrorist organizations seeking to acquire WMD."[73]

Several outside experts have asserted that while it is possible Iran could give WMD to terrorists, they believe this is highly unlikely. For example, Anthony Cordesman and Khalid Al-Radhan believe that, "plausible deniability is doubtful, and an opponent simply may not care if it can prove Iran is responsible."[74] Middle East expert Kenneth Pollack put it more bluntly: "The use of proxies or cutouts would not shield Iran from retaliation," and neither the United States nor any other victim would hesitate to respond with full force."[75]

Iran's Support of Terrorism: What Policymakers Need from U.S. Intelligence Agencies

The United States needs a range of information to adequately assess Iran's sponsorship of terror. Current events in Lebanon highlight the danger Iranian support for terrorist proxies, such as Hezbollah, poses for peace in the region and underscores the need for timely and accurate intelligence on a wide range of issues related to Iran, Hezbollah, and other groups that enjoy Iranian support. Iran's relationship with its proxies give it a global reach, which would be even more alarming should Tehran divert WMD to these groups.

Conclusion: Iran Is a Serious Security Threat on Which the United States Needs Better Intelligence

This report attempts to explain to the American people that, although intelligence is inadequate to develop a thorough understanding of the threat posed by Iranian activities, there is sufficient information available to conclude that Iran poses a serious threat to U.S. national security and to the security of our friends and allies. Based only on unclassified material, it is reasonable to assume that Iran has a program to produce nuclear weapons. The United States needs better intelligence to assess the status of Iran's nuclear program and how soon it will have an operational nuclear weapon. Iran's misleading reports to the IAEA about its nuclear research activities, many of which violate its treaty agreements, suggest hostile intentions. Iran's missile programs provide Tehran with the ability to strike targets far beyond its borders, as do its support of terrorism and meddling in Iraq. Moreover, the IAEA's belief that the Iranians may be testing missile reentry vehicles with nuclear applications poses the real possibility that Iran could spark a major regional war.

The July/August 2006 Hezbollah attacks against Israel sparked an outbreak of violence with major ramifications for peace in the Middle East. These attacks may be fully backed by Tehran and could mark the beginning of a new and more dangerous policy by Iran to use a terrorist proxy to inflict pain on Israel and the West. The U.S. Intelligence Community will play an important role in assisting American policymakers in ascertaining the extent and objectives of any Iranian role in the Hezbollah attacks.

The worst-case scenario is that Iran is run by a government into which we have little insight, and that this government is determined to acquire nuclear, chemical and biological weapons, support terrorism, and undermine political stability in Iraq. However, before we can conclude that this worst-case scenario is the reality faced by the United States, the Intelligence Community must provide policymakers with better insights into developments inside Iran.

The U.S. Intelligence Community will play a pivotal role before, during, and after any negotiations with Iran. Iran's August 22, 2006 response to the nuclear incentives package will need a thorough and complete evaluation. Policymakers will need high quality intelligence to assess Iranian intentions to prepare for any new round of negotiations on its nuclear program and for possible future discussions about the situation in Iraq. U.S. negotiators will need as complete an understanding as possible about the Iranian nuclear program, including its research facilities and its leaders' intentions. U.S. intelligence agencies will need to assess the likelihood of activities at undeclared nuclear facilities and how to verify Iranian compliance with a possible agreement on its nuclear program. If negotiations with Iran fail and a new set of trade sanctions are placed on Iran, the Intelligence Community will need to provide analysis and collection to verify international compliance with the sanctions. These and many other tasks will require a substantial commitment of collection and analytical resources by U.S. intelligence agencies.

Recommendations for the Intelligence Community

U.S. intelligence agencies need to take a wide range of steps to fill intelligence gaps and improve their collection and analysis of information on Iran, including:

1. Improve analysis. The IC's analysis on vital national security issues like Iran must be thorough and timely. Analysts must evaluate all contingencies and consider out-of-the box assessments that challenge conventional wisdom. Iran WMD analysis could improve once the DNI Iran and Counterproliferation mission managers integrate analysts more thoroughly with collectors and with their colleagues in other agencies. Iran analysts must also make greater use of open source intelligence on Iran, the availability of which is augmented by Iran's prolific (if persecuted) press.

2. Improve coordination on Iran-specific issues. To make effective use of the full range of tools and capabilities at its disposal, the Intelligence Community must ensure that each agency's efforts are fully coordinated and deconflicted. On the recommendation of the WMD Commission, the Director of National Intelligence established a Mission Manager for Iran to develop and implement a coordinated IC-wide strategy for Iran. This function, while still new, needs committed leadership and interagency cooperation to succeed. At a more operational level, individual agencies must ensure that their staffs—operators, analysts, targeters, and others— share information with each other and with their counterparts in other agencies to ensure that resources are allocated effectively and efforts are not duplicated by multiple agencies. The Mission Manager must focus in particular on filling the many intelligence gaps that prevent a thorough understanding and assessment of critical issues.

3. Improve coordination on counterproliferation issues. The DNI has directed that the National Counterproliferation Center (NCPC), created by the Intelligence Reform and Terrorism Prevention Act

of 2004, serve as the IC's Mission Manager for Counterproliferation. The NCPC can potentially play an important advisory role in improving proliferation analysis and collection. The NCPC and Iran Mission Manager must coordinate closely to ensure that they pursue consistent and complementary strategies on issues related to Iran's potential WMD programs. Furthermore, all IC experts should be called upon to bring their knowledge to bear on the problem. WMD experts at the Department of Energy National Labs, for example, should be more thoroughly integrated into the debates that take place inside the Beltway so others in the Intelligence Community can benefit from their in-depth expertise.

4. Enhance HUMINT capabilities. The DNI has recognized that the Intelligence Community needs to improve its human intelligence (HUMINT) capabilities writ large, both on foreign intelligence and counterintelligence matters. Certainly, the nature of the Iranian target poses unique HUMINT challenges; since American officials have so little physical access to Iran, it is difficult to collect information there.

5. Augment linguistic capabilities. Without question, the IC needs more staff who speak Farsi at a native or professionally proficient level.[76] HUMINT collectors need such language skills to operate effectively in Iranian communities around the world; signals intelligence (SIGINT) analysts need language fluency to understand intercepted communications; and analysts need language skills to read original documents and develop a feel for Iran's political system and culture. The Intelligence Community and the Defense Department should devote more resources to Farsi language training, but they should also work with other parts of the U.S. government to promote the teaching of Farsi and other critical foreign languages in civilian schools and universities. The country needs more high school and college graduates with critical language skills than the U.S. Government alone can train.

The Intelligence Community must also employ creative means of working around the shortage of skilled linguists. The National Virtual Translation Center (NVTC), created by the Intelligence Authorization Act for Fiscal Year 2003, has the potential to fill many of the Community's language shortfalls. The NVTC's use of contract linguists, many of whom have security clearances, gives it the flexibility to respond immediately to urgent taskings, augment capabilities provided by full-time IC staff, and provide real-time support to intelligence missions around the world. It is a unique and invaluable asset. The Director of National Intelligence must ensure that the Center receives the personnel and funding it requires to serve its IC customers in the coming fiscal years.

6. Strengthen counterintelligence efforts. We must assume that Iran attempts to collect intelligence on U.S. Government plans, strategies, and capabilities, as well as on sensitive technologies. The Intelligence Community must ensure that comprehensive counterintelligence training is given to professionals throughout the national security and scientific communities, both inside government and out, who are likely to be targeted by Iranian intelligence collectors.

7. Define goals and develop metrics. The DNI must clearly identify his goals for improving Iran-related collection and analysis so members of the Community know what they are supposed to achieve. He must also promulgate detailed performance metrics so Community managers can assess, on an ongoing basis, whether they are improving capabilities and making progress toward their critical intelligence objectives. The DNI should share these objectives and metrics with it so the legislative branch can conduct meaningful, continuous oversight of its activities regarding this critical national security challenge.

Notes

1. Remarks by Iranian President Mahmoud Ahmadinejad during a meeting with protesting students at the Iranian Interior Ministry, October 25, 2005.

2. Iranian President Mahmoud Ahmadinejad in a speech given in southeastern Iran, December 14, 2005.

3. Comments by Iranian President Mahmoud Ahmadinejad during a nationally televised ceremony, April 11, 2006.

4. Neil MacFaquhar and Hassan Fattah, "At crossroads, Hezbollah goes on the attack," *International Herald Tribune*, July 16, 2006, http://www.iht.com/articles/2006/07/16/africa/web.0717hezbollah.php; Michael Gordon, "Militants Are Said to Amass Missiles in South Lebanon," *New York Times*, July 16, 2006, http://www.nytimes.com/2006/07/16/weekinreview/16isra.html?_r=1&oref=slogin&pagewanted=print

5. Director of National Intelligence John D. Negroponte, "Annual Threat Assessment of the Director of National Intelligence," Testimony to the Senate Select Committee on Intelligence, February 2, 2006.

6. Interview of Director of National Intelligence John D. Negroponte with James Naughtie of the BBC, June 2, 2006. Available at http://www.dni.gov/interviews/20060602_interview.htm.

7. U.S. Department of State, Adherence and Compliance with Arms Control, Nonproliferation, and Disarmament Agreements, August 2005, pp. 55–56.

8. U.S. Department of State, Adherence and Compliance with Arms Control, Nonproliferation, and Disarmament Agreements, August 2005, pp. 20–21.

9. Director of National Intelligence John D. Negroponte, "Annual Threat Assessment of the Director of National Intelligence," Testimony to the Senate Select Committee on Intelligence, February 2, 2006.

364   ISSUE 19 / Is a Nuclear Iran a Global Security Threat?

10. Cited in Ray Takeyh, testimony before the Senate Committee on Foreign Relations, March 2, 2006.

11. A complete set of IAEA documentation on the Iranian nuclear program is available on the IAEA website at http://www.iaea.org/NewsCenter/Focus/IaeaIran/index.shtml.

12 IAEA Board of Governors Resolution, September 24, 2005, GOV/2005/77, http://www.iaea.org/Publications/Documents/Board/2005/gov2005-77.pdf.

13. IAEA Board of Governors document GOV/2006/14, February 4, 2006.

14. UN Security Council Presidential Statement, March 29, 2006, S/PRST/2006/15.

15. "Iran Reported Ready for Serious Talks on Nuclear Program," CNN.com, August 22, 2006, http://www.cnn.com/2006/WORLD/meast/08/22/iran.inspectors/

16. Commission on the Intelligence Capabilities of the United States Regarding Weapons of Mass Destruction ("The WMD Commission"), *Report to the President of the United States,* March 31, 2005, p. 4.

17. U.S. Department of State, Adherence and Compliance with Arms Control, Nonproliferation, and Disarmament Agreements, August 2005, p. 77.

18. "Implementation of the NPT Safeguards Agreement in the Islamic Republic of Iran: Report by the Director General." International Atomic Energy Agency, Vienna, Austria, GOV/2004/11, February 24, 2004, p. 8; CNN.com, March 10, 2005, http://www.cnn.com/2005/WORLD/asiapcf/03/10/pakistan.iran/index.html: CNN.COM, February 5, 2004, http://www.cnn.com/2004/WORLD/asiapcf/02/05/pakistan.nuclear/index.html.

19. Michael Laufer, "A.Q. Khan Chronology, Proliferation Brief, Volume 8, Number 8, Carnegie Endowment, 2006, http://www.carnegieendowment.org/publications/index.cfm?fa=view&id=17420.

20. "Implementation of the NPT Safeguards Agreement in the Islamic Republic of Iran: Report by the Director General." International Atomic Energy Agency, Vienna, Austria, GOV/2006/15, February 27, 2006, p. 15.

21. Reuters via DefenseNews.com, April 11, 2006, http://www.defensenews.com/story.php?F=1681098&C=mideast.

22. "Implementation of the NPT Safeguards Agreement in the Islamic Republic of Iran: Report by the Director General." International Atomic Energy Agency, Vienna, Austria, GOV/2003/75, November 10, 2003, p. 5.

23. "Implementation of the NPT Safeguards Agreement in the Islamic Republic of Iran: Report by the Director General." International Atomic Energy Agency, Vienna, Austria, GOV/2005/87, November 18, 2005, p. 2.

24. "Implementation of the NPT Safeguards Agreement in the Islamic Republic of Iran: Report by the Director General." International Atomic Energy Agency, Vienna, Austria, GOV/2006/15, February 27, 2006, p. 8.

25. Ibid.

26. "Implementation of the NPT Safeguards Agreement in the Islamic Republic of Iran: Report by the Director General." International Atomic Energy Agency, Vienna, Austria, GOV/2004/11, February 24, 2004, pp. 4–6.

27. "Implementation of the NPT Safeguards Agreement in the Islamic Republic of Iran: Report by the Director General." International Atomic Energy Agency, Vienna, Austria, GOV/2004/83, November 15, 2004, p. 19.

28. Thomas Wood, Matthew Milazzo, Barbara Reichmuth, and Jeff Bewdell, *The Economics of Energy Independence for Iran,* Los Alamos National Laboratory and Pacific Northwest National Laboratory, U.S. Department of Energy, March 2006.

29. Ibid.

30. Ibid.

31. "Implementation of the NPT Safeguards Agreement in the Islamic Republic of Iran: Report by the Director General." International Atomic Energy Agency, Vienna, Austria, GOV/2003/75, November 10, 2003, p. 10.

32. Bruno Schirra, "Atomic Secrets: The Man Who Knew Too Much." *Die Welt,* July 8, 2006, http://www.welt.de/data/2006/07/08/952138.html; George Jahn, "Iran Asks IAEA to Remove Chief Inspector," *Washington Post,* July 9, 2006, http://www.washingtonpost.com/wpdyn/. content/article/2006/07/09/AR2006070900192.html.

33. FoxNews.com, October 5, 2004, http://www.foxnews.com/story/0,2933,134550,00.html.

34. "Missile Survey: Ballistic and Cruise Missiles of Foreign Countries." Congressional Research Service Report RL30427, March 5, 2004, p.17.

35. Unclassified Report to Congress on the Acquisition of Technology Relating to Weapons of Mass Destruction and Advanced Conventional Munitions, July 1 Through December 31, 2003, November 2004.

36. Director of National Intelligence John D. Negroponte, "Annual Threat Assessment of the Director of National Intelligence," Testimony to the Senate Select Committee on Intelligence, February 2, 2006.

37 "Implementation of the NPT Safeguards Agreement in the Islamic Republic of Iran: Report by the Director General." International Atomic Energy Agency, Vienna, Austria, GOV/2006/15, February 27, 2006, p. 8.

38. General John Abizaid, Commander, U.S. Central Command, "2006 Posture of the United States Central Command," Testimony before the Senate Armed Services Committee, March 14, 2006.

39. Ibid.

40. See FBI Indictment on Khobar Towers bombing, June 21, 2001, available at http://www.fbi.gov/pressrel/pressrel01/khobar.pdf.

41. Vice Admiral Lowell E. Jacoby, USN, Director, Defense Intelligence Agency, "Current and Projected National Security Threats to the United States," Testimony to the Senate Select Committee on Intelligence, February 16, 2005.

42. Daniel Byman, "Iran, Terrorism, and Weapons of Mass Destruction," Testimony before the House Homeland Security Committee, Subcommittee on the Prevention of Nuclear and Biological Attacks, September 8, 2005.

43. BBC News website, Friday, March 17, 2006.

44. Jonathan Finer and Ellen Knickmeyer, "Envoy Accuses Iran of Duplicity on Iraq," *Washington Post,* March 24, 2006, page A12.

45. Director of National Intelligence John D. Negroponte, "Annual Threat Assessment of the Director of National Intelligence," Testimony to the Senate Select Committee on Intelligence, February 2, 2006; Nicholas Burns,

Under Secretary of State for Political Affairs, "United States Policy Toward Iran," Testimony before the House International Relations Committee, March 8, 2006; Scarborough, Rowan. "Rumsfeld Says Iran 'Allowing' Weapons Into Iraq." *Washington Times,* August 10, 2005.

46. Lionel Beehner, "Background Q&A: Iraq Militia Groups," Council on Foreign Relations, available at http://www.cfr.org/publication/8175/#6.

47. General George Casey, quoted in Tom Lasseter, "Iran Gaining Influence, Power in Iraq Through Militia," Knight-Ridder Newspapers, December 12, 2005.

48. Tom Lasseter, "Iran Gaining Influence, Power in Iraq Through Militia," Knight-Ridder Newspapers, December 12, 2005.

49. Edward T. Pound, "Special Report: The Iran Connection," *U.S. News & World Report,* November 22, 2004.

50. Kenneth Katzman, "Iran's Influence in Iraq," Congressional Research Service Report RS22323, November 30, 2005.

51. Lionel Beehner, "Background Q&A: Iraq Militia Groups," Council on Foreign Relations, available at http://www.cfr.org/publication/8175/#6.

52. President George W. Bush, speech to the Foundation for the Defense of Democracies, George Washington University, Washington DC, March 13, 2006.

53. John Negroponte, *Annual Threat Assessment of the Director of National Intelligence for the Senate Select Committee on Intelligence,* February 2, 2006, p. 13.

54. Department of Defense News Briefing with Secretary Rumsfeld and Gen. Pace, 14 March 2006, available at http://www.defenselink.mil/transcripts/2006/tr20060314-12644.html.

55. U.S. Department of State, *Country Reports on Terrorism 2004,* April 2005, pp. 88–89.

56. Secretary of State Condoleezza Rice, Roundtable With Australian, Indonesian and Latin American Journalists, March 9, 2006, available at http://www.state.gov/secretary/rm/2006/62968.htm.

57. State Department Coordinator for Counterterrorism Henry Crumpton, quoted in Dana Priest, "Attacking Iran May Trigger Terrorism," *Washington Post,* April 2, 2006, p. A1.

58. Paula DeSutter, Assistant Secretary of State for Verification and Compliance, Testimony before the U.S.-Israel Joint Parliamentary Committee, September 17, 2003.

59. Neil MacFaquhar and Hassan Fattah, "At crossroads, Hezbollah goes on the attack," *International Herald Tribune,* July 16, 2006, http://www.iht.com/articles/2006/07/16/africa/web.0717hezbollah.php.

60. Robin Wright, "Most of Iran's Troops in Lebanon Are Out, Western Officials Say," *Washington Post,* April 13, 2005, page A10. *Also* Kenneth Katzman, "Iran: U.S. Concerns and Policy Responses," Congressional Research Service Report RL32048, March 20, 2006, p. 21.

61. U.S. Department of State, *Country Reports on Terrorism 2004,* April 2005, pp. 89.

62. *Jerusalem Post,* August 13, 2006, http://www.jpost.com/servlet/Satellite?c=JPArticle&cid=1154525862648&pagename=JPost%2FJPArticle%2FShowFull;

STRAFOR.com, August 14, 2006, http://www.stratfor.com/products/premium/read_article.php?id=272526.

63. U.S. Department of State, *Patterns of Global Terrorism 2002*, April 30, 2003. Also Ari Fleischer, White House Press Briefing, March 25, 2002. Also, regarding Hezbollah as a source of funding for the Karine-A shipment, see "Iran and Syria as Strategic Support for Palestinian Terrorism," Israel Ministry of Foreign Affairs, September 30, 2002, available at http://www.mfa.gov.il/MFA/MFAArchive/2000_2009/2002/9/.

64. U.S. Department of State, *Country Reports on Terrorism 2004*, April 2005, pp. 89.

65. Associated Press, "Iran Promises Hamas $250 Million in Aid," *Ha'aretz*, 28 February 2006.

66. Matthew A. Levitt, "Sponsoring Terrorism: Syria and Islamic Jihad," Middle East Intelligence Bulletin, November–December 2002, available at http://www.meib.org/articles/0211_s1.htm.

67. Amos Harel, "Iran urging Islamic Jihad to attack Israel ahead of election," *Ha'aretz*, March 13, 2006.

68. Octavia Nasr, "Tape: Bin Laden Tells Sunnis to Fight Shiites in Iraq," CNN.com, July 1, 2006. available at http://www.cnn.com/2006/WORLD/meast/07/01/bin-laden.message/index.html.

69. R. Nicholas Burns, "U.S. Policy Toward Iran," Speech at Johns Hopkins University, Paul H. Nitze School of Advanced International Studies, Washington, DC, November 30, 2005.

70. Secretary of Defense Donald Rumsfeld, quoted in Associated Press, "US: Iran Gives Al-Qaeda Safe Passage," April 3, 2002.

71. Nicholas Burns, Under Secretary of State for Political Affairs, "United States Policy Toward Iran," Testimony before the House International Relations Committee, March 8, 2006.

72. Ibid.

73. *Country Reports on Terrorism 2005*, U.S Department of State, Publication 11324, April 2006, p. 173.

74. Anthony Cordesman and Khalid Al-Rodhan, *Iranian Nuclear Weapons? The Threats from Iran's WMD and Missile Programs* (Working Draft) (Washington: Center for Strategic and International Studies, February 21, 2006), p. 44.

75. Daniel Byman, "Iran, Terrorism, and Weapons of Mass Destruction," Testimony to the House Homeland Security Committee, Subcommittee on the Prevention of Nuclear and Biological Attacks, 8 September 2005, citing Kenneth Pollack, *The Persian Puzzle* (New York: Random House, 2004), pp. 420–421.

76. General John Abizaid, Commander, U.S. Central Command, "2006 Posture of the United States Central Command," Testimony before the Senate Armed Services Committee, March 14, 2006.

Office of Director of
National Intelligence

 **NO**

Iran: Nuclear Intentions
and Capabilities

Office of the Director of National Intelligence

The Director of National Intelligence serves as the head of the Intelligence Community (IC), overseeing and directing the implementation of the National Intelligence Program and acting as the principal advisor to the President, the National Security Council, and the Homeland Security Council for intelligence matters.

The Office of the Director of National Intelligence is charged with:

- Integrating the domestic and foreign dimensions of US intelligence so that there are no gaps in our understanding of threats to our national security;
- Bringing more depth and accuracy to intelligence analysis; and
- Ensuring that US intelligence resources generate future capabilities as well as present results.

National Intelligence Council

Since its formation in 1973, the National Intelligence Council (NIC) has served as a bridge between the intelligence and policy communities, a source of deep substantive expertise on critical national security issues, and as a focal point for Intelligence Community collaboration. The NIC's key goal is to provide policymakers with the best, unvarnished, and unbiased information—regardless of whether analytic judgments conform to US policy. Its primary functions are to:

- Support the DNI in his role as Principal Intelligence Advisor to the President and other senior policymakers.
- Lead the Intelligence Community's effort to produce National Intelligence Estimates (NIEs) and other NIC products that address key national security concerns.

From *National Intelligence Estimate*, November 2007, published by Office of the Director, National Intelligence Council. http://www.dni.gov/press_releases/20071203_release.pdf

- Provide a focal point for policymakers, warfighters, and Congressional leaders to task the Intelligence Community for answers to important questions.
- Reach out to nongovernment experts in academia and the private sector—and use alternative analyses and new analytic tools—to broaden and deepen the Intelligence Community's perspective.

National Intelligence Estimates and the NIE Process

National Intelligence Estimates (NIEs) are the Intelligence Community's (IC) most authoritative written judgments on national security issues and designed to help US civilian and military leaders develop policies to protect US national security interests. NIEs usually provide information on the current state of play but are primarily "estimative"—that is, they make judgments about the likely course of future events and identify the implications for US policy.

The NIEs are typically requested by senior civilian and military policymakers, Congressional leaders and at times are initiated by the National Intelligence Council (NIC). Before a NIE is drafted, the relevant NIO is responsible for producing a concept paper or terms of reference (TOR) and circulates it throughout the Intelligence Community for comment. The TOR defines the key estimative questions, determines drafting responsibilities, and sets the drafting and publication schedule. One or more IC analysts are usually assigned to produce the initial text. The NIC then meets to critique the draft before it is circulated to the broader IC. Representatives from the relevant IC agencies meet to hone and coordinate line-by-line the full text of the NIE. Working with their Agencies, reps also assign the level of confidence they have in each key judgment. IC reps discuss the quality of sources with collectors, and the National Clandestine Service vets the sources used to ensure the draft does not include any that have been recalled or otherwise seriously questioned.

All NIEs are reviewed by National Intelligence Board, which is chaired by the DNI and is composed of the heads of relevant IC agencies. Once approved by the NIB, NIEs are briefed to the President and senior policymakers. The whole process of producing NIEs normally takes at least several months.

The NIC has undertaken a number of steps to improve the NIE process under the DNI. These steps are in accordance with the goals and recommendations set out in the SSCI and WMD Commission reports and the 2004 Intelligence Reform and Prevention of Terrorism Act. Most notably, over the last year and a half, the IC has:

- *Created new procedures to integrate formal reviews of source reporting and technical judgments.* The Directors of the National Clandestine Service, NSA, NGA, and DIA and the Assistant Secretary/ INR are now required to submit formal assessments that highlight the strengths, weaknesses, and overall credibility of their sources used in developing the critical judgments of the NIE.

- *Applied more rigorous standards.* A textbox is incorporated into all NIEs that explains what we mean by such terms as "we judge" and that clarifies the difference between judgments of likelihood and confidence levels. We have made a concerted effort to not only highlight differences among agencies but to explain the reasons for such differences and to prominently display them in the Key Judgments.

Scope Note

This National Intelligence Estimate (NIE) assesses the status of Iran's nuclear program, and the program's outlook over the next 10 years. This time frame is more appropriate for estimating capabilities than intentions and foreign reactions, which are more difficult to estimate over a decade. In presenting the Intelligence Community's assessment of Iranian nuclear intentions and capabilities, the NIE thoroughly reviews all available information on these questions, examines the range of reasonable scenarios consistent with this information, and describes the key factors we judge would drive or impede nuclear progress in Iran. This NIE is an extensive reexamination of the issues in the May 2005 assessment.

This Estimate focuses on the following key questions:

- What are Iran's intentions toward developing nuclear weapons?
- What domestic factors affect Iran's decision making on whether to develop nuclear weapons?
- What external factors affect Iran's decision making on whether to develop nuclear weapons?
- What is the range of potential Iranian actions concerning the development of nuclear weapons, and the decisive factors that would lead Iran to choose one course of action over another?
- What is Iran's current and projected capability to develop nuclear weapons? What are our key assumptions, and Iran's key choke points/ vulnerabilities?

This NIE does *not* assume that Iran intends to acquire nuclear weapons. Rather, it examines the intelligence to assess Iran's capability and intent (or lack thereof) to acquire nuclear weapons, taking full account of Iran's dual-use uranium fuel cycle and those nuclear activities that are at least partly civil in nature.

This Estimate does assume that the strategic goals and basic structure of Iran's senior leadership and government will remain similar to those that have endured since the death of Ayatollah Khomeini in 1989. We acknowledge the potential for these to change during the time frame of the Estimate, but are unable to confidently predict such changes or their implications. This Estimate does not assess how Iran may conduct future negotiations with the West on the nuclear issue.

This Estimate incorporates intelligence reporting available as of 31 October 2007.

WHAT WE MEAN WHEN WE SAY: AN EXPLANATION OF ESTIMATIVE LANGUAGE

We use phrases such as *we judge, we assess,* and *we estimate*—and probabilistic terms such as *probably* and *likely*—to convey analytical assessments and judgments. Such statements are not facts, proof, or knowledge. These assessments and judgments generally are based on collected information, which often is incomplete or fragmentary. Some assessments are built on previous judgments. In all cases, assessments and judgments are not intended to imply that we have "proof" that shows something to be a fact or that definitively links two items or issues.

In addition to conveying judgments rather than certainty, our estimative language also often conveys 1) our assessed likelihood or probability of an event; and 2) the level of confidence we ascribe to the judgment.

Estimates of Likelihood. Because analytical judgments are not certain, we use probabilistic language to reflect the Community's estimates of the likelihood of developments or events. Terms such as *probably, likely, very likely,* or *almost certainly* indicate a greater than even chance. The terms *unlikely* and *remote* indicate a less then even chance that an event will occur; they do not imply that an event will not occur. Terms such as *might* or *may* reflect situations in which we are unable to assess the likelihood, generally because relevant information is unavailable, sketchy, or fragmented. Terms such as *we cannot dismiss, we cannot rule out,* or *we cannot discount* reflect an unlikely, improbable, or remote event whose consequences are such that it warrants mentioning. The chart provides a rough idea of the relationship of some of these terms to each other.

Remote	Very unlikely	Unlikely	Even chance	Probably/ Likely	Very likely	Almost certainly

Confidence in Assessments. Our assessments and estimates are supported by information that varies in scope, quality and sourcing. Consequently, we ascribe *high, moderate,* or *low* levels of confidence to our assessments, as follows:

- *High confidence* generally indicates that our judgments are based on high-quality information, and/or that the nature of the issue makes it possible to render a solid judgment. A "high confidence" judgment is not a fact or a certainty, however, and such judgments still carry a risk of being wrong.
- *Moderate confidence* generally means that the information is credibly sourced and plausible but not of sufficient quality or corroborated sufficiently to warrant a higher level of confidence.
- *Low confidence* generally means that the information's credibility and/or plausibility is questionable, or that the information is too fragmented or poorly corroborated to make solid analytic inferences, or that we have significant concerns or problems with the sources.

Key Judgements

A. We judge with high confidence that in fall 2003, Tehran halted its nuclear weapons program; we also assess with moderate-to-high confidence that Tehran at a minimum is keeping open the option to develop nuclear weapons. We judge with high confidence that the halt, and Tehran's announcement of its decision to suspend its declared uranium enrichment program and sign an Additional Protocol to its Nuclear Non-Proliferation Treaty Safeguards Agreement, was directed primarily in response to increasing international scrutiny and pressure resulting from exposure of Iran's previously undeclared nuclear work.

- We assess with high confidence that until fall 2003, Iranian military entities were working under government direction to develop nuclear weapons.
- We judge with high confidence that the halt lasted at least several years. (Because of intelligence gaps discussed elsewhere in this Estimate, however, DOE and the NIC assess with only moderate confidence that the halt to those activities represents a halt to Iran's entire nuclear weapons program.)
- We assess with moderate confidence Tehran had not restarted its nuclear weapons program as of mid-2007, but we do not know whether it currently intends to develop nuclear weapons.
- We continue to assess with moderate-to-high confidence that Iran does not currently have a nuclear weapon.
- Tehran's decision to halt its nuclear weapons program suggests it is less determined to develop nuclear weapons than we have been judging since 2005. Our assessment that the program probably was halted primarily in response to international pressure suggests Iran may be more vulnerable to influence on the issue than we judged previously.

B. We continue to assess with low confidence that Iran probably has imported at least some weapons-usable fissile material, but still judge with moderate-to-high confidence it has not obtained enough for a nuclear weapon. We cannot rule out that Iran has acquired from abroad—or will acquire in the future—a nuclear weapon or enough fissile material for a weapon. Barring such acquisitions, if Iran wants to have nuclear weapons it would need to produce sufficient amounts of fissile material indigenously—which we judge with high confidence it has not yet done.

C. We assess centrifuge enrichment is how Iran probably could first produce enough fissile material for a weapon, if it decides to do so. Iran resumed its declared centrifuge enrichment activities in January 2006, despite the continued halt in the nuclear weapons program. Iran made significant progress in 2007 installing centrifuges at Natanz, but we judge with moderate confidence it still faces significant technical problems operating them.

- We judge with moderate confidence that the earliest possible date Iran would be technically capable of producing enough HEU for a weapon is late 2009, but that this is very unlikely.

- We judge with moderate confidence Iran probably would be technically capable of producing enough HEU for a weapon sometime during the 2010–2015 time frame. (INR judges Iran is unlikely to achieve this capability before 2013 because of foreseeable technical and programmatic problems.) All agencies recognize the possibility that this capability may not be attained until *after* 2015.

D.   Iranian entities are continuing to develop a range of technical capabilities that could be applied to producing nuclear weapons, if a decision is made to do so. For example, Iran's civilian uranium enrichment program is continuing. We also assess with high confidence that since fall 2003, Iran has been conducting research and development projects with commercial and conventional military applications—some of which would also be of limited use for nuclear weapons.

E.   We do not have sufficient intelligence to judge confidently whether Tehran is willing to maintain the halt of its nuclear weapons program indefinitely while it weighs its options, or whether it will or already has set specific deadlines or criteria that will prompt it to restart the program.

- Our assessment that Iran halted the program in 2003 primarily in response to international pressure indicates Tehran's decisions are guided by a cost-benefit approach rather than a rush to a weapon irrespective of the political, economic, and military costs. This, in turn, suggests that some combination of threats of intensified international scrutiny and pressures, along with opportunities for Iran to achieve its security, prestige, and goals for regional influence in other ways, might—if perceived by Iran's leaders as credible—prompt Tehran to extend the current halt to its nuclear weapons program. It is difficult to specify what such a combination might be.
- We assess with moderate confidence that convincing the Iranian leadership to forgo the eventual development of nuclear weapons will be difficult given the linkage many within the leadership probably see between nuclear weapons development and Iran's key national security and foreign policy objectives, and given Iran's considerable effort from at least the late 1980s to 2003 to develop such weapons. In our judgment, only an Iranian political decision to abandon a nuclear weapons objective would plausibly keep Iran from eventually producing nuclear weapons—and such a decision is inherently reversible.

F.   We assess with moderate confidence that Iran probably would use covert facilities—rather than its declared nuclear sites—for the production of highly enriched uranium for a weapon. A growing amount of intelligence indicates Iran was engaged in covert uranium conversion and uranium enrichment activity, but we judge that these efforts probably were halted in response to the fall 2003 halt, and that these efforts probably had not been restarted through at least mid-2007.

G.   We judge with high confidence that Iran will not be technically capable of producing and reprocessing enough plutonium for a weapon before about 2015.

H.   We assess with high confidence that Iran has the scientific, technical and industrial capacity eventually to produce nuclear weapons if it decides to do so.

Table

Key Differences Between the Key Judgments of This Estimate on Iran's Nuclear Program and the May 2005 Assessment

2005 IC Estimate	2007 National Intelligence Estimate
Assess with high confidence that Iran currently is determined to develop nuclear weapons despite its international obligations and international pressure, but we do not assess that Iran is immovable.	Judge with high confidence that in fall 2003, Tehran halted its nuclear weapons program. Judge with high confidence that the halt lasted at least several years. (DOE and the NIC have moderate confidence that the halt to those activities represents a halt to Iran's entire nuclear weapons program.) Assess with moderate confidence that Tehran had not restarted its nuclear weapons program as of mid-2007, but we do not know whether it currently intends to develop nuclear weapons. Judge with high confidence that the halt was directed primarily in response to increasing international scrutiny and pressure resulting from exposure of Iran's previously undeclared nuclear work. Assess with moderate-to-high confidence that Tehran at a minimum is keeping open the option to develop nuclear weapons.
We have moderate confidence in projecting when Iran is likely to make a nuclear weapon; we assess that it is unlikely before early-to-mid next decade.	We judge with moderate confidence that the earliest possible date Iran would be technically capable of producing enough highly enriched uranium (HEU) for a weapon is late 2009, but that this is very unlikely. We judge with moderate confidence that Iran probably would be technically capable of producing enough HEU for a weapon sometime during the 2010–2015 time frame. (INR judges that Iran is unlikely to achieve this capability before 2013 because of foreseeable technical and programmatic problems.)
Iran could produce enough fissile material for a weapon by the end of this decade if it were to make more rapid and successful progress than we have seen to date.	We judge with moderate confidence that the earliest possible date Iran would be technically capable of producing enough highly enriched uranium (HEU) for a weapon is late 2009, but that this is very unlikely.

POSTSCRIPT

Is a Nuclear Iran a Global Security Threat?

The nuclear proliferation issue is a constant source of anxiety for nuclear and non-nuclear states alike. Who will join the club next? Are they a stable regime? What are their interests and goals, and would they be predisposed to using nuclear weapons to achieve their regional interests? Views about these issues are divergent and reflect the differences that exist in the global community. Most people believe that more nuclear powers mean a greater chance for a nuclear exchange. Most also believe that the control of nuclear weaponry by a few means that those states posses the upper hand on the adjudication of global issues and interests.

In the Middle East and the Persian Gulf, the stakes are even higher. Global oil supplies, the Israeli–Palestinian enmity, terrorism, Islamic fundamentalism, and U.S. geopolitical interests combine to make for a volatile and unstable mix. The only nuclear powers in the region are Israel, India, and Pakistan. If we exclude India and Pakistan for a moment, we see that a nuclear fundamentalist Iran forces the world community to examine several important questions. Would a nuclear Iran change the balance of power between Israel and its Arab neighbors? Would Israel allow such a development or pre-empt as they did in Osirak, Iraq, in 1979? Would Iran be predisposed to distributing nuclear technology to terrorist groups they support, like the Hezbollah of Lebanon?

Essentially, one must decide whether Iran would use nuclear weapons if they possessed them or would the weapons simply be a signal of pride and status for Iran in the regional and global communities. One school of thought, argued by many states that do not posses nuclear weapons, is that over 60 years only one state has used nuclear weapons in war, that is the United States, and that despite the growth of the nuclear club, no weapons have been launched. Thus, to assume that a nuclear Iran would be a global security threat is to ignore the fact that no evidence suggests they would use them in anger. Further, the argument is presented that painting Iran as a global security threat serves U.S. foreign policy but does not reflect Iranian regional or global interests.

The other school of thought contends that a nuclear Iran will bring nuclear weapons into the hands of religious extremists bent on obliterating Israel and spreading fundamentalism. Thus, regional states, U.S. military forces, and others are at risk of Iranian pre-emption to achieve their aims. Additionally, the "unstable" nature of a fundamentalist regime makes the use of nuclear weapons more likely and thus the possibility of a catalytic nuclear war a real threat. This view is certainly predicated on the assumption that a fundamentalist religious regime as in Iran would have less restraints on using said weapons to achieve their aims.

Whatever one's perspective, one fact is certainly clear. States like Iran, Saudi Arabia, North Korea, Syria, and others will get closer to having the ability to produce nuclear technology and weaponry. The current proliferation regime can mitigate these developments but probably cannot stop them. Thus, the world community will have to deal with nuclear proliferation and the real or perceived "threats" that these weapons create. The result will be a greater probability of a regional nuclear war.

Some interesting work here includes Michael Evans and Jerome Corsi's *Showdown with Nuclear Iran: Radical Islam's Messianic Mission to Destroy Israel and Cripple the United States* (Thomas Nelson, 2006), A. J. Venter's *Iran's Nuclear Option* (Casemate, 2005), and Scott Ritter's *Target Iran: The Truth about the White Houses Plans for Regime Change* (Nation Books, 2006).

ISSUE 20

Will China Be the Next Superpower?

YES: Shujie Yao, from "Can China Really Become the Next Superpower?" *China Policy Institute* (April 2007)

NO: Pranab Bardhan, from "China, India Superpower? Not So Fast!" *YaleGlobal Online* (October 25, 2005)

ISSUE SUMMARY

YES: Yao analyzes the current state of the Chinese economy and policy and postulates several possible scenarios for development. Ultimately, Yao surmises that China will develop as the next superpower by the mid twenty-first century.

NO: Bardhan argues that there are many variables and factors that can and will hinder China's development into a superpower, including vast poverty, weak infrastructure, and China's authoritarian government.

In 1979, after the death of Mao and the reign of the Gang of Four, Deng Sho Ping emerged as the supreme leader of the Chinese Communist party. At that moment he set China on a course of economic growth and expansion, military modernization and reform, and profound social and political change. The impact of this sea change in Chinese communist policy has been monumental. China now is one of the fastest growing economies on earth, producing goods and services at a rate of sustained growth unseen in the global economy. Its share of the export/import market has grown exponentially such that little is consumed or used that does not have a China link.

With this growth have come infrastructure development, urban expansion, monetary wealth creation, and profound societal change. While the Chinese Communist party maintains tight control, the society and economy continue to revolutionize themselves. Scholars and policymakers marvel at this change while trying to analyze its short- and long-term impact. Opinions vary as to how sustainable is this growth, and can it be managed and controlled by an authoritarian regime? Further, there is wide disagreement as to whether China's resurgence is creating a superpower or a paper tiger, and how strong is the educational, social, and political foundation on which this growth is based?

In the following section, two authors will explore a question that will be of primary focus for global scholars for the next decade. Will China be the next superpower? Yao summarizes his analysis determining that the probability of China's emergence as a superpower is great, given the presence of certain key variables. These include prudent and careful management of a mixed economy, available labor pool, access to resources, and of course, the capacity to innovate. Bardhan points to structural defects in the Chinese (and Indian) economies and systems that preclude superpower status. These include income inequality, infrastructure obstacles, bureaucratic inefficiencies, and a less-than-sophisticated notion of capital accumulation and reinvestment.

Fundamentally, both analyses agree that the potential is there, yet both see different scenarios as to how and in what form that potential will be realized.

YES

Shujie Yao

Can China Really Become
the Next Superpower?

This paper aims to answer the question whether China can really become the next superpower through assessing China's economic performance in the past three decades and evaluating the key constraints on China's future development. It presents a few possible scenarios to sketch how likely it is that China will become the next superpower towards the middle of the 21st century.

Introduction

China has been successful in the last three decades under economic reform and a policy of openness. The economic miracle has been due to Deng Xiaoping's gradualism and pragmatism in economic reforms and social changes, the smooth transformation to a mixed economy and the shift of development strategy from closed-door to openness.

China's fast growth has been accompanied by many difficult social, political and environmental problems. Rising inequality, persistence of absolute poverty, environmental degradation, corruption, and declining standards of traditional Chinese moral and social values are key constraints and challenges to China's further growth. China's future depends on its ability to solve these problems.

The most pessimistic scenario is that China is unable to face up to those challenges and constraints, rendering the country vulnerable to polarisation, corruption and financial/material crises with little hope of becoming a real superpower. The most optimistic scenario is that China is able to maintain high economic growth, to reduce inequality and poverty, to improve the natural environment, and to overcome the potential problems of energy and material shortage. In this scenario, China will overtake Japan by 2017 and the US by 2037. China will also become a world leader of science and technology, possessing the world's most advanced space, nuclear, computer, biological, medical, energy and military technologies.

From *China Policy Institute,* April 2007. Copyright © 2007 by Shujie Yao, China Policy Institute, School of Contemporary Chinese Studies/University of Nottingham. Reprinted by permission of the author. http://www.nottingham.ac.uk/china-policy-institute

What Constitutes a Superpower

The US and the former USSR are two examples of superpowers. The US has been the most powerful country in all aspects: the size of its economy, per capita gross domestic product (GDP), military strength, science and technologies, and international influence. The former USSR used to have huge military capability and influence over the world order. It was the only country able to challenge the US before the end of the cold war. Its economic strength was by no means comparable to that of the US. The key question is whether there will be another superpower in the next few decades, and if yes, which country? Russia, India, Japan or Germany is unlikely to become the next superpower for various reasons. Hence, one likely candidate must be China.

However, even if China can become the world's largest economy, it does not mean that China will automatically become a superpower. There are some other conditions for China to be a real superpower. Such conditions should include the level of per capita income, social justice and income equality, the ability to become a world leader of science and technology, and the ability to influence regional and global peace and order.

China's Rise and Its Significance in the World Economy

China's economic reform is the largest project in human history because it has affected a population 16 times that of the four Asian Tigers (South Korea, Taiwan, Singapore and Hong Kong) combined, and more than 10 times that of Japan.

During 1978–2006, China achieved an average annual growth of 9.6% in real GDP. Two different ways are currently used to measure GDP: in nominal dollars using official exchange rates and in PPP dollars using the actual buying power of currencies. Measured in PPP dollars, China's GDP in 2006 was $10.5 trillion, compared with $12.9 trillion for the US, $13.0 trillion for the EU, $4.1 trillion for Japan, $3.9 trillion for India, $2.6 trillion for Germany and $1.9 trillion for the UK. China is the third largest economic bloc after the EU and the US and the second largest economy after the US. PPP dollars tend to overstate the level of GDP for poor countries like China and India. Measured in nominal dollars, China was the fourth largest economy after the US, Japan, and Germany, with a total GDP of $2.72 trillion (20.94 trillion RMB) in 2006. China will overtake Germany to become the third largest economy in 2007 or 2008.

In the last thirty years, China's real GDP increased 13 fold, real per capita GDP over nine fold, and real per capita consumption more than six fold. Many consumer goods and services that were virtually unknown in 1978 have become daily necessities in Chinese households today, including colour TVs, telephones, motor cycles and computers. In 1978, China ranked number 23 in world trade. By 2006, China was the third largest trading nation in both imports and exports, with a total trade volume of

$1.8 trillion, generating a surplus of $177.8 billion. China had little foreign direct investment (FDI) before 1992 but has been competing with the US in recent years as the world's largest host of foreign capital.

China is the world's largest producer and consumer of many key industrial and agricultural products, including steel, cement, coal, fertilizers, colour TVs, cloth, cereals, meat, fish, vegetables, fruits, cotton and rapeseeds. By 2006, China had constructed 3.48 million km of highways and 45,460 km of motorways, or five times the total length of motorways in the UK. China is currently constructing the same length of the entire UK motorway system every two years. In 1978, China had only 598 universities recruiting 0.4 million students; by 2006, it had 1,800 universities recruiting over 5 million students and sending another 120,000 students abroad.

High and sustained economic growth has led to rapid industrialisation and urbanization. During 1978–2006, agriculture's share in national GDP declined from 28% to 11%, agricultural employment in national employment from 71% to 45%, rural population in national population from 82% to 57%.

Why China Succeeds

China's economic miracle can be attributed to its institutional reforms, transforming the former plan system to a mixed plan and market system. The approach of reform is gradual, guided by Deng's theory of 'Crossing the River by Feeling the Stones'. The reform was carefully managed with appropriate experimentation, accurate timing, correct sequence and manageable scale. Reforms progressed from agriculture and the countryside to the urban economy and state-owned enterprises, from the real economic sectors to the banking and other financial sectors, and from prices to the labour and capital markets, etc.

Adopting appropriate development strategies is another reason for China's success. Development strategies are shifted from import substitution to export-push and from closed-door to openness and globalisation.

China's reforms have been guided by some important development theories unavailable from existing economics text books. One such theory is 'Spots to Lead Areas' development, which is featured with some growing centres propelling the growth in the surrounding areas and then remote regions through the transmission of growth momentum incubated in the growth centres. In the early 1980s, China established the special economic zones and open coastal cities to be the country's growth centres.

Another theory is 'Walking with Two Legs' development to improve China's capability in science, technology and innovation. China has relied heavily on foreign technologies through direct purchase or indirectly through FDI to improve productivity. It has also invested heavily to improve its ability in technological innovation and knowledge creation at home.

Constraints and Challenges

Although China has made tremendous progress in the last thirty years, it is now faced with many challenges and constraints. The most important problems include high and rising inequality, corruption and persistency of poverty, environmental pollution, and over-dependency on non-renewable resources. All these problems could loom so large that China may become vulnerable to various crises. China's GDP is about 5% (14% in PPP terms) of the world total but it consumes more than one-third of the world's outputs of coal, steel and cement. China's past pattern of industrial growth is unlikely to be sustainable in the future.

Rising inequality and corruption are two major social and political issues which can render China vulnerable to social and political unrest, causing unwanted disruption to its economic progress.

Current Policies and Possible Scenarios

The government is aware of China's development constraints and challenges. Some policies have been implemented to resolve these problems through building a harmonious society and reducing income inequality. In agriculture, more land will be converted into forest and grass. Agricultural production will become more efficient and less dependent on chemical fertilisers and pesticides. More investments will be made in the rural areas to improve farm incomes and reduce urban-rural and inter-regional inequality. More effective measures are being adopted to combat corruption and strengthen the leadership of the Communist Party. Huge investments have been planned for the next 30 years to greatly improve the country's human capital, research and innovation capability in the strategic areas of space, energy, environment, computer and internet, biology and medicine, military affairs and defence, transportation and telecommunications, etc.

If the current policies are ineffective, China's growth can slow down, leading to higher unemployment and more poverty. In this scenario, the chance of China becoming a superpower will be small. If all policies are effectively implemented, China will be able to maintain high growth, to reduce inequality, poverty, and corruption, to improve production efficiency and the environment. In this scenario, China will overtake Japan to become the second largest economy by 2017 and the US by 2037, and will become another superpower. This prediction is based on the assumption that all countries continue to grow in the next 30 years following their own growth trends in the past three decades and that GDP is measured in nominal dollars, not in PPP dollars. By 2037, China will also become a world leader of science and technology and have sufficient military and/or diplomatic capability to compete with the US in maintaining regional and global peace and order.

Further Readings

Hu, Angang (2007), *'Five Major Scale Effects of China's Rise on the World'*, paper presented to the 18th Annual Conference of Chinese Economic Association (UK), April, University of Nottingham.

Hu, Angang (2007), 'National Life Cycle and the Rise of China', paper presented to the 18th Annual Conference of Chinese Economic Association (UK), April, University of Nottingham.

Yao, Shujie (2005), *Economic Growth, Income Distribution and Poverty Reduction in China under Economic Reforms*, RoutledgeCurzon, ISBN 0-415-33196-X.

Yao, Shujie and Kailei, Wei (2007), 'Economic Growth in the Present of FDI from a Newly Industrializing Economy's Perspective', *Journal of Comparative Economics*, 35(1), 211–234.

Yao, Shujie, L. Hanmer, and Zhongyi, Zhang (2004), 'The Implications of Growing Inequality on Poverty Peduction in China', *China Economic Review*, 15, 145–163.

Pranab Bardhan

 **NO**

China, India Superpower?
Not So Fast!

Despite Impressive Growth, the Rising Asian Giants Have Feet of Clay

The media, particularly the financial press, are all agog over the rise of China and India in the international economy. After a long period of relative stagnation, these two countries, nearly two-fifths of the world population, have seen their incomes grow at remarkably high rates over the last two decades. Journalists have referred to their economic reforms and integration into the world economy in all kinds of colorful metaphors: giants shaking off their "socialist slumber," "caged tigers" unshackled, and so on. Columnists have sent breathless reports from Beijing and Bangalore about the inexorable competition from these two new whiz kids in our complacent neighborhood in a "flattened," globalized, playing field. Others have warned about the momentous implications of "three billion new capitalists," largely from China and India, redefining the next phase of globalization.

While there is no doubt about the great potential of these two economies in the rest of this century, severe structural and institutional problems will hobble them for years to come. At this point, the hype about the Indian economy seems patently premature, and the risks on the horizon for the Chinese polity—and hence for economic stability—highly underestimated.

Both China and India are still desperately poor countries. Of the total of 2.3 billion people in these two countries, nearly 1.5 billion earn less than US$2 a day, according to World Bank calculations. Of course, the lifting of hundreds of millions of people above poverty in China has been historic. Thanks to repeated assertions in the international financial press, conventional wisdom now suggests that globalization is responsible for this feat. Yet a substantial part of China's decline in poverty since 1980 already happened by mid-1980s (largely as a result of agricultural growth), before the big strides in foreign trade and investment in the 1990s. Assertions about Indian poverty reduction primarily through trade liberalization are even shakier. In the nineties, the decade of major trade liberalization, the rate of decline in poverty by some aggregative estimates has, if anything, slowed down. In any case, India is as yet a minor player in world trade, contributing less than one percent of world exports. (China's share is about 6 percent.)

What about the hordes of Indian software engineers, call-center operators, and back-room programmers supposedly hollowing out white-collar jobs in rich countries? The total number of workers in all possible forms of IT-related jobs in India comes to less than a million workers—one-quarter of one percent of the Indian labor force. For all its Nobel Prizes and brilliant scholars and professionals, India is the largest single-country contributor to the pool of illiterate people in the world. Lifting them out of poverty and dead-end menial jobs will remain a Herculean task for decades to come.

Even in China, now considered the manufacturing workshop of the world (though China's share in the worldwide manufacturing value-added is below 9 percent, less than half that of Japan or the United States), less than one-fifth of its labor force is employed in manufacturing, mining, and construction combined. In fact, China has lost tens of millions of manufacturing jobs since the mid-1990s. Nearly half of the country's labor force remains in agriculture (about 60 percent in India). As per acre productivity growth has stagnated, reabsorbing the hundreds of millions of peasants will remain a challenge in the foreseeable future for both countries. Domestic private enterprise in China, while active and growing, is relatively weak, and Chinese banks are burdened with "bad" loans. By most aggregative measures, capital is used much less efficiently in China than in India, even though in terms of physical infrastructure and progress in education and health, China is better poised for further economic growth. Commercial regulatory structures in both countries are still slow and heavy-handed. According to the World Bank, to start a business requires in India 71 days, in China 48 days (compared to 6 days in Singapore); enforcing debt contracts requires 425 days in India, 241 days in China (69 days in Singapore).

China's authoritarian system of government will likely be a major economic liability in the long run, regardless of its immediate implications for short-run policy decisions. In the economic reform process, the Chinese leadership has often made bold decisions and implemented them relatively quickly and decisively, whereas in India, reform has been halting and hesitant. This is usually attributed to the inevitably slow processes of democracy in India. And though this may be the case, other factors are involved. For example, the major disruptions and hardships of restructuring in the Chinese economy were rendered somewhat tolerable by a minimum rural safety net—made possible to a large extent by land reforms in 1978. In most parts of India, no similar rural safety net exists for the poor; and the more severe educational inequality in India makes the absorption of shocks in the industrial labor market more difficult. So the resistance to the competitive process of market reform is that much stiffer.

But inequalities (particularly rural-urban) have been increasing in China, and those left behind are getting restive. With massive layoffs in the rust-belt provinces, arbitrary local levies on farmers, pervasive official corruption, and toxic industrial dumping, many in the countryside are highly agitated. Chinese police records indicate a sevenfold increase in the number of incidents of social unrest in the last decade.

China is far behind India in the ability to politically manage conflicts, and this may prove to be China's Achilles' Heel. Over the last fifty years, India's extremely heterogeneous society has been riddled with various kinds of conflicts, but the system has by and large managed these conflicts and kept them within moderate bounds. For many centuries, the homogenizing tradition of Chinese high culture, language, and bureaucracy has not given much scope to pluralism and diversity, and a centralizing, authoritarian Communist Party has carried on with this tradition. There is a certain pre-occupation with order and stability in China (not just in the Party), a tendency to over-react to difficult situations, and a quickness to brand dissenting movements and local autonomy efforts as seditious, and it is in this context that one sees dark clouds on the horizon for China's polity and therefore the economy.

We should not lose our sense of proportion in thinking about the rise of China and India. While adjusting its economies to the new reality and utilizing the new opportunities, the West should not overlook the enormity of the economic gap that exists between it and those two countries (particularly India). There are many severe pitfalls and roadblocks which they have to overcome in the near future, before they can become significant players in the international economic scene on a sustained basis.

POSTSCRIPT

Will China Be the Next Superpower

Over the past 30 years China has overcome its Maoist experiment and earlier colonial history to emerge as a vibrant growing economy. GDP growth rates alone have been between 8 and 15 percent per year for several years. The ingenuity, hard work, and vast resources of China have been unleashed in a mixed economic set of policies, and the result has been vast increases in production, huge amounts of foreign investment, and vast wealth creation that is transforming China. On these points, all scholars agree.

China's 1.3 billion people are also subjected to immense poverty in the countryside and in selected urban areas. They have significant infrastructure issues left over from the Communist era, and the political system leaves little room for expression and community empowerment for literally billions. China is in many ways the best global example of a dramatic play with important and broadly defined characters acting out on a global stage, and it is unclear as to where the story will go.

Several key variables will determine China's ultimate direction. First, China is in the midst of a strong growth and investment phase that is directly tied to this era of globalization. In fact, it would have been impossible for China to have grown so quickly in the last 15 years without the presence of globalization. This means that many factors outside of China's control will impact its development, including the direction of the U.S., European, and other economies and the ability of China to embrace technological changes.

Second, the enormous growth of a strong middle class in China raises questions as to the political expression for these tens of millions and what values this middle class will embrace. Will they be content with an authoritarian model, or will they demand greater forms of expressions that tear at the foundational fabric of the political system.

Third, can the current labor supply and costs in China be maintained amidst a growing and interdependent global economy? Already there are signs of breaks in the China advantage in this area as other regions of the world compete for manufacturing jobs based on cheap labor costs.

Fourth, will China be able to translate economic growth into political influence and power in places like the Middle East, Africa, and Latin America? Superpower status is in part a function of global influence and reach, and China has yet to show the will to exercise that reach and influence. Can China develop the military force structure for such power projection, and what drain will this place on the civilian economy? It remains an open question as to whether they aspire for such a role.

Certainly, China has the potential to be the next superpower, and it also has a well-thought-out plan for growth and modernization. Can China pull it off? Even the most generous analysis of the U.S. rise to super-power status admits that it was a process that took generations to come to fruition. The explosion of the atomic bomb was merely the culmination of a long path of industrialization, military expansion, and developing inter-nationalism among the political elite. China seems to be on the path, but whether they can sustain it and continue to embrace it remains an open question.

Some works that are illustrative include Susan Shirk's *China: Fragile Superpower: How China's Internal Politics Could Derail Its Peaceful Rise* (Oxford University Press, 2007); C. Fred Bergsten, Bates Gill, Nicholas Lardy, and Derek Mitchell's *China the Balance Sheet: What the World Needs to Know About the Emerging Superpower* (Public Affairs, 2006), and Ted C. Fishman's *China Inc: How the Rise of the Next Superpower Challenges America and the World* (Scribner, 2006).

Contributors to This Volume

EDITORS

JAMES E. HARF currently serves as Associate Vice-President and Director of the Center for Global Education at Maryville University in St. Louis. He is on leave from the University of Tampa where he is professor of government and world affairs. He spent most of his career at The Ohio State University where he holds the title of professor emeritus. He is coeditor of *The Unfolding Legacy of 9/11* (University Press of America, 2004) and coauthor of *World Politics and You: A Student Companion to International Politics on the World Stage,* 5th ed. (Brown & Benchmark, 1995) and *The Politics of Global Resources* (Duke University Press, 1986). His first novel, *Memories of Ivy* (Ivy House Publishing Group, 2005), about life as a university professor, was published in 2005. He also coedited a four-book series on the global issues of population, food, energy, and environment, as well as three other book series on national security education, international studies, and international business. His current research interests include tools for addressing international conflict and student strategies for maximizing study abroad experiences. As a staff member of the Presidential Commission on Foreign Language and International Studies in the late 1970s, he was responsible for undergraduate education recommendations. He also served 15 years as executive director of the Consortium for International Studies Education.

MARK OWEN LOMBARDI is the president and chief executive officer of Maryville University in St. Louis, Missouri. He is the coeditor and author of *The Unfolding Legacy of 9/11* (University Press of America, 2004) and the coeditor of *Perspectives of Third-World Sovereignty: The Postmodern Paradox* (Macmillan, 1996). Dr. Lombardi has authored numerous articles and book chapters on such topics as African political economy, U.S. foreign policy, and the politics of the cold war. He has given over 150 speeches to community groups and organizations and is a frequent commentator on local and national media on such topics as higher education reform, international affairs, U.S. politics, and U.S. foreign policy.

AUTHORS

GRAHAM ALLISON is director of the Belfer Center for Science and International Affairs at Harvard University. He has authored several books and numerous articles on international affairs and security studies.

RONALD BAILEY is science correspondent for *Reason* magazine and author of *ECOSCAM: The False Prophets of Ecological Apocalypse,* as well as an adjunct scholar with the Competitive Enterprise Institute.

PRANAB BARDHAN is a professor of economics at the University of California, Berkeley, and the chief editor of the *Journal of Development Economics.*

NAAZNEEN BARMA, MATTHEW KROENIG, AND ELY RATNER are Ph.D. candidates at the University of California, Berkeley.

DAVID BIELLO is Associate Editor for *Scientific American.*

DAVUID BRAIN is the president and CEO of Edelman Europe.

XIMING CAI is assistant professor of civil and environmental engineering at the University of Illinois at Urbana-Champaign. He earned his M.S. in hydrology and water resources at Tsinghua University in Beijing, China, and his Ph.D. in environmental and water resources at the University of Texas at Austin.

RED CAVANEY is president and chief executive officer of the American Petroleum Institute.

JANIE CHUANG is an international legal expert and practitioner-in-residence at the American University Washington College of Law.

SARAH A. CLINE is a former senior research assistant in the Environment and Production Technology Division of the International Food Policy Research Institute. She has also served as research assistant at Resources for the Future. She is currently a Ph.D. candidate in agricultural and resource economics at Colorado State University.

PETE ENGARDIO is a senior writer for *BusinessWeek* and coauthor of *Meltdown: Asia's Boom, Bust, and Beyond* in 2004. He joined *Business-Week* in 1985.

JULIA GALEOTA is a 20-year-old student whose essay as a 17-year-old won the 2004 Humanist Essay Contest.

H.T. GORANSON is the lead scientist of Sirius–Beta Corp. and was senior scientist with the U.S. Defense Advanced Research Projects Agency.

DANIEL T. GRISWOLD is assistant director of Trade Policy Studies for the Cato Institute.

DINA FRANCESCA HAYNES is an associate professor of law at the New England School of Law. She has published in the areas of international law, immigration law, human rights law, and human trafficking.

SUZANNE HOPPOUGH is a reporter for *Forbes* magazine.

ANDREW KEEN is a noted author and founder, president, and CEO of Audiocafe.com.

DAVID KRIEGER is president of the Nuclear Age Peace Foundation, and he is the coauthor of *Choose Hope, Your Role in Waging Peace in the Nuclear Age.*

MARK KRIKORIAN is the executive director of the Center for Immigration Studies and is also a regular contributor to *The National Review.* Prior to his current position he was editor of *The Winchester Star.*

JAMES HOWARD KUNSTLER is an urban planner and author of *The Long Emergency.*

PHILLIPE LEGRAIN is chief economist of Britain in Europe, the Campaign for Britain to Join the Euro. He is the author of *Open World: The Truth about Globalization* (Abacus, 2002).

RICHARD S. LINDZEN is the Alfred P. Sloan Professor of Meteorology in the Department of Earth, Atmosphere, and Planetary Sciences at MIT.

BJØRN LOMBORG is an associate professor of statistics in the Department of Political Science at the University of Aarhus in Denmark and a frequent participant in topical coverage in the European media. His areas of interest include the use of surveys in public administration and the use of statistics in the environmental arena. In February 2002 Lomborg was named director of Denmark's National Environmental Assessment Institute. He earned his Ph.D. from the University of Copenhagen in 1994.

MIA MacDONALD is a policy analyst and Worldwatch Institute senior fellow.

CAROL MATLACK is *BusinessWeek's* Paris bureau chief, after serving previously as Paris correspondent. Prior to Paris, she worked as a freelancer for *BusinessWeek* in Moscow.

ROBERT McDONALD is a postdoctoral fellow at Harvard University.

ROBERT S. McNAMARA was president of the World Bank Group of Institutions until his retirement in 1981. A former lieutenant colonel in the U.S. Air Force, he has also taught business administration at Harvard University, where he earned his M.B.A., and he served as secretary of defense from 1961 until 1968. He has received many awards, including the Albert Einstein Peace Prize, and he is the author of *In Retrospect: The Tragedy and Lessons of Vietnam* (Random House, 1995).

ROBYN MEREDITH is the senior editor for *Forbes* magazine in Asia

MICHAEL MEYER is senior editor for *Newsweek International.*

STEVEN W. MOSHER is president of the Population Research Institute.

JIM MOTAVALLI is editor of *E/The Environmental Magazine* and author of 3 books, including *Feeling the Heat: Dispatches from the Front Lines of*

Climatic Change (2004). He is also a frequent contributor to major newspapers on issues of the environment.

ETHAN NADELMANN is founder and executive director of the Drug Policy Alliance, the leading U.S. organization promoting alternatives to the war on drugs.

DANIELLE NIERENBERG is a research associate at the Worldwatch Institute.

DAVID PIMENTEL is a professor of insect ecology and agricultural sciences at Cornell University, and author of numerous related works.

JANET RALOFF is a writer for *Science News*.

MARK W. ROSEGRANT is director of the International Food Policy Research Institute's Environment and Production Technology Division. He has over 24 years of experience in research and policy analysis in agriculture and economic development, with an emphasis on critical water issues as they impact world food security and environmental sustainability. He earned his Ph.D. in public policy from the University of Michigan.

HUSSEIN SOLOMON is a lecturer at the University of Pretoria and the director of the Centre of International Political Studies.

SHIBLEY TELHAMI is the Anwar Sadat Professor for peace and development, University of Maryland, and non-resident senior fellow at Saban Center, Brookings Institute.

STEVEN WEBER is a professor of political science and the director of the Institute of International Studies at the University of California, Berkeley.

SHUJIE YAO is a professor of economics and Chinese sustainable development at the China Policy Institute, University of Nottingham.